The Early Years Reflective Practice Handbook

Edited by Avril Brock

Routledge
Taylor & Francis Group

LONDON AND NEW YORK

First published 2015
by Routledge
2 Park Square, Milton Park, Abingdon, Oxon OX14 4RN

and by Routledge
711 Third Avenue, New York, NY 10017

Routledge is an imprint of the Taylor & Francis Group, an informa business

British Library Cataloguing in Publication Data
A catalogue record for this book is available from the British Library

Library of Congress Cataloging in Publication Data
A catalog record for this book has been requested

ISBN: 978–0–415–52992–1 (hbk)
ISBN: 978–0–415–52993–8 (pbk)
ISBN: 978–0–203–11724–8 (ebk)

Typeset in Palatino
by Swales & Willis Ltd, Exeter, Devon

What do early childhood practitioners need to know about reflection and reflective practice?

Ongoing reforms in early childhood care and education social policy affect all aspects of young children's and their families' lives. Decisions are being undertaken at a rapid pace and there is a need for those working in the field of early years to consolidate and reflect on their knowledge and practice, building on what they already know.

This timely new book aims to support reflective practice for those working with young children in everyday work and in the wider political context, whatever their professional role and whatever level of qualification they hold. It takes a fresh look at a wide range of issues relating to early childhood care and education reflecting on policy, knowledge and practice.

Incorporating practical reflection activities, case studies, exemplar scenarios and questions in each chapter the book considers:

- policy developments and how these have affected young children and their families;
- issues around socio-culturalism, language, ethnicity, disposition, gender, inclusion and socio-economics when working with families;
- learning through play and the notions of quality, observation and assessment and continuity;
- contemporary issues that practitioners and students on placement may encounter in their everyday work;
- deepening reflective thinking and practice through ongoing and continuing professional development.

With practical guidance to help the reader reflect on their own practice, this text offers invaluable support to early years practitioners looking to develop their career and achieve higher qualifications at both undergraduate and Master's level. The book is a must for students on early years courses including early childhood studies, initial teacher training and early years teacher status.

Avril Brock is a principal lecturer in the Carnegie Faculty at Leeds Metropolitan University. She lectures in childhood and early years education teaching across undergraduate and postgraduate courses.

Contents

List of figures   ix

List of tables   x

Notes on contributors   xi

Foreword   xv
PAM JARVIS

Acknowledgements   xviii

Introduction   1
AVRIL BROCK

Part I: Setting the practice of reflection firmly in early childhood care and education   **5**

1. What is reflection and reflective practice?   7
AVRIL BROCK

2. Why is reflection important for early childhood educators?   22
AVRIL BROCK

3. Developing reflective writing   39
AVRIL BROCK

4. Practitioners, professionalism and reflection on role   51
AVRIL BROCK

5. What does professionalism mean for me?   65
AVRIL BROCK

Part II: The knowledge base for early childhood educators 77

6. Reflecting on children, families and policy 81
    AVRIL BROCK

    Sure Start children's centres: a study of the development of
    social capital 92
    ANDREA RICHARDSON

7. A children's centre manager's perspective 101
    JANE LEES

8. Reflecting on the role of graduates as pedagogical with children
    from birth to three 115
    MARY E. WHALLEY

9. Early years professionals' reflections on practice for two-year-old
    children from Kirklees case studies 130
    RACHAEL SINGLETON AND AVRIL BROCK

10. A deeper understanding of play 142
    LIZ CHESWORTH

    Focused reflection point: What's going on? The challenge of
    making sense of open-ended play 159
    ANDY BURT

11. Reflecting on school readiness 166
    AVRIL BROCK

12. Capable, confident children: a reception class teacher's pedagogical
    reflections 178
    AVRIL BROCK AND TINA THORNTON

13. Quality is in the eye of the beholder: developing early years
    provision using child-led quality indicators 203
    JO ARMISTEAD

Part III: Case studies of contemporary issues 223

SECTION 1: WHAT'S IT LIKE FOR A CHILD? 227

    Why are my friends so important? 229
    AVRIL BROCK

    What's it like for a black child in the classroom? 234
    GINA HOUSTON

Why are my stories so important to me? 240
AVRIL BROCK

Adyta – the silent period, as experienced by young bilingual learners 244
CAROLINE BLIGH

What is it like for a child living with violence? 249
NAOMI LEWIS

What is it like for a bereaved child? 254
AVRIL BROCK

SECTION 2: HOW CAN I DEVELOP MY PROFESSIONAL
KNOWLEDGE AND PRACTICE? 261

How can I cater for children's individuality? 263
RACHEL SPARKS LINFIELD

How do I develop children's understanding of the concept of time? 266
LYNDSEY SHIPLEY

Communication using new technologies – the tip of the iceberg 270
ALIX COUGHLIN

What should I do about young children's gun play? 275
RACHEL MARSHALL, NICOLA MILTON, PAULA RENDER AND JENNIFER SMITH

Reflecting on the process of learning how to teach reading using
systematic synthetic phonics 281
BEV KEEN

How do I observe and assess children's capabilities? 286
AVRIL BROCK

SECTION 3: WIDENING REFLECTIVE PROFESSIONAL
KNOWLEDGE: WHAT DO I NEED TO KNOW ABOUT THIS
ISSUE AND WHY IS IT IMPORTANT? 291

Dealing with racist incidents 293
GINA HOUSTON

How can an early years setting support the mental health of
young children and why is this important? 297
LUCY AKROYD

How to support asylum and refugee children in early years education   303
REBECCA WOOD

Does bullying really happen in early years?   306
MELANIE HENDERSON

Children with parents in prison   311
AVRIL BROCK

**Part IV: Continuing professional development and action research
on reflective practice**   **315**

14. Deepening reflection even further   317
AVRIL BROCK

15. On reflection: examining undergraduate reflective practice across two
higher education (HE) sector endorsed foundation degrees (FDs) and
BA (Hons) programmes within a further education (FE) provision   335
HELEN ROWE

16. Does the use of reflective practice enhance early years foundation degree
students' personal and professional development?   347
NICOLA FIRTH

Part V: Appendices   **357**

Appendix 1: Avril Brock's autobiography extract   359

Appendix 2: Reflective diary on the Personal and Professional Reflective
Practice module   364
MOBALANLE COLE

Appendix 3: Avril Brock's timeline   368

Appendix 4: Mobalanle's timeline   370

Appendix 5: Avril Brock's digital paperchase   372

Appendix 6: Pavla's paperchase   375

Index   378

Figures

1.1	Kolb's (1984) learning cycle	16
1.2	Gibbs' (1988) model of reflective practice	16
1.3	A process of reflection-on-reflection	19
2.1	Dimensions of knowledge for early childhood care and education	24
2.2	Critically reflecting with a colleague	29
2.3	A continual process of personal and professional development	30
3.1	Bev and Liz discussing student portfolios	44
6.1	Children's worlds – an ecological perspective	84
6.2	Happy families	88
7.1	Family Links Nurturing Programme being delivered in Urdu	108
7.2	See how Nafisa is both concentrating and enjoying an opportunity to get messy	110
8.1	Experimental play with water	119
8.2	Leadership qualities of the graduate leader	123
9.1	Kirklees EYPs presenting their case studies	132
9.2	Enabling environments: making space to be two	133
10.1	Open-ended play with boxes	161
11.1	Effective pedagogical strategies involve and enthuse children	173
12.1	Independent learning in the outside environment	181
12.2	Characteristics of effective learning	184
12.3	Tina at her most expressive	185
12.4	Now, children, what do we do next?	187
12.5	Exploring outdoors	190
13.1	A child's view	212
cs.1	Best of friends on a mission	229
cs.2	Oscar and James story sharing	240
cs.3	Superhero play	277
cs.4	A process of developing professional knowledge about the teaching of phonics	284
14.1	The Johari window	330
15.1	Sample's views on reflective skills	338

Tables

2.1	Reflecting-on-practice notes	26
5.1	Key professional interests of the early years educators	69
5.2	A model of professionalism for early years educators	70
5.3	Fay's model of professionalism	71
5.4	Blank model of professionalism	73
12.1	Early years foundation stage long term planning 2012–2013	197
13.1	Categories and themes of quality experiences from the point of view of children	213
13.2	Theme 1a: Adults at my nursery are important	214
13.3	Theme 7a: Learning and knowing about things and how to do things are important	214
13.4	Theme 7b: Knowing about nursery and understanding other people there is important	214
13.5	Stages of implementation	215
14.1	Some examples of images and metaphors	328
14.2	Johari window adjectives	331
15.1	Hubbs and Brand matrix	337
15.2	Action research table showing interviewee word associations before and after using the Hubbs and Brand matrix	343

Contributors

Jo Armistead is an associate lecturer at Leeds Metropolitan University. She has worked in early years, primary and special education settings and in a local authority early years service. Her doctoral research focused on young children's perspectives on the quality of their early educational experiences. The role of stakeholders in developing the quality of provision remains a research interest, along with children's perspectives and the co-construction of learning.

Avril Brock is a principal lecturer in the Carnegie Faculty at Leeds Metropolitan University. She lectures in the School of Education and Childhood and works with PhD, EdD, postgraduate and undergraduate students studying early education and childhood. Her PhD longitudinal research elicited early years educators' thinking about their professionalism and this has resulted in a typology of professionalism which has been developed across the early years interdisciplinary team. Avril has also written books and journal articles on bilingualism, early language development and play. She has worked in higher education since 1989 after being a deputy head, primary and early years teacher in West Yorkshire, often working with linguistically diverse children. Avril has participated in several Socrates, Comenius and Erasmus European-funded European international projects and is involved in interdisciplinary partnerships with colleagues in West Yorkshire and the USA.

Liz Chesworth has been working in the field of early childhood education for more than 20 years. She has worked with children from birth to seven years in schools and children's centres, mainly in inner-city Leeds. Liz has also been a local authority advisory teacher and a researcher for a national evaluation of services for young children and their families. She is currently the course leader for the BA (Hons) Early Childhood Education with QTS at Leeds Metropolitan University and also teaches on the university's postgraduate and Master's provision. Liz is nearing the completion of her PhD, which focuses upon multiple perspectives of play in an English reception class.

Nicola Firth works at Wakefield College as Higher Education Lead Co-ordinator and Curriculum Development Manager. She leads and teaches on the Foundation Degree in Young Children's Learning and Development and BA (Hons) Early Years Top-up. After working in the early years field for 15 years Nicola found herself drawn to teaching in the FE sector and quickly moved into teaching HE in an FE environment. It was then that she studied for her Master's degree and the concept of reflection and reflective practice developed students both personally and professionally became a real passion for her.

Pam Jarvis is currently a senior lecturer in the Department for Children, Young People and Families at Leeds Trinity University and an associate lecturer at the Open University. She teaches and publishes in the areas of human development and early years practice, with a particular interest in the historical development of education and care for children and their families. She has qualified teacher status and was awarded a PhD by Leeds Metropolitan University in 2005 for her thesis 'The Role of Rough and Tumble Play in Children's Social and Gender Role Development in the Early Years of Primary School'.

Jane Lees studied law at Warwick University, followed by a postgraduate diploma in Housing Administration. She then spent 15 years working in welfare rights, initially in London and then in Bradford. Since 2004 she has been working as the lead of Communityworks Children's Centre and Community Project in inner-city Bradford. In 2013 Jane completed an MA in Early Years at Leeds Metropolitan University. Her interests and passions are social justice and the alleviation of child poverty.

Helen Rowe has recently been appointed as Senior Lecturer in Education at York St John University, lecturing on foundation degree awards in Supporting Learning and Working with Children and Young People. Prior to this she worked at Harrogate College in the HE faculty. Her teaching experience with adults spans over 15 years and includes many different subjects including child development, reflective practice, leadership and management, and research skills. Her interest in reflective practice continues as she is about to commence an investigation into the impact of reflection on young children's metacognitive knowledge development as part of her doctorate research.

Rachael Singleton has been a teacher most of her life and has specialised in early years following some years as a primary school teacher. She now works as part of a busy consultancy team with a more recent professional background in quality improvement and leadership and management in early years. She is a trainer and consultant with a particular emphasis on these areas. Rachael is a steering group member for the National Children's Bureau's Quality Improvement Network, and also leads networks and training for childcare managers and early years professionals.

Tina Thornton is currently the Assistant Headteacher, Early Years Co-ordinator and Key Stage 1 Co-ordinator at Scholes Junior and Infant School in Kirklees. She has been teaching for over seven years, working in both reception and year 2 classes. Tina previously managed a pre-school playgroup and is now a committee member of the school's local pre-school. She has an NVQ level 3 in Early Years Education, a first-class honours degree in Historical Studies and an MA in Professional Development (Early Childhood Studies). Tina is also a guest lecturer on the initial teacher training courses at Huddersfield University.

Mary E. Whalley works as an independent consultant, having previously been a course tutor on both the Early Years Foundation Degree and BA (Hons) Childhood Studies at Harrogate College and Leeds Metropolitan University. She had long involvement as a tutor and assessor in the graduate leader programme for early years professional status and is currently undertaking doctoral research on the pedagogical role of the graduate leader with children from birth to 30 months.

Case study authors

Caroline Bligh is a senior lecturer and course leader for the MA in Childhood Studies and Early Years. Caroline draws upon her prior professional experiences as a primary teacher when writing her sociocultural research examining young children's experiences during the initial stage of additional language acquisition – the silent period. She is also a senior lecturer in the School of Education and Childhood, Carnegie Faculty at Leeds Metropolitan University.

Andy Burt is an experienced Early Years and Key Stage 1 teacher with a passion for developing open-ended play opportunities. His teaching career has spanned three different primary schools within the York area as well as four years work as an advanced skills teacher for York local authority. Andy co-wrote a book on understanding young children's learning through play with Professor Pat Broadhead of Leeds Metropolitan University, following extensive research into child-led approaches within his own setting. Andy is currently the deputy head teacher at Bishopthorpe Infant School in York.

Alix Coughlin observes that Douglas Adams said that any technology that is in the world when you're born is just part of how the world works, anything that's invented while you're 15 to 35 is new and exciting, while anything invented after you're 35 is against the natural order of things. Alix is not acting her age and still finds new technologies and the possibilities inspiring. She teaches on the BA/FD in Young Children's Learning and Development at Craven College, North Yorkshire.

Gina Houston is a retired early years educator who has been working with young children for over 40 years, currently doing a PhD to take time to listen to their voices in order to better understand this fascinating, joyful age group and what makes working with them so exciting.

Bev Keen is a senior lecturer at Leeds Metropolitan University. She is the course leader of the two-year route of the BA (Hons) Early Childhood Education course leading to qualifed teacher status. Prior to this Bev worked as an early years and primary teacher for 17 years in North Yorkshire. Her research interests are in young children's early reading and learning through the outdoors.

Andrea Richardson worked as a teacher in special schools and primary inclusion units, then moved to LEA support and improvement services. She managed the

Early Years SEN and Parent Partnership Services for Education Leeds, becoming the Quality and Standards Manager. She is presently part of the children's services transformation programme. Andrea is undertaking PhD study in how children's centres are engaging with parents to improve services.

Rachel Sparks Linfield has worked in education for over 25 years, teaching throughout the early years foundation stage, Key Stages 1 and 2, and in higher education at both the University of Cambridge and Leeds Metropolitan University. She has over 100 publications including a wide range of books and articles for early years and primary practitioners, and non-fiction texts for children. She is also a senior lecturer in the School of Education and Childhood, Carnegie Faculty at Leeds Metropolitan University.

Lucy Akroyd, **Melanie Henderson**, **Naomi Lewis** and **Rebecca Wood** completed their PGCE Early Childhood Education at Leeds Metropolitan University in 2013 and are now teaching in schools.

Lyndsey Shipley, **Rachel Marshall**, **Nicola Milton**, **Paula Render** and **Jennifer Smith** completed their BA (Hons) Early Childhood Education with QTS at Leeds Metropolitan University in 2013 and are now teaching in schools.

Alix, **Amanda**, **Elizabeth**, **Fay**, **Gail**, **Helen**, **Jackie**, **Jane**, **Mobalanle**, **Nicola**, **Pavla**, **Sakinah**, **Sarah** and **Sharon** successfully gained the MA Early Years/Childhood Studies at Leeds Metropolitan University, and they kindly provided their reflective thinking for my research.

Foreword

Pam Jarvis

The instigation of state-funded education in 1870 was initially based on an education system fashioned in the factory schools of the mid-nineteenth century, in which 'education' was completely driven by top-down directives. A typical class consisted of forty or fifty small children sitting in rows at desks with arms folded, or busily taking dictation notes on a slate, to various levels of accuracy. Classroom teachers transmitted isolated pieces of information by rote, based on their beliefs about what children needed to know to become very small worker 'cogs' within the huge 'wheel' of a newly industrialised society. This was caricatured by Charles Dickens in *Hard Times* (1854), most particularly in the character of the entrepreneur, Mr Gradgrind, who informs anyone who will listen that the only type of education that children need consists of hard facts and calculations.

However, social reformers appointed by school boards began to question the wisdom of such a system, which placed such heavy restrictions upon a child's daily environment at such an early age. Margaret McMillan (1860–1931) was one of these, and her battle with England's state education system at the turn of the nineteenth century eventually made a major and enduring contribution to the ethos of Britain's public services for children and families, in terms of both education and health. She relentlessly insisted that both education and care are needed within a state education system, particularly when dealing with children under ten, and that children's physical, emotional and social needs must be met in order for them to be receptive to learning. She proposed that if the state insisted children were to attend school purely to transmit and test teaching and learning, then the school (and the state) would become yet another abuser (Mansbridge, 1932). While we find far fewer children in poor physical condition in modern Britain than those in the classrooms of the late nineteenth century, the state education system continues in its distinct lack of interest in children's psychological health (UNICEF, 2007, 2013), and we can certainly echo McMillan's concerns on this basis.

McMillan eventually created a unique, pioneering nursery school in South London. Care lay at the heart of her ethos, demonstrated in her firm statement that 'it is not much use to little ones to rattle them in and out of school . . . They need nurture' (McMillan, 1929). McMillan introduced methods of teaching and learning that embodied the concept of 'educare', instigating a wide variety of modern child-centred practices in England. These practices subsequently underpinned the culture in which Susan Isaacs (1885–1948) could introduce play-based learning in her Malting House School, premised upon emerging evidence from psychological research, drawing her practice from the concept that 'play has the greatest value for the young child when it is really free and his own' (Isaacs, 1971: 133). It can be argued that, following the advent of the welfare state over the immediate post-Second World War period, the culmination of these 'care and education' developments was expressed most explicitly within the Plowden Report on primary education, which proposed that: 'At the heart of the educational process lies the child' (Department of Education and Science, 1967: 25). It is from this core ethos that modern conceptions of professionalism in early years emerge, and it is this tradition that this book draws upon, presenting some excellent examples of child-centred practice in the twenty-first century, within a national environment that is becoming less and less supportive to such endeavours. Consider, for example, from the early years foundation stage statutory guidance:

> Each area of learning and development must be implemented through planned, purposeful play . . . it is expected that the balance will gradually shift towards more activities led by adults, to help children prepare for more formal learning.
>
> (Department for Education, 2012: 6)

Such sentiments raise the spectre of Mr Gradgrind, standing at the gateway to an increasingly adult-directed early years approach, once again training children to become cogs, but this time within the modern post-industrial wheel of relentless consumption, with a view to teaching and learning rather than educare. This book therefore enters the market at a very opportune moment, to present new and existing early years practitioners with reflective, child-centred practice at its best, examining issues arising from a critical perspective within busy multi-agency environments, dealing with both care and education perspectives. The practical examples are drawn from the professional journals of reflective and, frequently, highly experienced practitioners, who understand that the genetic human heritage of the child provides (as Piaget proposed) an intrinsic motivation to actively seek out developmental opportunities, and that the most enabling response from an adult is to provide the wings for their thoughts and imagination to fly, rather than firmly tying them to the dreary ground of a time- and culture-bound politico-economic agenda.

A wholly adult-directed, perfunctory approach, such as that proposed by the children's minister Elizabeth Truss in her direction that, in early years settings 'children [should] learn to listen to a teacher, learn to respect an instruction, so that they are ready for school' (Williams, 2013, online), threatens the re-booting of a monolithic state education process devoid of holistic educare principles with the potential of becoming, in the words of Margaret McMillan, 'less of a boon than an outrage' (Mansbridge, 1932: 41–2).

This book is, by contrast, constructed by those who do not espouse a political agenda, but wish to deeply understand the theories underlying early years educare, and its practice in 'real world' situations; the true heirs of the child-centred practitioners trained in England by McMillan a century ago. The reader will be transported into the independent and imaginative world of the child in free, play-based learning, where childhood is celebrated as an important life stage that is not simply a preparation for an ideologically enslaved adulthood. They will begin to understand the creative potential of the collective child consciousness, where pirates, supermen and fairy princesses ride magic broomsticks to Never Never Land, learning how to interact constructively with each other; each player inputting to a rich, original narrative that is as far removed from the grey, didactic world of the factory school as Hogwarts (Rowling, 2001) is from Dotheboys Hall (Dickens, 1839), leading them along the road to creative, flexible adult cognition.

The practice concepts discussed within this book will provide an excellent handbook for every early years practitioner, both experienced and new to the field, who enters childcare and education with a desire to develop their understanding of early childhood development, and to inspire children at the beginning of their journey to innovative, self-motivated learning. As such, I am delighted to have this opportunity to heartily recommend it to the reader.

References

Department of Education and Science (1967) *Children and Their Primary Schools: Report of the Central Advisory Council for Education (England)*. London: HMSO.

Department for Education (DfE) (2012) *Statutory Framework for the Early Years Foundation Stage*. Runcorn: Department for Education. Available at: http://media.education.gov.uk/assets/files/pdf/e/eyfs%20statutory%20framework%20march%202012.pdf (accessed 20 October 2013).

Dickens, C. (1839) *Nicholas Nickleby*. Available at: http://www.gutenberg.org/ebooks/967 (accessed 20 October 2013).

Dickens, C. (1854) *Hard Times*. Available at: http://www.gutenberg.org/ebooks/786 (accessed 12 April 2012).

Isaacs, S. (1971) *The Nursery Years: The mind of the child from birth to sixth years*. London: Routledge.

Mansbridge, A. (1932) *Margaret McMillan: Prophet and pioneer*. London: J.M. Dent.

McMillan, M. (1929) Letter to Robert Blatchford, 20th February. University of Greenwich, Artefact A94/16/A1/74.

Rowling, J. (2001) *Harry Potter and the Philosopher's Stone*. London: Bloomsbury Publishing.

UNICEF (2007) *An Overview of Child Well-Being in Rich Countries*. Florence: UNICEF. Available at: http://www.unicef.org/media/files/ChildPovertyReport.pdf (accessed 8 April 2014).

UNICEF (2013) *Child Well-Being in Rich Countries: A comparative overview*. Florence: UNICEF. Available at: http://www.unicef-irc.org/publications/pdf/rc11_eng.pdf (accessed 20 October 2013).

Williams, M. (2013) 'Childcare minister Elizabeth Truss attacks unruly nurseries'. Available at: http://www.theguardian.com/education/2013/apr/22/childcare-minister-elizabeth-truss-nurseries (accessed 28 April 2013).

Acknowledgements

To Jonathan, my long-suffering husband who has been the chief cook and bottle-washer and kept the home running smoothly whilst I have been slaving away at this book.

To my daughters, their husbands and my grandchildren who are my delight and source of inspiration.

To all the practitioners, students, colleagues and professionals who have contributed to this book. They have all been personally recruited by me to be involved in it and I do hope they will be as pleased with the results as I am.

Many thanks to Elizabeth Tolchard and Pam Jarvis for being critical friends and reading and commenting on the manuscript of the book.

Introduction

Avril Brock

This book addresses the range of aspects that early childhood educators (ECE) need to know about reflection and reflective practice. It aims to support these practitioners in their reflective practice in their everyday work and study and in the wider political context. There continue to be ongoing reforms in early childhood care and education (ECCE) social policy that affect all aspects of young children's and their families' lives and therefore the remit of early years educators. Policy decisions are being undertaken at a rapid pace and there is a need for those working in ECCE to consolidate their knowledge and practice, building on what they already know. Early childhood educators need to continue to develop their professionalism and professional knowledge to meet the demands of change. The book takes a fresh look at a breadth of issues relating to ECCE, drawing on policy, knowledge and practice related to: (1) reflective practice theory and research; (2) policy, professionals, children and families; (3) curriculum and pedagogy; (4) social policy and contemporary issues; and (5) continuing professional development and reflective practice.

Who is the book for?

If you are a qualified early years/primary teacher, an early years professional (EYP), an early years teacher or an early years educator (EYE); a student on a course such as early childhood studies, qualified teacher training (QTS), early years training level 3–6; a childminder, or newly qualified or experienced practitioner; a leader or manager of an early years settings or foundation stage or reception teacher in nursery, children's centres or school; or an ECCE lecturer in further or higher education (HE), then this reflective practice handbook should be invaluable for you. It aims to be a handbook that will be useful whether you are training, working or further developing your career in ECCE. It promotes immediate and ongoing lifelong learning through providing a panorama of issues and contexts for reflective practice. 'Practitioner' is used throughout the book to include the diversity of ECCE professionals: childminders, early years educators, early years professionals, head teachers, nursery nurses, pedagogues, children's centre managers, teachers, and tutors in FE and HE. Early childhood educators (ECE) is used in the book to encompass the fundamental dual strands of the role – care and education – for those working in ECCE. Early childhood care and education (ECCE) forefronts care before education and it is the preferred acronym used throughout this book.

How should the book be used?

The child is at the centre of this book and the objective is to enable ECEs to critically reflect, examine and analyse the policy, theory, research and practice that affects a child's ECCE. It presents perspectives from professional practitioners, students, parents and the children themselves in order to create reflective processes that engage and involve all parties. In this way the book aims to create a multifaceted and holistic picture of the breadth of the complex issues that practitioners may meet throughout their career. This handbook of reflective practice can be both read and digested in 'one sitting' by professionals and students and then revisited throughout a career as a new or critical issue arises. The handbook is meant to be used at different times during a career, and aims to be a useful long-term purchase. It aims to be a resource that has ongoing professional relevance. The objective is to promote debate as well as critical thinking through the exploration of different perspectives. It should travel with the reader through training, into practice and onto continuing professional development and further qualification. It aims to entice readers to interact and reflect on the knowledge and interpret it for practice. Reflection-on-practice in ECCE is, as Appleby and Andrews (2011: 9) state, a 'never ending learning journey'.

Why is reflection important for ECCE practitioners?

Reflection is about analysis, about delving into an issue or problem to explore different perspectives from a range of aspects and standpoints. The more complex or tricky the problem or issue is, the deeper the analysis required, as you think around and into the heart of it, working out what feels right. Emotion and intuition also play important roles in the reflective process. The process of reflection through engaging in reading and research and developing professional, practical and personal experience generates knowledge and skills that enable understanding, empathy and professional practice that can make a difference to children and families. Reflection on practice is to generate thinking to improve practice. This is why this book contains such a range of different subjects and issues in order to develop, broaden and deepen what knowledge and understanding needs to be gained, what skills need to be developed and what needs to be encompassed to provide good-quality provision. What do we need to know about young children's learning development; individual needs; community and society demands; the impact of policy development and implementation? The challenge for the reflective practitioner is to interconnect understandings derived from tacit knowledge gained from experience and practice with explicit knowledge gained through education and training.

Who are the contributors?

This book draws on the research, study and practice of colleagues and partners at Leeds Metropolitan University. It also promotes the work of students' work on Master's, postgraduate and undergraduate Early Childhood Education and Childhood Studies courses. I am continually excited and impressed by the wealth of work that students produce, which often goes unpublished and unsung and so may often be lost for ever as they enter the pressurised world of work. In this book their academic and professional successes are celebrated and hopefully will inspire readers. Their writing celebrates reflective practice and effective provision. I have also elicited the voices of practitioners, parents and children, as listening to people is a key aspect permeating the book. The aim is to promote reflection on how practitioners listen to children and their parents to become cognisant of their rights and diversity in order to provide inclusive and appropriate practice.

Why is the book important for ECCE practitioners?

There are concerns that current policy may lead to the narrowing of qualifications and training for ECCE. Local authorities' continuing professional development teams are disappearing and practitioners may have to fall back on their own resources. The book presents many reflective questions and issues for the reader in today's contemporary practice. How will ECEs protect, develop and justify their values and beliefs in a way that promotes appropriate quality and effective practice? The book aims to be a timely support for those working in ECCE when stakeholders and policymakers may have a minimal understanding of quality and appropriate provision for young children.

The ECCE practitioner obviously cannot know everything, even though he or she might have been in the job for many years. Change is constantly adding new dimensions, expectations, problems and issues that have to be tackled in the best way possible in order to meet the demands of the clientele of children and families, local authority and governors. Yet there has never been a better time to access knowledge and information and determine what may be required as new issues and situations arise. This is where this book aims to be useful – it obviously doesn't include everything that a practitioner may need to know, but its aim is to be a handbook to point readers in appropriate directions. It provides information selected from what I believe is important, constructed from my professional and personal life. The book will be a supportive resource creating a holistic framework for readers to access, to read in-depth or to dip in and out of when the need arises. This might occur at different times of practice, through moving settings, changing roles, gaining qualifications or when experiencing exceptional circumstances. Some of the chapters are academic, some are research based and some are practical – this is so the reader gets the most benefit out of a breadth of reflective thinking, and experience from the individual writers is aimed to address the range of demands of reflective practice.

Structure of the book

The book is organised into five parts:

- Part I: Setting the practice of reflection firmly in early childhood care and education
- Part II: The knowledge base for early childhood educators
- Part III: Case studies of contemporary issues
- Part IV: Continuing professional development and action research on reflective practice
- Part V: Appendices

Each chapter includes:

- underpinning knowledge and theory;
- research and policy;
- practical examples from professional practice including case studies and vignettes.

Throughout the book readers will:

- participate in focused reflection point activities;
- reflect on key questions or issues raised;
- check a summary of knowledge gained;
- consider challenges for the future;
- engage in further reading.

The book is my inspiration drawn from 35 years of working in education as a teacher and as a lecturer in higher education. Throughout my career I have been inspired by an amazing array of individual children, students and practitioners and my aim is to pass on this inspiration to the readers of this book. I have had more than a little help from the writing contributors, who were all specially selected for their knowledge and expertise. I am grateful to the students who have been involved in my research, to the practitioners who have let me interview and observe them and to the children who have both shown and told me what to do!

References

Appleby, K. and Andrews, M. (2011) 'Reflective practice is the key to quality improvement', in Reed, M. and Canning, N. (eds) *Implementing Quality Improvement and Change in the Early Years*. London: Sage.

Setting the practice of reflection firmly in early childhood care and education

Chapter 1: What is reflection and reflective practice?

Avril Brock

This chapter develops both knowledge of what is reflection and also why it is so important. It justifies the fundamental nature of reflective thinking and practice. Readers will gain understanding of how and why reflective practice is beneficial and should have real purpose for the ECCE practitioner.

Chapter 2: Why is reflection important for early childhood educators?

Avril Brock

In this chapter readers will gain understanding of how and why reflective practice is beneficial and should have real purpose for the ECCE practitioner. It draws on the voices of real practitioners and demonstrates how to develop purposeful reflective thinking on practice.

Chapter 3: Developing reflective writing

Avril Brock

A key way of reflection is through a process of writing and this can be undertaken in a variety of ways. Reflective writing activities such as journaling, evaluations, self-assessment documents and portfolios are explored in this chapter.

Part I

Chapter 4: Practitioners, professionalism and reflection on role

Avril Brock

This chapter demonstrates the importance of developing a strong awareness of professionalism and the complexity of the professional role. This awareness involves knowledge of self, of professional standards and requirements set by government and professional bodies and of the professional role within the contexts of ECCE settings.

Chapter 5: What does professionalism mean for me?

Avril Brock

This chapter focuses on professionalism – what does this mean for early years practitioners and why is both a consensus of professionalism in the field and a personal understanding of professionalism important for ECEs?

What is reflection and reflective practice?

Avril Brock

This chapter develops both knowledge of what is reflection and also why it is so important. It justifies the fundamental nature of reflective thinking and practice. Readers will gain understanding of how and why reflective practice is beneficial and can have real purpose for the ECCE practitioner.

In order to do this the chapter commences with definitions of reflection and examines why we need to reflect. It examines perspectives from key theorists – Dewey, Schön and Eraut – as well as drawing on contemporary authors and researchers writing on reflection. It provides you with strategies and mechanisms to help you develop and improve your knowledge of reflection and how to participate in meaningful reflective thinking and action. This chapter, and the whole of this book in fact, is to enable you to make the connections through drawing on role models – theorists, researchers, mentors, colleagues and critical friends who can help put reflective thinking into practice.

What is reflection?

Reflection is not a new activity; in fact you can trace it back to the Greek philosophers – Socrates, Plato and Aristotle – whose philosophic debate was founded on critical thought and reflection. Yet 'reflection' has become a very contemporary demand in many professional fields. This is particularly the case in training, further and higher education where assessment occurs through reflective portfolios or learning journals and where reflective evaluations of practice are expected. There is pressure for contemporary professionals to reflect in and on their professional practice. Reflection and reflective practice are core values of professionals and have a key role in professional training. Reflection is promoted in a range of disciplines, particularly in education, health and social care, and is an essential part of professional practice (Moon, 2004). However, do you still hear 'forget what you have been taught at college or university – this is the real world' – yet how can practice and thinking about it have contradictory purposes (Paige-Smith and Craft, 2008: 13)? Early childhood educators (ECEs) need to be able to articulate not only their educational and pedagogical aims, but also their personal values to reflect on how they form their actions and responses in order to deliver a genuinely inclusive curriculum (Forde *et al.*, 2006). For reflection to be purposeful it needs to be meaningful and, for early years practitioners, it therefore needs to relate to their work with young children and their families.

Is there one definitive meaning of reflective practice that is normally regarded as good practice? Indeed, as Boud (2010: 25) argues, 'unreflective practice is certainly bad'. Bolton (2005, 2010) and Moon (1999, 2004, 2005) are key writers and researchers in the areas of reflection and reflective practice and they have both observed how interpretations of reflection can often be woolly and lack clarity, which sometimes results in practitioners not gaining a clear understanding of reflection. Ryan (2011) also observes that reflection can tend to be superficial and that it needs to be taught in a systematic way, in order for it to move from the everyday and immediate situation. There is a lot of truth in Ryan's (2011) observation that there can be a lack of clarity in terminology and definitions of reflection. Hickson (2011) defines reflection as a mirror image (in a mirror or water) to reflect thinking in order to analyse experiences and practice. She observes that, as there is no clear definition, it can be perceived from varying theoretical perspectives.

Frost's (2010: 16) internet search of 'reflective practice' brought up over half a million hits! The internet provides us with a large amount of information and requires us to develop new ways of thinking. However, more information is not necessarily better information and practitioners need to develop criticality in their search on the internet, in textbooks and in journal articles in order to gain a depth of knowledge and understanding. It is worth bearing in mind Powell's (2011: 202) view that although the internet enables us to access knowledge, solve problems and enable quick answers, it can lead to a lack of depth at times. A short-term quick answer may solve a problem quickly and easily but often more than one source will provide a balance, with varied complementary perspectives on issues. This chapter aims to present the differing perspectives on reflection and the following chapters aim to provide deeper reflective understandings on particular issues.

Why reflect? The purposes of reflection

Learning to become a truly reflective practitioner is like being a butterfly – the metamorphosis may hurt as new thinking often requires change – but this will result in a more advanced state: flying rather than crawling; professional understanding rather than just technical application! However, without purpose reflection can be random personal wanderings or even rather hollow (Jones and Shelton, 2011). Reflective thinking and practice may be demanded for:

■ becoming a professional practitioner through training: meeting professional standards in personal professional development learning journals, eportfolios or evaluations in practice files;

- everyday practice to improve own teaching/working with children and to provide quality provision and promote the most appropriate and enjoyable learning experiences for young children;
- furthering professional development through gaining promotion, leadership or higher qualifications as a leader of a setting, room or age range within the early years foundation stage (EYFS);
- compiling the Self Evaluation Document Form (SEF) for Ofsted which is required for ECCE settings, schools, universities and colleges.

So the demands are real and there are several powerful external motivating factors such as achieving qualifications or meeting the requirements of Ofsted. However, reflective practice should be absolutely integrated into what practitioners do, intrinsic for self and for the children with whom you work. Reflective practice should therefore be continual and ongoing, a real part of life and not just an abstract or temporal exercise.

How to reflect?

Reading theory in textbooks to develop knowledge about reflective practice can support understanding and help ensure it is not shallow and on only a surface level. Reading or seeing reflective writing being modelled are very useful ways of gaining understanding and application. Reflection is a dialogic process which may be within the self – listening to ourselves – or through interactive relationships with others through listening and sharing perspectives (Rinaldi, 2006). In order to get a real understanding of critical reflection it might be useful to engage in sustained shared thinking about reflection with colleagues, with a tutor or fellow students. A student, newly qualified practitioner or someone working towards further qualification is expected to reflect on their activities to talk them through with a mentor, trainer or manager and probably have to write about a selection in their formal evaluations, journals or essays. 'Real' reflective practice needs another person as mentor or professional supervisor, who can ask appropriate questions to ensure that the reflection goes somewhere (Atherton, 2011). Practitioners need to be able to reflect within the workplace and it can be beneficial if the reflective process is modelled by colleagues. Participating in a reflective practice with others enables a reconstruction of practice and in doing so makes thinking more explicitly formulated. This can occur through observing practice; using case studies and scenarios; shadowing colleagues/mentors; and engaging in discussion. See Chapter 14 for examples of writing exercises aimed at deepening reflective thinking and Chapters 15 and 16, where the authors introduce their action research projects.

Knights *et al.* (2007) argue that there are taken-for-granted assumptions about reflection and reflective practice and they question how reflection is different from thinking. Reflection has been assumed to happen inside people's heads and is an individualised view of learning. Bradbury *et al.* (2010: 4) believe that there is an urgent need to revisit ideas of reflection and reflective practice to return to the challenges and to take into account the complexity of the workplace and professional identity. They propose that there is a need to reclaim the radical ideas of Schön and other pioneers in order to develop more criticality and critical practice. Therefore this chapter now examines the theories generated by three key pioneers of reflective thinking – Dewey, Schön and Eraut.

Key pioneers in reflective thinking

John Dewey (1859–1952)

Dewey was an American philosopher, psychologist and educational reformer and his ideas continue to have relevance for all educational practitioners, because of his explorations of thinking and reflecting. He believed that reflection is an added dimension of people's thought processes and that people actively need to develop these. It is not only important to learn how to think effectively, but also to acquire the habit of doing reflection as purposeful action. Dewey believed that reflecting back over what we have done is important for extracting the meanings of what has occurred. In this way we develop the ability to build on this 'capital stock for intelligent dealings' with further experiences (Dewey, 1938: 110). Dewey observed that 'We do not learn from experience . . . we learn from reflecting on experience' (1933: 78).

In this way, he argues, reflection through thinking, and organising the thoughts derived through reflection, enable deeper intellectual understanding. Beliefs and values should be generated through knowledge, and rational thought should be based on evidence gained through reflective thinking.

Dewey's theories on reflection are about:

- thinking;
- a form of problem solving;
- an active and deliberate process;
- sequences of interconnected ideas;
- underlying beliefs;
- open-mindedness;
- reasoning and ordering of thoughts.

What does this mean for you?

Practitioners need to continually carefully consider how they practise and reflect upon their work with children. Dewey's (1933) thinking is still so contemporary today – he argued that if you do not operate as a reflective practitioner, then you risk basing practice on prejudice, on uninformed or outdated thinking. Through critically reflecting on practice, using skills such as observation and reasoning, practitioners should be able to ensure that their work is responsible and ethical.

Donald Alan Schön (1930–97)

Schön theorised that the ability to reflect on action is necessary in order to engage in a process of continuous learning and that this is a crucial characteristic of professional practice. Schön's (1976) 'knowledge-in-action' and 'knowledge-on-action' portrayed the need for theory embedded in practice, with reflexivity being the practical application of reflecting on practice and then engaging in the process of relating theories or ideas to practice. The professional depends on tacit knowing-in-action, when every competent practitioner makes innumerable judgements, yet may not be able to give adequate reasons for them (Schön, 1983). Schön's theories of tacit knowing-in-action and reflection-in-action are relevant to all professionals who need to make sense of what they think and do in their everyday practices. To reflect *in* action (while doing something) and *on* action (after you have done it) is an important feature of professional training in many disciplines (Atherton, 2011). Critical reflection on work with children is an important element of knowledge to enable the integration of theory and practice situated in experience.

Schön's theories on reflection are about:

- consonance between practice, knowledge and experience through:
  - □ tacit knowing-in-action
  - □ reflection-in-action
  - □ reflection-on-action;

- making sense of an action after it has occurred perhaps as a subconscious activity;
- reflective conversation in which continual re-adjustment and appropriate change occurs;
- critique, reflection, articulation of understanding and application;
- reflection as an effective method of improving performance;
- challenging of underlying assumptions;
- ways of coping.

Schön invented the phrase 'professional artistry' to promote the complexity of using this range of knowledge and skills in becoming reflective in and on practice. Schön's reflective practitioners use emotional response to complement their knowledge and understanding about a subject in order to refine and develop actions and relationships (Reed, 2011: 2). They are therefore thoughtful and contemplative, able to draw on their intuition, insight and artistry in order to be truly reflective professionals.

What does this mean for you?

Tacit knowledge and reflection-in-action guides practitioners' actions when they are working with children, even if they cannot necessarily access that knowledge when they are asked about it. Tacit theories are embedded in the practitioners' conscious and subconscious knowledge and thinking. They are not there by accident but will have been developed from knowledge gained through training and experience of working in settings with children and experienced colleagues, as well as drawing on their own personal life experiences. Of course all this knowledge is not drawn out within one particular day, activity or an incident that has significance for you. Alix, a Master's student and further education lecturer in ECCE, observed:

> *I think Schön's theory of reflection on/in action and the tacit knowing in action are particularly useful for early years educators; they have that knowledge but just aren't aware of what a skill it is and they need to recognise it and value it as it makes them good practitioners, and I've since seen quite a few people who just don't have that tacit knowledge and it's not something that can be taught. Alix*

Acquiring the tacit knowledge that underpins routines and intuitive decisions can be difficult to explain. Historically, ECCE practitioners have not been particularly articulate or assertive enough in justifying and promoting their beliefs and ideologies. According to Anning (2002) the professional knowledge of early years practitioners was often tacit and rarely exposed to public scrutiny. This 'tacit knowledge' (Schön, 1987) may be embedded deeply in practice as implicit theories, but that does not mean that the professional knowledge base is not complicated. The ongoing changes in educational policy aimed at improving practice require ECEs to continually engage in further training to develop knowledge and practice.

Michael Eraut (1940–)

According to Eraut (1994), theoretical professional knowledge and contextual practical knowledge need to be interlinked; theory is not divorced from practice and it helps generate deeper understanding. What is the difference between professional knowledge and practical knowledge? Eraut (1994: 19) argues that professional knowledge involves theory and practice, public and personal knowledge, propositional and process knowledge, and analytical and intuitive thinking (Eraut, 1994). Practical knowledge has often been considered to be context bound whereas theoretical knowledge is comparatively context free, but this cannot be correct. Knowledge is also gained through experience and Eraut (1994: 13) argues that practical knowledge is dependent on one's perceptions, cognitive understandings and expectations. Time devoted to reflection, making sense and linking experiences with other personal knowledge, makes practical knowledge as valuable as professional or theoretical knowledge. Perhaps the following are useful distinctions as to where the underlying knowledge bases are derived:

- Theoretical knowledge is normally acquired through education and study.
- Practical knowledge is gained on the job through training, experience and practice leading to competence.

- Personal knowledge is developed through combinations of personal previous experience, values and beliefs, education, training and practice.

When these knowledge bases are reflected upon, articulated and understanding is enhanced then professional knowledge is generated. It is essential to integrate reflection with personal and contextual understanding in order to identify the way to develop, change and improve practice. Eraut believes that working alongside others enables you to:

- observe and listen to others at work;
- participate in shared activities;
- learn new practices and perspectives;
- become aware of different kinds of knowledge and expertise;
- gain some sense of other people's tacit knowledge.

What does this mean for you?

Critical reflection is both a theory and a practice – the reflective thinking processes enable the making and remaking of knowledge.

Contemporary professionals need to continually gain and interrelate different aspects of knowledge and for many it is complex and multidimensional, crossing a range of expertise and skills. Professional practice is contextual and complex and reflective thinking can act as a tool for evaluating practice, helping to determine discrepancies between what is implicit and what is explicitly practised (Fook and Gardner, 2007). Critical reflection can effect change and improve practice and may occur as a subconscious activity, conversation with a colleague or through reflective writing.

Critical thinking

Critical thinking is a capacity to work with complex ideas whereby a person can make effective provision of evidence to justify a reasonable judgement. The evidence, and therefore the judgement, will pay appropriate attention to context.

(Moon, 2005)

There is not one established definition of critical thinking – there are some different views of, and approaches to, critical thinking with many models and frameworks available to describe the process. Critical thinking is obviously connected to learning processes but it is probable that the substance of the topic under consideration is complex and that deep thinking is required to gain a real understanding of the problem. The key is obviously in the use of 'critical'. The metacognitive processes involved in the critical thinking may involve personal feelings and emotions. Key points to note about critical thinking are:

- Critical thinking is to do with thinking and learning.
- It should evaluate and be constructive.
- It should be deep and not surface level processing.
- It is important when thinking through complex ideas.
- It involves reflexivity and may involve emotion.
- It supports justification and enables reasonable judgement based on evidence.
- It relies on understanding and knowledge through determining appropriate information related to context.

Focused reflection point

- Reflect on your learning processes and when you last had to engage in some difficult critical thinking in order to understand a new idea, theory or practice.
- You could reflect back on the last training session you attended, whether it was organised by the local authority, at college or university. Did it stretch your thinking?
- Or reflect back on the last essay you submitted for your most recent qualification. Did you have to work hard to accommodate new understanding to answer the assignment question or was it a case of building on and assimilating what you already knew?

Critical reflection

Critical reflection is putting critical thinking into practice through focusing on specific processes, ideas, issues or activities. According to Fook and Gardner (2007), critical reflection is both a theory and a practice based on an understanding of the individual in social contexts and links between an individual and society. Critical reflection enables professional development and personal empowerment, and should lead to deeper understandings and beneficial changes in practice. The purposes of critical reflection include:

- providing the means for both theory and processes to enable the making and remaking of knowledge to happen;
- providing a framework that enables you to manage knowledge, critical issues and current stresses;
- enabling you to be active in the organisation (work or study) through active, articulate participation;
- supporting understanding of emotions, power, politics, social structure and hierarchy;
- facilitating knowledge of how specific work 'cultures' are interpreted and maintained.

(Fook and Gardner, 2007: 10)

There are a number of theoretical models of the processes of critical reflection. Scanlon and Chernomas' (1997) three stages of reflection is quite easy to understand:

- awareness
- critical analysis
- new perspective.

As is Wong *et al.*'s (2000) levels of reflective ability:

- non reflectors
- reflectors
- critical reflectors.

Fook and Gardner (2007) have created a framework of three phases of critical reflection: moving from description to reflective questioning and leading to redeveloping practice theory. This requires a deeper look at thinking, actions and emotions with connections made between assumptions and the social world through:

1. The understanding of an individual in a social context.
2. The linking of theory and practice of critical reflection in the model.
3. The importance of linking changed awareness with changed actions.

In Moyles' (2010: 19) opinion critical reflection occurs on at least four different levels:

1. 'of the moment reflection', which she feels is related to Schön's reflection-in-action, drawing on practitioners' tacit knowledge and intuition;
2. 'retrospective reflection' on what has been, which she feels is related to Schön's reflection-on-action through looking back on events and considering what might have happened differently;
3. 'prospective reflection' on what might happen in the future;
4. 'reflection-on-reflection', which is a metacognitive process; reflecting on our own knowledge through the reflective process, usually with another.

Her second, third and fourth levels should enable a deeper thinking through reducing the pressure of making decisions in the immediate situation and enable the practitioner to draw on a broader and deeper knowledge base. The fourth level requires research through accessing other people's opinions, either through a critical friend or colleague or through reading relevant theory and ideas from books, journals or websites. Moyles (2010: 21) challenges the ECE practitioner to *retrospectively* reflect on intentions, decisions, feelings and perceptions; to *prospectively* consider values, alternative solutions or actions and knowledge or information; and for '*reflection-on-reflection*' to examine the learning gained and how thoughts and actions have changed through the reflection and review processes. There are a myriad of methods, tools, techniques and frameworks for reflective practice which can be used collegially in small or large groups or individually through textbooks or online training.

The most important thing a practitioner needs to know is that critical reflection requires working at in order to become adept at it. There are quite a number of models of how to develop the processes of critical reflection that can be used to organise thinking and develop criticality. These models can help facilitate the deepening of reflection. The most well-known reflective process models are Kolb's (1984a, 1984b) experiential cycle and Gibbs' (1988) reflective cycle.

Kolb's (1984) four stages in learning are cyclical, as can be seen in Figure 1.1: as you review or reflect on a practical or concrete experience on a personal basis, you may then apply theories, previous or new knowledge to help you describe the experience. In this way you engage in abstract conceptualisation which should lead you to actively experiment or try out what you have learned. This may happen quickly, or over days, weeks or months depending on the topic, and there may be a 'wheels within wheels' process at the same time (Atherton, 2013).

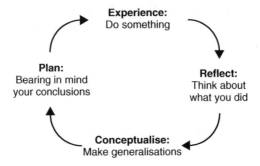

FIGURE 1.1 Kolb's (1984) learning cycle (LeedsMet University Skills for Learning).

However, you may find Gibbs' (1988) model to be more useful as it enables you to follow a six-stage plan of reflective practice in action. This enables you to move from simply describing what has happened, through a process of analysis and then on to developing future actions.

FIGURE 1.2 Gibbs' (1988) model of reflective practice.

Focused reflection point

Select either Kolb's or Gibbs' model and see if you can make it work for you whilst reflecting on an activity with children that you have undertaken recently. Which aspects of the cycle did you find most useful? Did it help reflective thinking more if just reflected on in your mind or if you created a written diagram to portray your thoughts?

Helen and Jackie used the reflective cycle models in their work as further education lecturers in ECCE:

> *These were useful, if a little overused within reflective practice. They provide access to the process of reflection though for some learners they need interpreting. Use of such templates encourages good habits, though I believe that they can also become too regimented and perhaps some of the more exciting creative thinking may get overlooked. Helen*

> *My research for the assessment and from class input allowed me to vastly broaden my understanding of the process of reflection and that it doesn't have to be a complicated procedure. That in essence it is the same process regardless of whether it's broken down into six stages or just three. Jackie*

Vikki found Gibbs' (1988) reflective cycle to be a very useful and manageable process for thinking things through about a messy play activity.

> *I was fairly skeptical about using this model of reflection as I wasn't sure how the six steps would link with each other and I was concerned about repeating myself in the conclusion and analysis sections. However, when I got into the writing I really felt that I was able to think more clearly about what had happened and why. I think the feelings section is extremely important as it kept the incident as a personal experience to me rather than an event or story that I was merely telling. It allowed me to access feelings and thoughts that would have otherwise gone un-noticed. Overall I found this model effective for me to think clearly and reflect upon what had happened. The action plan was a good way to organise my thoughts into what I would do if the same situation occurred again. This is, again, something I would have been less likely to do had I not written it in this reflection. However, I would question how important it is to write all six sections when reflecting in everyday life, especially with the demands of a career. It would be very time consuming and so perhaps might be best to use for reflection on personal life when time and thought can be put into it (Brock, 2010: 54). Vikki*

Kolb's and Gibbs' models illustrate how observation and reflection on practice can enable the forming of new thinking that can then be tested in ensuing and new situations. You can use either of these models and there are many more available on the internet, but why not create your own diagram that suits your style of reflective thinking. For critical reflection to be effective it needs to self-emanate from a desire to do it, having understood its value, and it can be, in Bolton's (2005: 3) view, the 'pearl grit in an oyster of practice and education'.

Focused reflection point

Dye (2005: 221) suggests drawing a diagram using the following three words:

EXPERIENCE   REFLECTION   LEARNING

Move the words around, add further words that are meaningful for you, use arrows or other graphics and in this way you will create your own model that has relevance for you. What is most important is that you use the model that is most appropriate for yourself – one that can support you and enable you to be reflective. You can even adapt any of the above to suit your own preferences.

Promoting critical reflection

Your process of reflection-*on*-reflection can take the form of a continuous learning journey and in this way will not only continue to enhance your provision, but will also promote feelings of personal and professional accomplishment and enhance job satisfaction, as your provision and children's achievements grow in quality. A process of reflection-on-reflection is demonstrated in Figure 1.3. The benefits of engaging in critical reflection include:

- developing an understanding of how to critically analyse;
- deepening thinking through becoming more skilful in reflecting – improve through doing;
- further developing knowledge of research and theory applied to personal practice;
- promoting change in practice and developing effective provision that meets children's needs;
- enhancing children's experiences, through understanding how to improve scaffolding of their learning and metacognition;
- promoting confidence in caring and teaching, and so increasing job satisfaction, as children learn and achieve;
- endorsing personal success, promoting professional accomplishments through an ongoing personal professional learning journey;
- facilitating articulation and advocacy through sharing knowledge of effective practice.

Conclusion

Purposeful reflection does not always come naturally and you may have to work at it, but it is most easy and valuable when it has meaning and purpose. This chapter has introduced you to notions, theories and research about reflection and reflective practice. You should by now have a sound founda-

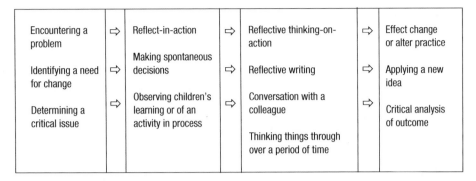

Encountering a problem	⇨	Reflect-in-action	⇨	Reflective thinking-on-action	⇨	Effect change or alter practice
Identifying a need for change	⇨	Making spontaneous decisions	⇨	Reflective writing	⇨	Applying a new idea
Determining a critical issue	⇨	Observing children's learning or of an activity in process	⇨	Conversation with a colleague	⇨	Critical analysis of outcome
				Thinking things through over a period of time		

FIGURE 1.3   A process of reflection-on-reflection.

tion of knowledge of these in order to move through the book. There will be many opportunities and focused reflection points when you will be requested to engage in reflection about specific activities or issues. Your reflectivity is bound to improve greatly if you participate in these, and your knowledge base will also further develop. The next chapter will provide you with purpose and justification of why reflective practice is so important for ECE practitioners and commence your journey towards putting it into practice on a regular basis.

Summary of knowledge gained

After reading and reflecting on this chapter you should now be very aware:

■ that there are varied definitions of reflection and reflective practice;
■ of the key theories that provide relevant knowledge and understanding about reflection;
■ of what processes to engage in to promote purposeful reflection;
■ that making time to engage in reflection is necessary to improve thinking and practice.

Challenges for the future

■ That you will continue to develop your knowledge and understanding about reflective practice.
■ To trial different reflective thinking cycles and to create your own model that works for you.
■ That you will engage in the focused reflection points presented throughout this book.

Further reading

Bolton, G. (2010) *Reflective Practice Writing Professional Development Book*. Third edition. London: Sage.

Moon, J. (2004) *Handbook of Reflective and Experiential Learning: Theory and practice*. London: Routledge Falmer.

Moyles, J. (ed.) (2010) *Thinking About Play: Developing a reflective approach*. Maidenhead: McGraw Hill/Open University Press.

References

Anning, A. (2002) 'Paper Two: Investigating the impact of working in integrated service delivery settings on early years practitioners' professional knowledge and practice: Strategies for dealing with controversial issues.' Paper presented at the Annual Conference of the British Educational Research Association, University of Exeter, England, 12–14 September 2002. The Effectiveness of Early Years Education Symposium.

Atherton, J.S. (2011) *Learning and Teaching: Reflection and reflective practice* (Online: UK), retrieved 11 April 2012 from http://www.learningandteaching.info/learning/reflecti. htm.

Atherton, J.S. (2013) *Learning and Teaching: Experiential learning* (Online: UK), retrieved 11 September 2013 from http://www.learningandteaching.info/learning/experience.htm.

Bolton, G. (2005) *Reflective Practice: Writing and professional development*. Second edition. London: Paul Chapman Publishing.

Bolton, G. (2010) *Reflective Practice: Writing and professional development*. Third edition. London: Sage.

Boud, D. (2010) 'Relocating reflection in the context of practice', Chapter 2 in Bradbury, H., Frost., N., Kilminster, S. and Zukas, M. (eds) *Beyond Reflective Practice: New approaches to professional lifelong learning*. London: Routledge.

Brock, A. (2010) 'The nature of practitioners' reflection on their reflections about play', in Moyles, J. (ed.) *Thinking About Play: Developing a reflective approach*. Maidenhead: McGraw Hill/Open University Press.

Bradbury, H., Frost, N., Kilminster, S. and Zukas, M. (2010) *Beyond Reflective Practice: New approaches to professional lifelong learning*. London: Routledge.

Dewey, J. (1933) *How We Think: A restatement of the relation of reflective thinking to the educative process*. Revised edition. Boston, MA: D.C. Heath.

Dewey, J. (1938) *Experience and Education*. New York: Collier Books.

Dye, D. (2005) 'Enhancing critical reflection of students during a clinical internship using the self-S.O.A.P. note', *The Internet Journal of Allied Health Sciences and Practice*, 3(4): 1–6.

Eraut, M. (1994) *Developing Professional Knowledge and Competence*. London: Routledge Falmer.

Fook, J. and Gardner, F. (2007) *Practicing Critical Reflection: A resource handbook*. Maidenhead: OUP/McGraw Head.

Forde, C., McMahon, M. and Reeves, J. (2006) *Putting Together Professional Portfolios*. London: Sage.

Frost, N. (2010) 'Professionalism and social change: the implications of social change for the "reflective practitioner"', Chapter 1 in Bradbury, H., Frost., N., Kilminster, S. and Zukas, M. (eds) *Beyond Reflective Practice: New approaches to professional lifelong learning*. London: Routledge.

Gibbs, G. (1988) *Learning by Doing: A guide to teaching and learning methods*. Further Education Unit, Oxford Brookes University, Oxford, retrieved 8 April 2014 from http://www.brookes.ac.uk/services/upgrade/study-skills/reflective-gibbs.html.

Hickson, H. (2011) 'Critical reflection: reflecting on learning to be reflective', *Reflective Practice*, 12(6): 829–39.

Jones, M. and Shelton, M. (2011) *Developing Your Portfolio: Enhancing your learning and showing your stuff. A guide for the early childhood student or professional*. Second edition. London: Routledge.

Knights, S., Meyer, L. and Sampson, J. (2007) 'Enhancing learning in the academic workplace through reflective team teaching', *Intellect Ltd*, 4(3): 237–47.

Kolb, D.A. (1984a) *Experiential Learning Experience as a Source of Learning and Development*. New Jersey: Prentice Hall.

Kolb, D.A. (1984b) *Learning Cycle*. LeedsMet University Skills for Learning, retrieved 8 April 2014 from http://skillsforlearning.leedsmet.ac.uk/local/reflection/models/02.shtml.

Moon, J. (1999) *Learning Journals: A handbook for academics, students and professional development*. London: Kogan Page.

Moon, J. (2004) *A Handbook of Reflective and Experiential Learning: Theory and practice*. London: Routledge.

Moon, J. (2005) 'Progression in higher education: a study of learning as represented in level descriptors', in Hartley, P., Woods, A. and Pill, M. (eds) *Enhancing Teaching in Higher Education*. London: Routledge Falmer.

Moyles, J. (2010) *Thinking About Play: Developing a reflective approach*. Maidenhead: OUP/McGraw Hill.

Paige-Smith, A. and Craft, A. (2008) *Developing Reflective Practice in the Early Years*. Maidenhead: Open University Press/McGraw Hill.

Powell, S. (2011) 'How can e-reflection help develop your practice?', Chapter 12 in McGregor, D. and Cartwright, L. (eds) *Developing Reflective Practice: A guide for beginning teachers*. Maidenhead: Open University Press.

Reed, M. (2011) 'Reflective practice and professional development', in Paige-Smith, A. and Craft, A. (eds) *Developing Reflective Practice in the Early Years*. Second edition. Milton Keynes: Open University Press/McGraw Hill, pp. 278–99.

Rinaldi, C. (2006) *In Dialogue with Reggio Emilia: Listening, researching and learning*. London: Routledge.

Ryan, M. (2011) 'Improving reflective writing in higher education: a social semiotic perspective', *Teaching in Higher Education*, 16(1): 99–111.

Scanlon, J.M. and Chernomas, W.M. (1997) 'Developing the reflective teacher', *Journal of Advanced Nursing*, 25: 1138–43.

Schön, D. (1976) *The Reflective Practitioner: How professionals think in action*. Aldershot: Arena.

Schön, D.A. (1983) *Educating the Reflective Practitioner*. San Francisco, CA: Jossey-Bass.

Schön, D. (1987). *Educating the Reflective Practitioner: Toward a new design for teaching and learning in the professions*. San Francisco, CA: Jossey-Bass.

Wong, K., Pine, R. and Tsang, N. (2000) 'Learning style preferences and implications for training programs in the hospitality and tourism industry', *Journal of Hospitality and Tourism Education*, 12(2): 32–40.

2

Why is reflection important for early childhood educators?

Avril Brock

This chapter asks you to reflect on your knowledge base as an ECE practitioner, to realise its complexity and the many varied components that you need to draw on in your everyday work. It will get you to explore your personal, practical and professional knowledge base. It aims to enable you to become a reflective practitioner, able to demonstrate reflexivity on your practice and your professional role. It will ask you to explore what is meant by constructive practice and how to deal with critical incidences and relationships. The issues in the chapter then move to the wider external relationships and why being articulate about your professional knowledge base and demonstrating your critical reflective thinking is important. The chapter presents perspectives from authentic voices of those at the forefront of practice – the ECCE practitioners and students who work with young children. It also aims not only to clarify the reflection process for you, but also to make it professionally and personally meaningful and purposeful.

Developing professional knowledge

The development of new knowledge, thinking, policy and practice occurs constantly and practitioners operate within the context of where and with whom they work, accepting or adapting to change. New developments might feel positive or negative to the individual practitioner, but whatever the immediate and personal/professional feelings she or he might have, it is necessary to engage in critical reflection on any change. It is a key professional attribute to be able to reflect on the impact of change on the children and families with whom you work and the effects on working practice.

Contemporary professionals need to continually gain and interrelate different aspects of knowledge, and for most it is complex and multidimensional, crossing a range of expertise and skills. Developing professional knowledge involves the interconnection of technical or subject knowledge, practical skills, values, beliefs, attitudes and awareness (Ovens, 1999).

> When these knowledge bases are reflected upon, articulated and understanding enhanced then professional knowledge is generated. It is essential to integrate reflection with personal and contextual understanding in order to identify the way to develop, change and improve practice.
>
> (Brock, 2010)

Stenhouse (1975) suggests that educators develop 'contextual knowing' which is the knowledge that is 'context specific' as practitioners articulate, understand and reflect on their practice. Early childhood educators are facilitators and partners in the process of the development of knowledge, and this is not just 'I do this' but the justification of purpose and intent in relation to developmental needs. Knowledge is seen as constructed and understood in relation to effective deployment of evidence to outside agencies and stakeholders, including parents and Ofsted.

Reflection should examine practice and underlying assumptions in order to identify the way to change and develop practice; however, by itself it is not sufficient for professional development to occur (Day, 1999). It needs to be integrated with the uniqueness of personal and contextual understanding (Hoyle and John, 1995). Professionals need to 'participate in a range of informal and formal activities which will assist them in a process of review, renewal, enhancement of thinking and practice, and, most importantly, commitment of the mind and heart' (Day, 1999: 1). Theory is implicit in professional practice, which can be improved by closing the gap between what is implicit and what is explicitly practised. Reflection on professional practice can help determine discrepancies between implicit and explicit assumptions.

A model of professional knowledge

Terms such as knowledge, beliefs, theories, thinking, values, principles and frames of reference are all used to characterise aspects of practitioners' thinking about their professional knowledge (Bennett *et al.*, 1997). Practitioners may draw upon the varied aspects of knowledge mentioned in this chapter – theoretical, craft, practical, personal and tacit knowledge. The ability to reflect on these contributes to professional knowledge. As research theories are examined, new thinking is offered and changing policy development occurs, so the demands intensify and increased professional knowledge is required. It is therefore important that questioning and debate among ECCE professionals occur in order to stimulate the growth of professional knowledge (NAEYC, 1993). Being a professional educator is not just about delivery or technical practice. When it is informed by principles and thinking, it becomes a professional act drawing upon a range of skills. Knowledge is drawn from a breadth of experiences gained through education, training and practice. Figure 2.1 offers a model of the scope of knowledge required by those working in the field of

Theoretical Professional Personal Practical Tacit Craft Wisdom Theoretical (*thinking and developing*) Practical application (*experiencing and doing*)

Knowledge of how children learn	Knowledge of individual children – meeting individual needs
Knowledge of child development	
Knowledge of pedagogy	Knowledge and practice of how educators teach including play-based pedagogy
Knowledge of curriculum models – EYFS, Reggio, Montessori, High/Scope, Steiner	Knowledge of pedagogical framing – putting ideology into practice that works for the children
Knowledge of EYFS curriculum content	Knowledge of what to teach, plan, resource
Knowledge of national and local legislation and initiatives	Knowledge of Ofsted inspection, assessment and testing requirements
Knowledge of ecological theory	Knowledge of implementing national and local policy
Knowledge of socio-culturalism – culture, ethnicity, language, inclusion, diversity	Knowledge of how policy impacts on the children and families with whom you work
Knowledge about special educational needs and inclusion	Knowledge about the specific needs and interests of the children, families and communities with whom you work – how to provide for inclusion and diversity
Knowledge about the varied professionals across the disciplines	
Knowledge of standards and competences	Knowledge of working with key people in your interdisciplinary team and developing specific relationships
Knowledge of leadership and management	
Knowledge of context of job and role – meeting the demands of professional roles, engaging in continuing professional development and training	Knowledge and skills of managing in action – leading a team and creating a vision

ACQUIRED THROUGH

Higher or further education courses and training days	Placement/field work
	Work/roles in setting
Mentors/teachers/lecturers	Mentors modelling
Reading textbooks/journals/periodicals	Working relationships with colleagues
Mentors with theories	Family, friends and acquaintances
Internet/media	Previous life history
Policy documents – national/local/setting	Visiting other settings

FIGURE 2.1 Dimensions of knowledge for early childhood care and education.

ECCE. Knowledge from both theory and practice contributes to practitioners' actions in their everyday roles and this model aims, in conjunction with the rest of this chapter, to validate ECE (early childhood educator) professionality through an exploration of knowledge base.

Reflecting in everyday practice

Cameron and Boddy (2006) note that there has been a lack of emphasis on the development of critical thinking and reflection in the training programmes for teaching assistants and those working with younger children. Potter and Hodgson (2007: 497) suggest that without such grounding some staff in early years settings may 'understandably struggle to take an enquiring approach to their work'. Whilst early years workers are motivated by their personal practical experiences, some may be 'distrustful and underestimate the value of their insights' (Cameron and Boddy, 2006: 58). Potter and Hodgson (2007: 497) have demonstrated how focused Sure Start training with a strong focus on critical thinking and reflection can enhance adult–child interaction. The Children's Workforce Development Council (CWDC) (2007: 58) required practitioners studying for the early years professional (EYP) qualification to 'reflect on and evaluate the impact of practice, modifying approaches where necessary, and taking responsibility for identifying and meeting their professional development needs'. Potter and Hodgson (2007) believe that it is crucial that all staff working with young children are able to reflect critically on what they do and why they are doing it. The ability to undertake critical thinking and reflection is therefore not just the prerogative of or a requirement for those working towards higher qualifications. In order to develop one's professional role, all early years practitioners need to understand and engage in the continual development of reflective practice.

So what do you need to reflect on in your everyday practice? Your reflective process may take different forms and focuses dependent on what is happening in your practice at any particular time – whether as a working practitioner or as a student. Many of you will be both working in a setting whilst undertaking ECCE qualifications for EYE (early years educator), for EYT (early years teacher) or for QTS (qualified teacher status). (See Chapter 4 for further discussions on these qualifications.) You may be a childminder studying for your Master's or a manager of a children's centre and gaining the National Professional Qualification in Integrated Centre Leadership (NPQICL). It may be difficult to reflect at a critical level because you have such a busy life, but reflecting on one's practice will develop and improve with experience and time.

There now follow some examples of what you might want to reflect on in your practice or your study. Select one or more that has meaning for you and have a go at thinking about what you could do to improve or develop your work. Use Table 2.1 to make reflecting-on-practice notes.

Focused reflection point

In practice you might reflect on how to:

- change the layout of your classroom or teaching area to improve children's access to resources;
- develop learning journeys of your key-worker children;
- promote positive behaviour with a challenging child;
- acquire and use some phrases of Polish language to enhance a group of children's additional language, promote self-esteem and develop bilingual language learning;

- encourage boys to go into the writing area and to be involved in emergent writing activities;
- improve the story corner through accessing the local authority's library provision;
- involve parents in observations of their children;
- reflect on your role within your setting and how to develop your responsibilities;
- work collaboratively with a challenging colleague;
- implement the EYFS development matters;
- compile observations for the foundation stage profile (FSP).

TABLE 2.1 Reflecting-on-practice notes

Key points raised	What I can put into practice now	Ideas to follow up

Focused reflection point

In study you might reflect on:

- which course to take that is most appropriate in meeting your needs and professional development;
- how to evidence standards in a personal professional development file;
- critical incidents that arise due to conflicts between work and study;
- how to evaluate learning activities that are analytical and not just descriptive;
- how to prove your capabilities to assessors, teacher mentors or placement tutors;
- how to create a learning journal or a reflective portfolio;
- how to write an academic essay at an appropriate level – where do you go for advice and how will you act on it to produce the correct standard and level;
- how to work collaboratively on a group PowerPoint presentation of a current issue;
- how to manage work–life balance and personal and professional relationships.

You might draw a mind map of your thoughts and ideas or you might find Table 2.1 useful as a work in progress. You can make notes of your initial thoughts and then keep adding to it as you return to further develop your reflective thinking on an activity.

Focused reflection point

It will be useful to have a go at critically analysing the following scenario. In critiquing this it can show you that you can reflect on and appraise your own practice. Reflect on answering these three questions after you have read the scenario:

- Do you find anything amiss with the practice?
- Would you advise the practitioners and the setting that practice could be improved?
- If you were a three-year-old what would you like to have been doing on this afternoon?

A stay and play session at a setting. A group of 16 three-year-olds were sitting in a circle around Glenys who was getting them to guess the day of the week. The children sit politely, some with their mums as it was an invitation play and stay afternoon at the private daycare nursery. Glenys recited the days of the week and the months of the year with most of the children making noises that were in tune, with one little girl getting the answers right. Opposites were next and the children were reminded of opposite concept words that were displayed in the room. This was quite an abstract activity as there were no practical resources used. Glenys read Monkey Puzzle *by Julia Donaldson and Axel Scheffler and the children listened and enjoyed this lovely story; however, not all could see the pictures as the book was flat on her knee rather than held up for all to see. During this time, Alice, the other early years practitioner for this group, had disappeared to do some other tasks and Cameron, who had his own way of participating, was allowed to do 'his own thing' around the room. After circle time the children were asked which area they wanted to play in and they were encouraged to make autonomous decisions. They were directed to an activity if they didn't choose for themselves. Alice returned and spent the next 30 minutes colouring in photocopied pictures with a group of children. Glenys had a rest and watched a mum reading to her child and baby. Another mum took her son to the water tray and made full use of the resources available in this wet area. The water was coloured green and the children were sailing boats, pouring water on them to determine floating and sinking. Only four children at a time were allowed in the water; there were four aprons. The children knew this meant only four children should be playing there; however, eight children were keen to play and either hovered or joined in without an apron. Probably three of these three-year-olds particularly needed some individual support for attention, behaviour and language needs. The ratio was eight children per adult and the practitioners were both quite young and had not yet gained a level three qualification. Glenys said at the end of the play and stay that she had had a lovely afternoon.*

The resources and the timetable for this setting were very good. There was some knowledge of the EYFS curriculum, but was the pedagogy appropriate? Were the practitioners under pressure and could they really cater for children's individual needs in a group this size? What should these practitioners know about adult–child interaction? Some of the boys had a star chart in operation to encourage good behaviour; could they have been a little bored with provision – does it lack challenge? Of course this is a snapshot of an hour in one afternoon; however, it was a time when visitors were present and one would have thought best practice would have been on offer. However, the children were happy and they were enjoying nursery; several had learned the alphabet and recited it to their parents; they had established good friendships and they could sit and listen well. What are your reflections on this scenario? Share them with a colleague or fellow student.

Self-evaluation should be an active process of considering what you do in your practice, including the active reflection that considers the possible gap between hope of intentions and what actually happens (Lindon, 2010: 5). This process of serious thought and constructive critical analysis of current practice leads to an informed judgement about strengths and considered plans for change that will bring about improvements. Lindon (2010: 6) advises that the ECCE profession is not one 'where you can take ten minutes out to analyse a problem of activity', as the work with young children is normally very intense and it is mostly necessary to 'make time to think back and analyse after the event'.

The reflective practitioner: reflexivity on practice and professional roles

The term reflective practitioner applies to all those ECCE practitioners regardless of their role, whether or not they work directly with young children (Paige-Smith and Craft, 2008). Engaging in study and gaining a professional knowledge base means that you can justify and articulate your practice to others – parents, managers, colleagues, head teachers, governors, assessors, Ofsted. Engaging in a process of reflection in a purposeful way and discussing it with a mentor, or having your reflective writing assessed by a tutor and seeing improvement in what you do, or achieving good feedback will promote your confidence, articulation and professionalism. This is not only important for achieving qualification, but also for gaining promotion, for doing well in Ofsted inspections or in supporting you in any requests for further resources or change in practice. As a professional ECE you need to be committed to your own professional growth and professional conduct and continue to develop your specialised knowledge of ECCE. Chapter 4 discusses further what professionalism means for ECE practitioners of all levels.

Reflection in an informal discussion with a critical friend or colleague can enable you to see different perspectives and can enable examination of taken-for-granted situations. Knowledge shared promotes understanding and a desire to use the knowledge to make a difference. A questioning of personal and professional values and practices can challenge one's thinking and so deepen understanding to further develop practice. Through dialogue and discussion with a 'learning partner' you can engage in a co-construction of knowledge. We know that children learn more effectively through contextualisation and active learning and the same is the case for most adults. Reflexivity on practice requires acute observation and a process of deep questioning that explores and teases out events or actions. This process of analytical thinking should also include appraisal of one's feelings and values. You should also explore varied perspectives in an interactive dialogic process with others.

Reed (2010: 8) warns of the dangers in thinking that there are simple answers to questions about reflective practice. It is important that personal interpretation for evaluation and redefining our individual professional role occurs within a particular context, space or time. In Reed's opinion practitioners need to engage in meta-reflection which involves defining and redefining one's individual professional 'identity' as reflective thinkers. Reed (2010: 16) found his students to be willing 'to research different perspectives and to use these to self evaluate and to inform personal change'. He acknowledges the struggle that many have to 'construct personal meanings within someone else's framework and expectations' and in developing a voice when being assessed. However, he assures us that this is essential for 'your development of your identity, competence and confidence' (Reed, 2010: 16). Reflection is more than simply thinking about experiences and needs to involve critiques of one's assumptions about beliefs and values and how these have developed. The reflective practitioner needs to understand experiences in the social context and how this can be used to develop future practice (Hickson, 2011: 831). Hickson's 'structured uncertainty' is a really useful phrase to show how, when she reflects on her values, experiences, influences, people or interactions, she continually asks herself 'why' as she believes each thought and reflection is important and relevant. In her opinion this 'mining deeper' into reflective thinking has the potential to invigorate and empower through recognising personal ability and skill along with the learning.

This book aims to promote constructive practice – you need to make decisions as to when and how you want to use it. It aims to be a handbook to not only support you as you train but also to travel with you through the educational process and into practice and on to continuing professional development. It aims to *entice* you into reflectively interacting with what you meet in the book and interpret in practice.

FIGURE 2.2 Critically reflecting with a colleague.

Constructive practice

Jones and Shelton (2011: 1) argue that 'constructive practice – hands-on, interactive, social collaborative – is so engaging' as practitioners can 'construct their own knowledge' and take responsibility for their own learning. Constructivism is about learning and how knowledge is acquired, continued and further developed. Constructive practice is influenced by social and cultural factors existing in the workplace environment and influenced by the people with whom you work and by policymakers who may demand specific outcomes. Purposeful engagement with others in learning is a shared activity demanding investment of effort and time (Jones and Shelton, 2011: 12). You need to be active agents in your own learning, modifying and developing through your experience and existing understanding; constructing and reconstructing your understanding. Information transformation has the potential for deep-level learning and through this transformation comes ownership, knowledge and an understanding of underlying principles and processes (Jones and Shelton, 2011: 16). As well as reviewing the 'what' and 'how', professionals also need to address the 'why' – going through a continual process of re-affirming and/or re-accommodating their ideology through reflecting on their knowledge, beliefs, values and ethics (Brock, 2010). The diagram in Figure 2.3 demonstrates that reflective professional development is a continual process.

Your personal philosophy or ideology is developed through knowledge; interaction with others; practical experiences; engagement in tasks; observations of practice and of children; personal, biographical experiences. All these create:

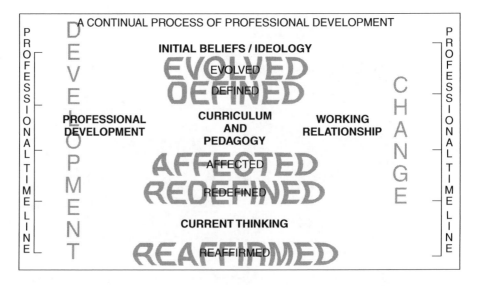

FIGURE 2.3   A continual process of personal and professional development (Brock, 2010: 49).

- who we are;
- what we think;
- what we believe;
- what we do;
- what we are interested in/like to do;
- what we think we are capable of;
- what challenges we can rise to;
- what our ambitions are.

Social change has to be understood through individual action and in this way professional identity might be reformed and translated into new or reaffirmed professional practice (Fook and Gardner, 2007). Forde *et al.* (2006: 66) argue that it is valuable to focus on learning *in* rather than *away from* practice, as 'using critical reflection will allow practitioners to identify what they do well and what they need to do to improve their practice'. A good place to start is to determine what your values are – what is important to you and what do you believe in?

Focused reflection point

Why not have a go at determining what your value statements would be. Use the following prompts to develop your thinking:

- Who am I and what is my sense of identity?
- What do I believe in?
- What about my interpersonal relationships – who has a similar ideology to me?
- Who are my critical friends – who do I contact and have conversations to explore my problems and critical issues?
- What are my relationships with employers, leaders/managers, colleagues, clients?
- Do I have a mentor?
- Do I work in anti-oppressive practice where everyone's culture and identity is valued?
- Do I feel empowered in my work or study?

Reflection-on-reflection indicates an extra dimension to a practitioner's reflective process in that it requires dissemination to a critical friend, researcher or tutor who will actively listen or read the reflections and then respond in ways that further develop the reflective process itself. The 'reflectee' is aware that there is an interested party who is evaluating the reflections and may comment on insights, observations, knowledge or relationships. The process is not meant to make judgements on the practice but to act like a mirror for the 'reflectee' and so aims to deepen understanding of the practice or the event (Brock, 2010).

Critical incidents

The purpose of reflection on a critical incident is to focus on a specific incident or situation – a particular event, experience, encounter, activity or issue that might be causing you some disequilibrium. You may feel nervous, worried or unsettled about an experience. You might find you need to look at yourself, or others, in a new light, or to re-evaluate your practice. In the context of reflective practice an incident is 'critical' in the sense that the reflector has chosen to spend some time reflecting on it. The critical incident can be anything from, for example, a mundane routine or habit to a more emotionally charged incident. It can be an event which made you stop and think, raised questions for you or impacted on your beliefs or on your personal and professional learning. A critical incident that might happen in the workplace as a student or practitioner might be:

- a parent challenging your behaviour management, toilet training or assessment of their child;
- a colleague criticising one of your learning activities or tidiness around a wet resource area;
- a manager disapproving of your time management;
- a tutor querying the depth of your written observations;
- Ofsted commenting that you need to make critical changes to your practice.

If you are using critical incidents to help you reflect it may be useful to consider why you chose the incident. When writing about a critical incident you would briefly describe the incident but the primary focus should be on what you learned or realised and why. Smyth's (1989) four-step reflective process is a valuable and easy to access way of engaging in reflection on critical incidents:

1. What did I do? (Providing detailed description)
2. What does this mean? (Examining from different perspectives)
3. How did I come to be this way? (Examining any assumptions from contextual and political factors)
4. How might I do things differently? (Considering alternatives and future actions)

Students on a Master's course reflected on their use of critical incident theory to analyse particular experiences that had happened to them, that had caused them concern or that they wanted to explore in more depth after the situation, action or experience had happened:

> The critical incident theory had an enormous, positive impact on me personally as it enabled me to come to terms with some disturbing events that occurred in my professional life, which subsequently went on to affect my personal life. I wasn't able to make the connection before this exercise. Sakinah

> The investigation of critical incident theory was interesting and thought provoking. It gave direction and focus to the reflective process and encouraged real

and in-depth exploration of an incident from many perspectives. It was useful to appreciate that incidents could be both positive as well as negative. Helen

Reflecting on critical incidents was useful in terms of allowing me not only to look at incidents from my own point of view but also from others' viewpoints. I tend to write this type of reflection when reflecting on professional matters, therefore found it useful particularly from a work point of view. Nicola

---

Focused reflection point

Why not select one of the following examples to engage in a focused reflection. Either use Table 2.1 (reflecting-on-practice) notes on pages 25–6 or just spend five or ten minutes thinking about it and then perhaps share it with a colleague or fellow student.

- An experience where you were less than satisfied about how you resourced an activity.
- How you dealt with two children quarrelling over a toy.
- Concern about the level of learning achieved by the children in the role play area.
- Concern about the health and safety of the outdoor environment.
- That a child with SEN is not participating with other children.

It is vital that your reflections go beyond purely describing learning experiences to draw out how the experiences have changed the way you look at something. The aim is to evoke new comprehensions about the event, and the outcome should be that it is more understandable or acceptable. You might need to change elements of your thinking or practice to restore yourself to a state of equilibrium. In order to reflect effectively on a critical incident, consider the following:

- the context of the experience;
- a description of what happened;
- how you felt about the experience when it was happening;
- how you felt about it afterwards;
- why the experience was critical to you;
- what you have learned and/or decided to change in your practice.

Another idea is to focus on non-critical incidents to gain insight by respecting the reflective processes to enlighten what most needs examining (Bolton, 2005). It does not matter that you do not depict what actually happened, or what you, your student or client thought. What does matter is that you have brought what you do understand and think about this person into the forefront of your mind. In Sharkey's (2004) opinion, 'we need to attend to the untold' (Bolton, 2005: 12).

I liked the critical incident theory, which I initially thought would have to be something major to be critical, but it turns out that a small decision can be something critical if it has an impact on the way you think. Alix

This was very interesting as this is something that examined how you dealt with difficulties when they arise. Whether you 'on reflection' consider your actions to have been appropriate. I always thought that you should put your own feelings to one side and not act on them till you have been able to think things through and be calm, but it was discussed that feelings shouldn't be ignored and that subjectivity can be part of reflecting, which was a new concept to me. Jackie

Insight is gained by respecting the reflective and reflexive processes to light upon and enlighten that which needs examination (Bolton, 2005). Joy-Matthews *et al.* (2004) recommend writing what you do not remember. We often focus on negative incidents, those which we find painful in some way, to try to find out what went wrong. However, it is also useful to reflect on positive incidents, for example to identify how the positive effects can be reproduced elsewhere, or to question routines and why a certain practice has become a habit, and would an alternative be preferable? Critical incident writing can:

- help you deal with really critical issues/incidents;
- get you in touch directly with your feelings, giving your ideas and thoughts a flow of expression;
- enable you to acknowledge the importance of the incident;
- draw on links not thought of purely in discussion;
- stimulate you to find peer support/mentoring through on-line conferencing.

You might find McGregor and Cartwright's (2011: 275) five steps of writing about critical incidents supportive in deepening your level of reflexivity:

1st   Being able to identify and describe a critical incident or happening (the *what* of a situation).

2nd Being able to explain *why* you did it the way you did or why the critical incident arose.

3rd Being able to recognise there were *different* ways to act in the critical happening or incident.

4th Being able to devise a way of *finding* out whether one approach was better than another leading up to that type of critical incident.

5th Comparing the evidence to decide which *approach* worked best, to avoid an incident arising again, and why.

Reflecting on situations and writing down one's thinking can reduce anxiety and stress, but they are not meant to be confessions (Bolton, 2005: 62). However, there are times when individuals experience traumatic, critical events that challenge their understanding of their world and their place in the world. This understanding has been referred to as a worldview. As a result of their traumatic encounter a person may have difficulty integrating their worldview as they wish it would be and their worldview according to their experience (Fay, 1998). The incident has emotional impact on an individual due to the meaning a person ascribes to that event. Narrative psychological theory suggests that developing a story about oneself and your reaction to a critical or sub-critical incident can be very supportive. Practitioners have observed children role-playing 9/11 by flying model planes into a tower of bricks or building imaginary fires after the Bradford football match fire. Developing reflective thinking about a traumatic occurrence or observation through externalising conversations may be valuable and cathartic – think about refugee and asylum children who have observed war; children who have experienced domestic violence, bereavement or whose parent may be in prison. The case studies in Section 3 will provide some relevant information about children who may have had one or several of these experiences. You may then want to go through the reflective processes in your professional role and see how to make a difference to these children. Doing the research and gaining relevant knowledge is only the first step!

Critical relationships

Many of us might have experienced professional issues in our working environment. We may have felt that our expertise has not been valued or felt that there was poor leadership in a school or ECCE setting. We might have felt that our ideas for change and development were not listened to or accepted. A colleague's body language, facial expressions and perhaps hidden or overt criticism might have prevented effective relationships or change from happening. Open discussions and leading people supportively through change is important. Staff need to feel involved in reflective discussions about change to avoid their using such phrases as 'I'm sorry but . . .' or 'We've done that before and it didn't work.' Claire Walden (2012) describes how 'Fishface' in a staff meeting can prevent things from happening and how leaders have to rise to the challenge of moving staff positively forward from feeling demoralised or uninspired. Leaders need to reflect on their working relationships with staff and develop a personal inner resilience to feeling hurt about the erection of hurdles or barriers or feeling personally criticised. Useful advice is to undertake 'silent pedagogy' through not directly interfering, but modelling and providing positive support and promoting reflective thinking in a non-critical way. Some practitioners resist being pushed into being reflective as they may feel that their job is mainly intuitive and tacit. They know what to do and feel they do not need to engage in ongoing reflection, and may say 'I haven't got time' or 'We've always done it this way.' It is possible to compel someone to imitate reflection to meet professional standards, but this will not be effective if the reflections are not meaningful. It requires personal motivation and understanding to see need and understand purpose. Look at Chapter 8 for examples of graduate leadership and how they involved staff in making a real difference for two-year-olds in settings. No matter what resistance is encountered it is important to be seen as supportive and constructive; as Lindon (2010: 7) advises, you may be taking apart 'cherished assumptions of practice' that may have emotional consequences. Reflective practice should enable thoughtful practitioners to address important questions such as 'I believe my practice is child-centred. But what makes me so sure?' 'What makes the inspectorate happy?' 'What will make the children happy?'

Reflection within a climate of policy change

Reflection is very important for ECCE practitioners when they need to examine their professional role, status, autonomy and voice when challenged by others. During the last 35 years, early years practitioners have experienced numerous changes in policy and frameworks which have varyingly caused some educators to feel destabilised and so question their beliefs and values. Reflective thinking can help practitioners keep a balance on perspectives and help examine one's own space in a setting and in local and national society. As stated earlier in this chapter, tacit knowledge does not mean that the professional knowledge base is not complicated. Working with young children is one of the most enjoyable and fulfilling professions but it can also be a stressful occupation – not necessarily from the pressures of normal day-to-day working with children, which creates both physical and mental demands, and not only due to curriculum, assessment or paperwork requirements, but often due to external pressures imposed through testing, reporting, inspection or through significant others (teachers; managers; inspectors) challenging beliefs and values. When we work with young children we are normally very involved in what we do and we have strongly held values about working for the best outcomes for young children and families. Furthermore, target-driven policy can create a disjunction between professional and organisational values; as Frost (2010: 23) observes, 'true critical reflection cannot occur in isolation', otherwise it will become separate from the reality in which practitioners operate. Moss (2008: xii) warns against a narrow interpretation of reflective practice as it can be used as a means to govern early childhood professionals or used to assess personal 'conformity to externally imposed norms' in a mechanistic way. In order to deal with external demands ECEs will need to engage with the wider social and political context and develop a strong sense of professionalism and professional identity. This will be explored in Chapters 4 and 5.

Conclusion

Reflection can be an exhilarating journey (Bolton, 2005) but there may be tensions arising from your reflection-*on*-reflection with others; whether it is because an academic tutor or an external assessor is assessing your work; whether you are having to justify changes to a line manager who seems to be unconvinced; or whether you are just finding it hard to articulate your ideas at this stage in time. Remember: it will get easier the more you do, as it becomes a natural reflective process. Critical reflection can develop knowledge and understanding and reflection-on-practice can therefore refresh or change practice for practitioners aiming for higher quality provision. Keeping up to date with the developments in knowledge, empirical research, practice and policy is important and it is stimulating for the field of ECCE that it is now informed by so many respected practice researchers who have worked with young children and can draw on their professional experiences. This is even more important today with the many changes that are constantly occurring in ECCE with the effects of an austerity climate impacting on young children and their families. This is not only the case for the UK but also throughout many European countries, the USA, South America, Africa and China to name a few. Your process of reflection-on-reflection should take the form of a continuous learning journey and, in this way, will not only continue to enhance your provision but will also promote feelings of personal and professional accomplishment and enhance job satisfaction.

Summary of knowledge gained

After reading and reflecting on this chapter you should now be very aware:

- of why reflective thinking and practice is important to you as an ECCE practitioner;
- of what processes to engage in to promote purposeful reflection;
- that you can select your own strategy of engaging in reflection including discussing with a colleague.

Challenges for the future

- To ensure that reflective thinking becomes part of your everyday practice.
- To make decisions to take a focused reflective approach on a particular aspect as the need arises.
- To reflect with colleagues and to take advantage of different practitioner perspectives on critical issues.

Further reading

If you are interested in developing your knowledge of engaging in reflection further, why not read the following:

Lindon, J. (2010) *Reflective Practice and Early Years Professionalism: Linking theory and practice.* London: Hodders.

Page-Smith, A. and Craft, A. (eds) (2011) *Developing Reflective Practice in the Early Years.* Second edition. Milton Keynes: Open University Press.

Reed, M. and Canning, N. (2011) *Implementing Quality Improvement and Change in the Early Years.* London: Sage.

References

Bennett, N., Wood, L. and Rogers, S. (1997) *Teaching Through Play: Teachers' thinking and classroom practice.* Buckingham: Open University Press.

Bolton, G. (2005) *Reflective Practice: Writing and professional development.* Second edition. London: Paul Chapman Publishing.

Brock, A. (2010) 'The nature of practitioners' reflection on their reflections about play', in Moyles, J. (ed.) *Thinking About Play: Developing a reflective approach.* Maidenhead: McGraw Hill/Open University Press.

Cameron, C. and Boddy, J. (2006) 'Knowledge and education for care workers: what do they need to know?' in Boddy, J., Cameron, C. and Moss, P. (eds) *Care Work: Present and future.* London: Routledge.

Children's Workforce Development Council (CWDC) (2007) *Early Years Professional National Standards.* Leeds: CWDC.

Day, C. (1999) *Developing Teachers: The challenges of lifelong learning.* London: Routledge Falmer.

Fay, J. (1998) 'A narrative approach to critical and sub-critical incident debriefings'. PSyD Dissertation, American School of Professional Psychology. Retrieved 9 April 2014 from http://www.wcpr2001.org/pdf/JoelDissertation.pdf.

Fook, J. and Gardner, F. (2007) *Practising Critical Reflection: A resource handbook.* Maidenhead: Open University Press/McGraw Hill.

Forde, C., McMahon, M. and Reeves, J. (2006) *Putting Together Professional Portfolios.* London: Sage.

Hickson, H. (2011) 'Critical reflection: reflecting on learning to be reflective', *Reflective Practice*, 12(6): 829–39.

Hoyle, E. and John, P.D. (1995) *Professional Knowledge and Professional Practice.* London: Cassell.

Jones, M. and Shelton, M. (2011) *Developing Your Portfolio: Enhancing your learning and showing your stuff. A guide for the early childhood student or professional.* Second edition. London: Routledge.

Joy-Matthews, J., Megginson, D. and Surtees, M. (2004) *Human Resource Development.* Second edition. London: Kogan Page.

Lindon, J. (2010) *Reflective Practice and Early Years Professionalism: Linking theory and practice.* London: Hodders.

McGregor, D. and Cartwright, L. (eds) (2011) *Developing Reflective Practice: A guide for beginning teachers.* Maidenhead: Open University Press.

Moss, P. (2008) 'Foreword', in Paige-Smith, A. and Craft, A. (2008) *Developing Reflective Practice in the Early Years.* Maidenhead: Open University Press/McGraw Hill.

National Association for the Education of Young Children (NAEYC) (1993) *A Conceptual Framework for Early Childhood Professional Development: A position statement of the National Association for the Education of Young Children.* Washington DC: NAEYC.

Ovens, P. (1999) 'Can teachers be developed?' *Journal of In-Service Education*, 25: 275–306.

Paige-Smith, A. and Craft, A. (2008) *Developing Reflective Practice in the Early Years.* Maidenhead: Open University Press/McGraw Hill.

Potter, C. and Hodgson, S. (2007) 'Nursery nurses reflect: Sure Start training to enhance adult child interaction', *Reflective Practice*, 8: 4: 497–509.

Reed, M. (2010) 'Children's centres and children's services', in Reed, M. and Canning, N. (eds) *Reflective Practice in the Early Years.* London: Sage, pp. 99–113.

Sharkey, J. (2004) 'Lives stories don't tell: exploring the untold in autobiographies', *Curriculum Enquiry*, 34(4): 495–512.

Smyth, J. (1989) 'A critical pedagogy of classroom practice', *Journal of Curriculum Studies*, 21(6): 483–502.

Stenhouse, L. (1975) *An Introduction to Curriculum Research and Development.* London: Heinemann.

Walden, C. (2012) 'Inspiring the workforce to inspire children'. Paper presented to TACTYC Conference, *Developing Early Years Practice: Reflecting on developments in practice and research*, 10 November 2012, Birmingham.

3

Developing reflective writing

Avril Brock

Introduction

One of the key ways of reflection is through a process of writing and this can be undertaken in a variety of ways. Reflective writing activities such as journaling, evaluations, self-assessment documents and portfolios have become expected forms of demonstrating knowledge to achieve higher qualifications or receive professional judgements from assessors and Ofsted inspectors. Reflective writing is required by most levels of professional training yet, as Bolton (2005: 1) argues, the use of the terminology of 'reflective practice' has 'lost some credence' as it has become a 'catch-all name for a wide range of activities from deep life, work and organisation'. Because of this there is a concern that 'rote box-ticking practices seeking to make professionals accountable' are replacing critical thinking and analysis (Bolton, 2005: 1). When undertaking reflective writing for assessment purposes, the writer should understand the purpose and benefits of the writing activities. Otherwise it may be purely descriptive without engaging in a process of critical reflective thinking and decision making about how to improve one's professional role.

Reflective writing has become standard in initial and continuing professional education and development. This chapter aims to ensure that you see reflective writing as both meaningful and valuable and supportive of the deepening of reflective thinking processes. It focuses on 'How to reflect purposefully?' through exploring methods often selected in professional development qualifications – journaling; keeping diaries; undertaking evaluations. This chapter, and Chapters 5, 9, 12, 15 and 16, will draw on the experiences of a range of ECCE practitioners and students on undergraduate, postgraduate and Master's modules.

Reflective writing: levels of engagement

Without meaningful understanding a 'student' may just do the writing required in order to satisfy the assessment procedures and may not perceive the benefits and reasons for the process. If this is the case then, as Bradbury *et al.* (2010) observe, reflections can often be superficial and procedural rather than questioning and challenging. Reflective practice has been formalised by regulatory bodies as a way of developing the professionalism of practitioners and students through assessments and professional development. Bradbury *et al.* (2010: 3) argue that if reflection is used mainly as a tool for assessment rather than for conceptual debate, is it really possible to promote truly reflective practice when it is probably often perceived as 'just a procedure'? They believe this has led to a range of teaching and learning activities which have unfortunately all been grouped under a single category labelled reflection.

Reflective writing will benefit from practice and good feedback from a mentor or tutor. There may be a perception that academics are remote and are distant from practical experience; however, although tutors might not have recent practical experience, the knowledge they are imparting and the reflective processes they are advocating have most likely been developed from previous practical experience with children. Tutors will have engaged in ongoing theoretical reading and should be able to critically analyse what works in a range of settings with diverse children and families. Academics will aim to develop criticality in students so they can be selective as to what is purposeful. It is most beneficial if tutors enable students to be open, flexible and reflective on practice and thinking, and this may be developed through a range of activities.

> *As a tutor in both HE and FE I was very aware of the significance of reflective practice for practitioners and also for my own teaching practice. I had a reasonable grasp of several key theories and felt fairly confident about applying these. On the other hand I believed that many learners viewed reflecting as part of their personal professional development modules within the foundation degree to be tedious and repetitive. Helen*

> *I remember that I thought it was important. I was already convinced that it was valuable from my prior studies – the certificate in education and the BA in Professional Training and Development. I believed it improved my work as both a teacher and a health visitor. I was involved in the teaching of modules that involved the encouragement of reflective writing within my role as a teacher and I had experienced resistance in students to embrace reflection. This puzzled me. Sarah*

Reflective writing activities for external agencies

This chapter reflects on activities that may be demanded by external agencies to achieve qualifications, such as journaling, eportfolios, activity evaluations and the self-evaluation form (SEF). Time to explore and discover in depth is important to enable the reflector to frame personal thinking. There are many varied strategies of reflective processing in journals, including diary entries, activity evaluations and critical incident analysis. There may be the inclusion of children's pictures, photos, mind maps, planning, academic research, dialogues and even doodles! Types of journaling include:

- logs, which can record events, calculations or readings and be useful as aide-memoires;
- diaries, which can contain stories of happenings, memories, thoughts, ideas, poems, or dialogues;
- journals, which may be records or explorations of events and include thoughts and feelings about specific aspects.

All these can reflect thought processes and analysis related to practice or just to thinking things through. The choice and style of journaling depends on writers' needs and inclinations and can be structured or unstructured, personal or professional forms of reflective writing (Bolton, 2005).

This could be time-consuming; however, once started it was informative and an effective aide-memoire. The diary itself became most successful as a reflective tool once I reflected back on the entries and made notes and asked questions of myself. I have recently encouraged this mode of reflection with level 2 learners and encouraged entries on any subject just to get the process of reflecting going. I have been amazed at the level of reflection which they have mastered once they were in control of the subject and language and images that they could include. Helen

I wrote a diary for a week at work and it made me realise how much I cram into every day and why I reflect at home! Jane

Journaling

Writing in an organised way in a journal can be undertaken for personal or professional purposes and can be both descriptive and analytical. Keeping a log of what happens on an everyday basis can be done through simple notes, and the power of this can be through looking back at events for patterns, repetition of events or consequences of particular activities. Journaling places the writer at the heart of the learning process, able to focus on their own experience, which makes the learning more deliberate (Moon, 2004). Journaling has become an accepted way of documenting reflective thinking and analysis of workplace actions for assessment purposes across a range of academic disciplines. This has been particularly the case in ECCE for qualifications such as the National Professional Qualification in Integrated Centre Leadership (NPQICL), early years professional status (EYPS) and the most recent professional role of early years teacher (EYT). The use of reflective journals on training courses has therefore become a popular form of getting practitioners to engage in reflective thinking.

An important intention of reflective practice is to improve what we do and the contents of a journal need to facilitate the building of a relationship between reader and writer. The actual process of reflective writing can help you:

- think purposefully on a specific activity, experience or incident;
- clarify thoughts as you write things down rather than them just floating around in your head;

- enable improvement and further development of an activity;
- assess children's involvement and learning;
- make sense through observing, analysing and then applying.

Creating a journal is a learning event and can improve motivation to learning (Hargreaves, 2004). As Moon (1999) observes, being reflective habitually becomes easier with time, enables one to be in charge of your own learning processes, and no one type of learning results from its use.

> *I have become much more confident in my teaching of reflective practice and have a deeper knowledge and understanding of the subject matter. I believe it is essential to reflect on practice both personally and professionally (I just wish I had more time to do so and keep actual written reflections; however, I tend to reflect on my practice and bullet point notes in order to develop/alter practice). I still feel that some people do not understand the concept fully and believe that it either comes naturally to a person who is quite self-analytical or those who do not like to look too deeply at themselves struggle to be reflective. Nicola*

The advantages of journaling are that it can really help clarify thoughts and develop self-awareness. The aim is to encourage a 'deep' approach to learning, link everyday experiences to study and so create a dialogue between student and tutor. The objective of journaling is to demonstrate justification and accountability for practice. It should facilitate new insights and understandings, and connect present, future and past experiences and possible changes in thinking and action, informing future thinking and development.

> *Journaling – looking at my professional working week, which highlighted the diversity of my role and how useful reflection really is for me in my profession. Sakinah*

> *Journal entries opened up new avenues to self discovery as well producing an intellectual space where I could siphon my thoughts, struggles and understanding, eureka moments in my learning, relationships with others and honest reflections of my feelings. Sharon*

Journaling can be a vehicle to test assumptions and evaluate significant episodes, and can be therapeutic; however, it may also be unsettling (Bolton, 2005). 'Ironically, it seems that the very requirement to write in the first person singular may be an important reason why journals contribute to improve learning' (Moon, 1999). Journalers should consider their own interests and take responsibility for their learning, address issues of concern and take account of their previous knowledge and ongoing experience. It is important to make the links between thinking and action and engage in relevant connected academic reading to underpin thinking and discussions. The problem with journaling for some people is that it can be time-consuming, detailed and wordy. Reflecting regularly in a journal is often difficult in a busy academic and working routine. Journaling should not be just streams of consciousness; reflective journal writers question, explore and analyse personal experiences, actions and even emotions. Obviously time, active participation and commitment are crucial for effective journaling to occur.

Thorpe (2004: 328) suggests that 'reflective thinking requires a trusting relationship if one is required to write about individual thoughts, feelings and experiences honestly'. She raises concerns that these aspects are often an integral part of being assessed and this raises issues about confidentiality of entries and the ethics of grading personal reflections that may be highly emotional. It is important that participants choose what they want to divulge and share.

> *I was a little anxious as reflective practice can be quite personal in the sharing of information as I am naturally a private person, so this took a bit of getting over for me. I am not so good at talking about my experiences as some of the others in the group, but I am happy to write about them. Amanda*

Bain *et al.* (2002: 171) found that their students valued reflecting on their teaching placement through weekly journal writing and found the 'feedback that focuses on the level of reflection attained was more effective in bringing about improvement in journal writing than feedback focused on teaching issues.' It is important to be informed about the rationale of journaling for assessment, for evaluation or both; however, reflecting-on-actions with children should enable the practitioner to build on successes, as well as improve practice.

Eportfolios: reflecting electronically

Eportfolios are becoming a popular way of providing evidence for professional courses. E-personal development planning can provide a level of flexibility for students' participation. They can comprise collections of many aspects of study and work and students can scan observations, photographs and practice evaluations from mentors or tutors. Students can cut and paste from documents and are also able to cross-reference through hyperlinking. They may engage in online conversations and electronic exchanges, which can be done anywhere and in their own time (Powell, 2011: 202). Ongoing dialogues can take place through social networking, Skype, Facebook, MSN Chat or Twitter. However, students, practitioners and academics must all be aware of the need for confidentiality and the ethics of using these, as engaging in social networking can result in overly informal and inappropriate conversations if participants forget the purpose of what they are doing.

Tutors in ECE at LeedsMet University use varied virtual learning environment software according to the needs of the course and students. They share their views on using eportfolios with students for their personal professional development in order to compile evidence for QTS standards. The tutors were very positive and were reflecting on ways of how to further improve students' success.

FIGURE 3.1 Bev and Liz discussing student portfolios.

Eportfolios

Eportfolios are a way of collecting information together for practice and to share with tutors, mentors, assessors and parents. They're an effective way of keeping everyone informed and the parents of the children can see this and participate. They're great for learning as adults and tracking one's own development. However, some people worry about having more than one piece of technology to get used to. My advice is to look for one that's easy to use and that has a familiar format. Vanessa

Pebblepad Plus

Students can save anything in an asset store and tag each item against the standards. They then blog to pull all these together. These might reflect good teaching or child observations and they link in the relevant documents – they can include displays, planning and photos. Some students engage really well but some haven't engaged enough and need to input more. Unfortunately you don't find this out until the end. Some students input work continually and progressively whilst others leave it until the last minute. Some have not always used their time well and have over inputted – submitting reams and reams, whereas some input very little. Liz

Smart Notebook

This software will also be used by students in the classroom when they become NQTs. The students write reflective accounts of how they have met the different standards in different ways. They write on pages then link to relevant documents for evidence. They choose significant things to reflect standards and their progress. I think it is good and it works well. The students like it too, particularly as they will need to use it as teachers. The quality of student reflection varies according to each student. I think we might adapt the procedures so that they get a mark rather than a pass/fail, as this will provide an impetus that a small number of students might need to engage more fully and produce better quality of work. Bev

Activity evaluations

Individual evaluations of lessons, activities and experiences planned, delivered and assessed by students on initial teacher education and level three practitioner courses have always been seen as a very important element of working with children. However, it is necessary to ensure you are not just descriptive. It is not enough to write 'the children did this and they enjoyed the activity'. How do you know they enjoyed it? What criteria are you basing your conclusions on? The objectives of activity evaluations are not to just be descriptive about what went on, but also to demonstrate an understanding and an ability to analyse.

- What went well?
- What did the children do?
- What could I do to improve this activity?
- What shall I do next?

Hayes (2011: 126) observes that newly developing practitioners are more likely to reflect-on-action rather than reflect-in-action, but he advises that 'over time and with perseverance' practitioners will be able to keep a 'running commentary'. McGregor (2011: 1) argues that 'reflectively pondering and questioning what you do can improve your achievements in life', which is quite empowering, and 'there can be few better ways of elevating your life than by thinking about, and reflecting upon' working with, caring for and educating children. She (McGregor, 2011: 4) reminds us of Dewey's three important attributes: open-mindedness to new ideas; wholeheartedness to engage with fresh approaches; and responsibility to be aware of the consequences of one's actions. McGregor (2011: 1) advises that it is necessary to 'reflect determinedly to improve practice' and warns that this requires 'effort and sustained, focused thinking centred on a particular issue', as 'initial thoughts of what happened when and how can be purposeless until you make them more constructive through questioning'. It is important to not only think about what happened and what went well, or what didn't work effectively, but also why it happened in a particular way, asking yourself what you would alter, or should you have reacted differently to the children's responses? In this way the evaluations of your own actions and of the children's participation will enable you to make adjustments to what you say and do through reflecting on:

- How well did the children learn?
- Did they initiate their own learning
- How did I intervene, interfere, involve?

Your planning will generally have taken the following aspects into account:

- the focus of the activity, whether child initiated, adult initiated or adult led;
- what resources are available, whether freely chosen from any area or specifically selected;
- time allowed and whether open-ended continuous provision or finite activity;
- position of the activity in a resource area, carpet space or outdoor play activity;
- number of children in the activity – individual, small, large task or open access.

However, to deepen your knowledge and understanding about what is most effective for the children's learning it is really valuable to reflect on specific aspects. You need to be selective about your reflection-on-action post activity, so select one or two focus reflection points. Keep a checklist to determine if you have analysed your provision from varied perspectives during a placement or each month of your practice to answer these questions. Through making this a natural part of your practice you will be able to address impact, achievement and individual children's needs.

Focused reflection points

It is important to reflect on the many varied aspects of activities with children before, during and after. Reflect on an activity that you have done with children and select key aspects to think about from the list below. Be purposeful about which aspects you choose and vary your focus of reflection each time you do this activity. Remember that it should be meaningful for you and purposeful for your practice. So, how effective were you in determining the following aspects:

- grouping of the children considering their interests, friendship, gender and ability;
- support for individual needs (see the differentiation section in Chapter 12);
- language targeted with clear support for children with EAL and SEN;
- pace of adult delivery in the activity and amount of time for children's thinking, participation and accomplishment;
- language used by children and opportunity to document their responses;
- children's levels of involvement, concentration and persistence;
- development and depth of children's thinking elicited and learning progress achieved;
- children's collaboration with each other;
- children's enjoyment and levels of excitement during the activity;
- opportunities for observations and assessment;
- extensions of the activity into further developments or other areas of provision.

Should you reflect on these aspects before, during or after an activity? Think about what works best for you. Is it more difficult to reflect-in-action or more time-consuming to reflect-on-action?

Early years self-evaluation form (SEF)

The SEF (self-evaluation form) is an Ofsted demand that settings must complete to evaluate the quality of registered early years provision and ensure continuous improvement. The form states that 'self-evaluation is important in helping you to consider how best to create, maintain and improve your setting so that it meets the highest standards and offers the best experience for young children' (Ofsted, 2013: 4). The SEF enables managers, owners and staff to evaluate practice against the judgements inspectors will make. Each setting completes the form to provide evidence of quality of provision, demonstrating perceived strengths and areas for development and how self-reflection is undertaken to demonstrate commitment to continuous improvement. This is completed prior to an Ofsted visit and the inspector will plan from it and consider how the setting evaluates the service offered to children and the compatibility of this to the judgements made (Ofsted, 2013: 5).

Part A of the form requests the details of the setting and the views of those who use it or work there.

Part B requests evidence and grading for:

- the quality and standards of the early years provision;
- how well the early years provision meets the needs of the range of children who attend;
- the contribution of the early years provision to children's well-being;
- the leadership and management of the early years provision;
- the overall quality and standards of the early years provision.

You will be asked to write critical reflections on your provision and to grade the setting's practice as:

- Outstanding: my practice is exemplary;
- Good: my practice is strong;
- Satisfactory: my practice is reasonable but could be better;
- Inadequate: my practice is not good enough and I know it needs to improve.

Ofsted advises that settings use the statutory framework for the EYFS (DfE 2012), Development Matters in the Early Years Foundation Stage and the Ofsted Inspection Framework. Claudia is an owner manager of an early years private day nursery and she reflects on what she needs to do to prepare for an Ofsted inspection and what to write in the SEF.

Reflection of a private daycare owner for SEF

We are due an Ofsted inspection soon as it is three years since our last one, for which we received outstanding. We need to reflect on our provision and I am going to ask all our practitioners their thoughts and opinions on what we do well and what we need to improve. I think we have a problem with outdoor play because everyone accesses the outdoor play area at the same time. The children need their own sunscreen and outdoor footwear on and this takes an awful lot of time. It may be really beneficial if the parents put it on before the children come to nursery and they would also know it has been applied properly. Either that or a member of the team applies it to everyone first thing in the morning. We are losing lots of valuable play and activity time through this. We need to timetable the outdoor play area as well as develop the outdoor provision in terms of activities and resources. The area is rather small and the older children can knock over the younger ones as they dominate the play area. What's really good is the way the babies get an outdoor sleep in their pushchairs and this is a really healthy outdoor activity to get vitamin D. We have an established forest school area in the woods and twice a week we have a forest school leader who takes ten three- and four-year-olds to the wooded area to build fires, cook marshmallows and make hot chocolate. They create models and animal houses, explore, climb, make dens etc. Children obviously love it and parents really value it. We have a huge display in the nursery to inform everyone. This is a real plus for us as no other nursery in the area has this provision. Our garden area is fantastic as it produces food. The children plant all the vegetables in spring ready for summer – peas, beans, radishes and strawberries – the children pick them and we use them the next day. We also have a pond area with wildlife such as tadpoles and the children watch the frogspawn grow and provide stones for the small frogs to move amongst. We also have chickens and the children feed them and collect the eggs. However, the outdoor play area is too small. There is a huge sandpit which needs reducing in size, the slide is in a poor position and needs moving round and the whole area could be better managed with more exciting activities. Claudia, owner manager, Little Stepping Stones Nursery

The SEF can be downloaded from the Ofsted website and it is worth examining to gain a picture, not only of the requirements for an inspection, but also of the breadth of decisions and reflections on practice required to provide quality provision. It will be seen that is it not a small task to complete the SEF, but nor is it a small task to undertake continuous reflective practice!

The Ofsted inspection process for schools was revised in 2012. A school will receive a phone call from the Lead Inspector on the inspection team and a summary of the school's self-evaluation needs will be made available. The NAHT (2013) advises that there are two very useful documents on the Ofsted website – 'Preparing a school self-evaluation summary' and 'Subsidiary Guidance' – and advises that the section of the template entitled 'The context of the school' will be of particular interest to inspectors.

Conclusion

This chapter has demonstrated how important reflecting on practice is, in both academic study for gaining qualifications and in professional roles in the workplace. Reflecting and evaluating in and on practice is obviously demanding. If you are interested in continuing professional development and deepening your reflective thinking and action, go to Chapter 14 as it provides activities that can be used individually, in staff training in a setting and on courses of academic study at all levels. Taking ownership of one's reflection in order to improve practice must be key to being a professional. The next chapter explores what it means to be a professional in ECCE in contemporary times.

Summary of knowledge gained

After reading and reflecting on this chapter you should now be very aware that:

- reflective writing makes a difference and can develop reflective thinking and practice;
- reflective thinking and writing can be enjoyable and personally and professionally enhancing;
- evaluation and reflection are key components of practice and required by Ofsted and other stakeholders.

Challenges for the future

- Have a go at journaling and reflect on your entries.
- Participate in writing SEFs.
- Aim to improve your written evaluations.

Further reading

If you are interested in developing your knowledge of engaging in reflection further, why not read the following:

Arnold, C. (ed.) (2012) *Improving Your Reflective Practice through Stories of Practitioner Research.* London: Routledge.

Jones, M. and Shelton, M. (2011) *Developing Your Portfolio: Enhancing your learning and showing your stuff. A guide for the early childhood student or professional.* Second edition. London: Routledge.

McGregor, D. and Cartwright, L. (2011) *Developing Reflective Practice: A guide for beginning teachers.* Maidenhead: Open University Press.

References

Bain, J., Mills, C., Ballantyne, C. and Packer, J. (2002) 'Developing reflection on practice through journal writing: impacts of variations in the focus and level of feedback', *Teachers and Teaching: Theory and Practice*, 8(2): 171–96.

Bolton, G. (2005) *Reflective Practice: Writing and professional development.* Second edition. London: Paul Chapman Publishing.

Bradbury, H., Frost, N., Kilminster, S. and Zukas, M. (eds) (2010) *Beyond Reflective Practice: New approaches to professional lifelong learning.* London: Routledge.

Department for Education (DfE) (2012) *Statutory Framework for the Early Years Foundation Stage.* Runcorn: Department for Education.

Hargreaves, D.H. (2004). *Learning for Life: The foundations for lifelong learning.* Bristol: Policy Press.

Hayes, D. (2011) 'Establishing your teacher identity', in Hansen, A. (2011) *Primary Professional Studies.* Exeter: Learning Matters.

McGregor, D. (2011) 'What can reflective practice mean for you . . . and why should you engage in it?' Chapter 1 in McGregor, D. and Cartwright, L. (eds) *Developing Reflective Practice: A guide for beginning teachers.* Maidenhead: Open University Press.

Moon, J. (1999) *Learning Journals: A handbook for academics, students and professional development.* London: Kogan Page.

Moon, J. (2004) *A Handbook of Reflective and Experiential Learning: Theory and practice.* London: Routledge.

National Association of Head Teachers (NAHT) (2013) *School Self-Evaluation: Preparing for Ofsted.* Retrieved 9 April 2013 from http://www.naht.org.uk/welcome/advice/advice-home/accountablity-and-community-advice/school-self-evaluation-preparing-for-ofsted.

Ofsted (2013) *The Framework for School Inspection.* Retrieved 9 April 2014 from http://www.ofsted.gov.uk/resources/framework-for-school-inspection.

Powell, S. (2011) 'How can e-reflection help develop your practice?' Chapter 12 in McGregor, D. and Cartwright, L. (eds) *Developing Reflective Practice: A guide for beginning teachers.* Maidenhead: Open University Press.

Thorpe, K. (2004) 'Reflective learning journals: from concept to practice', *Reflective Practice,* 5(3): 327–43.

4

Practitioners, professionalism and reflection on role

Avril Brock

This chapter will help you to understand the importance of what it is to be a professional, developing a strong awareness of your professionalism and the complexity of the professional role. This awareness involves knowledge of self, professional standards and requirements set by government and professional bodies and of the professional role within the context of ECCE settings. There should be a continual process of reflection of all these but there will be particular times when you make a conscious effort to appraise your professionalism. This may be at points of assessment before achieving qualification; during an inspection process; challenge by a colleague/line manager; or when thinking about promotion or a new job.

This chapter recognises the diversity and roles of the practitioners who comprise the professional group of 'early childhood educators' (ECEs). I use this 'title' to encompass the fundamental dual strands of the role – care and education – for those working in ECCE. This has demanded much thought, as demonstrated in this chapter, as in the UK in 2013 the titles for ECCE practitioners have changed. This section contains quite a number of questions for you to ponder in order to stimulate your reflective thinking on your professionalism and professional identity, so do select those questions which have meaning and interest for you and pass on those that do not.

Who are the ECCE professionals?

In England the debates about professionalism, status, title and role seem set to continue. There has never been such an important time for ECCE practitioners to become aware of their professionalism and affirm what it comprises. Aiming for a triumvirate of As – to be accountable, to be articulate and to advocate – should be of the highest importance for all practitioners working in care and education for young children, whatever the ECCE setting and whatever the professional role. This chapter provides perspectives on the qualifications and titles, standards and expectations of stakeholders, as well as exploring specific critical issues that these ECCE practitioners may meet in their professional role. All these are key aspects upon which reflection will be required at particular points in time in your career.

A professional working in early years has always had a range of titles and qualifications and has been described as an early childhood educator, teacher, pedagogue or practitioner (MacNaughton, 2003). The roles of ECEs are complex and wide ranging, as they may work across the two disciplines of care and education, and this may affect multidisciplinary practice in nearly everything they do. According to MacNaughton (2003) they deploy their knowledge not as individuals, but as members of the social institution of the early childhood profession and as employees of the early childhood setting. They are accountable for the provision of curriculum and pedagogy and the management of the human resources of staff, families, children and professional services. The challenge of being an ECCE professional is deciding how to put this into practice and how to interpret social policy within an organisation (MacNaughton, 2003). The roles of practitioners are not one-dimensional, but both multifaceted and transdisciplinary.

On reflecting on the diversity of the professional roles of those working in ECCE it is useful to consider the following:

- Who are the early childhood educators in today's society?
- How do their professional roles balance the two key aspects of care and education and do these compete for priority in actual practice?
- What are the qualifications, competences or standards required for each professional role?
- What are the expectations and demands of each professional role in the diverse settings?
- What are the implications of the DfE (2013) changes to ECE qualifications and titles?
- What particular issues may arise for your professional role?
- What does this mean for the individual's professionalism?

Teachers with qualified teacher status (QTS) had, for many decades, been called early years teachers, but now this title of early years teacher is replacing the early years professional (EYP) qualification. Early years QTS were unhappy about the title of EYP as it seemed to take away the 'professional' dimensions of their job, and now it is quite confusing that the title of teacher is being awarded to non-QTS practitioners. The title early years educator (EYE) has been used in Brock's (2006a, 2011, 2013) research for the last decade to encompass the professional roles of the participants – nursery nurses, level three practitioners, teachers, children's centre managers and early years lecturers. The research participants felt strongly about their professionalism and perceived themselves to be professional and capable. The findings demonstrated that there was a unity of thinking among the sample across their different roles and they shared similar knowledge and values. It is interesting that the government has now decided to use this title of EYE for those ECCE practitioners with qualifications achieved at level 3.

The *Foundations for Quality* (Nutbrown, 2012) independent review of ECCE qualification drew on contributions from a range of ECE professionals. Nutbrown's aim was to improve the quality of ECCE for young children so that:

■ every child is able to experience high-quality care and education whatever type of home or group setting they attend;
■ early years staff have a strong professional identity, take pride in their work, and are recognised and valued by parents, other professionals and society as a whole;
■ high-quality early education and care is led by well-qualified early years practitioners; and
■ the importance of childhood is understood, respected and valued.

(Nutbrown, 2012: 10)

One of Nutbrown's objectives was to provide clarity for ECE qualifications and end the disparity between EYPS and QTS. She argues that the new title of EYT suggests they will have the same role and status as qualified teachers, but actually these practitioners working with younger children are being offered a lesser status and level of pay (Nutbrown, 2013). The government commissioned the Truss Report, *More Great Childcare* (DfE, 2013) in response to the Nutbrown Review – the aim being to create more affordable childcare through increasing adult/child ratios. However, many ECCE professionals and academics argued it would have a dramatic effect on the quality of ECCE. Nutbrown criticised the government's proposals, arguing that they would:

shake the foundations of quality provision for young children . . . Whilst I felt that my recommendations taken together would enhance quality, I am not at all convinced that accepting just five, and tinkering with many others, will achieve the outcomes for children and for their professional practitioners that many had hoped for.

(Nutbrown, 2013: 3)

Nutbrown was particularly critical of the plans to introduce non-QTS early years teachers, to relax ratios, and not to require childminders to hold formal qualifications as they:

will not have the same status as teachers of children over five years of age. The hoped-for parity with primary and secondary school teachers will not be realised . . . Early years carers and educators are professionals who themselves need continually to develop their own knowledge, skills and understanding. They need to be confident in their own work with children and in engaging with parents and professionals, such as health visitors and social workers.

(Nutbrown, 2013: 6)

The government response (DfE, 2013) to the recommendations of the Nutbrown Review (DfE, 2012) affirms that the title of 'early years educator' will offer a recognised badge of quality for qualifications which meet the new 'full and relevant' criteria 'considered against the requirements of the EYFS' (DfE, 2013: 29). Wild *et al.* (2013: 141) argue that the Nutbrown Review (2012) and *More Great Childcare* (2013) propose that the strong consumer market-based model of practice portrayed in the documents has worrying 'implications for professionalism of workforce and quality of children's experiences'. They argue that there is a lack of emphasis on professionalism in the government's documentation, and that this is possibly because they do not want a costly workforce. There are enormous implications for the future for ECCE professionals. It is therefore so important for all practitioners to gain knowledge, understanding and voice about their professionalism.

What different issues or challenges does each particular role carry? Obviously all early years practitioners are concerned with the breadth of aspects related to quality of provision, children's individual needs and working relationships with other professionals, but there are specific perspectives that each of the varied practitioner roles might need to particularly examine, reflect upon and address. Each practitioner role brings its own standards to gain each qualification and these will be presented in the following sections. But there may also be specific reflective points that each particular role may need to address. There are challenges arising through changes in government policy that affect the education of young children.

Ongoing reflective thinking will be required to enable you to address those questions that have purpose and that have interest for you. You will gradually develop your professional thinking to create professional knowledge and practical application. It is through a continual process of reflection in and on knowledge and practice that your professional understanding will occur. First of all you should reflect on professional identity – where you site yourself and which direction you are going. Isn't this obvious, you ask – well, is it?

Focused reflection point

Take a little time at this point to reflect on one of the following issues that you think may impact on your professional role. You will meet these issues again in the chapters in Part II.

- How will teachers meet the demands of the Coalition Government's school readiness agenda?
- What further training on curriculum and appropriate pedagogical approaches will be available for EYTs?
- How will children's centre managers meet the demands of changes to a setting's provision in financially challenging times?
- What is the impact of local authority cuts to early years services and how will the new super output areas be reconfigured?

■ Will a deregulation of childminders result in a loss of professionalism, status and high-quality provision?

There has never been a more important time to ensure that early years practitioners are aware of what ECCE professionalism entails.

Focused reflection point

■ Compare the sets of standards and qualifications criteria for qualified teacher status (QTS) (DfE, 2012); the new early years teacher qualification (NCTL, 2013a) and those for early years educator (NCTL, 2013b). They can be respectively found at:

  □ http://www.education.gov.uk/schools/teachingandlearning/review ofstandards;
  □ https://www.gov.uk/government/publications/early-years-teachers-standards;
  □ https://www.gov.uk/government/publications/early-years-educator-level-3-qualifications-criteria.

■ The QTS standards obviously cover teachers across the EYFS, primary and secondary education, but wouldn't many early childhood education teachers be delighted with the emphasis on some of the standards in the early years teacher framework?
■ If you compare the early years teacher standards with those for EYPs (DfE, 2012) you will find them very similar without the demands for leadership, but has the phrasing of many of the standards changed for the better or worse?
■ Do you think there is less mention of children's individual needs?
■ Look at the comprehensive nature of the EYE (NCTL, 2013b) standards – they are wide-ranging and expect a valuable degree of knowledge about children's everyday needs, holistic development and high-quality provision.
■ Would you like to create your own set of standards? What would you take from each of these to suit your own professional role and ideology?

Focused reflection point

Here are some further questions you might like to reflect on:

■ Do the standards focus mainly on a competence-based approach?
■ How much can professionals develop their autonomy in practice derived through their professional knowledge base?
■ Will the training for level three practitioners promote reflective thinking and practice and develop the professional knowledge base of the role?
■ Where are professional ethics and values acknowledged in the standards?

- What are the implications for training of these practitioners with continuing professional development teams disappearing from local authorities?
- Will there be a reduction in expectation of quality and will practitioners get thrown back on their own resources?
- Is the current climate different now – how well-established is a pedagogy of play in the revised EYFS? Where are the structures now for interdisciplinary working?

Underpinning the implications of all these questions is how important reflective thinking and practice will be for all early childhood educators and how important is an understanding of one's own professional role.

The professional role: what does reflective practice mean for me?

There will be particular times, according to your position, study and interests when you will need to reflect on issues relevant to your professional role. This section presents three key reflective professional issues that you may be interested in reflecting on individually, with colleagues or with fellow students. In recent years the changes in educational policy have been effective in improving practice through developments with regard to practitioners' knowledge development and there are more opportunities for further training and qualification in ECCE than ever before. Engaging in Schön's (1983) reflection *in* and *on* practice is important for practitioners to translate policy into practice. To be truly professional, critical reflection needs to be continual, taking on board new ideas and thinking to inform professional knowledge.

Key reflective professional issue: where is the ethic of care and a reflective approach situated in early years training?

Taggart (2011: 87) proposes that there has been a lack of focus on 'care' and 'caring' in standards and that effective early years provision involves more than providing care through 'a warm and stimulating environment and well-placed optimism' as recommended by the CWDC (2007: 8). In Taggart's opinion (2011: 85) the CWDC 'uses language which most practitioners described above would find appealing, such as "care for", "nurture", "warm", "loving", "flourish"'; however, he argues that they are used in a way that

> suggests a hierarchy of skills, attitudes and behaviours, some of which are more professional and some of which are less so. In this conceptualisation, the provision of care is seen as part of a 'taken-for-granted' assemblage of lower skills which acts as a platform upon which the higher skills of

professionalism can be built . . . Yet this is not the view of practitioners themselves. In contrast to this competence-based version of professionalism based on discursive principles, the ethic of care is highly prized within the informal discourse of practitioner professionalism.

(Taggart, 2011: 85)

A discourse of professionalism in England often omits the inclusion of ethics (Brock *et al.*, 2011) and excludes the ethical vocabulary of care (Taggart, 2011). Taggart (2011: 85) argues that ECCE has a 'legitimate aspiration to be a "caring profession" like others such as nursing or social work defined by a moral purpose' and drawing on 'an ethic of care as evidence of their professionalism'. He suggests that practitioners need to demonstrate a critical understanding of their practice as 'emotion work' and to champion 'caring' as a central dimension of professionalism with skills and competence, not just as the 'maternal' element of a keyworker. He argues that a 'political ethic of care' should be at the heart of practice and in this way 'the personal vocabulary of hope, passion and love becomes enlisted in the cause of community and social justice' (Taggart, 2011: 85). Professional behaviour (or lack of it) may also depend on the extent to which the practitioner draws on ethical qualities such as patience, courage, persistence or care in a flexible way. Because these cannot be assimilated to discursive reason, these qualities are often absent from codes of practice and assessment standards (Taggart, 2011: 87).

Drudy (2008: 56) found that 'it is significant that the terms "care", "caring" or "an ethic of care" do not appear, even once, in any of the six major European policy documents examined' in her research. Taggart (2011: 87) argues that this absence of ethic and care is 'puzzling in the face of evidence that such qualities as passion, care and love are often characteristic' of excellent practitioners. This mirrors Brock's (2006b) and Brock *et al.*'s (2011) research which found that the early years professional status standards of 2006 did not really emphasise an ethic of care. Brock *et al.* (2011) created ten tenets of ethical practice for ECCE professionals:

1. Adherence to a professional code of conduct and/or self regulating code of ethics.
2. Consideration of standards, which may include measures of what is quality.
3. Beliefs, values and principles – applicable and acceptable to workers and clients – consistent with inclusiveness rather than exclusiveness.
4. Ethical relationships between practitioner and client, centred on pre-eminence of an individual's needs, interests, rights and opinions.
5. Responsibility to the well-being of individuals or society respecting confidentiality.
6. Moral integrity with elements of vocation, altruism or 'good work' informing values.
7. Promotion of well-being, truth, democracy, fairness and equality for both clients and society.

8. Trustworthiness in professional knowledge and practical wisdom developed through experience and continuing professional development.
9. Commitment to working in collaboration with colleagues and sharing of expertise.
10. Collective and collaborative action regarding ethical practice through articulating professional voice and engaging in advocacy.

(Brock *et al.*, 2011: 17)

Potter and Hodgson (2007) argue that the requisite for a reflective approach for those working with young children has not been apparent. They believe that there is a lack of emphasis on the development of critical thinking in training programmes for staff in early years settings and they will therefore 'understandably struggle to take an enquiring approach to their work' (Potter and Hodgson, 2007: 498). Engaging in critical thinking and reflecting on one's role is an important element of being a professional. Both Potter and Hodgson (2007) and Cameron and Boddy (2006) question how early years practitioners can trust their tacit knowledge if they are not trained how to reflect on it and test if their practice is effective and appropriate through critical analysis of what they do. Potter and Hodgson (2007: 495) demonstrate how a twelve-week reflective training approach resulted in some major changes in practice. It provided extensive opportunities for reflection in and on action through the use of both video clips and work-based support sessions, and the training greatly increased reflection in this key area of early years activity. Developing both an ethic of care and an ability to engage in reflective thinking must be key to developing professionalism in ECCE.

Key reflective professional issue: should personal autonomy have relevance for early years teachers with QTS?

During the last thirty years the teaching profession has experienced a range of prescriptive frameworks, which have varyingly caused some teachers to feel destabilised and so to question their beliefs and values. The introduction of a National Curriculum (DfES, 1989), followed by national Standard Assessment Tests and League Tables, caused many early years teachers to feel perturbed and challenged by demands they believed were inappropriate for young children in the early years of schooling. However, the introduction of the Foundation Stage and its Curriculum Guidance with a focus on children being at the centre of the educational process was deemed to have been positive by EYEs (Keating *et al.*, 2002). Its introduction resolved many of the conflicts of teachers of young children through re-affirming a play-based pedagogy. In Hargreaves and Hopper's (2006: 181) opinion the Curriculum Guidance for the Foundation Stage was 'a major step towards the professionalisation, and potentially enhanced status of EY teachers'.

This cycle of instability, questioning and reaffirmation of principles and values seems set to continue for ECEs. There are now new challenges ahead that may cause qualified teachers in the early years to again question their professional knowledge, values and beliefs. There are at least three key issues that raise concerns – first, what does the future hold for qualified teachers in the early years? The new EYT replaces the status qualification; what will this mean for those who have qualified teacher status who work with young children as early years teachers? What will the future be for initial teacher training? At the present time the status, pay and qualification of teachers is the same whether in early years, primary or secondary. The second issue relates to who leads on pedagogy and curriculum and where does care sit? The new EYFS (DfE, 2012a) is developed from the well-received 2008 version, but does play-based pedagogy still receive the same strong focus? (see Chapters 10, 11 and 12). The third issue is regarding the emphasis on school readiness in much of the recent government documentation and how this will affect the practice of early years teachers (see Chapter 11).

Traditionally the UK has been at the forefront in requiring that teachers of children – within foundation stage, primary school and secondary education – are educated to degree level and have qualified teacher status. The findings of the New Labour government-funded EPPE (Effective Pedagogy in the Early Years) Project (Siraj-Blatchford *et al.*, 2002) indicated that well-qualified staff, in particular trained teachers, encourage children to engage in activities with high cognitive challenge, use more direct teaching and are more effective in their interactions with the children (Sammons *et al.*, 2004). This indicates that effective teacher interaction results in children gaining higher cognitive outcomes. At the time of writing this book, the government is aiming to improve the standards of teachers and the qualifications for those wishing to become teachers. Yet Michael Gove, the secretary for education, announced in 2012 that it would no longer be a requirement for teachers in academies to have qualified teacher status. Schools are able to use unqualified people to teach lessons on both a temporary and permanent basis.

> The evidence from around the world shows us that the most important factor in determining the effectiveness of a school system is the quality of its teachers. The best education systems draw their teachers from the most academically able, and select them carefully to ensure that they are taking only those people who combine the right personal and intellectual qualities. These systems train their teachers rigorously at the outset.
>
> (DfE, 2010)

An overemphasis on educational achievement has produced conflicts for teachers when they have had to meet aspects of curriculum and pedagogy that might challenge their values and beliefs. In Wood's (2004: 361) opinion the policy frameworks in ECCE in the UK 'have created tensions and dilemmas for teachers as they strive to reconcile their professional knowledge with increasingly prescriptive frameworks'. Wood and Bennett's (2000: 647) research examines how teachers construct and reconstruct their knowledge and it finds that there is a requisite for a 'greater professionalism for early childhood teachers in order for them to become agents of change and articulate the theories that underpin their practice'.

Focusing on educational achievement may lead to less emphasis on individual young children's personal, social and emotional needs, and children may not gain the emotional well-being that is so important for holistic learning and development. The Coalition Government has a strong emphasis on school readiness and its requirements that children in Year 1 take a phonics screening check that contains nonsense or pseudo words may lead to unreasonable expectations of some young children (see discussion on this in Chapter 11 and see the case study on teaching phonics on page 281).

Key reflective professional issue: how will new policy developments affect our practice when working in an interdisciplinary team?

The National Professional Qualification in Integrated Centre Leadership (NPQICL) (NCSL, 2005), introduced to enhance professional leadership in the new children's centres, is currently under review (NCTL, 2012). The NPQICL (NCSL, 2005) standards, focused on management and leadership knowledge and skills, suggested that it promoted narrow interpretations, omitting factors connected to ethics, relationships and commitment (Brock, 2006b). Children's centre managers do not necessarily require knowledge, qualification or experience of working with young children, yet, as Keating *et al.* (2002: 201) advise, a knowledge of early years principles and the needs of young children are important for head teachers, governors and other managers, so they are not overly focused on the government's political agenda intent on measuring success by results. Aubrey *et al.*'s (2007) investigation into early childhood leadership with integrated centre managers, foundation unit coordinators and managers in the private and voluntary sectors found that higher initial qualifications have a significant impact, and that effective leaders were goal-oriented in their approach, involved teams in decision making, and were professionally knowledgeable, supportive, warm and kind (Rankin and Butler, 2011).

The UK government policy has required a focus on working across professional and organisational boundaries as there is the potential to help complex societal problems (Rankin and Butler, 2011). Leaders of ECCE centres therefore have roles that may be central to a community and require the confidence to be advocates for children and families (Muijs *et al.*, 2004; Brock, 2006b). This indicates the complex issues connected to professionalism for EYEs and how knowledge, expertise, ethics, skills, education and training are key elements in the debates.

Brock and Rankin's (2011) book demonstrates how acknowledgement of one's own professionalism and professional role, alongside knowledge of other professional roles, is important for effective practice in an interdisciplinary team. Communication and joint reflection are key! The title of multiprofessional 'indicates a degree of inter-agency and interdisciplinary co-operation' and 'shared cultural belonging where meanings, values and understandings can be explored' (Powell, 2005: 78).

Research by Anning (2002) finds that an overview of everyone's work is difficult and there are sometimes tensions between staff from different disciplines and backgrounds. This indicates the dilemmas for practitioners in contending with their changing roles. Anning (2002) proposes that professionals' changing identities require skilful management to ensure real integration of services and so improve ECCE provision. In Oberhuemer's opinion:

> These emerging shifts in the practitioner role demand a radical reappraisal both of the formal level, the organization and the content of initial training, and of the system of in-service education and supporting networks for professional development.
>
> (Oberhuemer, 2004: 18)

Warin (2007: 90) also expresses concern about the problems that different professionals face in collaborating with each other and suggests there are 'cracks below the rhetoric of seamlessness'. Undoubtedly there are problems with partnership and joined-up thinking; as Frost (2001) found, in his research on front-line working with children and families, co-location does not solve all the problems. It is therefore important for all ECE professionals to establish and reflect on, have confidence in and be able to articulate their own professional identity.

Conclusion

This chapter has provided information about the diverse roles of those working in ECCE, their qualifications, standards and key issues. It should have enabled you to realise that it is valuable to have a strong awareness of your own professionalism and what this entails, so that you can truly become accountable, articulate and able to advocate where you see the need arising or an issue to be addressed. Some of the key issues mentioned in this chapter have implications and challenges for all the ECCE practitioners, so if these issues have concerns for you – and you should be able to raise other pertinent personal professional issues – then this should prompt you to answer the question as to why an understanding of your own professionalism is so important. Therefore read the next chapter which will help you reflect on and establish your own professionalism.

Summary of knowledge gained

■ Why it is important to establish your own professionalism and advocate for your professional role.

■ Why having your professionalism acknowledged and respected is important for the children and families with whom you work.

■ Why it is valuable to have an understanding of the professionalism of other practitioners across a range of services.

Challenges for the future

Now you have read this chapter reflect on the following questions:

■ Does the government consider professionalism for ECE practitioners to be important?

■ Do you have knowledge and understanding of other practitioners working in the ECCE team?

■ How will you ensure you can establish your own professional identity?

Further reading

Jarvis, P., George, J. and Holland, W. (2012) *The Early Years Professional's Complete Companion.* Second edition. Harlow: Pearson Longman.

Miller, L. and Cable, C. (2008) *Professionalism in the Early Years.* London: Hodder and Stoughton.

Miller, L. and Cable, C. (2011) *Professionalization, Leadership and Management in the Early Years.* London: Sage.

References

Anning, A. (2002) *Paper Two: Investigating the impact of working in integrated service delivery settings on early years practitioners' professional knowledge and practice: strategies for dealing with controversial issues.* Paper presented at the Annual Conference of the British Educational Research Association, 12/14 September, University of Exeter, Exeter, England.

Aubrey, C., Harris, A., Briggs, M. and Muijs, D. (2007) *How do they manage? An investigation of early childhood leadership.* End-of-award report award number RES 000-22-1121. Childhood Research Unit, University of Warwick.

Brock, A. (2006a) *Eliciting early years educators' thinking: how do they define and sustain their professionalism?* Paper presented to the European Early Childhood Education Research Association (EECERA) conference, Reykjavik, Iceland, 30 August–2 September 2006.

Brock, A. (2006b) *Dimensions of early years professionalism – attitudes versus competences?* Reflection paper on Training Advancement and Co-operation in the Teaching of Young Children (TACTYC) website: www.tactyc.org.uk.

Brock, A. (2011) 'Perspectives on professionalism', Chapter 3 in Brock, A. and Rankin, C. (eds) *Professionalism in the Early Years Interdisciplinary Team: Supporting young children and their families*. London: Continuum.

Brock, A. (2013) 'Building a model of early years professionalism from practitioners' perspectives', *Journal of Early Childhood Research*, 11(1): 27–45.

Brock, A. and Rankin, C. (2011) *Professionalism in the Early Years Interdisciplinary Team: Supporting young children and their families*. London: Continuum.

Brock, A., Swiniarski, L. and Rankin, C. (2011) 'Are we doing it by the book? Professional ethics for teachers and librarians in the early years', in Campbell, A. and Broadhead, P. (eds) *Working with Children and Young People: Ethical debates and practices across disciplines and continents*. New International Studies in Applied Ethics. Peter Lang.

Cameron, C. and Boddy, J. (2006) 'Knowledge and education for care workers: what do they need to know?' in Boddy, J., Cameron, C. and Moss, P. (eds) *Care Work: Present and future*. London: Routledge, p. 197.

Children's Workforce Development Council (CWDC) (2007) *Early Years Professional National Standards*. Leeds: CWDC.

Department for Education (DfE) (2010) *The Importance of Teaching: The schools white paper*. Norwich: The Stationery Office.

Department for Education (DfE) (2012a) *Statutory Framework for the Early Years Foundation Stage*. Runcorn: Department for Education.

Department for Education (DfE) (2012b) *Teachers' Standards*. Runcorn: Department for Education.

Department for Education (DfE) (2013) *More Great Childcare: Raising quality and giving parents more choice*. Runcorn: Department for Education.

Department for Education and Science (DfES) (1989) *The National Curriculum for England and Wales*. London: DfES.

Drudy, S. (2008) 'Professionalism, performativity and care: whither teacher education for a gendered profession in Europe?' Chapter 2 in Hudson, B. and Zgaga, P. (eds) *Teacher Education Policy in Europe: A voice of higher education institutions*. University of Umeå, Sweden: Faculty of Teacher Education, pp. 46–62.

Frost, N. (2001) 'Professionalism, change and the politics of lifelong learning', *Studies in Continuing Education*, 23: 5–17.

Hargreaves, L. and Hopper, B. (2006) 'Early years, low status? Early years teachers' perceptions of their occupational status', *Early Years: An International Journal of Research and Development*, 26: 171–86.

Keating, I., Basford, J., Hodson, E. and Harnett, A. (2002) 'Reception teacher responses to the Foundation Stage', *International Journal of Early Years Education*, 10: 193–203.

MacNaughton, G. (2003) *Shaping Early Childhood: Learners, curriculum and contexts*. Maidenhead: Open University Press.

Miller, L. and Cable, C. (eds) (2008) *Professionalism in the Early Years*. London: Hodder and Stoughton.

Muijs, D., Aubrey, C., Harris, A. and Briggs, M. (2004) 'How do they manage? A review of the research on leadership in early childhood', *Journal of Early Childhood Research*, 2: 157–69.

National College for School Leadership (NCSL) (2005) *National Standards for Leaders of Children's Centres*. London: HMSO.

National College for Teaching and Leadership (NCTL) (2012) *National Standards for Leaders of Children's Centres*. London: HMSO.

National College for Teaching and Leadership (NCTL) (2013a) *Teachers' Standards (Early Years) from September 2013*. Reference: NCTL-00108-2013. London: NCTL.

National College for Teaching and Leadership (NCTL) (2013b) *Early Years Educator (Level 3): Qualifications criteria*. Retrieved 10 April 2014 from https://www.gov.uk/government/publications/early-years-educator-level-3-qualifications-criteria.

Nutbrown, C. (2012) *Foundations for Quality: The independent review of early education and child-care qualifications. Final report*. Runcorn: Department for Education.

Nutbrown, C. (2013) *Shaking the Foundations of Quality? Why 'childcare' policy must not lead to poor quality early education and care*. Sheffield: University of Sheffield.

Oberhuemer, P. (2004) 'Controversies, chances and challenges: reflections on the quality debate in Germany', *Early Years: An International Journal of Research and Development*, 24: 9–21.

Potter, C. and Hodgson, S. (2007) 'Nursery nurses reflect: Sure Start training to enhance adult child interaction', *Reflective Practice*, 8(4): 497–509.

Powell, J. (2005) 'Multiprofessional perspectives', in Jones, L., Holmes, R. and Powell, J. (eds) *Early Childhood Studies: A multiprofessional perspective*. Maidenhead: Open University Press, pp 77–89.

Rankin, C. and Butler, F. (2011) 'Issues and challenges for the interdisciplinary team in supporting the 21st century family', Chapter 2 in Brock, A. and Rankin, C. (eds) *Professionalism in the Early Years Interdisciplinary Team: Supporting young children and their families*. London: Continuum.

Sammons, P., Eliot, K., Sylva, K., Melhuish, E., Siraj-Blatchford, I. and Taggart, P. (2004) 'The impact of pre-school on young children's cognitive attainments at entry to reception', *British Educational Research Journal*, 30: 692–707.

Schön, D.A. (1983) *Educating the Reflective Practitioner*. San Francisco, CA: Jossey-Bass.

Siraj-Blatchford, I., Sylva, K., Muttock, S., Gilden, R. and Bell, D. (2002) *Researching Effective Pedagogy in the Early Years*. London: Institute of Education.

Taggart, G. (2011) 'Don't we care? The ethics and emotional labour of early years professionalism', *Early Years*, 31(1): 85–95.

Warin, J. (2007) 'Joined-up services for young children and their families: papering over the cracks or re-constructing the foundations?' *Children and Society*, 21: 87–97.

Wild, M., Leeson, C., Silberfield, C., Nightingale, B. and Calder, P. (2013) *More? Great? Childcare? A discourse analysis of recent social policy documents relating to the care of young children in England and Wales*. Paper presented to EECERA conference, Tallinn, Estonia, 29 August–1 September 2013.

Wood, E. (2004) 'A new paradigm war? The impact of national curriculum policies on early childhood teachers' thinking and classroom practice', *Teaching and Teacher Education: An International Journal of Research and Studies*, 20(4): 361–74.

Wood, E. and Bennett, N. (2000) 'Changing theories, changing practice: exploring early childhood teachers' professional learning', *Teaching and Teacher Education*, 16: 635–47.

5

What does professionalism mean for me?

Avril Brock

This chapter focuses on professionalism – what does this mean for early years practitioners and why is both a consensus of professionalism in the field and a personal understanding of professionalism important for ECEs? Who is entitled to be called a professional and what constitutes her or his professional knowledge? The chapter aims to develop your knowledge of your own professionalism and ability to articulate this professionalism for yourself and to other people. Reflection is an important part of this process as you will be thinking about what contributes to your professional practice and the quality of provision. The chapter explores definitions of professionalism, professionalisation and professional identity for ECEs, drawing on Brock's (2006, 2011, 2013) research in exploring dimensions of professionalism. Above all, why is all this important for you?

This chapter asks you to reflect upon what it is to be a professional, why it is important to be considered to be a professional, and asks you to think about these five questions:

1. Why do *you* require an understanding of your own professionalism?
2. Why is this so important now and in the future?
3. What are *your* personal professional values and ethics with regard to your practice?
4. What do *you* perceive are your needs for your ongoing and continuing professional development?
5. What is your professionalism?

I propose to you that there has never been a more important time for ECCE practitioners to develop an understanding of their own professionalism. Develop your knowledge, establish your personal professional values and understand ethics with regard to your practice, and aim to achieve the three As of accountability, articulation and advocacy! My research, eliciting practitioner voice and thinking, has generated a typology of professionalism which has been employed to enhance the professional role. This will be explored later in this chapter as its aim is to support your individual sense of professionalism and an understanding of the complexity of your professional role.

Who or what is a professional?

Professionalism theory and research can be found in the domains of sociology, philosophy and history. It is a very contemporary and contentious issue and has been the concern of several fields of discipline: management; education; health professions; social work; journalism; early childhood educators. The need to define professionalism has become a key concern of the role of the professional and has merited recent study from researchers in early years education such as Brock (2006, 2011, 2013); Osgood (2004, 2006); Miller and Cable (2008) and Urban (2009). Professionals in ECCE work in interdisciplinary teams in children's centres, schools, health centres and across a range of services. These different professionals need to work together and it is valuable to gain a sense of each other's professionalism as well as asserting and establishing one's own personal professionalism (Brock and Rankin, 2011).

There has been much debate about what constitutes the professions and how they should be defined, yet despite the widespread use of the term 'professional' in the media and the everyday discourse of professional people, 'it defies common agreement as to its meaning' (Hoyle and John, 1995: 1). There is not a single explanatory trait or characteristic of professionalism – it is not a generic concept, but a concrete, changing, historical and national phenomenon (Friedson, 1994, 2001). The lack of consensus occurs because perspectives on professionalism can vary, both pragmatically and conceptually, as society changes and becomes ever more complex. The terms 'profession' and 'professional' are now often applied with considerable abandon to a wide variety of occupations with elusive and continual reinterpretation of the concepts (Helsby, 1996). To 'professionalise' is to make an occupation professional, which implies that, with the right conditions, any occupation could become a profession. To be a professional is a phrase often in use in the contemporary workplace and may relate to competence and punctiliousness. There is a clear distinction between 'being a professional', which includes issues of status, reward and public recognition, and 'behaving professionally', which implies dedication, standards of behaviour and a strong service ethic (Helsby 1996: 138). Professionalism is related to proficiency – the knowledge, skill, competence or character of a highly trained professional, as opposed to amateur status or capability. However, professionalism can also be 'attitudinal' – there may be professional and unprofessional garage mechanics and hairdressers, just as there are professional and unprofessional teachers, lawyers and doctors (Helsby, 1996: 137). Components of pay, recognition and reward depict 'professionalisation', whilst characteristics of ethics, standards and commitment represent 'professionalism' (Osgood, 2006).

The following is an extract from Elizabeth's portfolio submitted for assessment on the MA Childhood Studies degree. She reflects on the attributes of professionalism we had discussed at university:

My experience of the tutors at Leeds Met has been one of true professionalism, and I think this is in part due to their being reflective practitioners, a noticeable difference between the tutors from years ago (accepting my maturity and experience adding to this conclusion). I thought the lecture on professionalism would be about teachers' professionalism. However, Avril's interesting introduction used the video of Captain Sullenberger, the pilot of the plane landing on the Hudson River in New York in 2009. As someone commented on YouTube about Captain Sullenberger, 'you can tell just by the way he talks', 'very professional, humble too'. I had never really thought about the definition of 'professionalism' yet felt that I had carried out this role for many years. After some reflection, the definition of professionalism to me was 'acting in accord with one's profession, job role and company'. To be 'considerate, fair, polite and act with dignity'. I learnt there is in fact a distinction between 'being a professional' and 'behaving professionally' (Brock, 2011). Some of the attributes described match those of Helsby (1996: 138) where the description of 'behaving professionally' implies dedication, standards of behaviour and a strong service ethic. Reading further into professionalism helped me understand more fully Brock's Seven Dimensions of Professionalism (2011) and how this could relate to many professions. Schön (1976) also describes various elements of professionalism in different areas. Elizabeth

The discourse of professionalism

The discourse of professionalism is a part of a sense of self and it is attractive for workers to perceive themselves as professionals in order to gain 'cultural capital' (Bourdieu, 1990). Occupations seek recognition as professions as this should lead to enhanced esteem, status, remuneration and power (Hoyle and John, 1995). It is therefore very important in contemporary society for occupations to be established as professions, with the implications for both career and personal success. In the UK there has been an ongoing and complex struggle by ECE professionals to negotiate their professional status with employers, governments, clients and the general public (Frost, 2001). Many groups have faced challenges to their authority, legitimacy and inevitably their professionalisation. Furthermore, the salary level and social status of some professions have constrained their progress towards professional status. As Evetts (2009) advises, there needs to be a further analysis of the discourse of professionalism reconstructed within professional occupational groups. It can be problematic in the caring professions of education, nursing and social work, where it is evident, as Forster (2000) observes, that there is still a greater concentration of women. Those working in ECCE have perhaps had the hardest battle to gain recognition as professionals, not only because they work with the youngest members of society, but also because they are a predominantly female group.

It would seem timely to promote a reconceptualisation of early years professionalism through research that 'explores issues of professional roles and identity' (Woodrow, 2007: 241). In 2003 Campbell (2003: 243) argued for a 're-conceptualisation of professionalism in the context of the early years' and it can be seen with all the changes and concerns surrounding ECCE that this reconceptualising needs to be ongoing. The voices of those working in the field therefore need to continue to be elicited to create a more comprehensive perspective of professionalism for ECCE. Reflecting on and evaluating one's professional role and its practical application is key to professionalism (Hughes and Menmuir, 2002). The previous chapter aimed to demonstrate how important it is for ECE practitioners to engage in professional discourse and to address issues at policy level. Early childhood care and education requires a knowledgeable, highly qualified and articulate workforce to do this and knowing what your own professionalism entails is key.

Professionalism is complex

Definitions of professionalism are definitely complex! Aldridge and Evetts (2003) argue that being professional is not one concept but a cluster of related ones. In 1985 Katz suggested eight concepts of professionalism for ECCE: social necessity; altruism; autonomy; code of ethics; distance from client; standards of practice; prolonged training and specialised knowledge. Oberhuemer (2005) proposed a model of four professional activities of: interacting with children; care management and leadership; partnership with parents; and knowledge base. Cable and Miller (2008: 172) find that the following six themes underpin professionalism: quality, standards, expertise, reflection, identity and social status. Friedman (2007: 126) acknowledges the complexity of defining professionalism and proposes that it is 'like a ball of knotted string' that requires such 'knots' as gender and power, ethics, leadership and change to be opened and untangled.

Brock's (2013) literature search across definitions of professionalism from varied disciplines gave rise to the following being key aspects of a professional's work. It:

- is esoteric, complex, and discretionary in character;
- requires theoretical knowledge, skill and judgement that ordinary people do not possess or comprehend, and cannot readily evaluate;
- requires a demanding period of training; higher education; commitment to knowledge and skill;
- is especially important for the well-being of individuals or society at large;
- is altruistic and values good work for the client group;
- requires professional development as a lifelong process;
- is pleasurable, interesting and valuable.

Brock's empirical study research presents a model of professionalism that has been developed through longitudinal research in ECCE in England. It has been formulated through both the theoretical framework and findings from the empirical study 'Eliciting early years educators' voices: how do they define and sustain their professionalism?' (Brock, 2006). The research explores professionalism in the field, promoting recognition of the complexities of the roles of those who work with young children, and has developed a generic model of professionalism for ECCE. The study elicited the voices and thinking of a group of early years educators (EYEs) diverse in age, gender, role, ethnicity, training and length of service:

- nursery nurses (level three practitioners);
- reception/foundation stage/early excellence teachers;
- nursery and independent school head teachers;
- private day-care and Sure Start managers in workplace/community-based nurseries;
- lecturers in further and higher education;
- professionals working in the interdisciplinary team – early years professionals; speech and language therapists; early years librarians;
- students on Master's, postgraduate and undergraduate early childhood education courses.

Focused reflection point

The EYEs involved in the research raised many professional aspects and those that received most interest can be seen in Table 5.1. Which of these topics are professionally relevant for you? Do they indicate the complexity and qualities of your work? Do you think they portray your understanding of professionalism and professional knowledge?

TABLE 5.1 Key professional interests of the early years educators

Professional issues	Working relationships	Curriculum and pedagogy
Appropriate training: courses; qualifications; CPD	National directives	Curriculum content
	Initiatives/funding	Play-based pedagogy
Practical knowledge and expertise	Local authorities	Foundation Stage Curriculum
Professional aspects of role	Community liaison	Developmentally appropriate practice
Significant mentors	Parents – involvement; information sharing; partnership; outreach;	Individual needs and inclusion
Acclaim; status; pay; value	Staff relationships within a setting and working in a team	'Too Much Too Soon' and school readiness
Change: pressure; conforming; collegiate	Challenges from colleagues	Transition from the foundation stage
Environment: ethos; interest; commitment; enjoyment	Multidisciplinary teams/liaison with other services	Curriculum models – High/Scope; Montessori; Reggio Emilia; Forest schools
Skills: managing; organising; planning; assessing; observing; monitoring	In-house staff development and personal/professional CPD	

The aim was to determine the professionalism of the respondents through eliciting their professional thinking and practical knowledge. It is important to elicit the voices of the professionals themselves in order to get a true understanding of what each role entails. The research enabled them to reflect on any areas of interest and critical issues arising from their professional roles through a range of techniques aimed at eliciting their voices. In order to gain a holistic and thorough understanding of early years education professionals, varied data collection strategies were used to elicit their thinking: personal/professional timelines; questionnaires; semi-structured interviews; video reflective dialogues; focus group meetings. Each strategy elicited different aspects of the EYEs' professionalism and this was crucial to gain a breadth and depth of their thinking and generated seven dimensions of professionalism: knowledge; education and training; skills; autonomy; values; ethics; and reward. The typology or model of professionalism demonstrating the content of these seven dimensions is shown in Table 5.2.

TABLE 5.2 A model of professionalism for early years educators

KNOWLEDGE *What do you need to know?*	Systematic body of knowledge, as well as knowledge gained through experience
	Professional knowledge integrated with practical experience to develop expertise in the field
	Knowledge from varied theoretical premises
	Recognition of the knowledge of the expertise of the parties involved
EDUCATION and TRAINING *How you have achieved knowledge and expertise*	Qualifications gained through FE and HE and apprenticeship through working in the field, applying knowledge to practical experiences
	Appropriate training with regard to young children's learning and development
	Training to deliver flexible, developmentally appropriate services and curriculum that demanded a high level of pedagogic knowledge
	Self-directed continuing professional development to further develop knowledge and expertise
SKILLS *What you need to do*	Well-developed complex multidisciplinary skills that encompass the demands of the role
	Effective teamwork, with different professionals, creating an inclusive ethos
	Ability to exercise significant judgements with regard to appropriate practice and skill exercised in new problems and situations
	Monitoring and evaluating effectiveness to inform practice and provision
	Effective communication of aims and expectations to the many and varied stakeholders
	Ability to critique, reflect and articulate understanding and application
AUTONOMY *Your voice and advocacy – being allowed to do the job*	Stronger voice in the shaping of relevant policy and practice
	Consulted as experts with recognition of professional knowledge and expertise
	Autonomy over professional responsibilities and recognition of professionalism, promoting status and value in the field
	Ability to exercise discretionary judgement regarding service
	Vocational aspects recognised and endorsed
VALUES *What informs and sustains you?*	Sharing of a similar ideology based on appropriate knowledge, education and experience
	Beliefs in principles for appropriate provision that meets children's and families' needs
	Altruistic orientation through commitment to professional values and vocation built on moral and social purposes
	Public service and accountability to the community and client group of children and families
	Creating an environment of trust and mutual respect inherent in the professional role

ETHICS	Ethical principles and engaging with values consistent with the discipline
What are your moral guidelines and codes?	High level of commitment to professional role and to the client group of parents, carers and children
	Commitment to collaborative and collective behaviour
	Inclusiveness whilst valuing diversity in all working relationships, including children, families and communities
	Self-regulating code of ethics
REWARD	Personal satisfaction, interest and enjoyment in the work
Why you do the job	Commitment to professional role
	Being valued and gaining acclaim for the professional expertise by the client group and by policymakers
	Forming strong and supportive relationships
	Pay – financial remuneration; stability and security of tenure
	Passionate about working with children

Source: Brock, 2011

A typology of professionalism

The typology has been used as a mechanism for exploring what professionalism entails with students on Master's courses (Brock, 2010) and with other professionals in the ECCE interdisciplinary team (Brock and Rankin, 2011). The typology is useful to facilitate professionals' engagement in debate about their professionalism.

> *It was useful to consider these dimensions and to contemplate how they impacted upon my views of self and also of others. The whole concept of professionalism provided debate and led to a critical reflection of different facets of my role as a teacher. Helen*

Fay adapted the typology to reflect her own perspective on her professional dimensions. Fay had begun her professional career on BTEC training as a nursery nurse, moving on to a BA in Childhood Studies, then after completing her MA in Early Years she gained qualified teacher status and later taught early years in a primary school.

TABLE 5.3 Fay's model of professionalism

KNOWLEDGE	The knowledge to be a successful teacher can never be complete. I feel the best teachers continue to gain knowledge every day throughout their career. I do, however, have a sound foundation to start me off. I have a vast amount and huge variety of children of all different ages and in different settings. As well as six years of specific knowledge of education about children and childhood which goes hand in hand with experience.
What do you need to know?	
EDUCATION and TRAINING	I did my BTEC in Early Years with level 6 Nursery Nurse qualification. I then did my undergraduate in Childhood Studies and including the Master's in Early Years I will have had five years' worth of education specifically to do with childhood, child development, education, and the importance of the early years.
How you have achieved knowledge and expertise	

TABLE 5.3 *Continued*

SKILLS *What you need to do?*	A good teacher needs to be someone who is academically able to teach and equally cares about the well-being of children. She should be well organised, a successful planner, who is flexible and follows children's individual interests and needs. A good teacher must be approachable for children, staff and parents, and excel in communication skills. Good imagination and creativity are important and they must offer support and respect all children, be well balanced, relaxed around children, act 'firm but fair', be in control of a classroom and be committed to teaching. Importantly teachers need to be a good role model for children who are hugely influenced by the attitudes and values of others.
AUTONOMY *Your voice and advocacy – being allowed to do the job*	All the experience and knowledge I have gives me the independence to have my own thoughts and ideas as a teacher and the confidence to make my own decisions and guide others, both children and adults. Whilst still being happy and seeing the usefulness to seek advice from others.
VALUES *What informs and sustains you?*	The importance of the early years as children learn the most in the first five years of their life and therefore these first few years need to be the most stimulating. Children need the opportunities to excel in these early years and have a rich environment and teacher. I also want to make a difference to children in their literacy learning due to the struggle I had with reading and writing as a child.
ETHICS *What are your moral guidelines and codes?*	A clear set of classroom rules, so all children and staff know the behaviour expectations and the behaviour management policies. To go into my classroom everyday with the children's best interests as priority. Also that every child's individual needs are met and that all children have equal opportunities.
REWARD *Why you do the job*	I want to work with children because it is a hugely rewarding job, which I have always wanted to do. I want to make a difference in children's lives. I will hugely enjoy the job and the children will in turn enjoy their learning and reach their highest learning potential. If it's teaching a child how to read, or helping them understand how to do simple addition this will make the foundation for their future education and life chances, it is a huge responsibility but something I can't wait to do.

The challenges for ECE practitioners

The challenges mentioned earlier in this chapter demonstrate the need for ECCE professionals' expertise and knowledge to be recognised and respected and that they should be contributing to shaping policy. The students on the module reflected on using the typology and on their further development of their perceptions on their own professionalism since participating in the research:

> Presenting a portfolio of analytical reflections helped me to demonstrate my understanding of concepts of professionalism and critical reflection. The different pieces of writing helped me to recognise the impacts and influences upon my deepening personal and professional development. Brock (2011) puts forward the argument that 'the emphasis on interdisciplinary work has profound implications for how we think about professionals and professionalism.' Brock (2011) uses seven key themes to support understanding of perspectives of professionalism and future interdisciplinary

practice. It has been universally accepted that professional development is essential for individuals if they wish to respond to the demands of an ever changing early years context. Using Brock's (2011) model of professionalism certainly heightened my awareness of what professionalism involves for individuals working with children and their families. Whilst I believe that I have certainly increased my knowledge, skill and education, how I will be able to have a voice in shaping policy in interdisciplinary partnerships and practice will remain a challenge. Especially where practice asks teams to work together to achieve common goals but values and professional ethics may differ to mine. Whilst definitions of professionalism may vary between policy and practice, Brock (2011) argues that it is important that 'voices of diverse professionals are elicited for their perspectives on their professionalism'. From a childhood education perspective many practitioners found that an outcome-driven curriculum did not necessarily meet the learning needs of young children, where governments undermined the autonomy of early years teachers. A concept where awareness of the knowledge, skills and expertise of diverse early years professionals can only be a positive thing, if we are expected to unify professional expertise to achieve better outcomes for children and families. Sharon

---

Focused reflection point

Now have a go at adding your own professional attributes within each of the seven dimensions in this blank table:

TABLE 5.4 Blank model of professionalism

KNOWLEDGE *What do you need to know?*	
EDUCATION and TRAINING *How you have achieved knowledge and expertise*	
SKILLS *What you need to do*	
AUTONOMY *Your voice and advocacy – being allowed to do the job*	
VALUES *What informs and sustains you?*	
ETHICS *What are your moral guidelines and codes?*	
REWARD *Why you do the job*	

After much thought and discussion with colleagues, the concept of professionalism began to unfold and I then found it an interesting journey to map, document, and validate who I am as a professional in this field, and to realise the many skills and abilities that I possess. It has also been an exhilarating experience to learn from the other students. I feel that I have given much thought as to what skills and abilities that I hold with regard to each section in my portfolio, and this has involved a great deal of self-reflection and evaluation. It has also helped to consolidate my concept of who I am . . . Reflection is essential to a fully lived professional life (Boreen et al., 2000). Gail

---

Focused reflection point

What are your dimensions of professionalism?
   Would they be:

- education and training
- knowledge
- skill
- ethics
- values
- autonomy
- reward

What would you delete or what would you add?

Conclusion

Adopting a critical and self-reflective approach to practice is key to an individual's professional identity. Rankin and Butler (2011: 56) argue that reflection is important to make sense of the knowledge and understandings we have already learnt – 'our own values as practitioners will affect how we approach reflective enquiry'. Practitioners can become more articulate, secure and able to justify practice when they feel ownership of their own professionalism and professional knowledge in the face of challenges. Taking a reflective approach can develop the ability to understand situations and dilemmas, and becoming confident about these can lead to deeper understanding and potential changes in our working relationships and professional practice. Continuing professional development supports this reflection-on-reflection activity – it is not just an 'academic' exercise but a part of the reflective journey essential for a deep-thinking professional who is interested in further developing knowledge and competence (Brock, 2010). Hopefully, having read this chapter you should have a stronger understanding of your own professionalism. You should now be ready to move on to the next sections in this book and be keen to reflect on the range of the professional knowledge base and the diversity of issues that have importance for ECCE.

Summary of knowledge gained

After reading and reflecting on this chapter you should now be very aware:

- that professionalism is a complex concept and can be interpreted differently;
- that professionalism can consist of seven dimensions: knowledge, education and training, skills, autonomy, values, ethics and reward;
- that having professional status is important in ensuring your acquisition of the three As of accountability, articulation and advocacy.

Challenges for the future

- Is establishing your professionalism important to you?
- What are your key dimensions of professionalism?
- What do you consider to be your professional ethics?
- Why should ongoing professional development be important for you?

Further reading

Bradbury, H., Frost, N., Kilminster, S. and Zukas, M. (eds) (2011) *Beyond Reflective Practice: New approaches to professional lifelong learning.* London: Routledge.

Brock, A. and Rankin, C. (2011) *Professionalism in the Early Years Interdisciplinary Team: Supporting young children and their families.* London: Continuum.

Lindon, J. and Lindon, L. (2011) *Leadership and Early Years Professionalism: Linking theory and practice.* London: Hodder and Stoughton.

References

Aldridge, M. and Evetts, J. (2003) 'Rethinking the concept of professionalism: the case of journalism', *British Journal of Sociology*, 54: 547–64.

Boreen, J., Johnson, M.K., Niday, D. and Potts, J. (2000) *Mentoring Beginning Teachers: Guiding, reflecting, coaching.* Portland, ME: Stenhouse Publishers.

Bourdieu, P. (1990) *The Logic of Practice.* Cambridge: Polity Press.

Brock, A. (2006) *Eliciting early years educators' thinking: how do they define and sustain their professionalism?* Paper presented to the European Early Childhood Education Research Association (EECERA) conference, Reykjavik, Iceland, 30 August–2 September 2006.

Brock, A. (2010) 'The nature of practitioners' reflection on their reflections about play', in Moyles, J. (ed.) *Thinking About Play: Developing a reflective approach.* Maidenhead: McGraw Hill/Open University Press.

Brock, A. (2011) 'Perspectives on professionalism', Chapter 3 in Brock, A. and Rankin, C. (eds) *Professionalism in the Early Years Interdisciplinary Team: Supporting young children and their families.* London: Continuum.

Brock, A. (2013) 'Building a model of early years professionalism from practitioners' perspectives', *Journal of Early Childhood Research*, 11(1): 27–45.

Brock, A. and Rankin, C. (2011) *Professionalism in the Early Years Interdisciplinary Team: Supporting young children and their families.* London: Continuum.

Cable, C. and Miller, L. (2008) 'Looking to the future', in Miller, L. and Cable, C. (eds) *Professionalism in the Early Years.* London: Hodder, pp. 167–77.

Campbell, A. (2003) 'Developing and evaluating early excellence centres in the UK: some issues in promoting integrated and "joined-up" services', *International Journal of Early Years Education*, 11: 235–44.

Evetts, J. (2009) 'New professionalism and new public management: changes, continuities and consequences', *Comparative Sociology*, 8: 247–66.

Friedman, R. (2007) 'Listening to children in the early years', in Wild, M. and Mitchell, H. (eds) *Early Childhood Studies: Reflective reader.* Exeter: Learning Matters, pp. 81–94.

Friedson, E. (1994) *Professionalism Reborn: Theory, prophecy and policy.* Oxford: Polity Press.

Friedson, E. (2001) *Professionalism: The third logic.* Cambridge: Polity Press.

Forster, N. (2000) 'A case study of women academics' views on equal opportunities, career prospects and work family conflicts in a British University', *Women in Management Review*, 15, 316–27.

Frost, N. (2001) 'Professionalism, change and the politics of lifelong learning', *Studies in Continuing Education*, 23: 5–17.

Helsby, G. (1996) 'Professionalism in English secondary schools', *Journal of Education for Teaching*, 22: 135–48.

Hoyle, E. and John, P.D. (1995) *Professional Knowledge and Professional Practice.* London: Cassell.

Hughes, A. and Menmuir, J. (2002) 'Being a student on a part-time early years degree', *Early Years Journal of International Research and Development*, 22: 147–61.

Katz, L. (1985) 'The nature of professionalisms: where is early childhood education?' Addresss presented at the Early Childhood Organisation Conference in honour of Miss E. Marianne Parry, OBE, Bristol Polytechnic, England, September. Printed in *Talks with Teachers of Young Children.* Norwood, NJ: Ablex Publishing Corp., pp. 219–35.

Miller, L. and Cable, C. (2008) *Professionalism in the Early Years.* London: Hodder.

Oberhuemer, P. (2005) 'Conceptualising the early childhood pedagogue: policy approaches and issues of professionalism', *European Early Childhood Education Research Journal*, 13: 5–16.

Osgood, J. (2004) 'Time to get down to business? The responses of early years practitioners to entrepreneurial approaches to professionalism', *Journal of Early Childhood Research*, 2: 5–24.

Osgood, J. (2006) 'Deconstructing professionalism in early childhood education: resisting the regulatory gaze', *Contemporary Issues in Early Childhood Journal*, 7: 5–14.

Rankin, C. and Butler, F. (2011) 'Issues and challenges for the interdisciplinary team in supporting the twenty-first-century family', Chapter 2 in Brock, A. and Rankin, C. (eds) *Professionalism in the Early Years Interdisciplinary Team: Supporting young children and their families.* London: Continuum.

Schön, D. (1976) *The Reflective Practitioner: How professionals think in action.* Aldershot: Arena.

Urban, M. (2009) 'Rethinking professionalism in early childhood: untested feasibilities and critical ecologies', *Contemporary Issues in Early Childhood*, 11(1).

Woodrow, C. (2007) 'W(h)ither the early childhood teacher: tensions for early childhood professional identity between the policy landscape and the politics of teacher regulation', *Contemporary Issues in Early Years*, 8: 233–43.

The knowledge base for early childhood educators

Now use the techniques and advice in Part I to reflect on and further develop your practice. The chapters in Part II present an overview of ECCE in the UK to provide you with key knowledge and research from the guest contributors' perspectives on what are their important issues. This section is for anyone who is at the forefront of practice, both those who are just commencing work with children and those who are very experienced, as everyone needs to be a reflective practitioner. As an ECE practitioner you will make a considerable number of decisions every day – some intuitive, some based on successful practice, some spontaneous in response to a new situation. It is important to engage in ongoing questioning and reflection to become professional at your work. The focus of each of the chapters has been specifically determined to provide you with a balance and range of perspectives of what you need to reflect on to ensure high-quality provision for whatever age range or professional role you have within the field of ECCE.

Chapter 6: Reflecting on children, families and policy

Avril Brock

The chapter addresses ECCE and family policy to examine the political and social issues that are impacting on ECCE today. This is a complex area and practitioners need to develop critical and reflective perspectives on what will affect their practice and provision.

Chapter 7: A children's centre manager's perspective

Jane Lees

This chapter is a professional practitioner perspective from a children's centre manager, who interprets how recent policy has impacted upon children's centres, ECCE and the young children and families who use her setting.

Chapter 8: Reflecting on the role of graduates as pedagogical with children from birth to three

Mary E. Whalley

This chapter informs and examines the new graduate leader role and investigates understanding of 0–30 months pedagogy and the impact on practice with children under three, with a view to identifying or signposting some effective ways forward to ensure that the EYP role does encompass the whole of the EYFS age range, birth to five.

Chapter 9: Early years professionals' reflections on practice for two-year-old children from Kirklees case studies

Rachael Singleton and Avril Brock

This chapter presents reflective case studies from three graduate leaders regarding how they have further developed their practice with two-year-olds.

Chapter 10: A deeper understanding of play

Liz Chesworth

This chapter provides contemporary and seminal theory, research and practice regarding the all-important role of play in young children's learning and presents innovative research that used video as a means of listening to young children's perspectives of their play in an English reception class. The chapter offers insights and approaches to actively involving children as participants in the research process.

Focused reflection: What's going on? The challenge of making sense of open-ended play

Andy Burt

Chapter 11: Reflecting on school readiness

Avril Brock

School readiness seems to be high on the government agenda and this is a cause for concern for many early years practitioners, trainers, researchers and parents. This chapter reflects on how ECCE is provided for young children when they enter the formal school system.

Chapter 12: Capable, confident children: a reception class teacher's pedagogical reflections

Avril Brock and Tina Thornton

This chapter interconnects theory, research and policy with the professional thinking of an 'expert' reception teacher's practice. It has been written through a partnership between the editor and Tina Thornton, a reception class teacher in a Yorkshire rural infant and primary school. The chapter is structured around Tina's eight key aspects of her reception class provision.

Chapter 13: Quality is in the eye of the beholder: developing early years provision using child-led quality indicators

Jo Armistead

The chapter is written from a social constructionist viewpoint, which understands early years settings as spaces for children and communities of practice. It argues for a way of viewing and developing quality early childhood education from the perspective of children.

Focused reflection

What do you think is important for you as a reflective practitioner? These chapters aim to underpin and deepen your existing knowledge and to develop it further into new thinking and reflections on practice. In order to help you focus on what you are eliciting from the chapters in Part 2, it would be beneficial to use the framework below to make notes as you read the chapters and this will then become useful both as a reflective tool and as an aide-memoire to refer back to in the future.

Key points raised	What I can put into practice now	Ideas to follow up

6

Reflecting on children, families and policy

Avril Brock

This chapter addresses ECCE and family policy to examine the political and social issues that are impacting on ECCE today. It reflects on how to capitalise on partnerships with families and to develop the strengths of varied cultural and social expectations. The ECCE area is complex and practitioners need to develop critical and reflective perspectives on what will affect their practice and provision in their work with young children. The chapter aims to enable you to understand why it is complex and why reflection on policy impact is important.

ECCE: a political perspective

During the last two decades, early childhood has been high on the global political agenda, shaping children's and their families' daily and future lives through policy development. This has evolved through the growing awareness of the significance of the first five years of life for intellectual, social and emotional development. There has been a steady growth of interest and research in these early years from the disciplines of psychology, education, social policy, social care and neuropsychology. Policy development for ECCE has continually undergone revision and change – sometimes due to knowledge developed from contemporary research and practice; sometimes due to economic and political ideologies. Recently the economic recession that has affected many countries globally has resulted in a reduction in funding for early childhood services.

The social, political and cultural environment influences how professionals work and how they develop their personal professional values and ethics. The policy changes that have impacted on young children and their families have been both numerous and rapid for the last three decades across three different governments in the UK – Conservative (1979–97); New Labour (1997–2010) and the Conservative and Liberal Coalition Government (2010–). This chapter explores family policy and how this affects the social and cultural capital of young children and their families. Action for Children is a UK-wide charity that aims to support the most vulnerable and neglected children to break free from injustice, deprivation and inequality, so they can achieve their full potential. The charity's 'As Long As It Takes' report (2008) researched the number of policy changes that related to children and young people and found that over 400 different policies and funding initiatives were likely to have had impact upon the lifetime of a 21-year-old, which averages out at twenty new initiatives every year.

Reflecting on how policy can impact on children

In 1989 the United Nations Convention on the Rights of the Child (UNCRC) afforded all children the same range of civil, political, economic, social and cultural rights as adults and was adopted worldwide by governments with the exceptions of the USA and Somalia. It came into force in the UK in 1992 and it details what every child needs to have for a safe, happy and fulfilled childhood respecting the dignity and worth of each individual, regardless of race, gender, language, religion, opinions, wealth or ability. The UNCRC requires that services for children develop policies that are responsive to the wide range of children's needs that encompasses all spheres of their lives (Lewis and Lindsay, 2000). Children are seen as rightful recipients, who should have the right to express views on all matters of concern to them, and inclusive practice should require that children should take part in any decision-making processes that concern them (Nutbrown and Clough, 2006). Examples of this can be seen in Chapters 10 and 13, where Liz Chesworth and Jo Armistead respectively demonstrate how children's voices can be accessed and their interests addressed. But how are children really seen by policy-makers – local and national? The UK Coalition Government seems to have a strong focus on school readiness and there may be a lack of understanding of the needs of young children (see Chapter 12 by Brock and Thornton). Do government and policymakers really listen to children's opinions? Brock (2011) demonstrates that some groups have been very effective in listening to children and families and acclaims the 'Good Childhood Inquiry' (The Children's Society, 2007); the 'Children and Mental Health Services' (CAMHS, 2008) review; the 'Lamb Inquiry for Special Educational Needs and Parental Confidence' (DCSF, 2009); and 'Support for All: the Families and Relationships Green Paper' (DCSF, 2010).

The 'More Great Childcare' report (DfE, 2013b) (you will remember reading about this in Chapter 4) policy document was revised to 'More Affordable Childcare' in July 2013 (DfE, 2013a), after strong reservations from Nick Clegg, the deputy prime minister. Imogen Parker (ippr, July 2013) believes that this year-long commission on ECCE 'does not really provide any new approaches to reform' with most of the changes 'unlikely to substantially reduce costs, boost quality or widen access to early years provision'. Wild et al.'s (2013) research considers the overt and covert discourses in the Nutbrown Review (2012) and 'More Great Childcare' (DfE, 2013b) as they are policy documents that advocate a number of significant changes to early years provision. They found:

> a significant shift in concepts of quality, professionalism and childcare. The positioning of child as investment is a strong feature of the discourse within the latter of these documents as well as an increase in top down frameworks of surveillance and control.
>
> (Wild *et al.*, 2013: 1)

Wild *et al.* (2013) argue that both these policy documents see children as a commodity, as 'money in the bank', with the aim being cheaper childcare while still achieving quality. Both the documents assert that quality and professionalism will occur only if there is strong top-down regulation and inspection (Wild *et al.*, 2013). They argue that this mirrors Osgood's (2010) views on rhetoric as enterprise, that the government seems to believe that the alternative to accountability and competition is laziness. They believe this will affect the position of children and families.

It can be seen how so many factors impact on young children and all this reflects Bronfenbrenner's theory, developed three decades ago. Bronfenbrenner (1979) explains that children are situated within the socio-cultural context of the family and community, and that the ECCE setting, policy development and broader society all impact on their development, well-being, education and life experiences. Bronfenbrenner's (1979) model places the universal child at the centre of concentric circles of influence and demonstrates the significance of the macrosystem of policies and events in the wider world affecting the microsystem where young children and their families are situated. Reflective practitioners realise that their professional knowledge needs to be developed from a critical understanding of how policy and provision impacts on providing appropriate services for young children and their families. Figure 6.1 (Brock, 2011) provides a perspective of how professionals in universal and targeted services impact on children's lives.

Developments such as the Sure Start programme of interagency working to meet needs of children under four years of age and their families provided good early years practice and the integration of family support services. Young children and their families do not 'see their needs for early education, health care, literacy support, job or housing advice as separate silos and neither should the professionals working with them' (Rankin and Butler, 2011). All children in the United Kingdom will have contact from birth with a range of health professionals – midwife, general practitioner, health visitor and dentist; some children will encounter paediatricians, dieticians, physiotherapists or speech and language therapists. The majority of children will have early childhood education and care experiences with childminders, early years professionals, nursery nurses or teachers. They will then enter the

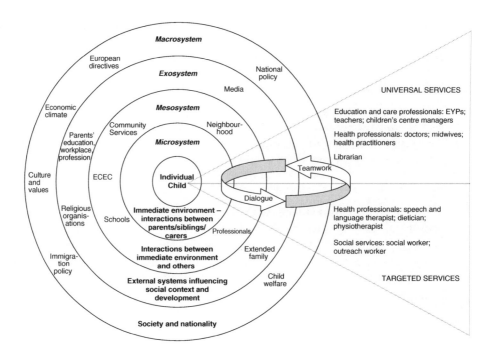

FIGURE 6.1   Children's worlds – an ecological perspective (Brock, 2011).

state education system, be educated in the independent sector or be home educated. Some children will have interventions from social services and may encounter varied social workers, outreach workers, police officers and even lawyers (Brock, 2011).

Supporting Families in the Foundation Years

In 2011 the Department for Education and the Department of Health produced *Supporting Families in the Foundation Years*, which contained the government's vision for the services that were required to support families with children in the early foundation years. It states that the focus is on child development; that families should be placed at the heart of services and that early intervention and help would be provided wherever there was a need. The government aimed to establish a new relationship that enables skilled professionals 'to do what they believe is best' (DfE/DoH, 2011b). Five key government-funded independent reviews are at the heart of the document: Field's (2010) report on poverty and life chances *The Foundation Years: Preventing poor children becoming poor adults*; Marmot's *Fair Society, Healthy Lives* (Marmot, 2010); Allen's (2011) report *Early Intervention: The next steps*; Munro's (2011) *Review of Child Protection: Final report, a child-centred system* and Tickell's (2011) review of the EYFS *The Early Years: Foundations for life, health and learning*. The DfE and DoH (2011a) also produced an evidence pack of resources, research and policy entitled *Families in the Foundation Years*, which provides the underpinning verification for the key aspects raised.

The introduction to the evidence pack (DoE/DoH, 2011a: 2) opens with a 'commitment to developing evidence-based policy' and states that it has been informed by a 'wide range of robust evidence sources'. It asserts that the early years of a child's life are critically important and that 'high quality health services, early education, and care for young children and their families make a real difference' (DoE/DoH, 2011a: 2).

> We have found overwhelming evidence that children's life chances are most heavily predicated on their development in the first five years of life. It is family background, parental education, good parenting and the opportunities for learning and development in those crucial years that together matter more to children than money, in determining whether their potential is realised in adult life.
>
> (Field, 2010: 5)

> Different parts of the brain develop in different sensitive windows of time. The estimated prime window for emotional development is up to 18 months, by which time the foundation of this has been shaped by the way in which the prime carer interacts with the child. Emotional development takes place throughout childhood, and there is a further reorganisation during early adolescence.
>
> (Allen, 2011: 16)

Key factors emerging from these reports that significantly impact on young children's development and life chances are ECCE; physical health, mental health and emotional well-being; socio-economic factors; effective parenting; and early intervention issues. The next sections will expand on these factors and reflect on the implications of these for early years practitioners who work with young children and their families.

Early childhood care and education

Over the past decade, many countries have expanded and developed their policies for their early childhood care and education. Early childhood education and care (ECEC) has become 'increasingly used by governments and international organisations worldwide, because it encapsulates the different national systems of both care and education for children from birth to eight years' (Gammage, 2006: 237). In Northern Ireland the Department of Children and Youth Affairs (DCYA) established in 2011 prefers to use the phrase 'early childhood care and education' (ECCE), which forefronts care before education, and it is the preferred acronym used throughout this book.

In Gammage's (2006: 236) view 'impoverished early experiences' can have a 'debilitating effect, eroding relationships, inhibiting learning and creativity', and a 'good start' in early education may compensate for negative effects of a child's early developmental context (Sylva *et al.*, 2002). Whilst there now seems to be international agreement that investment in ECCE is important, the different approaches countries have adopted mean that children's early education and care experiences can differ greatly (Neuman, 2005; Gammage, 2006). Some children have the statutory right to attend full-day care from six months, some have state provided pre-school, whereas others have no access to education or care experiences outside the home environment. Children therefore may attend different centres for different lengths of time at different ages, experiencing different models, quantities and qualities of ECCE. Furthermore, traditionally in many countries, education and care have been separate systems. A research report compiled by the Centre for Research in Early Childhood (CREC) with the DfE (Pascal *et al.*, 2013) provides 'A Comparison of International Childcare Systems' and aims to:

- provide a short contextual commentary for fifteen selected study countries plus the UK on changes in the five structural indicators of their early education system over the last five years and also on the child physical well-being data for each country;
- analyse patterns within, and between, the set of five structural indicators in centre-based pre-school provision across the fifteen selected study countries, plus the UK.

(DfE/CREC, 2013)

The CREC states that the strength of this research

lies in its capacity to describe how both European and non-European countries are responding to demands for a more highly structured, professionalised and regulated early education system which has the capacity to address socio-economic disadvantage, provide strong economic returns on investment and create more inclusive, stable and higher achieving societies.

(Pascal *et al.*, 2013: 4)

ECCE in the UK

Theorists, researchers and practitioners in the field of ECCE often define early childhood education from birth to eight years (Gammage, 2007). Few institutions in England would have children throughout this age range on roll; however, this will be changing if the government's desire to place two-year-olds in school settings becomes the norm. Young children may have their ECCE experiences in the private, voluntary or public sector in a combination of the following:

childminder; children's centre; crêche; day nursery; early excellence centre; forest nursery; Foundation Stage Unit; home environment; Montessori school; independent school; nursery class in school; nursery school; playgroup; private day care; reception class; special needs school; Steiner school; Sure Start setting (which may be situated in one of the other settings); workplace nursery; wrap-around care in schools.

Most children experience at least two different settings over this period and possibly different educational and care practices (Saracho and Spodek, 2003). For example, Oscar has been in the same full-time daycare from the age of ten months to three years nine months, whilst James stayed with his mum at home with visits to 'Mums and Toddlers' until he was two years three months, then he attended a toddler group for two mornings with one afternoon each with maternal and paternal grandmothers; and at two years six months also attended two full days of private daycare. In England all three- and four-year-olds are entitled to 15 hours of funded early education from the aforementioned list of settings that meet the requirements of the EYFS and Ofsted inspection. This is for 38 weeks of a year until they reach compulsory school age (the term following their fifth birthday). Two-year-olds labelled as disadvantaged can also receive funding for 15 hours of childcare in settings that achieve at least 'good' in their Ofsted inspections. Research (Maisey *et al.*, 2013) found that where children attended higher quality settings, there was a positive impact on language ability, and on their parent–child relationship (2-year-old pilot). Some parents believed that their parenting skills, their relationships and the ability to provide a more stimulating learning environment at home with their children also improved.

> From September 2013, children from families meeting the criteria also used to decide eligibility for free school meals, and looked after children, will be eligible – this will be around 20 per cent of all two-year-olds in England, although the percentage will vary from area to area.
>
> (DfE, 2013a)

The Bercow Report (2008) and Roulstone *et al.*'s (2011) research both demonstrate that a 'child's communication environment influences language development' and that this is a 'more dominant predictor of early language than social background' and can strongly influence 'performance at school entry'. The number of books available to the child, frequency of visits to the library, parents teaching a range of activities, the number of toys available and attendance at pre-school are all important predictors of children's vocabulary at the age of two (Siraj-Blatchford, 2010). Children's understanding and use of language at age two predicts how well they perform on school entry assessments including reading, maths and writing. From September 2014 the Coalition's aim is to increase the number of those eligible to around 40 per cent of all two-year-olds. The policies surrounding childcare and funding are continually changing. Working parents on low income may be able to get extra tax credits to help with the costs. Parents can find out about funding on the websites of the Department for Education, Parental Choice, GOV.UK and local authority websites.

Good-quality ECCE has a significant positive effect on early cognitive development and longer pre-school experience can benefit literacy outcomes. Smith *et al.* (2009) found that quality, the provider's reputation, concern with the care given with staff characteristics as to whether they were affectionate or well trained were the most important values when choosing a provider. Hunt *et al.*'s (2011) research demonstrated that a good-quality early years setting can compensate when children do not experience a strong home learning environment. Skilled practitioners working with parents and carers supporting the quality of home learning improves children's progress and their relationships with parents and carers.

Families, life chances and educational achievement

A child's life chances are most heavily predicated on their development in the first five years of life. Family background, parental education, good parenting and the opportunities for learning and development in the early years have more impact on children's emotional and social development than money and so determine potential and attainment (Field, 2010). The concept and structure of families are constantly changing and each family has its own individual

FIGURE 6.2 Happy families.

culture, needs and priorities. 'Parent' can encompass a wide diversity and variety of parenting cultures and the social context within which families operate can vary greatly. An understanding of families is crucial for those who work with young children and twenty-first-century families can constitute nuclear families, stepfamilies, extended families, multigenerational family households and same-sex partnerships (the *Focus on Families* report, Smallwood and Wilson, 2007). The 'traditional' view of the family is of a married couple with children and this is still mainly the norm, but increasingly families with children may consist of a cohabiting couple or a single parent (Brock, 2011). Recent trends include the delay of marriage and childbearing and an increase in divorce, cohabitation and births outside marriage, and so reconstituted families are formed.

According to Utting (2009), effective, warm, authoritative parenting gives children confidence, a sense of well-being and self-worth whatever the constitution of a modern family may be. Utting (2009) finds that parents who are confident, flexible and have good participative communication skills tend to manage stress well and help their families to do the same. Parents who lack emotional warmth or operate negative or inconsistent discipline risk their children developing emotional or behavioural problems. Parental involvement in a child's education from an early age has a significant effect on educational achievement and the home learning environment (HLE) is crucial in supporting children's achievements. The EPPE Project (Sylva *et al.*, 2002) proved that young children attending a high-quality ECCE setting can have a lifelong effect on social development and educational attainment and this is particularly important for children from disadvantaged backgrounds.

The effects of living in poverty

Field's (2010) *Independent Review on Poverty and Life Chances* acknowledged that the first five years of young children's lives are those which predict their future life chances. In recent years policy regarding young children and their families has been concerned with reducing poverty, getting parents into employment, and increasing training, aspiration and educational achievement, but the recession has created even more difficulties. Recent statistics state that more children than ever are living in poverty in the UK. Both the New Labour and Coalition governments made pledges to end child poverty and between 1998 and 2012 the number of children in relative poverty in the UK fell. Butler (2013) quotes the government's Work and Pensions Secretary Iain Duncan Smith:

> While this government is committed to eradicating child poverty, we want to take a new approach by finding the source of the problem and tackling that. We have successfully protected the poorest from falling behind and seen a reduction of 100,000 children in workless poor families.

At least one out of every six children in the UK lives in relative poverty, according to the Department for Work and Pensions. In 2011/12, 17 per cent of children

(2.3 million) were in households in the UK with incomes below 60 per cent of contemporary median net disposable household income before housing costs and 27 per cent (3.5 million) after housing costs. However, the Institute for Public Policy Research (IPPR) and children's campaigners argue that many children moving into the poverty bracket are in families where people are working and that the number of children living in absolute poverty is now one in five children in the UK. Headlines on the BBC news website on 30 May 2013 quoted a study by Church Action Poverty and Oxfam that stated that 'more than half a million UK people may rely on food banks' and blamed 'benefit cuts, unemployment and the increased cost of living for the growth in hunger and poverty'.

> Every day people in the UK go hungry for reasons ranging from redundancy to receiving an unexpected bill on a low income. Trussell Trust foodbanks provide a minimum of three days' emergency food and support to people experiencing crisis in the UK. In 2012–13 foodbanks fed 346,992 people nationwide. Of those helped, 126,889 were children. Rising costs of food and fuel combined with static income, high unemployment and changes to benefits are causing more and more people to come to foodbanks for help.
>
> (Trussell Trust, 2014)

Families who are trapped in a cycle of poverty may be suffering from lack of employment; poor housing; overcrowding; lack of resources leading to poor health and diet; post-natal depression; mental health and learning difficulties (Raffo *et al.*, 2007, cited in Brock, 2011). Low socio-economic status does not mean low aspiration, but it is more likely there are barriers to achievement (Hirsch, 2007). Feinstein's (2003) research found that children from high socio-economic status at twenty-two months overtook the children from low socio-economic status as their age increased at forty months, five years and ten years of age. The Sutton Trust funded report (2010) showed that children in the poorest fifth of families were already nearly a year behind children from middle-income families in vocabulary tests. This research by Waldfogel and Washbrook (2010) indicates that children's educational achievements are strongly linked to parents' income and low income may be a barrier to social mobility.

Melhuish *et al.*'s (2008, 2010) research finds that HLE has a greater influence on a child's intellectual and social development than parental occupation, education or income. What parents do with their children is more important in terms of the children's outcomes than who they are in terms of social class and income. Siraj-Blatchford *et al.*'s (2011: 33) comprehensive study explores why some 'at-risk' children 'succeed against the odds' while others fall further behind. Disadvantaged children significantly benefit from good quality pre-school experiences and Siraj-Blatchford *et al.*'s (2011) research finds that this is the case internationally. This *Effective Provision of Pre-School, Primary and Secondary Education 3–16* (EPPSE) study finds that the evidence from France indicates that pre-school appears to reduce socio-economic inequalities and in Switzerland the expansion of ECCE has improved intergenerational educational mobility.

In September 2013 the National Children's Bureau (NCB) called for urgent action to address the poverty and disadvantage that still wreaks havoc on children's lives, causing them to lag far behind their more affluent peers in almost all areas of their lives, from health to education, early development to housing. The NCB comparison with other developed nations found that a staggering number of children suffer unnecessarily and that there is a risk that patterns of disadvantage were becoming permanent features of UK society. The research, entitled *Greater Expectations* (NCB, 2013), compares data on different aspects of children's lives today with a ground-breaking national cohort study of eleven-year-olds published in 1973. It finds that significantly more children grow up in poverty today, 3.5 million compared to 2 million, and these children suffer devastating consequences throughout their lives. According to research by the Joseph Rowntree Foundation (Hanley, 2009), public awareness of the extent and reality of UK poverty is limited. Real-life stories and the voice of people in poverty are effective and powerful in engaging the public, but severely under-represented in media. Did you know that:

- the UK has one of the worst rates of child poverty in the industrialised world;
- the majority of poor children live in a household where at least one adult works;
- 43 per cent of poor children live in a household headed by a lone parent;
- the majority of poor children live in a household headed by a couple;
- 42 per cent of children in poverty are from families with three or more children?

Focused reflection point

- What do you know about children who live in poverty? What are your perspectives?
- Undertake an internet search to find out more about poverty and develop your understanding as to why food banks, payday loans and which area of the country you live in affects young children living in or on the edge of poverty.
- Find out what is the difference between absolute poverty and relative poverty?
- Access this weblink – http://www.ncb.org.uk/greaterexpectations – and download the document *Greater Expectations*. You should then watch the powerful video clip of the same name on the NCB website.

Families are important: the relevance of social capital

Richardson's (2013) research explores how social capital has developed in individuals using the services of four Sure Start children's centres in a large urban city in northern England. Whilst the development of children's centres has been debated over the last ten years, the individual voices of parents and staff describing the complexity of their social experience and change is rarely represented. Richardson's research uses the theoretical models around social capital offered by Bourdieu (1984) and Woolcock (1998) to provide a framework to analyse and disseminate the intricacy of relationships and interaction; the motivations and reasons why individuals behave as they do. She found that the reciprocity described in the staff/parent relationships and the value of the services offered strongly emerged through the detailed personal perspectives of the staff and parents. This provided insight into the challenging circumstances and complexities of individual lives, and a framework for how social capital develops. Richardson's research demonstrates how Sure Start children's centres have enormous potential for supporting individual progress and possibilities for generating social change.

Focused reflection point

Here are some extracts from Richardson's (2013) study on the development of social capital in four children's centres. They should help you understand what is meant by social capital as well as providing an insight into how complex and difficult life can be for some families with young children. The parents volunteered to participate in the research and their names have been changed to respect confidentiality.

Read about their situations and reflect on the powerful impact that listening to real voices provides. Then share your reflections with a colleague.

Sure Start children's centres: a study of the development of social capital

Andrea Richardson

The voice of parents

Anne fled serious domestic violence, after having her baby and eventually being moved to a new city a long way from family and friends. She was re-located to a new city because of the significant risk to her own and her son's safety from a violent partner.

> *Before only I could understand him but now a lot of people can understand him now, so he's done a hell of a lot better here than at the other place. I've been coming here since January, since we've come here things have got a hell of a lot better, everything's better so it's worked for the reason that he started going to nursery, my life changed. I used the counselling and the play and stay, they also got me on a course with the NSPCC and on a volunteering course as well. I've only just done that, but then I can do volunteering here. It's helped to meet other parents and make networks. Anne*

Groups and networks

> *I used the play and stay, it helped to meet other parents and make networks.*

Aisha came to England four years ago with her two children and father, fleeing from a difficult marriage where her husband drank and was physically violent.

She came into an equally difficult life in England, staying at first with relatives who dominated and verbally abused her. She struggled to begin her new life for herself and her family, moving a number of times before she ended up attending the children's centre. She was quite dependent on the centre for a while, but now has established herself and her family.

> Elise was well cared for, she was with Sara (key worker), she had people she liked. You know when you get into a room and you just have a good feel about it. I felt the aura, I felt very at ease here. I let go slowly, it was a process, it didn't happen overnight, I get panic attacks sometimes. I came to parenting groups, used nursery. It was also cooking groups – lovely groups. I find the open door policy very approachable, that's made it easier. Aisha

Social cohesion and inclusion

> I find the open door policy very approachable that's made it easier. I think if it's open it makes it easier for parents, its good. Some don't have, they have closed doors, it's difficult then to discuss any worries, so that was good.

Mat has been a single parent since Ryan's mother died from drug use. He has been using services at Hollyoaks Sure Start children's centres for around three years. Although Mat has a large family, seven sisters, they live in the Midlands and south of England. He had a long history of drug and alcohol use; he stopped using heroin when his partner died. His son Ryan went to school six months ago.

> I used to drink. Jan and Helen sat me down and it was informal, having a laugh. I had many problems, so I felt like I want to tell them, I wanted to. They got me involved in the alcohol dependency unit, you know you don't want to hide anything, you want to talk 'cause you know they've got advice. I don't know of any other place like this, everyone on the estate knows about it, Jan is always walking around, going to visits, telling people what's going on or if they need any help. That's the good thing. Instead of having the information just here it's actually going out and talking, Jan knows everyone. Mat

Trust and solidarity

> The main people I talk to are Jan and Helen, I felt I could talk to and be open with them.

Collective action and co-operation

> This morning you get veg, good quality, cheaper stuff; I give them a hand with that. It makes you want to come in and get involved.

Steve is a single parent who had recently taken on the full care of his two children. Their mum had been unable to care for them because of long-standing mental health problems and substance abuse. He gave up work to look after the children and moved back to the community where he had grown up, where his sister and old friends lived.

> I keep my kids active then I ask what they've done as they say we've been planting seeds, so we go home then and do it, go to the shops. We've grown

sunflowers; we talk about feelings and emotions, checking they understand things. Steve

Information and communication

I'm here quite a lot. I enjoy coming here because I get good news and they tell me about things, do I want to do this or that, give you leaflets. They're as helpful as possible I mean in my position you need a bit of help.

Jen uses the childcare services at Sunningdale Children's Centre, as she works full time. She described herself as 'getting into trouble' when she was younger. She had Annie when she was seventeen and had great support from her mum, but she described episodes in her life when she was the victim of sexual abuse and domestic violence.

I had a domestic violence incident so I had my confidence knocked but I'm like a bouncing ball. I'm back on my feet again. I know what it's like not to have confidence, from being here, seeing things like that and how it affects people; I don't want it to affect me like that. I know the best way to go through it now. I have learned a lot. At first I struggled a lot, even though I lived with Mum; when I was pregnant I was only 17. When I had her I made my mum push her then I thought . . . I bounced back . . . I thought she's my baby, I'm not a bad mum, although I thought I was. She's clean, she's healthy, she's mine. Jen

Empowerment and political action

I know what it's like not to have confidence, from being here, seeing things like that and how it affects people. I don't want it to affect me like that. I know the best way to go through it now. So I just help myself and bounce straight back up again.

Physical health, mental health and emotional well-being

Physical, intellectual, social and emotional development is obviously founded in early childhood, but what happens during these early years has lifelong effects on many aspects of health and well-being (Marmot, 2010). Dyson *et al.* (2009) affirm that 'healthy early childhood development strongly influences many aspects of well-being, such as obesity/stunting, mental health, heart disease'. Regular support from a health visitor has a positive impact on both parents' and children's well-being and mental health. The Healthy Child Programme (DoH, 2009b) includes breastfeeding support and a range of proven preventive services. The Family Nurse Partnership programme (DoH, 2009a) is regarded as a most effective early childhood home visiting programme that demonstrates reductions in children's injuries, child abuse and neglect; increases in fathers' involvement; increases in maternal employment; reductions in welfare dependency; and better parenting. The Department of Health (2011) considers that these early intervention programmes have substantial benefits for children, including improved cognitive development; school readiness and academic achievement; and emotional and behavioural development. The government announced the policy 'Giving all children a healthy start in life' (DoH, 2013) in March 2013, which builds on the successes of the Healthy Child Programme, health visitors and the Family Nurse Partnership.

> Giving every child the best start in life is crucial to reducing health inequalities across the life course. The foundations for virtually every aspect of human development – physical, intellectual and emotional – are laid in early childhood. What happens during these early years (starting in the womb) has lifelong effects on many aspects of health and well-being, educational achievement and economic status.
>
> (Marmot, 2010: 22)

Children's health is strongly influenced by their parents' health and healthy behaviour, and factors such as breastfeeding, smoking, immunisation and diet all have impact on children's development. Children of 'mothers with mental ill health are five times more likely to have mental health problems themselves, resulting in both emotional and behavioural difficulties' (Meltzer *et al.*, 2003) (see the case study on children's mental health in Part III for further information). The availability of high-quality health services, early years education and support through the Sure Start programme has resulted in families experiencing better child health, parenting, home learning environments and life satisfaction than families in non-Sure Start areas (Melhuish *et al.*, 2010).

What is early intervention?

Early intervention works on the basis that the care a child receives in the first three years can largely determine future outcomes. This means that it is important to intervene to tackle any problems emerging for children as soon as possible, such as diagnosed disabilities or developmental delays so that they receive resources to maximise development. This can be through providing targeted services and support universally to all children and families or through targeted support for those more likely to suffer poor outcomes (reflect back on Figure 6.1). Government-funded research finds that:

> Like the reviews led by Graham Allen MP, Dame Clare Tickell, and Rt Hon Frank Field MP, this review has noted the growing body of evidence of the effectiveness of early intervention with children and families and shares their view on the importance of providing such help. Preventative services can do more to reduce abuse and neglect than reactive services.
>
> (Munro, 2011: 7)

The Centre for Excellence and Outcomes in Children and Young People's Services (C4EO) is a valuable resource that provides support for practitioners and their senior management team to promote excellence in local practice and transform lives. The Centre informs about national research and supplies data about 'what works' to improve children's lives, to close the gap in educational achievement and to improve emotional resilience for children and young people with additional needs. It is the belief of C4EO that 'early intervention and prevention for vulnerable children, young people and families poses one of the greatest challenges for local services and society at large' (C4EO, 2013).

The aim of the Common Assessment Framework (CAF) process is to gather and assess information related to individual children's developmental needs as well as the family environment. The CAF was developed for practitioners from a range of backgrounds to unite in a multidisciplinary 'team around the child' (TAC) to determine an appropriate course of action to provide the services needed (DfE, 2012). Identification and assessment should involve parents and children themselves, as it is important to respect the diversity of families and communities. For children with disabilities or complex health needs, the Early Support Programme can offer the joined-up support that families need. The Lamb Enquiry on Special Educational Needs and Parental Confidence (DCSF, 2009) reported that Early Support was widely welcomed by parents for its family-centred, multi-agency approach and the support of a key worker.

Conclusion

There are critics who believe that early intervention can be overly viewed from a deficit perspective that sees families as being at fault if their child is not succeeding according to Western developmental milestones. It is therefore important to continually and critically reflect on policy and practice that affects children and their families and to see them as individuals within society. The issues are definitely many and complex. Acquiring information and developing an understanding of implications will take time. This chapter has presented an overview of policy issues; the next chapter presents the perspective of a children's centre manager working at the forefront with young children and their families.

Summary of knowledge gained

After reading and reflecting on this chapter you should now be aware that:

- political and social issues impact on ECCE and that it is important to ascertain how these can impact on a setting;
- families are very different and will have varied cultural and social expectations;
- families experience diverse life chances and socio-economics, health and early childhood care and education experiences which all impact on children's future educational achievement.

Challenges for the future

- You should now be developing reflective perspectives on what affects your practice and provision in your work with young children and their families.
- Determine to keep up to date and develop knowledge of relevant political and social issues.
- Keep an open mind and reflect on issues with colleagues or other students on a regular basis.

Further reading

Baldock, P. (2010) *Understanding Cultural Diversity in the Early Years.* London: Sage.
Baldock, P., Fitzgerald, D. and Kay, J. (2013) *Understanding Early Years Policy.* London: Sage.
Miller, L. and Hevey, D. (2012) *Policy Issues in the Early Years.* London: Sage.
Papatheodorou, T. (2012) *Debates on Early Childhood Policies and Practices: Global snapshots of pedagogical thinking and encounters.* London: Routledge.

References

Action for Children (2008) *As Long As It Takes: A new politics for children.* Watford: Action for children.
Allen, G. (2011) *Early Intervention: The next steps.* London: Cabinet Office.
Bercow Report (2008) *A Review of Services for Children and Young People (0–19) with Speech, Language and Communication Needs.* Nottingham: DCSF Publications.
Bourdieu, P. (1984) *Distinction: A social critique of the judgement of taste.* London: Routledge and Kegan Paul.
Brock, A. (2011) 'The child in context – policy and provision', Chapter 1 in Brock, A. and Rankin, C. (eds) *Professionalism in the Early Years Interdisciplinary Team: Supporting young children and their families.* London: Continuum.
Bronfenbrenner, U. (1979) *The Ecology of Human Development.* Cambridge, MA: Harvard University Press.
Butler, P. (2013) 'Poverty rose by 900,000 in coalition's first year', *The Guardian*, 13 June. Retrieved 11 April 2014 from http://www.theguardian.com/society/2013/jun/13/1million-more-people-poverty-coalition-first-year.
Centre for Excellence and Outcomes in Children and Young People's Services (C4EO) (2013) *C4EO theme: Early intervention.* http://www.c4eo.org.uk.
Children and Mental Health Services (CAMHS) (2008) *Children and Young People in Mind: The final report of the National CAMHS Review.* London: DCSF and DoH.
Children's Society, The (2007) *Good Childhood Inquiry.* London: The Children's Society.
Department for Children, Schools and Families (DCSF) (2009) *Lamb Inquiry for Special Educational Needs and Parental Confidence.* Nottingham: DCSF Publications.
Department for Children, Schools and Families (DCSF) (2010) *Support for All: The Families and Relationships Green Paper.* Norwich: The Stationery Office.
Department for Education (2012) *Team Around the Child (TAC).* Retrieved 11 April 2014 from

http://www.education.gov.uk/childrenandyoungpeople/strategy/integratedworking/a0068944/team-around-the-child-tac.

Department for Education (2013a) *More Affordable Childcare*. London: Department for Education. Retrieved 11 April 2014 from https://www.gov.uk/government/publications/more-affordable-childcare.

Department for Education (2013b) *More Great Childcare: Raising quality and giving parents more choice*. London: Department for Education. Retrieved 11 April 2014 from https://www.gov.uk/government/publications/more-great-childcare-raising-quality-and-giving-parents-more-choice.

Department for Education and Department of Health (2011a) *Families in the Foundation Years: Evidence pack*. Runcorn: Department for Education. Retrieved 11 April 2014 from https://www.gov.uk/government/publications/supporting-families-in-the-foundation-years.

Department for Education and Department of Health (2011b). *Supporting Families in the Foundation Years*. Runcorn: Department for Education. Retrieved 13 April 2014 from https://www.gov.uk/government/publications/supporting-families-in-the-foundation-years.

Department of Health (2009a) *Family Nurse Partnership Programme*. Retrieved 11 April 2014 from https://www.gov.uk/government/publications/family-nurse-partnership-programme-information-leaflet.

Department of Health (2009b) *Healthy Child Programme: Pregnancy and the first five years of life*. Retrieved 11 April 2014 from https://www.gov.uk/government/publications/healthy-child-programme-pregnancy-and-the-first-5-years-of-life.

Department of Health (2011) *The Evidence Base for Family Nurse Partnership*. Retrieved 11 April 2014 from https://www.gov.uk/government/publications/evidence-base-for-family-nurse-partnership-fnp.

Department of Health (2013) *Giving All Children a Healthy Start in Life*. Retrieved 11 April 2014 from https://www.gov.uk/government/policies/giving-all-children-a-healthy-start-in-life.

Dyson, A., Hertzman, C., Roberts, H., Tunstill, J. and Vaghri, Z. (2009) *Childhood Development, Education and Health Inequalities: Task group report to the Strategic Review of Health Inequalities in England Post 2010 (Marmot Review)*. London: University College London.

Feinstein, L. (2003) 'Inequality in the early cognitive development of British children in the 1970 cohort', *Economica*, 70: 73–98.

Field, F. (2010) *The Foundation Years: Preventing poor children becoming poor adults. The report of the Independent Review on Poverty and Life Chances*. London: Cabinet Office. Retrieved 11 April 2014 from http://webarchive.nationalarchives.gov.uk/20110120090128/http://povertyreview.independent.gov.uk/media/20254/poverty-report.pdf.

Gammage, P. (2006) 'Early childhood education and care: politics, policies and possibilities', *Early Years: An International Journal of Research and Development*, 26: 235–48.

Gammage, P. (2007) 'None so blind: early childhood education and care – the connective tissue', *Forum*, 49(1&2): 47–56.

Hanley, T. (2009) *Engaging Public Support for Eradicating Poverty in the UK*. York: Joseph Rowntree Foundation.

Hirsch, D, (2007) *Chicken and Egg: Child poverty and educational inequalities*. London: Child Poverty Action Group.

Hunt, S., Virgo, S., Klett-Davies, M., Page, A. and Apps, J. (2011) *Provider Influence on the Home Learning Environment*. Report to the DfE. London: Family and Parenting Institute.

Lewis, A. and Lindsay, G. (2000) *Researching Children's Perspectives*. Buckingham: Open University Press.

Maisey, R., Speight, S., Marsh, V. and Philo, D. (2013) *The Early Education Pilot for Two-Year-Old Children: Age five follow-up research report March 2013*. NatCen Social Research, Department for Education.

Marmot, M. (2010) *Fair Society, Healthy Lives*. London: The Marmot Review.

Melhuish, E.C., Sylva, K., Sammons, P., Siraj-Blatchford, I., Taggart, B. and Phan, M. (2008) 'Effects of the home learning environment and preschool center experience upon literacy and numeracy development in early primary school, *Journal of Social Issues*, 64(1): 95–114.

Melhuish, E., Belsky, J., Leyland, A.H. and Barnes, J. (2010) *The Impact of Sure Start Local Programmes on Five Year Olds and Their Families*, November 2010, NESS Research Report 28. London: DCSF; HMSO.

Meltzer, H., Gatward, R., Corbin, T., Goodman, R. and Ford, T. (2003) *The Mental Health of Young People Looked After by Local Authorities in England*. London: The Stationery Office.

Munro, E. (2011) *The Munro Review of Child Protection: Final Report: A child-centred system*. London: Department for Education/The Parliamentary Bookshop.

National Children's Bureau (NCB) (2013) *Greater Expectations: Raising aspirations for our children*. London: National Children's Bureau.

Neuman, M. (2005) 'Governance of early childhood education and care: recent developments in OECD countries', *Early Years: An International Journal of Research and Development*, 25: 129–41.

Nutbrown, C. (2012) *Foundations for Quality: The independent review of early education and childcare qualifications. Final Report*. Runcorn: Department of Education.

Nutbrown, C. and Clough, P. (2006) *Inclusion in the Early Years: Cultural analyses and enabling narratives*. London: Sage.

Osgood, J. (2010) 'Negotiating professionalism: towards a critically reflective emotional professionalism', *Early Years: an International Journal of Research and Development*, 30(1): 119–34.

Parker, I. (2013) 'The coalition still isn't rising to the challenge on affordable childcare', New Statesman ('The Staggers' blog), 16 July. Retrieved 13 April 2014 from http://www.newstatesman.com/politics/2013/07/coalition-still-isnt-rising-challenge-affordable-childcare.

Pascal, C., Bertram, T., Delaney, S. and Nelson, C. (2013) *A Comparison of International Childcare Systems*. London: Department for Education/Centre for Research Early Childhood. Retreived 11 April 2014 from http://www.crec.co.uk/DFE-RR269.pdf.

Raffo, C., Dyson, A., Gunter, H., Hall, D., Jones, L. and Kalambouka, A. (2007) *Education and Poverty: A critical review of theory, policy and practice*. York: Joseph Rowntree Foundation and University of Manchester.

Rankin, C. and Butler, F. (2011) 'Issues and challenges for the interdisciplinary team in supporting the 21st century family', Chapter 2 in Brock, A. and Rankin, C. (eds) *Professionalism in the Early Years Interdisciplinary Team: Supporting young children and their families*. London: Continuum.

Richardson, A. (2013) *Sure Start Children's Centres: a study of complex social change*. Paper presented at 23rd European Early Childhood Education Research conference, 'Values, Culture and Contexts', Tallin, Estonia, 28–31 August 2013.

Roulstone, S., Law, J., Rush, R., Clegg, J. and Peters, T. (2011) *The Role of Language in Children's Early Educational Outcomes*. Research Report DFE- RR134. Sheffield: Department for Education.

Saracho, O. and Spodek, B. (2003) *Studying Teachers in Early Childhood Settings*. Greenwich, CN: Information Age Publishing.

Siraj-Blatchford, I. (2010) 'Learning in the home and in school: how working class children succeed against the odds', *British Educational Research Journal*, 36(3): 463–82.

Siraj-Blatchford, I., Mayo, A., Melhuish, E., Taggart, B., Sammons, P. and Sylva, K. (2011) *Performing against the odds: developmental trajectories of children in the EPPSE 3–16 study*. Research Report DFE-RR128. London: Department for Education/Institute of Education.

Smallwood, S. and Wilson, B. (eds) (2007) *Focus on Families*. Basingstoke: Palgrave Macmillan.

Smith, R., Purdon, S., Schneider, V., La Valle, I., Wollny, I., Owen, R. and Bryson, C. (2009) *Early Education Pilot for Two Year Old Children: Evaluation*. London: DCSF.

Sylva, K., Siraj-Blatchford, I., Taggart, B., Sammons, P., Elliot, K. and Melhuish, E. (2002) *The Effective Provision of Preschool Education (EPPE) Project: Summary of findings*. London: DfES and Institute of Education, University of London.

Tickell, C. (2011) *The Early Years: Foundations for Life, Health and Learning*. An Independent Report on the Early Years Foundation Stage to Her Majesty's Government.

Trussell Trust (2014) 'UK Foodbanks', *The Trussell Trust*, retrieved 10 April 2014 from http://www.trusselltrust.org/foodbank-projects.

Utting, D. (2009) *Parenting Services: Assessing and meeting the need for parenting support services*. London: Family and Parenting Institute literature review.

Waldfogel, J. and Washbrook, E. (2010) *Low Income and Early Cognitive Development in the U.K.* London: The Sutton Trust. Retrieved 11 April 2014 from www.suttontrust.com/our-work/research/download/35/.

Wild, M., Leeson, C., Silberfield, C., Nightingale, B. and Calder, P. (2013) *More? Great? Childcare? A discourse analysis of recent social policy documents relating to the care of young children in England and Wales*. Paper presented to EECERA conference, Tallinn, Estonia, 29 August–1 September 2013.

Woolcock, M. (1998) 'Social capital and economic development: towards a theoretical synthesis and policy framework', *Theory and Society*, 27: 151–208.

7

A children's centre manager's perspective

Jane Lees

Introduction

This chapter is a professional practitioner perspective from a children's centre manager, who interprets how recent policy has impacted upon children's centres, ECCE and the young children and families who use her setting.

During the General Election campaign of 2010, Sure Start children's centres (SSCCs), which had been a flagship policy of the Labour Party, were a key area of debate. Conservative leader David Cameron assured the public, 'Yes, we back Sure Start . . . [it's] something that really matters' (*The Independent* (internet), 5 May 2010). The aim of this chapter is to focus on the policies of the Coalition Government and seek to understand their impact on SSCCs as providers, as well as on children and families.

A short history of SSCCs

The origins of Sure Start came from the 1998 Comprehensive Spending Review led by Norman Glass, an economist, who had no experience of early years. He was asked to quantify expenditure on young children and the effectiveness on outcomes for children. The review was extremely comprehensive involving 11 different government departments (Glass, 1999; Lewis, 2011a; Eisenstadt, 2011) and examined evidence from America including Head Start and the Perry pre-school programme (Eisenstadt, 2011) as well as UK research in child health. The review concluded that the early years were the most important for a child's development and children were more vulnerable to external adverse environmental conditions than had been realised. It also found that the issue of young children experiencing multiple disadvantage was severe and growing and there was a strong correlation with social exclusion as an adult. It found that there was not a consistent approach to provision for children under four in terms of quality or quantity and that providing a comprehensive community-based programme incorporating early intervention, alongside support for the family and based on existing good practice, could impact on child development. It would also help families and thereby break the cycle of deprivation, ultimately reducing government expenditure over the long term (Melhuish and Hall, quoted in Belsky *et al.*, 2007).

The result was a £542 million anti-poverty intervention strategy called Sure Start local programmes (SSLPs). It was targeted at families with children under four, living in the most disadvantaged communities in England. The key characteristics of SSLPs included the targeting of areas with high concentrations of the most deprived children aged 0–4 as identified using the Index of Multiple Deprivation (IMD). It was decided a ring-fenced budget, over a 10-year period, for a defined geographical area, which brought together professionals particularly from statutory providers such as health, education and social care, as well as the voluntary sector, was the way forward to provide integrated, or 'joined up' multidisciplinary services that were child-centred. The SSLPs needed to be user, not provider led and managed by a local partnership of local professionals from across the range of services working with children and families, and parents should be key decision-makers at this strategic level (Anning and Ball, 2008). They should involve families by building on their strengths, and promote participation in the design and delivery of service provision (Weinberger *et al.*, 2005).

The funding for SSLPs came directly from central government, bypassing local government (Melhuish and Hall, quoted in Belsky *et al.*, 2007) and this local autonomy allowed for innovation and creativity in service delivery. However, there were ambitious targets to achieve such as increasing breastfeeding and access to maternity services and also improving children's language development. '[T]he centre of government would define certain outcomes in exchange for freedom to innovate on the inputs that would achieve the outcomes' (Eisenstadt, 2011: 35). Education Secretary David Blunkett saw SSLPs as a means of building social capital, which empowered parents and communities, often with an emphasis on the voluntary sector (Bagley, 2011; Eisenstadt, 2011). Indeed 'successful Sure Start local programmes demonstrated a core "style", the essence of which was valuing people' (Anning and Ball, 2008).

Initially there were 60 'trailblazer' SSLPs, with a further 250 planned offering outreach, home visits, family support – both individual and through parenting programmes – and support for good-quality play and learning, along with advice on health and special needs. There was freedom to develop other initiatives that met local needs (Lewis, 2011b). The fact that SSLPs were individually tailored made their evaluation very difficult (Belsky *et al.*, 2007; Eisenstadt, 2011). Anning and Ball (2008), who were both principal investigators for the National Evaluation of Sure Start, found that 'reach figures for SSLPs were disappointing . . . rarely higher than 26 per cent. A further dilemma was that those who would have benefited most from Sure Start were the least likely to be reached' (p. 167). However, before SSLPs had had sufficient time to be established, Labour policy by 2003 had changed to developing children's centres, also interchangeably known as Sure Start children's centres (SSCCs).

The new agenda was the provision of universal services and no longer purely focused on specifically defined areas with high concentrations of deprivation. The policy goal was to end child poverty by reducing the number of children living in workless households, through the provision of affordable, good-quality childcare and employment support to get parents, especially lone parents, into work. The children's centre core offer, for those based in areas where the majority of children were in the 30 per cent most deprived areas (IMD), included the requirement to provide fully integrated childcare and education, alongside specific provision from JobcentrePlus. ' A focus on support for children and their parents gave way to an emphasis on children's cognitive development on the one hand, and parents' employment on the other' (Lewis, 2011a, b). The death of Victoria Climbié and subsequent development of the Every Child Matters Framework, in 2003, significantly determined policy change, stressing the importance of prevention, educational attainment and integrated services for children. The five outcomes, which were based on consultations with children, young people and families, were:

- being healthy: enjoying good physical and mental health and living a healthy lifestyle;
- staying safe: being protected from harm and neglect;
- enjoying and achieving: getting the most out of life and developing the skills for adulthood;
- making a positive contribution: being involved with the community and society and not engaging in anti-social or offending behaviour;
- economic well-being: not being prevented by economic disadvantage from achieving their full potential in life.

To achieve these outcomes, local authorities, via newly appointed Directors of Children's Services, had direct accountability to government. Glass (2005) argued that these changes marked the abolition of Sure Start, while Lewis (2011a: 77) concluded that the Labour Government presented the transition from Sure Start local programmes to children's centres 'as a continuation of the "essence" of Sure Start', enabling them to claim success for their flagship programme, notwithstanding the negative findings of the National Evaluation (Belsky *et al.*, 2007) and the change in approach. By the time of the 2010 General Election, there were 3,578 SSCCs, covering the whole of England, including Phase 3 SSCCs, which were established in the 70 per cent more affluent areas (IMD) of the country. The Apprenticeships, Skills, Children and Learning Act 2009 included a provision which embedded SSCCs in legislation, making the provision of children's centres a statutory requirement for local authorities. Lewis *et al.* note that '[t]he fact that a (SS)CC is not necessarily a building but rather a service umbrella is not always apparent from the government documents' (2011: 35). This would prove significant for the Coalition Government when it introduced unprecedented cuts to public spending.

The Coalition Government and SSCCs

When the Coalition Government was formed in May 2010, within three days the Department for Children, Schools and Families (DCSF) had been renamed the Department for Education. For a leader of an SSCC, working with children and families, it signalled a chilling departure. However, four key independent reviews from Field (2010), Allen (2011), Tickell (2011) and Munro (2011) were commissioned, as described in Chapter 6, and all strongly asserted the importance of the early years. Notwithstanding the Coalition's endorsement of these reviews and personal commitments from both David Cameron and Nick Clegg about supporting SSCCs, key policy changes have adversely affected children and families, and SSCCs. The most significant policy changes are outlined in the headings below, although they are, in many cases, interlinked and to understand the full picture should be seen as a whole.

Funding of SSCCs

The introduction of children's centres, by the previous Labour Government, had already resulted in a significant reduction in the level of investment per child (Lewis, 2011: 74), with the Public Accounts Committee 'fearing the implications for disadvantaged areas'. Children's centres were funded from a general early years funding stream 'with the expectation that the most generously funded children's centres would be in the poorest areas' (Eisenstadt, 2011). Previously Sure Start local programmes funding was 'ring-fenced', which meant that it could only be spent on Sure Start provision. The Coalition Government introduced the Early Intervention Grant, which combined previous funding streams to local authorities for Sure Start local programmes and children's centres as well as all other activities for children aged 0–19. This 'ring-fence' has been removed, allowing local authorities to make decisions on how to prioritise their expenditure. This has allowed national government to insist that it has provided sufficient funding and that local decision making has determined allocations of expenditure. Watt, quoting Eisenstadt (*Guardian* (internet), 14 November 2011), stated that 'Sure Start is being cut, anyone who says otherwise is wrong.' It should be noted that if the ring-fence was still in place it would have been insufficient to cover the financial requirements of SSCCs, as it applied only to SSLPs and not to children's centres. However, by removing the ring-fence it has paved the way for a reduction in funding of SSCCs.

When the Coalition Government removed all the various funding streams for children and young people aged 0–19 and combined them into the Early Intervention Grant (EIG), it was cut by 10.9 per cent from £2,483m in 2010–11 to £2,212m in 2011–12. The transfer of funding for the 2 Year Old Offer (discussed below) from the EIG to the Dedicated Schools Grant reduced the size of the EIG from 2012, effectively ring-fencing funding away from SSCCs and youth provision. In 2013–14 the total 'EIG' was £1,708m, and in 2014–15 it will be £1,600m. This represents an overall reduction of £883m; although, 'from April 2013, the

EIG has been abolished and funding for early intervention and family services is now being provided as part of the "General Fund"' (Report from the All Party Parliamentary Sure Start Group, July 2013). This effectively means that local authorities could spend this money on anything, as there is now no segregation of income for children and young people's services.

Notwithstanding the Coalition Government's decision to adopt the term 'foundation years', the recommendation to gradually move funding to the early years, advocated by Field and Allen, has not happened. The SSCCs have suffered significant cuts and these are expected to get worse. Reductions in grants to local authorities have not been apportioned consistently across England. The Coalition Government has succeeded in transferring public anger to local authorities by devolving decision making on budgets. Coalition Government transparency around funding of the 2 Year Old Offer has intensified the strain on budgets in the cities with the highest levels of child poverty. Bradford has been one of the hardest hit, having already suffered £100m cuts in the last two years. Bradford is among many local authorities that have strived to protect SSCCs from cuts. Bradford Council has recently announced a proposal to cut the SSCC budget by 25 per cent over the next two financial years. The proposal includes closing 7 of 12 Phase 3 SSCCs (those in the most affluent areas) and further reductions to the rest with a stronger weighting of funding to the most deprived areas.

> More than 400 SSCCs have closed during the first two years of Coalition Government; with over half of those still open no longer providing any onsite childcare . . . London (126) and the south-east (62) are the regions that have seen most closures, according to Labour's figures, which were obtained through parliamentary questions. Ministers have said that of the 401 closures, only 25 were what it termed 'outright closures'. The other 376 centres were reduced by reorganisations, including the merger of two or more centres.
>
> (Butler, 2013)

'Closing' SSCCs has proved very emotive, as Sheffield City Council discovered in 2013, when they reorganised 36 SSCCs into 17 'hub centres'. The council made the decision to cut £3.5m from the SSCCs' budgets for 2013/14. This caused an outcry with hundreds of people marching through the streets and a petition of 10,000; however, the cuts were implemented. There have been significant cuts to individual SSCCs and there has also been some deregulation of SSCCs such as the removal of 'the requirement for professionals in SSCCs in the most disadvantaged areas to have both Qualified Teacher and Early Years Professional status [which] will mean they have the flexibility to make better use of the resources available to them' (DfE (internet), 16 November 2010). Funding to the Children's Workforce Development Council was also withdrawn, during the same announcement. This contradicts the evidence from research by Sylva *et al.* (2004: 7), which found that:

> Having trained teachers working with children in pre-school settings (for a substantial proportion of time, and most importantly as the curriculum leader) had the greatest impact on quality, and was linked specifically with better outcomes in pre-reading and social development at age 5.

The emphasis and message is that SSCCs 'should re-focus on their original purpose and identify, reach and provide targeted help to the most disadvantaged families' (Field, 2010: 7). Field advocates Blunkett's social capital vision, with the proviso that SSCCs must not become a service for poor families. 'Progressive universalism' (Ed Balls, quoted in Lewis, 2011a) was already being advocated by the Labour Government in 2005. In fact the Marmot Review stated: 'To reduce the steepness of the social gradient in health, actions must be universal, but with a scale and intensity that is proportionate to the level of disadvantage. We call this proportionate universalism' (Marmot, 2010: 16). The struggle between universal and targeted SSCC services, in the current economic climate, continues to trouble each local authority trying to meet the needs of children and families and is unachievable. Everyone wants more for less funding from their SSCCs and while other support services are cut, such as smoking cessation, road safety and JobcentrePlus, SSCCs have to cover their roles too.

Focused reflection point

Take a little time at this point to reflect on one of the following issues that you think may impact on your professional role.

- Has the freedom given to SSLPs to design their own services resulted in creative solutions at a local level or has it weakened the evidence of the effectiveness of Sure Start – thereby making it more vulnerable to cuts?
- Do you think that the expansion from Sure Start local programmes to Sure Start children's centres 'continued the essence' of the original vision?
- Has the cost of universal provision compromised the effectiveness of narrowing the achievement gap for the poorest children?
- Do you believe in 'progressive universalism' or targeted provision for SSCCs?
- Given the evidence from Allen, Field and Marmot, should we be cutting services for children under three?

---

2 Year Old Offer

The decision by the Coalition Government to offer 15 hours of free childcare to the most deprived 40 per cent (IMD) of two-year-olds was based on pilots commissioned by the previous Labour Government. It is a positive decision which should help the very poorest children access high-quality education and care. The Coalition Government announcement promised extra resources for the poorest families; however, local authorities were shocked to discover that these 'extra resources' are, in large part, being taken from the Early Intervention Grant and forming a 'ring-fenced' part of the Dedicated Schools Grant. The implications in areas of the country with relatively low numbers of children entitled to the 2 Year Old Offer (2YOO) are fairly insignificant. However, in places such as Bradford the picture is different. Some £6.1m of EIG which was expected to be used to fund SSCCs and other children's services has been hived off to cover the cost of the 2YOO, effectively taking away the money that was being used to provide services for one set of poor children to give to another set of poor children. The Coalition are putting in additional funding (the exact amount is difficult to quantify); however, the cities with high levels of child poverty have had their budgets diverted by central government, which contradicts the Coalition Government's policy of decentralisation.

The implementation of the 2YOO is extremely challenging. Bradford has to expand from 300 to 5,400 places by September 2014. There was initially no capital funding from government to achieve these places, only an offer of loans; however, there have now been small amounts of capital allocated. There are two major challenges: the first is that only those rated by Ofsted as 'good' or 'outstanding' nurseries are able to be providers of the 2YOO; and the second is the training of sufficient numbers of early years practitioners to deliver 2YOO. The proposal by Elizabeth Truss to extend the ratios of adults to children from 1:4 to 1:6 for two-year-olds was met with total abhorrence by 95 per cent of the early years profession and has since been dropped. The Coalition Government, at the time of writing, has yet to announce the criteria for the 2YOO. However, it is expected to include families with an earned income of under £16,190, as well as families where no adult is working and children who have special educational needs.

Core purpose of SSCCs

The core purpose of children's centres is to improve outcomes for young children and their families and reduce inequalities between families in greatest need and their peers in:

- child development and school readiness;
- parenting aspirations and parenting skills; and
- child and family health and life chances.

(SSCC's Statutory Guidance, April 2013: 7)

Every Child Matters outcomes, which were at the heart of SSCC provision after the Laming Enquiry, are no longer mentioned. However they still exist with two noticeable changes in emphasis and form the basis of the delivery element of the Ofsted Inspection Framework.

Improve the well-being of young children in the following areas:

- physical and mental health and emotional well-being;
- protection from harm and neglect (Stay Safe);
- education, training and recreation (Enjoy and Achieve);
- the contribution made by them to society; and
- social and economic well-being.

(SSCC's Statutory Guidance, April 2013: 8)

The core purpose is intended to have a three-pronged approach of services which are 'universal, targeted and specialist', the last of these being focused on families experiencing multiple risk factors including 'children in need and "troubled" families'. This links SSCC provision with the Coalition Government's Troubled

FIGURE 7.1 Family Links Nurturing Programme being delivered in Urdu: an evidence-based programme used extensively in Bradford.

Families initiative, which aims to target 'dysfunctional families' (Conservative Manifesto, 2010) and move them into employment, as a solution to their situation. It is based on Payment By Results, which was also piloted for SSCC funding, but in March 2013 a decision was made not to pursue this approach.

One of the positive outcomes of the austerity measures has been a revitalisation of the determination to work together across all providers delivering services for children and families. In Bradford an Integrated Care Pathway is being launched which should significantly improve the relationships between midwifery, health visiting and SSCCs, based on best practice at a local level, which currently varies considerably across the district. There is a stronger emphasis on 'evidence-based programmes' as prescribed by Allen (2011). Children are no longer permitted merely to enjoy themselves but should be getting ready to start school. The pressure to achieve results that evidence outcomes for children has increased and Michael Gove (currently Secretary of State for Education) has rightly insisted that children from disadvantaged backgrounds should be supported to achieve the same good level of development as their more affluent peers. However, what he does not seem to understand is the distance that many of these children need to travel in order to achieve this goal and the resources needed to secure high-quality support to facilitate the aspiration.

Focused reflection point

Stop and think about these questions at this point in time:

- Is it your experience that austerity measures have resulted in genuine opportunities for better integrated working across the professions?
- Are school readiness and enjoyment through play compatible?

Welfare reforms and a local perspective

The Coalition Government has clarified the emphasis on targeting vulnerable children and child poverty, which was lost with the transition from Sure Start local programmes to children's centres, where 'lack of strategic direction' (Lewis, 2011b) was an issue. However, the welfare reforms have substantially increased the number of children in poverty. The Institute of Fiscal Studies (IFS) predicts an increase of 200,000 children in poverty by the end of the Coalition Government's term in office in 2015 and by a further 200,000 by 2020 (Brewer *et al.*, 2011). Once Universal Credit is introduced and the number of disabled people declined Personal Independence Payments grows (there is a target of a 20 per cent reduction from those currently claiming Disability Living Allowance) we will see great pressure on families and services. Levels of debt will increase dramatically as people will be expected to manage with one monthly payment to cover all their outgoings. Levels of financial literacy are extremely low – other than people knowing about robbing Peter to pay Paul – but Universal Credit denies that opportunity. The most significant factors affecting poverty are the decisions to cap benefit increases to a maximum of 1 per cent for the next three years as well as index linking benefits to the consumer price index (CPI) measure of inflation rather than the retail price index (RPI). It is well known that the CPI usually gives a lower estimate of the rate of inflation than the RPI. The Child Poverty Act 2010, passed with cross-party support, makes the target to eradicate child poverty by 2020 a legal requirement. The IFS estimates that in 2020 relative child poverty will be at its highest rate since 1999 and absolute child poverty will be at its highest rate since 2001.

In my SSCC reach 99.8 per cent of children are in the poorest 15 per cent in the country. People start queuing for the Benefits Advice session more than an hour before the session starts, as otherwise they might not be seen. The number of women disclosing themselves as experiencing domestic abuse is on the increase, as is the number of referrals to the foodbanks. Within the last 12 months the number of people receiving food, from the largest of four food-banks in Bradford, has risen from 70 to 770 per month. We now offer meals to families as part of our Stay and Play provision and feed our children when they arrive at 9am for their 2YOO place. Making a decision about targeting the most vulnerable, when the grant to provide SSCC services has gone down but the number of children in the area has increased from 880 to 1,062, is challenging to say the least; particularly as deprivation has got worse.

We used to have a nursery with 80 per cent fee payers; we now have a handful, who are all part-time. The decision to reduce the maximum amount of tax credits from 80 per cent to 70 per cent has made childcare less affordable. The recommendations in *More Affordable Childcare* have been universally rejected by the profession. The number of families where no one is in paid employment was always high in our reach area. When the economic downturn hit, those without qualifications and work experience now had to compete with people who have lost their job; which makes their position even more difficult. We have people coming through our doors every day wanting help and advice to gain

FIGURE 7.2 See how Nafisa is both concentrating and enjoying an opportunity to get messy.

employment. Communityworks Children's Centre and Community Project is based one mile from the centre of Bradford. We were the hub of the community before the Coalition Government required it of us. We aim to work together with local people to improve their life chances and have seen numerous examples over the years. Although the area is primarily of Mirpuri Pakistani heritage, we have been successful in attracting a diverse range of families which reflects all backgrounds represented in the community. Within learning in the early years foundation stage, Communication and Language and Knowledge and Understanding of the World are the greatest challenges for the majority of children and their families; including White British. These are massive barriers children have to overcome in order to narrow the achievement gap with their middle-class peers. We provide a wide range of activities for children and their parents from Stay and Plays to Triple P (a one-to-one parenting programme), to four different English classes for parents, to baby massage and participation in Core Group meetings with families under social care. We have made a significant impact but Ofsted want more.

The Ofsted Inspection Framework

The Apprenticeships, Skills, Children and Learning Act 2009 brought security to SSCCs by making them part of the statutory provision for children's services, and it also brought Ofsted inspections. Ofsted have been inspecting SSCCs since April 2010 and the Inspection Framework is now in its third re-write. The latest Ofsted statistics indicate that 30 per cent of SSCCs 'require improvement' (formerly described as 'satisfactory') while 1 per cent are 'inadequate'. Only 13 per cent were found to be 'outstanding' and 56 per cent 'good' (Ofsted website, statistics to June 2013). Under the latest framework only 'good' or above will suffice and as an SSCC manager I strongly believe that we should be providing the very best services to children and their families. When we were inspected in 2011, it was a challenging but positive experience. However, there is a danger that managers and local authorities focus too much on pleasing Ofsted rather than meeting the needs of children and families.

The new Ofsted Inspection Framework introduced from April 2013 has raised the expectations of SSCCs substantially at a time when the majority are experiencing cuts in funding. There is a much stronger emphasis throughout on targeting vulnerable groups with evidence that 65 per cent of these groups are 'participating regularly' as well as the requirement to evidence that 80 per cent of families with young children 'are known'. Unlike schools, where judgements are made on the children at the school, SSCCs have the additional challenge of relying on partnerships with health service providers to establish the names and addresses of the families with young children in their 'reach area' and this data is subject to parents giving consent to their information being passed to SSCCs. They are also expected to evidence 'exceptionally well-established' information sharing between its partners, which means 97 per cent of families with young children 'are known' in order to have a chance of being judged as 'outstanding'. It also needs to be taken into account that the most vulnerable families tend to have high levels of mobility and are considered 'hard to reach'.

The overall effectiveness of an SSCC under the present framework is based on three key judgements:

1. access to services by young children and families;
2. the quality and impact of practice and services;
3. the effectiveness of leadership, governance and management.

(Ofsted, 2013a: 5)

Leading an SSCC has never been more challenging, and evidencing progress through the tracking of children and families where the starting points are so very low compared to national averages is extremely difficult. The cuts to public services have resulted in some managers being responsible for three or four SSCCs, all with reduced budgets. Unfortunately SSCC leaders are currently feeling that they are being overwhelmed by the combination of diminishing resources and unachievable targets. In Bradford we also have rising birth rates, an increase in the number of vulnerable families due to welfare reforms and increasing numbers of Eastern European families, particularly Roma families. Ofsted provides a snapshot of what appears to be happening at an SSCC, but what really matters is what we do every day and how much difference that makes to children and their families to enable them to have the best possible opportunities in life. Ofsted and governments need to be mindful that parents are the primary educators of their children, and many do so really well and without choosing to participate in their local SSCC – although I would strongly recommend they do get involved.

> **Focused reflection point**
>
> ■ Is the focus within your setting firmly set on meeting the needs of children and their families – or meeting the Ofsted Inspection Framework requirements?
> ■ Do you think that the Coalition Government has backed Sure Start or is this the beginning of the end?

Conclusion

To conclude, Marmot (2010: 94) asserted: 'In short, we need a second revolution in the early years.' Investing in the early years is the most cost-effective way of improving life chances for children and reducing the overall cost to the state over the lifetime of the individual (Field, 2010; Allen, 2011). By their very nature governments take a short-term view and want immediate results (Eisenstadt, 2011). It needs to be remembered that Sure Start only began in 1999; the earliest school in England dates back to 597 (King's School, Canterbury). In the last 14 years we have moved to a position where 'there are ongoing debates about what kind of early years services the nation needs, but no longer arguments about whether the nation needs these services at all' (Eisenstadt, 2011: 3). The current economic crisis threatens to reduce the very potential that SSCCs could realise if given the funding and commitment from local partnerships, at the same time as the government's own statistics are predicting substantial increases in child poverty. High-quality provision is expensive to deliver and good outcomes for children can only have a lasting effect if SSCCs are given the necessary investment to work intensively with children and their families, where *their* needs are paramount. There needs to be a real commitment to invest in the foundation years in order to narrow the gap by reducing the number of children in poverty and increasing the number of children reaching a good level of development. The Coalition Government say that they back Sure Start, but the evidence is that SSCCs are experiencing a reduction in resources, while the numbers of children in poverty is increasing; pressure is mounting to target the 'most vulnerable' while high-quality provision is becoming harder to achieve. We have not secured our second revolution.

> **Summary of knowledge gained**
>
> After reading and reflecting on this chapter you should now be very aware:
>
> ■ of the origins of Sure Start and the transition into SSCCs that offer universal provision;
> ■ of the impact of austerity measures on children and families and the services they use;
> ■ that Coalition Government decisions have prioritised austerity, meaning levels of child poverty have increased, particularly through welfare reform;
> ■ that research commissioned by the Coalition Government advocating increased investment in the Early Years has not been implemented;
> ■ that SSCCs are experiencing significant cuts and significantly more rigorous inspection.

Challenges for the future

- To ensure that the needs of children and families remain the first priority.
- With child poverty increasing, making sure that local authorities invest their reduced budgets in the areas of highest need while maintaining sufficient provision on preventative services.
- To create genuine interdisciplinary methods and solutions which ensure that every child has the very best start in life.
- Securing our second revolution.

Further reading

The first two of the following books will give you much greater detail about the origins of Sure Start and how it developed, while the third is a report produced by MPs which brings together various ideas for the future:

Anning, A. and Ball, M. (2008) *Improving Services for Young Children from Sure Start to Children's Centre*. London: Sage.
Eisenstadt, N. (2011) *Providing a Sure Start*. The Policy Press.
Best Practice for a Sure Start: The Way Forward for Children's Centres – Report from the All Party Parliamentary Sure Start Group 4Children, July 2013.

References

All Party Parliamentary Sure Start Group (July 2013). *Best Practice for a Sure Start: The way forward for Children's Centres*. London: 4Children.
Allen, G. (2011) *Early Intervention: The next steps. An independent report to Her Majesty's Government*. London: The Cabinet Office, HM Government.
Anning, A. and Ball, M. (2008) *Improving Services for Young Children from Sure Start to Children's Centre*. London: Sage.
Bagley, C. (2011) 'From Sure Start to Children's Centres: capturing the erosion of social capital', *Journal of Education Policy*, 26(1): 95–113.
Belsky, J., Barnes, J. and Melhuish, E. (eds) (2007) *The National Evaluation of Sure Start: Does area-based early intervention work?* Bristol: The Policy Press.
Brewer, M., Browne, J. and Joyce, R. (2011) *Child and working-age poverty from 2010 to 2020*. London: Institute for Fiscal Studies.
Butler, P. (2013) 'Hundreds of Sure Start centres have closed since election, says Labour', *The Guardian* (internet), 28 January. Retrieved 17 April 2014 from http://www.theguardian.com/society/2013/jan/28/sure-start-centres-closed-labour.
Department for Education (2010) *Free childcare for disadvantaged 2-year-olds to be guaranteed in law*, DfE (internet), 16 November. Retrieved 17 April 2014 from https://www.gov.uk/government/news/free-childcare-for-disadvantaged-2-year-olds-to-be-guaranteed-in-law.
Department for Education (2013a) *Sure Start children's centres statutory guidance: for local authorities, commissioners of local health services and Jobcentre Plus*, DfE (internet), 15 April.

Retrieved 17 April 2014 from https://www.gov.uk/government/publications/sure-start-childrens-centres.

Department for Education (2013b) *More affordable childcare*, DfE (internet), 16 July. Retrieved 17 April 2014 from https://www.gov.uk/government/publications/more-affordable-childcare.

Eisenstadt, N. (2011) *Providing a Sure Start*. Bristol: The Policy Press.

Field, F. (2010) *The Foundation Years: Preventing poor children becoming poor adults. The report of the Independent Review on Poverty and Life Chances*. London: The Cabinet Office, HM Government.

Glass, N. (1999) 'Sure Start: the development of an early intervention programme for young children in the United Kingdom', *Children and Society*, 13, 257–64.

Glass, N. (2005) 'Surely some mistake', *The Guardian* (internet), 5 January. Retrieved 17 April 2014 from http://www.theguardian.com/society/2005/jan/05/guardiansocietysupplement.childrensservices.

Independent (2010) 'The fourth debate: you ask the questions to the leaders of the three main parties', *The Independent* (internet), 5 May. Retrieved 17 April 2014 from http://www.independent.co.uk/news/uk/politics/the-fourth-debate-you-ask-the-questions-to-the-leaders-of-the-three-main-parties-1962810.html.

King's School, Canterbury (internet) *History*. Retrieved 17 April 2014 from http://www.kings-school.co.uk/document_1.aspx?id=1:31658&id=1:31637.

Lewis, J. (2011a) 'From Sure Start to Children's Centres: an analysis of policy change in English early years programmes', *Journal of Social Policy*, 40(1): 71–88.

Lewis, J. (2011b) 'Making the transition from Sure Start local programmes to Children's Centres, 2003–2008', *Journal of Social Policy*, 40(3): 595–612.

Lewis, J., Cuthbert, R. and Sarre, S. (2011) 'What are Children's Centres? The development of CC Services, 2004–2008', *Social Policy and Administration*, 45(1): 35–53.

Marmot, M. (2010) *Fair Society, Healthy Lives: The Marmot review of health inequalities in England post 2010*. London: The Marmot Review.

Munro, E. (2011) *The Munro Review of Child Protection-Final Report: A child-centred system*. London: Department for Education, HM Government.

Ofsted (2013a) *The framework for children's centre inspection from April 2013*, Ofsted (internet), 21 March. Retrieved 17 April 2014 from http://www.ofsted.gov.uk/resources/framework-for-childrens-centre-inspection-april-2013.

Ofsted (2013b) *Official statistics: children's centres inspections and outcomes*, Ofsted (internet), 5 September. Retrieved 17 April 2014 from http://www.ofsted.gov.uk/resources/official-statistics-childrens-centres-inspections-and-outcomes.

Sylva, K., Melhuish, E., Sammons, P., Siraj Blatchford, I. and Taggart, B. (2004) *The Effective Provision of Pre-School Education (EPPE) Project: Findings from pre-school to end of Key Stage 1*. Institute of Education. Retrieved 17 April 2014 from http://eppe.ioe.ac.uk/eppe/eppepdfs/TP10%20Research%20Brief.pdf.

Tickell, C. (2011) *The Early Years: Foundations for life, health and learning. An independent report on the Early Years Foundation Stage to Her Majesty's Government*. London: Department for Education, HM Government.

Watt, N. (2011) '124 Sure Start centres have closed since coalition took power', *The Guardian* (internet), 14 November. Retrieved 17 April 2014 from http://www.theguardian.com/society/2011/nov/14/sure-start-centre-closures-coalition?INTCMP=ILCNETTXT3487.

Weinberger, J., Pickstone, C. and Hannon, P. (eds) (2005) *Learning from Sure Start: Working with young children and their families*. Maidenhead: Open University Press.

8

Reflecting on the role of graduates as pedagogical with children from birth to three

Mary E. Whalley

This chapter focuses on the role of graduate leaders of practice with children from birth to thirty months (B–30m) in England. From 2006 to 2013 this role was carried out by early years professionals (EYPs) and from September 2013 the name and status changed to that of early years teacher. This chapter reflects on the challenges for graduates in roles of pedagogical leadership with the youngest children in early childhood education and care settings. The chapter presents the theory, research and policy that affect the graduate leader (GL) role. Much of the literature refers to 'birth to three' and every attempt is made to sift out the relevance to the B–30m age range. The feminised pronoun is used throughout to refer to the young child, though the application is to both girls and boys.

Introduction: graduate leadership in the early years

Early years professional status (EYPS) was introduced by the Labour Government in 2006 as a new strategic leadership role seen as key to improving workforce skills, knowledge and competencies and raising the quality of young children's experiences in early years settings (Children's Workforce Development Council (CWDC), 2010). Early years professionals (EYPs) are all graduates who have met the Standards defined for the role (CWDC, 2010; Department for Education (DfE), 2012). By 2013, there were over 11,000 EYPs working across maintained, private, voluntary, independent and home-based settings for children from birth to five years within the early years foundation stage (EYFS) (DfE, 2013a). The early years teacher status replaced EYPS in September 2013 and EYPS remains recognised as the equivalent of this qualification. The remit for these graduate roles is to be 'specialists in early childhood development ... with babies and young children from birth to five' (DfE, 2013c). Graduates 'lead practice' or are pedagogical leaders, where pedagogy is seen as all that happens to and with young children which contributes to their learning and development (Stephen, 2010).

A number of studies to date (Walker *et al.*, 2009; Hadfield *et al.*, 2012; Mathers *et al.*, 2011) highlight positive benefits of the graduate leader role of EYP and status to the graduates themselves, especially in enhanced skills, knowledge and understanding and the effects of these on practice. However, the Hadfield *et al.* (2012) and Mathers *et al.* studies (2011) also identified a number of ongoing challenges, especially in defining the EYPs' role in leading practice. The Mathers *et al.* study was the only one to consider the impact of early years professional status on the different age groups defined within the role's remit: babies (0–18 months), toddlers (18 months to three years) and young children (three to five years). Mathers *et al.* (2011: 7) found the greatest impact of the EYP role to be on practice with young children, three to five, with 'little evidence that graduate leaders were having impact on the quality of provision for younger children (birth–30 months)'. This reflects findings from other countries, too, that practice with babies and toddlers is less likely to be graduate led (Oberhuemer, 2008).

In the majority of literature referring to children B–30m, the terms 'babies' – or 'infants' – and 'toddlers' are used. Here, 'babies'/'infants' refers to children from birth to 18 months and 'toddlers' to the 18-month to three-year age range. The focus in this chapter covers both babies and toddlers from birth to 30 months. Powell and Goouch (2012) suggest that around one-third of babies under one and half of children from one to two will be in some form of non-parental care setting for at least part of the week. However, as the 2011 Mathers *et al.* study suggests, it is the B–30m age group with which graduate leaders are less likely to be found.

Children from birth to thirty months

Defining a child of B–30m is less problematic than that of the wider concept of 'childhood' – which is largely socially and culturally constructed (Jones, 2009) – and refers to the period when universally the child is dependent on adults for all her needs. Two-year-olds have featured sharply in recent government initiatives both in terms of increased targeted provision, especially for those in disadvantaged neighbourhoods (Clegg, 2012) and in the introduction of assessment for all two-year-olds as part of the revised EYFS Framework (DfE, 2012: 1) to 'pick up early any problems in a child's development of special educational needs' and share key information with parents. Thus, it could become a key area of practice for the early years graduate leader.

There is a global paucity of literature relating to processes and practices with children from birth to three within the field of ECCE (David *et al.*, 2003; Nutbrown and Page, 2008) and the studies that do exist are mainly from disciplines other than education. Nutbrown and Page (2008) provide a helpful overview of recent research on the development of babies' and toddlers' thinking, aided by enhanced visual and audio brain technology which enables researchers to create a fuller picture about young children. There is growing awareness of the cognitive capacity of very young children with a number of studies (such as Gopnik *et al.*, 1999; Gopnik and Schulz, 2004) suggesting that babies very quickly recognise familiar faces. Meltzoff and Prinz (2002) illustrate babies' ability to understand and imitate the actions of others, using this as an important tool in learning social behaviours, while Gammage's study (2006) intimates that curiosity is present from birth. Such research, mainly from neuroscience, is contributing to the growing bank of knowledge about very early development. An early years graduate leader of practice is expected to support the healthy development of children from birth to five and practitioner knowledge and experience is needed to balance the tentative theorising from research (Nutbrown and Page, 2008).

Focused reflection point

■ How confident are you about your knowledge of young children's development in the birth-to-three age range?

■ Do you think you need to engage in further reading or visit other settings to further develop your knowledge and experience?

Babies' and toddlers' rights and competencies

What emerges strongly from recent studies is the view of the child from birth to 30 months as having rights and as capable and competent. The 1989 United Nations (UN) Convention on the Rights of the Child (UN, 2012) – particularly Article 29a's reference to a child's right to 'education' – is taken to include learning from birth. The Reggio Emilia understanding of the child is of one 'rich in potential, strong, powerful . . . and most of all connected to adults and (other) children' (Malaguzzi, cited in Penn, 1997: 117). It is this connectedness, developed over time, which allows the child the 'hundred languages of expression' (Malaguzzi, 1997: 3) – in recognition of the diverse ways in which children interpret and make sense of their world.

The Reggio approach shares an understanding of the young child with that embedded in the *Te Whāriki* approach to early learning (New Zealand Ministry of Education, 1996) which recognises the whole child and acknowledges that the child's wider world of family and community are core to her experience of childhood. Practice in England, particularly that of the key person approach (Goldschmied and Jackson, 2004), recognises the importance of working in partnership with families to ensure the well-being of the child. Indeed, underpinning this stance are well-respected theories of interactional, relational learning, such as Bandura's (1986) 'reciprocal determinism' – where learning is viewed as an interaction between three components: the child's own psychological processes, the child's own behaviour and the actual environment, including the adults in it – and the neo-Vygotskian Rogoff's (1990) notion of 'guided participation' whereby children are seen as active learners acquiring new knowledge and skills through their participation in 'meaningful activities alongside parents, adults or other more experienced companions' (Gauvain, 2001). Such models are considered central to effective practice with B–30m children.

Some important work is emerging about very young children's rights to a pedagogy of care (Rockel, 2009) which firmly positions support for and with young children's learning in a caring framework. Learning begins at birth and babies and toddlers in non-parental care settings have the right to practitioners who are working under strong pedagogical leadership, where the holistic needs of young children are paramount.

B–30m pedagogy

The concept of 'pedagogy' with such young children still does not enjoy widespread currency in the English context despite being commonly used in other parts of the world (Allen and Whalley, 2010). Moyles *et al.* (2002: 5) define pedagogy as 'encompassing both what practitioners actually DO and THINK and the principles, theories, perceptions and challenges that inform and shape these . . .'. Stewart and Pugh (2007: 9) suggest that early years pedagogy is 'rooted in values and beliefs about what we want for children, and supported by knowledge, theory and experiences'.

Early years pedagogy is multi-dimensional, and these definitions apply across the birth to five years age range. For children B–30m, the historical legacy of the so-called 'care versus education' divide remains significant (McDowell Clark and Baylis, 2012). Practice in B–30m was considered to be 'childcare' – staffed by overwhelmingly female workers whose basic training had prepared them to look after young children who are away from their parents through ordered and pre-determined routines (Chapman, 2003). Any notion of 'education' for babies and toddlers was subsidiary at best. Oberhuemer (2008) observed that 'early education' – for older children – had generally higher status, while 'childcare' had a correspondingly lower status. Such a legacy is unhelpful in a discussion of contemporary B–30m practice and, in England, the division was, to a large extent, bridged in 2001 by a uniting in administration and inspection of all children's services (ATL, 2004). Now the articulation of an appropriate pedagogical paradigm for work with children B–30m is long overdue.

A pedagogy of care

The concept of 'educare' was first mooted by the New Zealand academic, Anne Smith, in 1988. Although the actual term has had only minimal take-up globally, the concept is one to which the majority of early years educators would now subscribe as it signifies the utter inseparability of these two core strands of provision for B–30m children. There is currently a groundswell of argument for a pedagogy of care (Rockel, 2009) which incorporates both caring and learning, particularly for B–30m children. Powell and Goouch's recent study (2012) highlights contemporary discourse on the ethic of care with babies.

The notion of a pedagogy of care draws on the work of several reconceptualist scholars such as Dahlberg and Moss (2005: 3), who argue cogently for a challenge to the dominant discourse of early years provision as 'technical practice' – with measurable indicators of quality and outcomes – and emphasise instead the development of a child who will be 'flexible and developmentally ready for the uncertainties and opportunities of the 21st century'. Promulgating the notion of pre-schools as 'loci of ethical practice', Dahlberg and Moss (2005: 86) take a postmodern ethical approach and propose a move towards a new paradigm of interconnected themes which place the individual at the heart: 'responsibility, relationships, situatedness and otherness are particularly important' (Dahlberg and Moss, 2005: 69). An appropriate contemporary pre-school pedagogy, thus, is based on respectful, responsible relationships with each other and the environment. Such a pedagogy of care fits well with the needs of children from birth to 30 months.

The approaches to babies' and toddlers' learning and development evident from Reggio Emilia, Italy and New Zealand – and, arguably, also in the short-lived *Bt3M* framework in England (DfES, 2002) – can be seen to offer a reconceptualisation of care within an educational framework, which positions learning firmly as starting from birth (Rockel, 2009). Much of the literature around the graduate leader role describes it as that of effecting change (CWDC, 2010) so it is not unreasonable, therefore, to expect graduate leaders themselves to be at the forefront of engagement with a pedagogy of care.

FIGURE 8.1   Experimental play with water.

Frameworks for early learning

One of the key functions of the early years graduate role is to 'lead the delivery of the Early Years Foundation Stage (*EYFS*)' (DfES, 2006) – the framework for learning and development across the birth-to-five age range which was first introduced in 2008 (DCSF, 2008) for all Ofsted-registered settings, with a revised framework introduced from September 2012 (DfE, 2012). In England there has been government intervention on the shape of learning in pre-compulsory school age settings since 1996 though it was not until the introduction of *EYFS* in 2008 that this included children from birth to three. A non-statutory framework for the youngest children had been introduced in 2003, *Birth to Three Matters* (*Bt3M*) (DfES, 2002), though this was later subsumed into the *EYFS*. Unlike the frameworks for children from three to five years, *Bt3M* focused on aspects and components – rather than discrete areas – of learning and development, mirroring and probably influenced by approaches in other countries, such as New Zealand's *Te Whāriki* framework.

Although *Bt3M* had only a short life (2003 to 2008), it was considered to be highly significant at the time and was very well received by practitioners (David *et al.*, 2003). The *EYFS* shares a principled approach with New Zealand's *Te Whāriki* though there is a divergence as the *EYFS* flows into discrete areas of learning which can be seen to be subject-based while *Te Whāriki* is more broadly based and focuses on the competencies for holistic development which are seen in Moyles *et al.*'s (2002) and Stewart and Pugh's (2007) definitions of early years pedagogy.

Focused reflection point

- Why not explore New Zealand's *Te Whāriki* ideology further? You can find many interesting resources and policies regarding *Te Whāriki* on the internet.

In considering the needs of children from birth to 30 months, the approach in the *EYFS* with its focus on areas of learning is questioned. Indeed, House (2011: 4) represents a growing number of protesters about the 'insidious ideology of "schoolification" (in the *EYFS* framework) . . . and "too much too soon"', which clearly resonates with the concerns from many practitioners working with B–30m children about the extent to which the essence of *Bt3M* has been lost within the *EYFS*. Conclusions from a recent analysis of majority world early learning frameworks (Victorian Curriculum and Assessment Authority (VCAA), 2008: 47) indicate two key findings: that the 'strongest early education programs have clear well-defined principles . . . understood by educators, families and . . . communities' – again picking up on the notion of relational learning (Bandura, 1986; Rogoff, 1990) – and that the prevailing view of early years educators is that 'teachable moments' occur within the context of children's natural play and experiences rather than around pre-determined standards or goals (VCAA, 2008: 48). Such findings can be seen as highly applicable to practice with B–30m children.

The leader of practice with children from birth to 30 months

The concept of 'professionalism' was embedded in the title of early years professional, and McGillivray (2008), Osgood (2012), Miller and Cable (2011) and Brock and Rankin (2011) have all made significant contributions to this discourse in identifying both the present opportunities and a range of barriers to the establishment of a high-status, graduate-led workforce. McGillivray's (2008: 245) perception of the 'dichotomy between a workforce . . . construed as caring, maternal and gendered as opposed to professional, degree educated and highly trained' has particular relevance for graduate leaders' work with B–30m children where, as we have seen, care practices are an integral (and historically dominant) part of the (principally female) role. However, if a pedagogy of care can be articulated and embedded into B–30m practice then this should also support the professionalisation of the workforce, especially for those who are leading practice.

Manning-Morton (2006) suggests that, despite the increase of the key person role in B–30m practice since the 1990s, there is still much evidence to suggest that

> organisational and individual practices . . . (arguably the 'care tasks' with very young children) . . . often prevent practitioners from fully meeting the needs of the youngest children . . . early years practitioners must develop a professional approach that combines personal awareness with theoretical knowledge.
>
> (Manning-Morton, 2006: 42)

Arguing cogently for the emergence and consolidation of a 'holistic professional identity from a dualist history' (Manning-Morton, 2006: 44), which combines mutual respect for all aspects of caring and depth of knowledge, she promotes a new paradigm of professionalism which refutes the prevailing notion that values knowledge more than skills (Saks, 1983). Manning-Morton (2006: 50) further asserts that such professionalism will result in B–30m practitioners as 'critically reflexive, theoretical boundary-crossers' which, again, sits well with the graduate leader role in effecting change.

That word 'leadership'!

Good leaders are generally considered to be people who are able to think and act creatively in routine and non-routine situations and who set out to influence the actions, beliefs and feelings of others (Doyle and Smith, 1999) and, as such, this would apply to the role of early years professional and early years teacher. However, as we noted at the outset of the chapter, research studies on the graduate leader role to date suggest ongoing challenges in defining the *leadership* element of the role. Most of the theoretical understanding of leadership belongs more appropriately to the worlds of finance, commerce, business and politics (Whalley, 2011a), with the emphasis on organisational leadership. It is helpful, though, to consider some of these briefly, not least in order to highlight what the graduate early years leader is not!

Four main 'generations' of leadership theory are often described (Doyle and Smith, 1999), though these are not mutually exclusive or totally time-bound (Van Maurik, 2001): trait (leaders exhibit particular characteristics); behavioural (leaders behave in specific ways); situational (leaders respond according to the variable context); and transformational (the leader is an agent of change). All can be seen to have some relevance to the early years graduate leader role though it is the last – transformational leadership, particularly the work of Bass and Avolio (1994) – which is particularly apt, given the charge to the graduate leader to effect change.

Bass and Avolio (1994) believe the transformational leader can raise the levels of others' awareness and consciousness about the significance and value of designated outcomes and ways of reaching them, can encourage others to transcend self-interest for the good of all concerned, and can expand others' range of wants and needs (Wright, 1996). Although this is lofty rhetoric, the reality is more complex and many graduate leaders report strong resistance to change, citing factors such as staff's reluctance to accept new ideas, inadequate resources/time, and levels of social disadvantage and parental involvement, though there is also substantial evidence that early years professional status has had 'significant impact on practitioners' ability to effect change' (CWDC/University of Wolverhampton, 2011: 33–4).

Graduate leadership in the early years

Despite the plethora of traditional and emerging theories of leadership, the concept of 'leadership of *practice*' is a distinctive element to the role of early years professional and early years teacher and, in England, offers a new paradigm of professional leadership in early years – pedagogical leadership. However, as the early evaluations indicated (Walker *et al.*, 2009), there was some confusion about what this meant originally and challenges remain, particularly in the graduate leaders' own perception of themselves as leaders and the way the role is perceived across the early years sector (Lloyd and Hallet, 2010; McDowall Clark, 2012).

Since the introduction of early years professional status, it has been important to distinguish between the leader of an early years *setting* and the leader of *practice*. This has been challenging for a number of reasons: many of the 11,000-plus graduate leaders to date are themselves the leader (or manager – which can lead to greater confusion!) of a setting. Indeed, there is important wider discussion here about the differences between 'leader' and 'manager' (Law and Glover, 2000). The prevailing understanding of the graduate leader as 'in charge' is unhelpful in any discussion of the early years professional and early years teacher role which calls for a reconceptualisation of leadership.

Since 2000, a bank of global research evidence relating to early years leadership is emerging. The existing reviews of literature on leadership in early years to date (Muijs *et al.*, 2004; Dunlop, 2008) and studies such as that by Siraj-Blatchford and Manni (2007) focus principally on leadership of *settings*, though Siraj-Blatchford and Manni (2007: 9) come closer with their concept of 'leadership for learning' which requires: contextual literacy (i.e. specific response to a particular situation – fitting well with the mainstream theory of 'situational leadership', Fiedler and Garcia, 1987); a commitment to collaboration; and a commitment to improving outcomes for all children.

Focused reflection point

■ Reflect on the leadership qualities in Figure 8.2 and apply them to yourself.
■ Do they accurately reflect your abilities? Would you remove or add anything to the model?

McDowall Clark and Murray's (2012) work indicates a great reluctance among many early years practitioners to embrace the leadership element of the early years graduate role when seen against normative constructs of leadership. They offer a new paradigm of 'leadership within' which is characterised by catalytic agency (a willingness to take action, albeit sometimes in very small ways), reflective integrity (the capacity for reflection is seen as essential to the leadership role) and relational interdependence (with leadership seen as a shared process). Such a paradigm can be seen to empower a new generation of early years graduate leaders.

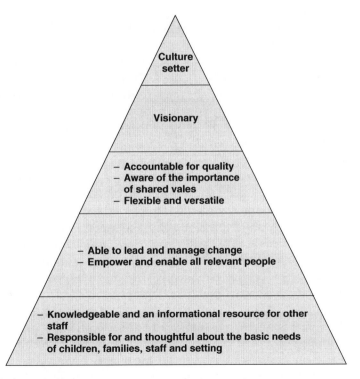

FIGURE 8.2 Leadership qualities of the graduate leader.

Source: adapted from Moyles, 2006: 21–2.

The work of seminal writers such as Rodd (1997, 2006) and Aubrey (2007) cannot be underestimated and has been influential in raising consciousness about leadership skills within early years; yet even here the emphasis is on effective leadership in a setting. Moyles' (2006) work, too, has informed understanding of early years leadership of settings, though she does make an important distinction between management *skills* and leadership *qualities*, and the model in Figure 8.2 (based on Maslow, 1954) shows how these qualities might be applied to the graduate leadership task.

The graduate leader's self-perception as leaders of practice with B–30m children

It is the graduate leaders themselves who need to articulate the new paradigm of leader of practice (Stamopoulos, 2012; Whalley, 2011b). There are multiple challenges here: the diverse roles and settings where early years professionals and early years teachers are to be found mean it is difficult to establish the concept of early years graduate leadership in the wider public consciousness. Aligned with this, though, has been the huge difficulty in establishing professional identity and a clear career path for graduate leaders (Lloyd and Hallet, 2010; CWDC/ University of Wolverhampton, 2011). This is in sharp contrast to those other areas of work with which early years professional status and early years teacher status have comparability (Lloyd and Hallet, 2010) – teachers in schools and social workers. This is compounded and confused further by early years teacher status not carrying qualified teacher status. School teachers and social workers have a clearly mapped progression route to leadership roles whereas this is embedded into early years graduate leadership from the outset.

Our youngest children need knowledgeable and professional educators who understand all children's needs, are well informed about early cognitive development and understand different theories of learning (Edgington, 2005). Powell and Goouch's research (2012) found, though, that many practitioners in baby rooms felt neglected, undervalued and under-supported. They concluded that the training, support and guidance needed for practitioners working with babies needed to be much more specific, and argued strongly for more funding to be targeted to this area of early years. McDowall Clark and Baylis (2012: 231) believe that, because the notion of graduate-led practitioners is relatively new to England, the perception remains that for maximum 'value', energies should concentrate on pre-school children (three- to four-year-olds). However, they argue that this actually underlines a 'historical remnant' which undervalues under-threes themselves and that graduate leaders have a crucial role to play as 'thoughtful agents' (Appleby and Andrews, 2011: 59) with babies and toddlers – reflecting on and seeking to improve the quality of provision.

Establishing the graduate leader voice especially in pedagogical practice with children from birth to 30 months remains aspirational – given the historical legacy of an undervalued, under-resourced caring role, especially with such young children. Graduate leaders themselves can begin to create 'shared meaning' about the role (Blumer, 1969) collectively, as part of communities of practice (Lave and Wenger, 1991), reflecting on the meaning of their leadership role and articulating this authentically.

Conclusion: the child, the practice, the professional leader

Although there is a growing respect for professionals working with babies and toddlers (Goouch and Powell, 2011; McDowall Clark and Baylis, 2012), there remains the historical remnant of the undervaluing of those who work with children from birth to 30 months and thus, implicitly, an undervaluing of the babies and toddlers themselves. Key questions around why there are few graduate leaders working principally with such young children need to be asked as there is a danger here of failure to recognise the critical importance of work with very young children in creating and sustaining 'democratic encounters with children from babyhood onwards' (Pascal and Bertram, 2009: 258). Nutbrown and Page (2008: 176) believe that 'the younger the children, the more crucial it is that their close adults are informed, alert, sensitive and reflexive . . . Adults who can articulate their pedagogy make the best educators' (2008: 176). Renewed understanding of the child from birth to 30 months is required: she is seen as both competent and capable yet also in need of high-quality care. The conceptualisation of a pedagogy of care (Dahlberg and Moss, 2005) is called for in which the child's holistic needs – and those of her parents – are taken into consideration and met. This requires committed and dedicated professional leadership from early years graduates who will rise to this complex task (Abbott and Langston, 2005) and be 'thoughtful agents' (Appleby and Andrews, 2011: 59) for and with B–30m children.

The chapter has advised graduate leaders to become empowered through engaging in the high-level critical reflection necessary to establish a new paradigm of early years leadership with children from birth to 30 months within a pedagogy of care. The discourse round the content and shape of provision for the child in her earliest years, and the one who leads such practice, should be of critical importance. Therefore the next chapter draws on the voices of graduate leaders themselves.

Summary of knowledge gained

This chapter advises graduate leaders to become empowered through engaging in the high-level critical reflection necessary to establish a new paradigm of early years leadership with children from birth to three years within a pedagogy of care. In becoming more empowered, it is the graduate leaders themselves who can shape and transform practice and the understanding of leadership. The discourse round the content and shape of provision for the child in her earliest years, and the one who leads such practice, should be of critical importance.

Challenges for the future

- Reflect on how to forefront a pedagogy of care for B–3 years whilst reading the next chapter, which provides case studies of good practice.
- Reflect on how graduate leaders can promote high-level critical reflection in the people with whom they work in a setting.
- How can they encourage staff to develop their knowledge and qualifications through participating in further training and facilitating their ongoing professional development?

Further reading

Hallet, E. (2013) '"We all share a common vision and passion": Early Years Professionals reflect upon their leadership of practice role', *Journal of Early Childhood Research*, 11: 312–25.

Murray, J. and McDowall Clark, R. (2013) 'Reframing leadership as participative pedagogy: the working theories of early years professionals', *Early Years*, 33(3): 289–301.

Whalley, M.E. (2011) *Leading Practice in Early Years Settings*. Exeter: Learning Matters.

References

Abbott, L. and Langston, A. (eds) (2005) *Birth to Three Matters: Supporting the framework of effective practice*. Maidenhead: Open University Press.

Allen, S.F. and Whalley, M.E. (2010) *Supporting Pedagogy and Practice in Early Years Settings*. Exeter: Learning Matters.

Appleby, K. and Andrews, M. (2011) 'Reflective practice is the key to quality improvement', in Reed, M. and Canning, N. (eds) *Quality Improvement and Change in the Early Years*. London: Sage.

Association of Teachers and Lecturers (ATL) (2004) *Right from the Start: Early years educational policy and practice*. London: ATL.

Aubrey, C. (2007) *Leading and Managing in the Early Years*. London: Sage.

Bandura, A. (1986) *Social Foundations of Thought and Action*. Englewood Cliffs, NJ: Prentice-Hall.

Bass, B.M. and Avolio, B.J. (eds) (1994) *Improving Organisational Effectiveness through Transformational Leadership*. Thousand Oaks, CA: Sage Publishing.

Blumer, H. (1969) *Symbolic Interactionism: Perspective and method*. Englewood Cliffs, NJ: Prentice-Hall.

Brock, A. and Rankin, C. (2011) *Professionalism in the Early Years Interdisciplinary Team: Supporting young children and their families*. London: Continuum.

Chapman, L. (2003) *In a Strange Garden: The life and times of Truby King*. Auckland: Penguin Books.

Children's Workforce Development Council (CWDC) (2010) *On the Right Track: Guidance to the Standards for the Award of Early Years Professional Status*. Leeds: CWDC.

Children's Workforce Development Council (CWDC)/University of Wolverhampton (January 2011) *First National Survey of Practitioners with EYPS*. Leeds: CWDC. Retrieved 11 April

2014 from https://www.gov.uk/government/uploads/system/uploads/attachment_data/file/181641/EYPS-SURVEY.pdf.

Clegg, N. (2012) 'Nick Clegg hails a revolution in pre-school education'. London: Office of the Deputy Prime Minister. Retrieved 11 April 2014 from https://www.gov.uk/government/news/nick-clegg-hails-a-revolution-in-free-pre-school-education.

Dahlberg, G. and Moss, P. (2005) *Ethics and Politics in Early Childhood Education.* London: Routledge.

David, T., Goouch, K., Powell, S. and Abbott, L. (2003) *Birth to Three Matters: A Review of the Literature compiled to inform The Framework to Support Children in their Earliest Years.* Research Report 444. Nottingham: DfES. Retrieved 11 April 2014 from http://webarchive.nation-alarchives.gov.uk/20130401151715/https://www.education.gov.uk/publications/eOrderingDownload/RR444.pdf.

Department for Children, Schools and Families (DCSF) (2008) *The Early Years Foundation Stage (framework).* Nottingham: DCSF Publications.

Department for Education (DfE) (2012) *Early Years Foundation Stage (EYFS).* Retrieved 11 April 2014 from https:/www.education.gov.uk/publications/standard/AllPublications/Page1/DFE-00023-2012.

Department for Education (DfE) (2013a) *Graduate Leaders in Early Years: Early Years Professional Status.* Retrieved 11 April 2014 from http://www.education.gov.uk/childrenandyoungpeople/earlylearningandchildcare/h00201345/graduate-leaders.

Department for Education (DfE) (2013b) *The Early Years Foundation Stage (EYFS).* Retrieved 11 April 2014 from http://www.education.gov.uk/schools/teachingandlearning/curriculum/a0068102/early-years-foundation-stage-eyfs.

Department for Education (DfE) (2013c) *Early Years Initial Teacher Training (ITT).* Retrieved 11 April 2014 from http://www.education.gov.uk/childrenandyoungpeople/earlylearningandchildcare/h00201345/eyitt/teachers'-standards-early-years.

Department for Education and Skills (DfES) (2002) *Birth to Three Matters: A framework for supporting children in their earliest years.* London: DfES/Sure Start.

Department for Education and Skills (2006) *Children's Workforce Strategy: The government's response to the consultation.* Nottingham: DfES.

Doyle, M.E. and Smith, M.K. (1999) *Born and Bred? Leadership, heart and informal education.* London: YMCA George Williams College/The Rank Foundation.

Dunlop, A.-W. (2008) *A Literature Review on Leadership in the Early Years.* Livingston: Learning and Teaching Scotland. Retrieved 11 April 2014 from http://www.educationscotland.gov.uk/publications/a/leadershipreview.asp.

Edgington, M. (2005) *The Foundation Stage Teacher in Action: Teaching 3, 4 and 5 year olds.* Third edition. London: Paul Chapman Publishing.

Fiedler, F.E. and Garcia, J.E. (1987) *New Approaches to Leadership, Cognitive Resources and Organizational Performance.* New York: John Wiley and Sons.

Gammage, P. (2006) 'Early childhood education and care: politics, policies and possibilities', *Early Years,* 26(3): 235–48.

Gauvain, M. (2001) *The Social Context of Cognitive Development.* New York: Guilford Press.

Goldschmied, E. and Jackson, S. (2004) *People under Three: Young children in daycare.* Second edition. London: Routledge.

Goouch, F.K. and Powell, S. (2011) *The Baby Room Project.* Paper published by the Association for the Professional Development of Early Years Educators (TACTYC). www.tactyc.org.

Gopnik, A.N. and Schulz, L. (2004) 'Mechanisms of theory-formation in young children', *Trends in Cognitive Science,* 8(8): 27–39.

Gopnik, A.N., Meltzoff, A. and Kuhl, P. (1999) *The Scientist in the Crib: Minds, brains and how children learn.* New York: William Morrow.

Hadfield, M., Jopling, M., Needham, M., Waller, T., Coleyshaw, L., Emira, M. and Royle, K. (2012) *Longitudinal Study of Early Years Professional Status: An exploration of progress, leadership and impact. Final report.* DfE Research Report: RR249c, DfE/CeDare, University of Wolverhampton. Retrieved 11 April 2014 from http://www.cedare-reports.co.uk/eyps/index.php.

House, R. (2011) 'A summary of Critical Commentary on *Reforming the Early Years Foundation Stage: Government Response to the Consultation*', TACTYC. Retrieved 11 April 2014 from www.tactyc.org.uk/pdfs/Reflection-House.pdf.

Jones, P. (2009) *Rethinking Childhood.* London: Continuum.

Lave, J. and Wenger, E. (1991) *Situated Learning: Legitimate peripheral participation.* Cambridge: Cambridge University Press.

Law, S. and Glover, D. (2000) *Educational Leadership and Learning: Practice, policy and research.* Buckingham: Open University Press.

Lloyd, E. and Hallet, E. (2010) 'Professionalising the Early Childhood Workforce in England: work in progress or missed opportunity', *Contemporary Issues in Early Childhood*, 11(1): 75–88.

Malaguzzi, L. (1997) 'No way. The hundred is there', in Fillipini, T. and Vecchi, V. (eds) *The Hundred Languages of Children: Narratives of the possible.* Reggio Emilia, Italy: Reggio Children.

Manning-Morton, J. (2006) 'The personal is professional: professionalism and the birth to three practitioner', *Contemporary Issues in Early Childhood*, 7(1): 42–52.

Mathers, S., Ranns, H., Karemaker, A., Moody, A., Sylva, K., Graham, J. and Siraj-Blatchford, I. (2011) *National Evaluation of the Graduate Leader Fund: Final report.* Research Report DFE-RR 144, London: Department for Education. Retrieved 11 April 2014 from https://www.education.gov.uk/publications/standard/publicationDetail/Page1/DFE-RR144.

McDowall Clark, R. and Baylis, S. (2012) '"Wasted down there": policy and practice with the under-threes', *Early Years*, 32(2): 229–42.

McDowall Clark, R. and Murray, J. (2012) *Reconceptualising Leadership in the Early Years.* Maidenhead: Open University Press/McGraw Hill.

McGillivray, G. (2008) 'Nannies, nursery nurses and early years professionals: constructions of professional identity in the early years workforce in England', *European Early Childhood Education Research Journal*, 16(2): 242–54.

Meltzoff, A.N. and Prinz, W. (2002) *The Imitative Mind: Development, evolution and brain bases.* Cambridge: Cambridge University Press.

Miller, L. and Cable, C. (2011) 'The changing face of professionalism in the early years', in Miller, L. and Cable, C. (eds) *Professionalization, Leadership and Management in the Early Years.* London: Sage.

Moyles, J. (2006) *Effective Leadership and Management in the Early Years.* Maidenhead: Open University Press.

Moyles, J., Adams, S. and Musgrove, A. (2002) *The Study of Pedagogical Effectiveness in Early Learning (SPEEL).* DfES Research Report 363. London: DfES.

Muijs, D., Aubrey, C., Harris, A. and Briggs, M. (2004) 'How do they manage? A review of the research in early childhood', *Journal of Early Childhood Research*, 2(2): 157–69.

New Zealand Ministry of Education (1996) *Te Whāriki: He Whāriki Mātauranga mō ngā Mokopuna o Aotearoa: Early Childhood Curriculum.* Wellington: NZ Government Print.

Nutbrown, C. and Page, J. (2008) *Working with Babies and Children: From birth to three.* London: Sage.

Oberhuemer, P. (2008) 'Who is an early years professional? Reflections on policy diversity in Europe', in Miller, L. and Cable, C. (eds) *Professionalism in the Early Years.* London: Hodder and Stoughton.

Osgood, J. (2012) *Narratives from the Nursery.* London: Routledge.

Pascal, C. and Bertram, T. (2009) 'Listening to young citizens: the struggle to make real a participatory paradigm in research with young children', *European Early Childhood Research Journal*, 17(2): 249–62.

Penn, H. (1997) *Comparing Nurseries, Staff and Children in Italy, Spain and the UK*. London: Paul Chapman Publishing.

Powell, S. and Goouch, K. (2012) 'What in the world is happening to babies? A critical perspective of research'. Presentation at the TACTYC (Association for the Professional Development of Early Years Educator) conference *Developing Early Years Practice: Reflecting on developments in practice and research*, Birmingham, 10 November 2012.

Rockel, J. (2009) 'A pedagogy of care: moving beyond the margins of managing work and minding babies', *Australian Journal of Early Childhood*, 34(2): 1–8.

Rodd, J. (1997) 'Learning to be leaders: perceptions of early childhood', *Early Years: An International Journal of Research and Development*, 18(1): 40–4.

Rodd, J. (2006) *Leadership in Early Childhood*. Third edition. Maidenhead: Open University Press.

Rogoff, B. (1990) *Apprenticeship in Thinking: Cognitive development in social context*. Oxford: Oxford University Press.

Saks, M. (1983) 'Removing the blinkers? A critique of recent contributions to the sociology of the professions', *Sociological Review*, 31(1): 1–21.

Siraj-Blatchford, I. and Manni, L. (2007) *Effective Leadership in the Early Years Sector: The ELEYS study*. London: Institute of Education, University of London.

Smith, A.B. (1988) 'Education and care components in New Zealand children centres and kindergartens', *Australasian Journal of Early Childhood*, 13(3): 31–6.

Stamopoulos, E., (2012) 'Reframing early childhood leadership', *Australian Journal of Early Childhood*, 37(2): 42–8.

Stephen, C. (2010) 'Pedagogy: the silent partner in early years learning', *Early Years*, 30(1): 1–14.

Stewart, N. and Pugh, R. (2007) *Early Years Vision in Focus, Part 3: Exploring pedagogy*. Shrewsbury: Shropshire County Council.

Teaching Agency (2012) *Early Years Professional Status Standards – September 2012*. London: Teaching Agency. Retrieved 11 April 2014 from http://www.education.gov.uk/publications/standard/publicationDetail/Page1/TA-00083-2012.

United Nations (2012) 'Chapter IV Human Rights, Section 11, Convention on the Rights of the Child'. *United Nations Treaty Collections*. Retrieved 11 April 2014 from http://treaties.un.org/pages/ViewDetails.aspx?src=TREATY&mtdsg_no=IV-11&chapter=4&lang=en.

Van Maurik, J. (2001) *Writers on Leadership*. London: Penguin.

Victoria Curriculum and Assessment Authority (2008) *Analysis of Curriculum/Learning Frameworks for the Early Years*. Retrieved 11 April 2014 from http://docs.education.gov.au/system/files/doc/other/analysis_of_curriculumlearning_frameworks_for_the_early_years_birth_to_age_8.pdf.

Walker, M., Straw, S., Harland, J., Jones, M., Mitchell, H., Springate, I., Philips, L. and Baginsky, M. (CWDC) (2009) *Evaluation of the Career Developments of Early Years Professionals (EYPs)*. Leeds: Children's Workforce Development Council. Retrieved 11 April 2014 from http://www.nfer.ac.uk/publications/REYZ01/REYZ01_home.cfm.

Whalley, M.E. (2011a) *Leading Practice in Early Years Settings*. Second edition. Exeter: Learning Matters.

Whalley, M.E. (2011b) 'Leading and managing in the early years', in Miller, L., Drury, R. and Cable, C. (eds) *Extending Professional Practice in the Early Years*. London: Sage with the Open University.

Wright, P. (1996) *Managerial Leadership*. London: Routledge.

9

Early years professionals' reflections on practice for two-year-old children from Kirklees case studies

Rachael Singleton and Avril Brock

This chapter present the voices of some graduate leaders – all with early years professional status – as they reflect on their provision: in setting layout and child access; working with parents; and in pedagogical leadership. It draws on three graduate leaders in Kirklees Local Authority as they reflect on how they have become their setting's pedagogical leader of children from birth to 30 months (B–30m). The emphasis is on children aged two years and this group of graduate leaders may be the exception that proves the rule, as it is, as Mary Whalley avers in Chapter 8, unusual that practice with babies and toddlers will be graduate led.

As stated in Chapter 6, the aim of the Early Education Pilot for Two Year Old Children (Smith *et al.*, 2009) was to improve young children's social and cognitive outcomes skills and reasoning ability for over 13,500 disadvantaged two-year-olds through the provision of free early years education. Children attended a variety of early years settings such as nurseries and playgroups and with child-minders. The results suggested that a positive impact on child outcomes was normally only achieved in high-quality settings. Two-year-olds now labelled as disadvantaged can receive funding for 15 hours of childcare in settings that achieve at least 'good' in their Ofsted inspections. Maisey *et al.*'s research (2013) found that where children attended higher quality settings, there was a positive impact on language ability, and on their parent–child relationship (two-year-old pilot). From September 2014 the Coalition's aim is to increase the number of those eligible to around 40 per cent of all two-year-olds.

The reflective practitioners in this chapter all epitomise the three 'As' of accountability, articulation and advocacy. They all work within Kirklees Local Authority in West Yorkshire, northern England – an authority that places great emphasis on supporting their graduate leaders and effective provision in their ECCE settings. These graduate leaders are at the forefront of addressing pedagogical leadership in their settings, and their reflective processes and professional development journeys are articulated in this chapter. The very committed Early Years Learning Consultancy team, including Rachael Singleton, in Kirklees LEA successfully gained funding for sector-specific specialist support through the National Children's Bureau (NCB) Peer to Peer support programme developed as part of a C4EO (Centre for Excellence and Outcomes) and NCB specialist support assignment. Debbie Garvey and the local authority team delivered a programme of CPD for an enthusiastic group of graduate leaders. It had the two main threads of:

1. development of graduate leaders as leaders of practice;
2. development of quality provision for two-year-old children and their families.

The participants had undertaken a reflective assignment and this had been supported by the DfE Improving Outcomes for Children, Young People and Families' fund, the aim of which is to determine what works to improve children's outcomes and life chances.

In early March 2013 Rachael organised the Early Years Professional Symposium entitled 'Leading 2gether' and warmly invited graduate leaders to present their case studies of high-quality leadership and practice. The NCB (funded through the Centre for Excellence and Outcomes) worked in partnership with the local authority to support graduate leaders as leaders of practice in settings that receive free early childhood care and education funding for two-year-olds. At the symposium the pack of graduate leaders' case studies was launched that showcased the reflective stories of eighteen EYPs working in a range of settings: private day nurseries in small and large companies; pre-school playgroups; pre-schools; hospital settings; early years centres; and child-minding (C4EO, 2014). The case studies were also designed to encourage other graduate leaders to undertake similar inspirational reflective practice in their settings to improve children's outcomes and life chances. In the following case study extracts it can be seen how the Kirklees team supports practitioner research and is developing a successful network and membership for all graduate leaders in the authority.

The introduction to the case study pack reminds us what it is to be: 'Uniquely Two'; 'Positively Two'; 'Enabled to be Two'; and 'Learning to be Two'. These draw on Manning-Morton and Thorp's (2001) two-year-old characteristics:

- physical and emotional development;
- growing mobility, dexterity and independence;
- growing sense of themselves as individuals;
- interest in developing social relationships with their peers;
- need for close relationships;
- drive to communicate;

FIGURE 9.1   Kirklees EYPs presenting their case studies.

- curiosity and desire to explore the world around them;
- ability to be creative through imitating, imaging and representing their thoughts and feelings.

Graduate leaders need to join in with two-year-olds' play; verbalising and supporting their schema; engaging and supporting children's fascinations and drive to understand their world. Being 'Positively Two' is developed through close relationships with a key person, developing independence and a strong sense of well-being. Promoting an enabling environment is key for two-year-olds to become 'Enabled to be Two' through the provision of multisensory first-hand experiences in a safe, secure, nurturing and exciting setting. A two-year-old's brain development is extremely rapid as the child repeats and refines knowledge, and in this way the brain's neural pathways are strengthened. 'Learning to be Two' is through young children playing, repeating and practising their skills through playful learning experiences until they master what they set out to do.

Three of the eighteen excellent case studies are now presented and they exemplify these aforementioned attributes of a two-year-old. The case studies by Holly, Sally and Bev, and Yvonne represent the professional work of the graduate leaders in Kirklees. They communicate the reflective processes they engaged in to improve and further develop their provision for the two-year-old children in their settings. Working closely with parents and being effective as a team in the setting are key elements of these case studies. Each of the three case studies provides the graduate leader's rationale, developmental journey and reflections on the process and outcomes.

Focused reflection point

- Read the following three case studies and reflect on how each of the practitioners has determined an issue to be resolved through an area of provision that needed further development.

FIGURE 9.2 Enabling environments: making space to be two.

Case study 1

Enabling environments: 'Making Space to be Two'

Holly Guite

I am the owner/manager of a 32-place nursery and have a team of fourteen staff, several of whom hold degrees. The children in our setting come from a variety of backgrounds, a few having English as their second language. The majority of our parents are very involved with the setting.

Rationale

The catalyst for the change was an ITERS (Infant and Toddler Environment Rating Scale) and ECERS (Early Childhood Environment Rating Scale) audit twelve months ago. The audit was at my request. At the time I felt that we were an excellent setting with a 'Green' support rating, level 3 National Day Nurseries Association 'E Quality Counts' accreditation and a very good Ofsted inspection. However, a grade of 'Outstanding' always seemed to evade us and I felt that we could really benefit from some external input and a different perspective on the nursery and the service we provide.

Development journey

The main purpose of the audit was to question the basis of the layout of the setting. At this time we had two separate baby rooms at opposite ends of the setting separated by the main playroom (a large space) where the two- to four-year-olds were based. As a consequence, the baby room staff found it difficult to behave as one team, often feeling isolated. Resources were duplicated and the two-year-olds struggled to find a space of their own. They were often observed disrupting the play of the older children, knocking down their elaborate towers, castles and other fantastic creations and generally causing chaos when playing independently.

The solution was to transform one of the baby rooms into a space for the over-twos and install a room divide splitting the main play area into two. Staff became involved through staff meetings and then worked in three teams on planning an area of provision. We had a staff training day at Easter and we used that day to implement all the changes and re-organise the nursery in one day. A local authority consultant, who had been involved with the audit, worked with the staff, turning their ideas into a reality. We opened for business the next day.

Parents were informed of the pending changes by newsletter and by talking to their child's key person. Following the re-organisation we held a parent forum to discuss the changes and a questionnaire was sent out to all parents to gather feedback. We then organised a number of 'stay and play' sessions, so that the parents could see the new layout actually in use. These sessions worked very well and are something we have continued to do on a regular basis. The parents benefited from observing first-hand how their children play and engage with the environment and their friends, and the sessions served to dissipate some of the concerns they had initially over the changes made.

The result was significant and meant that the under-two provision could be totally re-organised to incorporate distinct areas for learning including mark making, messy play, sand and water, construction and small world in the open space behind the room divide, and quieter activities such as home bay, sensory, reading corner, maths and science in the room that was already a baby room. Sleeps also take place in this room because the door can be shut and all the noise from the nursery excluded.

The additional room adds a whole new dynamic and has reduced the noise levels in the nursery significantly, with children freely moving between areas. Consequently, we have observed that the children focus on one particular activity for longer periods of time and they seem calmer. The two-year-olds play alongside their older peers and have the space to express themselves without frustrating the older children.

Reflection

Without the ITERS and ECERS audit we would not have had the foresight to think out of the box and totally re-organise the nursery. We have not gained any more physical space but have gained so much by using that space more effectively. We were very much a reflective practice but had accepted the basic layout of the environment in which we worked.

I believe that the success of the project depended on involving all interested parties. The staff designed the new layout and worked hard to organise the nursery to reflect their plans. The parents were kept fully informed and given the opportunity to voice their opinions. Parental engagement in their child's learning, both at the setting and at home, has improved significantly through the 'stay and play' sessions, which have enabled the parents to observe how their children learn at nursery and continue this learning at home and extend it too. Parents (including dads) now visit to share stories with small groups of children, which they all love! Staff observed the children playing in the new space and changes have been made to improve it and respond to how the children integrate with their environment. Practice around transition and meal times has improved. We continue to review our practice and improvements to provision.

My role as a graduate leader is, and continues to be, one of facilitator. I led the practice in terms of identifying the need for external support and arranging the audit. I organised the process for thinking about the new layout and supported the team to be reflective in their roles and work together to find a solution. I ensured that all parties felt included and consulted (staff, children and parents). The funding received for the project has been used to finance staff meetings, parent forum meetings and stay and play sessions.

Focused reflection point

- Would a particular area of the learning environment within your provision benefit from improvement?
- What similarities are there to this case study?
- Would you address it in a different way?

Case study 2

Strengthening ties with parents, practitioners and partnership working

Sally Blake and Bev Dearnley

We are both managers of two separate 26-place pre-schools that provide full daycare. Even though the pre-schools are based in different communities, we are finding that we face similar challenges and experience comparable types of need. The pre-schools both endeavour to ensure that partnerships with parents are strong and meaningful; however, we are now striving to ensure we are engaging all of the families in the children's learning, including those families accessing the two-year-old funding.

Rationale

The focus of our change was to help practitioners understand and overcome barriers which are preventing families from engaging in their children's learning. This was planned through enabling our teams to access 'Parents in Early Years and Learning' (PEAL) training, which challenges preconceptions about family contexts, and also through networking with a similar setting facing similar difficulties.

Development journey

We jointly planned a four-hour training programme using the materials and activities so that the practitioners had the chance to share different experiences. We felt that if the practitioners instigated their own ideas concerning parental involvement in their child's learning, they would be more enthusiastic. Therefore the training was practical, and offered plenty of opportunity for discussion and reflection. The training was delivered over two two-hour evening sessions. The one consistent theme that ran throughout all of the practitioners' discussions was how paramount relationships are in establishing positive partnerships. All practitioners, including ourselves, realised that the training was just the beginning of our journey.

Although one of the pre-schools had already begun to introduce home visits, practitioners from the other team began to learn from them the positive impact homes visits can have. The setting has now introduced home visits and as a result they have become an effective part of our transition procedures. The home visit has also had a positive impact of developing relationships; feedback from parents indicates that they feel so much more at ease, know they have someone to talk to (and who to talk to) and are happy that they and their child have met their key person before they begin their settle sessions.

Other strategies we have recently introduced to support parents in engaging in their children's learning include the use of Facebook and weekly 'stay and play' sessions where we supported engagement through our partnership working. For one setting, a consultation event was supported by the local children's centre, where the settings and the local children's centre gifted books for the children to every family attending a briefing about the 'Bookstart corner project'. One hundred per cent of families attended the consultation evening and briefing, and as a result all of the children now have a scrap book that can be used to record photos, children's pictures and words used at home.

For both settings social networking has been an excellent tool in engaging all parents in their children's learning. Home learning links are posted onto the site on a weekly basis; the children's families comment on the status about what they have been doing at home with their children and tag photos of the children at the park, finding pine cones, or buns they have baked and much more. Not only is this excellent evidence of both settings striving for engagement but it also provides superb information for the children's learning journeys without even asking the parents to contribute to them, which can be overwhelming for some.

Reflection

Practitioners reflected on current relationships with families and improvements to regular and effective communication. We began a discussion on how communication with the children's families meant much more than having parents' evenings, termly newsletters, displays and invitations into the setting. We concluded that, although these are important strategies in informing parents, something more was needed to ensure that we were reaching out to and engaging all of the children's families on a consistent and regular basis.

Practitioners reflected on how their own assumptions about particular parents may have had an impact on establishing good-quality relationships. We reflected on journeys to work in a morning to understand why some of the children may be late for pre-school, why they may be hungry/thirsty/tired and why the parents do not have time to chat or even phone to say their child will be late or not coming in at all. Through doing this practitioners began to show an understanding of the many challenges our families face and discuss ways in which we could be supportive without being patronising, such as introducing a family breakfast on a regular basis where the children and their families can enjoy a stress-free mealtime together.

We recognise that this is just the beginning of our setting's learning journeys on how we can continue to strengthen ties. The PEAL project has had a significant impact on the practitioners' attitudes to parental engagement. As graduate leaders, we have become 'change agents' rather than the person changing practice: we have provided the practitioners with 'tools' to take ownership of changes themselves. The project has been invaluable in changing practitioner attitudes, forming a better understanding of the unique needs each and every family has, particularly for the families accessing the two-year funding. Overall the project has had a huge impact on the practice at both settings. We now consider ourselves as 'partners' and hope to continue to work in partnership with each other on similar projects in the future so that the practitioners from both settings can continue to share good practice in the future.

Focused reflection point

- Are there similarities to your own practice within this case study?
- Do you think there are any barriers in your provision that may prevent families from engaging in their children's learning?
- How can you form more effective partnerships in your setting?

Case study 3

'Now I am 2, look what I can do!' The importance of movement play

Yvonne Shaw

I work in a 48-place private day nursery and am a graduate leader and Deputy Manager, Special Educational Needs Coordinator (SENCO) and Toddler Room Senior.

Rationale

As the graduate leader I wanted to ensure that all children's needs were being met through age and stage appropriate provision. I also wanted to ensure that the children who had additional needs were being fully supported and challenged. The setting is currently being supported by the Kirklees Inclusion Team, who recently delivered a movement play session. After observing the session and asking our practitioners to complete a questionnaire, I realised that regular movement sessions would benefit all of the children in the Toddler Room. These sessions would provide regular physical development activities and form part of the toddlers' regular daily routine. However, physical play opportunities often decline in the winter months.

The revised early years foundation stage (EYFS) highlights physical development as one of the prime areas of learning, thus emphasising how this should be a priority for practitioners working with the youngest children. Physical play opportunities alongside Personal, Social and Emotional and Communication and Language development ensure that all children gain a solid foundation in their learning before the specific areas of development can be added to them.

Early on in the project I also held a room meeting with the team to evaluate daily routines and how circle time sessions were approached. It was clear that the practitioners didn't plan effectively for circle time sessions, which were often rather chaotic, and practitioners decided what to cover as they went along. This meant that sessions could be a little disorganised, although some of the sessions had worked well in the past. The daily routine in the room did have some basic structure and worked reasonably well; however, we felt that the less confident children may benefit from a visual timetable. As a team we came up with several ideas and we decided to work out a more structured routine. These two aspects of physical play and quality circle times became interconnected as I reflected on the needs of our two-year-olds in my setting.

Development journey

I took the ideas we had come up with at the meeting and used them to design three clearly defined adult-led activities for the children on a daily basis. The first aimed to welcome all of the toddlers and to help them get to know each other. The second aimed to increase their physical development and mobility. The third was a more calming session where the practitioner would either sing or read a story using movement rhymes and songs.

I led the sessions for a whole day and modelled to the team how enjoyable these times can be for both children and practitioners. The following day I supported and observed other members of the team when delivering them. One of the high points was when a practitioner said, 'I really enjoyed that singing session; all of the children were really focused and not distracted.' The involvement levels of the children were also much higher.

As Deputy Manager it is one of my roles to help assess planning. It was evident from the group activity plans that some practitioners had higher, unrealistic expectations of what children could do at certain ages and stages of development. This had also been evident in the child development questionnaires carried out at the start of the project. The majority of the practitioners only allocated around 50 per cent of the statements to the correct age group. After talking with practitioners their answers were based on parental expectations and the pressure they felt under to deliver these. It was decided that the best way to inform parents and give them a clearer understanding of child development was to create a display and provide leaflets clearly setting out development norms. This would help to clear up any misconceptions of when children should be able to achieve certain goals. Now the practitioners are independently able to plan and implement activities to develop and challenge all children appropriately, and movement play is an area of continuous provision on a daily basis. The practitioners commented that it has already had an impact on the children's confidence and concentration levels, and physical development such as a sense of balance, all of which have significantly increased. The children are now more aware of their daily routine and can follow the visual timetable to predict what will come next. Practitioners feel more empowered and confident when speaking with parents about child development and realistic goals.

Reflection

Generally the project went to plan, although it became not just about establishing clear routines but also about supporting practitioners to be more knowledgeable and independent when communicating with parents. A large emphasis was also placed on physical and development movement play and incorporating this on a daily basis to prepare children and equip them with the skills they will require for school.

I have realised that less confident practitioners will shy away from more challenging situations and step back to let others deal with any issues. I feel that this project has empowered practitioners to become more confident when speaking with parents about child development and what is appropriate for the age and stage of the children they are working with. My next steps will be to deliver the Parents, Early Years and Learning (PEAL) training, which I attended as part of this project, to all practitioners in the setting to strengthen their skills with parents. It will also enable them to support future parents of two-year-old children.

Focused reflection point

- How inclusive would you rate the setting in which you practice?
- Does the setting provide regular physical development activities as part of the regular daily routine throughout the year?
- How confident is everyone in the setting to speak to parents about relevant aspects of child development?

Conclusion

It is essential that practitioners reflect on the complexities of their role and the quality of provision for children and families. This is even more so for graduate leaders who are charged with 'leading practice' within their teams. The local authority has helped to support reflective practice through its strategy of challenge, support and training and has played an important role in bringing individuals together to form learning communities in projects and interventions. It is the corporate nature of reflection that has had the greatest impact within micro-cultures that stimulate, challenge and foster trust. Coupled with individual professionalism and integrity, graduate leaders have been supported in their change agency to raise standards and given recognition of their work and role, which has meant a great deal to them.

The role of Early Learning Consultant and strategic planning from the local authority has enabled facilitation of the project and ongoing collaboration as good practice visits continue and new projects begin. Both local and specialist knowledge from the consultant were highly valued by the group, who wanted to 'know what we need to know'. The structures and planning processes in place from the consultancy team were used to support reflection, such as requiring an action plan. For some, this provided a much-needed focus and tool for time management, but for others this proved a barrier and it became appropriate to respond flexibly and remove this requirement. Through conversations it was clear that, for some, more time to think and read was necessary, and subsequent clarity was gained through further CPD and action learning sets. In these instances, both graduate leader reflection and agency was generally richer. The project was used as a basis for an MSc, in which the following themes were most prominent:

- recognition or external validation;
- reflection;
- training, knowledge and continued professional development;
- being in a professional group – the learning community.

Project data also clearly showed the move away from graduate leaders delivering change personally, to empowering staff in settings and raising practitioner confidence. As one graduate leader put it:

> The project has enabled me to continue to develop my skills as a leader of practice and to support my staff team in continuing to be reflective about practice. I felt more able to engage the staff team in active learning following examples from the project.

The symposium presentations and case studies offered a clear demonstration of early years leaders who are accountable, articulate and passionate advocates for our youngest children and families.

Summary of knowledge gained

After reading and reflecting on this chapter you should now be very aware that:

- qualification, skill, knowledge, professional development and leadership for early years practitioners are crucially important for working with two-year-olds;
- reflective practice is key and skilled practitioners are engaging in it every day in order to improve practice;
- the Centre for Excellence and Outcomes in Children and Young People's Services shares evidence of best practice and provides practical 'hands on support' to help local areas make full use of this evidence.

Challenges for the future

- Make the connections between Chapters 6, 7, 8, 10, 11 and 13 that are relevant to practice and provision for two-year-olds.
- How will you ensure you continually reflect on your practice and when you may need to effect a significant change in your provision?
- What is the next step of your learning journey?
- Which qualification are you going to work for next in your career?

Further reading

Bradford, H. (2012) *Planning and Observation of Children under Three.* London: Routledge.

Hutchin, V. (2013) *Effective Practice in the Early Years Foundation Stage: An essential guide.* Maidenhead: Open University Press.

Page, J., Clare, A. and Nutbrown, C. (2013) *Working with Babies and Children: From birth to three.* Second edition. London: Sage.

References

Centre for Excellence and Outcomes in Children and Young People's Services (C4EO) (2014) *C4EO theme: Early Years. A project approach to supporting leadership of high quality childcare for funded two year old children and their families, Kirklees.* London: C4EO. Retrieved 13 April 2014 from http://www.c4eo.org.uk/themes/general/vlpdetails.aspx?lpeid=479.

Maisey, R., Speight, S., Marsh, V. and Philo, D. (2013) *The Early Education Pilot for Two Year Old Children: Age five follow-up research report March 2013.* NatCen Social Research, Department for Education.

Manning-Morton, J. and Thorp, M. (2001) *Key Times: A framework for developing high quality provision for children under three years old.* Camden Under Threes Development Group and The University of North London.

Smith, R., Poole, E., Perry, J., Wollny, I., Reeves, A., Coshall, C., d'Souza, J. and Bryson, C. (2010) *Childcare and Early Years Survey of Parents 2009.* Department for Education Research Report RR054.

10

A deeper understanding of play

Liz Chesworth

Introduction

This chapter will consider some issues and challenges associated with play in the early years and will explore why it is important for practitioners to reflect upon the social and cultural contexts for play within their classrooms and settings. It will draw upon examples from a recent study to propose that listening to children's perspectives can facilitate a deeper understanding of the motivations and meanings that young children bring to their play. The children's perspectives will be used to illustrate four key themes that emerged from the research: identity, reciprocity, possibility and resilience. These themes resonate with sociocultural approaches to understanding young children's learning and development (see for example, Carr *et al.*, 2010) that focus upon the dispositions associated with play as opposed to emphasising predetermined developmental outcomes.

Play and curriculum

The ideology of ECCE in the UK has traditionally emphasised the importance of play as central to young children's learning. However, there is compelling empirical evidence to suggest that the realities of implementing a play-based approach can be complex and problematic (Moyles *et al.*, 2002; Rogers and Evans, 2008) and that there is often a mismatch between the ideology of play compared to the reality of children's classroom experiences (Adams *et al.*, 2004; Moyles and Worthington, 2011). This mismatch has been fuelled by nearly three decades of political intervention with a focus upon a top-down approach to raising educational standards, thus creating competing discourses for ECCE that require practitioners to focus upon predetermined curriculum outcomes (Moss, 2007) whilst also acknowledging the ideologies of a playful approach to learning. A recent study in reception classes (Moyles and Worthington, 2011) highlights the tensions that this creates in practice. The findings suggest that, whilst practitioners extol the importance of play in the classroom, in reality children's experiences are often dominated by the requirements of the prescribed curriculum rather than by their current interests and motivations.

The recently revised early years foundation stage (EYFS) (DfE, 2012) continues the legacy of conflicting discourses by promoting a play-based approach whilst at the same time requiring practitioners to monitor and assess children's progress towards prescribed early learning goals. The EYFS identifies 'play and exploration' as one of three characteristics that underpin effective learning and advises practitioners to 'ensure children have uninterrupted time to play and explore' (Early Education, 2012: 6). However, the EYFS also places considerable emphasis upon school readiness (Papatheodorou and Potts, 2012) and the assessment of children using the EYFS profile.

There are ideological tensions associated with a curriculum that promotes play and playful approaches whilst at the same time emphasising the role of ECCE in preparing children for formal education. The notion of school readiness is a debated subject that is open to different interpretations (Papatheodorou and Potts, 2012), but in England it has come to be associated with an outcomes-driven ideology of education (Moss, 2012). As a result, play within early years settings has, arguably, come to be colonised by adult priorities in relation to curriculum delivery and children's attainment. As Rogers and Evans (2008, 15) propose, 'the provision of play activities with sound educational purpose is, then, the order of the day.' With practitioners being required to demonstrate their accountability for children's progress, understanding children's motivations for play has perhaps become overshadowed by pressure to demonstrate how outcome-led priorities are being met through playful experiences (Goouch, 2008; Rogers, 2010; Wood, 2010). As Broadhead (2006) argues, predetermined goals alone cannot encapsulate the sum total of a child's potential, yet there is a risk that an outcomes-driven agenda may place limitations on how we interpret and understand children's play in our early years classrooms and settings.

The implications for the reflective practitioner are significant: how to meet the requirements of the statutory curriculum and be accountable for children's progress whilst at the same time enabling children to engage in meaningful play experiences that reflect their genuine interests and motivations. There are no easy solutions to such dilemmas. However, this chapter proposes that developing a deeper understanding of play can enable practitioners to articulate and defend the place of play within early childhood and later I will present how my research into children's perspectives enabled me to bring a deeper level of reflection to my thinking about play. First, the discussion will focus upon some theoretical perspectives that encourage us to consider the significance of the social and cultural contexts for play.

Focused reflection point

- In your own experience have you found in reception and Year 1 classes that children learning through play and following their own interests and motivations is overruled by the requirements of the prescribed curriculum?
- Reflect with a colleague or fellow student on what good practice you have seen where learning through play has a high priority.

Limitations of developmental perspectives

Notions of play within early childhood education, at least from a Western perspective, have traditionally been informed by Piagetian theory, which views the child as 'a becoming individual' progressing through developmental stages towards adulthood. Piaget's theory of development is based upon the premise that all children pass through predetermined and universal developmental stages (Piaget, 1936). For Piaget, the child's learning was therefore determined, and consequently limited by, the stage they had reached towards maturity.

Hence, from a Piagetian stance, 'development was seen to determine learning' (Whitebread and Bingham, 2011: 1) and, as Pramling Samuelsson and Asplund Carlsson (2008) argue, play from this developmental viewpoint is seen as a vehicle to support children's progress through these internalised, biologically determined developmental stages towards maturation. Within the context of early childhood education, play from this perspective is often understood and described in terms of its potential to support children's progression through these predetermined developmental stages. It is this developmentally informed interpretation of play that continues to influence English educational policy and that underpins the dominant perspective of play within the EYFS discussed earlier in the chapter.

Piaget's developmental theories have been an enduring influence upon the positioning of play within early childhood education, and offer important insights into how play supports development (Hedges, 2010). However, as early childhood education has shifted to acknowledge children's diverse social and cultural heritages, the universal assumptions underpinning Piaget's developmental stages have come under examination (Edwards, 2007; Fleer, 2005). The assumed relevance of his theory for all children has been challenged and Wood (2010), for example, argues that the pursuit of developmental stages, norms and milestones privilege certain (Western, middle-class) groups and place others in a disadvantaged position. Furthermore, Piaget's developmental theory has been criticised for its failure to recognise the importance of cultural and social influences upon early learning and development (Dahlberg *et al.*,1999; MacNaughton, 2005).

Playing in a community of learners

The rejection of some key aspects of Piaget's theoretical arguments have been associated with a wider recognition of the sociocultural influences upon learning and a corresponding shift in the ways in which play is conceptualised within ECCE environments (Rogers, 2011; Brooker and Edwards, 2010; Wood, 2010). Underpinning this shift in thinking is a recognition that learning takes place within communities of learners and that it is essentially participatory in nature (Rogoff, 1994). Fleer, drawing upon Bodrova (2008, cited in Fleer, 2011), contests that play is a key activity through which children participate within their cultural and social communities. Broadhead presents a similar case for the possibilities that play offers young children to 'engage with learning in communities of learners' (2006: 192).

Participatory approaches to pedagogy require practitioners to reflect upon how their practices can foster a sense of belonging for children. However, the focus upon developmental outcomes within the early years foundation stage (DfE, 2012) presents some challenges for bringing such a sense of belonging into the heart of early years practice. By contrast, the New Zealand *Te Whāriki* curriculum has been developed from a sociocultural stance, and includes as one of its five curriculum strands a strand of 'belonging', wherein practitioners are urged to consider, from the child's perspective, '*do you appreciate and understand my interests and abilities and those of my family?*' (Carr and May, 2000). This approach to pedagogy places belonging at the heart of learning and development. Wenger (1998) proposes three connected modes of belonging within the learning community. These are: *alignment*, which considers the relevance of community activities to children's lives beyond the classroom; *engagement*, which emphasises the importance of social relationships and interests; and *imagination*, which Wenger argues is about children's awareness of multiple possibilities.

Bridging cultures

Wenger's mode of alignment reminds us that the extent to which ECCE environments offer opportunities for children to make connections with their home and cultural communities seems to be an important factor in forging a sense of belonging. This carries important implications for play. For example, Brooker (2010) highlights that learning through play takes on different meanings in different cultural situations. The transition from home to an ECCE environment will require the child to become a novice participant within this new community, and to develop the skills, knowledge and attitudes required to become an expert. For some children, the values and goals at home may be very different to those encountered at nursery or school (Brooker, 2002), and not all children will join as expert players (Broadhead and Burt, 2012). It is consequently essential for practitioners to recognise children's diverse family and cultural experiences and to be proactive in developing meaningful connections between the different communities in which young children participate as learners and players.

Wertsch (1998, cited in Carr *et al.*, 2010) introduces the idea of 'living in the middle' to describe the significance of the space between an individual and their social and cultural contexts. This space is 'occupied by the relating: the recognising, adapting, editing, recontextualising, improvising, constructing, enjoying, puzzling about, and taking up of (or ignoring) opportunities in the environment' (Carr *et al.*, 2010: 6–7). Carr *et al.* develop Wertsch's notion of 'living in the middle' to argue that this is the space where identity is formed and reformed. Walker and Nocon's (2007) research relating to children's boundary-crossing competencies proposes a similar notion by examining the role of cultural brokers (people and artefacts) in developing children's 'ability to function competently in multiple contexts' (2007: 178). Hence, identity is conceptualised as complex and dynamic, with children constructing and reconstructing multiple identities (Brooker and Woodhead, 2008).

It is argued here that play has the potential to act as a powerful cultural broker to bridge the space between young children's home and school cultures. Hedges (2010) suggests that one way in which practitioners can use play to develop meaningful connections between home and school cultures is through developing a deeper awareness of the interests, experiences and competencies that children bring from their families and communities. Arguing that 'children's foundational knowledge is based upon their unique family and community experiences' (2010: 28), Hedges applies Moll *et al.*'s model to suggest the potential that *funds of knowledge* (Moll *et al.*, 1992, cited in Hedges, 2010) can offer for enriching our understanding of children's play interests, and to consider how such interests are rooted in engagement in everyday experiences and interactions with others. Hence, a deeper consideration of children's play interests in relation to their family, community and cultural experiences can enhance the reflective practitioner's understanding of play within our early years classrooms and settings.

Anning (1998) has critiqued early years practitioners' avowed focus on supporting children's interests and suggests that, in reality, some interests are privileged over others: whilst certain play themes are encouraged and supported in the classroom, others are suppressed by adults and viewed as inappropriate. Anning argues that teachers' own backgrounds (predominantly white, female and middle class) serve to create an idealised, adult-oriented version of children's interests that fails to acknowledge children's genuine interests; interests that are often acquired through participation in family, social and cultural experiences. It is important to stress that play can provide a meaningful context for children to develop positive cultural identities only if their genuine interests and preoccupations are acknowledged.

Focused reflection point

- Select two children with whom you work or teach and reflect on what you know about their play interests and motivations. It would be useful to select a girl and a boy of quite different personalities. Reflect with a colleague and challenge yourself as to how much you know or do not know about the children.

Playful engagement in the learning community

Broadhead and Burt's recent research (2012) cites numerous examples of the diverse ways in which children's collaborative play can support the development of positive self-image and cultural identity through the utilisation of open-ended resources as cultural tools. Corsaro's (2005) research suggests that sociodramatic role-play is of particular significance for children's participation in their peer culture and in developing an orientation to adult culture. The relationships, friendships, conflicts and negotiations that take place as children play together consequently become an important area for consideration, and it is this important aspect of play that the discussion will now address.

Friendships are important for children, just as they are for adults. Reciprocal relationships with adults and peers underpin children's sense of belonging within their classroom community. However, many studies into early friendships have given little consideration to children's participation in cultural communities (Corsaro, 2003; Howes, 2011), and their capacity for forming and sustaining friendships has consequently been underestimated:

> A big reason that developmental psychologists underestimate the friendship knowledge and skills of young children is that they focus on outcomes. That is, they identify and classify children at various stages in the acquisition of adult friendship knowledge in relation to their age or other developmental abilities. There is an assumption here that kids must acquire or internalize adult concepts of friendships before they can really have complex friendship relations.
>
> (Corsaro, 2003: 67)

Corsaro's own studies reveal a very different scenario, and suggest that young children participate in complex social worlds in which they simultaneously engage in peer and adult cultures as they play. Early friendships form an important part of the child's engagement in social relationships and offer a context for communication as a cultural tool (Faulkner and Miell, 1993), as well as contributing to emotional well-being (Broadhead, 2004). Children use play to construct their own understanding of what is meant by friendship (Avgitidou, 2001; Broadhead, 2004; Dunn, 2004; Löfdahl, 2010), and play can strengthen friendships through children's engagement in shared endeavors and interests (Broadhead, 2004). Indeed, nearly a century ago, those interested in play were already beginning to recognise its capacity for supporting close and stable friendships (Isaacs, 1937, cited in Howes, 2011).

Conflict, power and play

Whilst there is strong evidence to support the notion that young children are very capable of developing and sustaining friendships during their play, it is equally important to avoid creating a romanticised image of young children playing harmoniously within a conflict-free environment. Anyone who has spent time in an ECCE environment will know that this is often not the case. In common with all communities, young children's peer culture also involves falling out, disagreements and the exercise of power and social control (Corsaro, 2003, 2005). Shared community norms, values and attitudes emerge in children's play through interaction, including those less harmonious interactions associated with conflict and control (Corsaro, 2003; Löfdahl, 2010).

Young children's conflicts are often related to disputes around the ownership and use of objects and materials (Wheeler, 1994; Cobb-Moore *et al.*, 2008), and Broadhead (2009) draws upon Vygotskyan theory to argue that one significant way in which children cooperate in their play is through negotiating the use and ownership of objects in order to sustain their play. This perspective supports Avgitidou's notion of freely chosen play as an 'interpersonal co-constructed activity' (1997: 6) which offers opportunities for children to cooperate with each other, negotiate meaning and exchange information as they engage in shared experiences. Such experiences afford important opportunities for children to explore the inter-subjectivity of meaning as they engage reciprocally with their peers, and it is towards this important aspect of play that the discussion will now turn.

Play and reciprocity: the co-construction and re-construction of meaning and ideas

This section builds upon Vygotsky's (1978) notion of the Zone of Proximal Development (ZPD) and develops the argument that play acts as a context for children to maintain a ZPD for each other as they negotiate and co-construct meaning. Van Oers and Hannikainen (2001) have adopted the term 'togetherness' to conceptualise those activities and experiences that involve collaboration, and define it as

> a quality of an activity that does not break down when problems have to be faced and when conflicts have to be settled in the context of that activity. Instead, the participants in that activity demonstrate an implicit or explicit wish to continue their shared activity.
>
> (Van Oers and Hannikainen, 2001: 105)

This definition resonates with evidence from Broadhead's (2004, 2009) research that conceptualises play as a cooperative experience. Likewise, Brennan (2008: 73) draws upon her study of preschool sociodramatic play to argue that play is an 'exercise in collective reconstruction'. Such an exercise requires participating children to be both cognitively and emotionally aware and respectful of self and others, and involves the self-regulation of behaviour in order to negotiate meaning and sustain the play. Bruner (1995) refers to such experiences as *joint involvement episodes* and argues for their importance in enabling children to explore different perspectives and priorities.

The dialogue that takes place between players forms a key element of such shared experiences, and, as Carr *et al.* argue, 'dialogue within a shared language opens up endless future possibilities for play and learning' (2010: 33). This is well illustrated by Cohen's (2009) study of pretend play, which drew upon Bakhtin's model of dialogic process (Bakhtin 1981, 1986, cited in Cohen, 2009) to analyse a range of play episodes within preschool classrooms. Cohen's research identified that children 'appropriated and assimilated others' words in play' (2009: 331) through their dialogue, thus contributing to shared meaning-making and the enrichment of the play. This resonates with Rogoff's notion of young children's predisposition to 'pick up the interpretation and viewpoint of others' (Rogoff, 1990: 73) within the community of learners. This does not, however, mean that children always reach a consensus in their play and certain voices will often emerge with more power in the play than others. Sawyer (1997), also drawing upon Bakhtin's dialogic model (1981, cited in Sawyer, 1997), explored the notion of heteroglossia in children's fantasy play to propose that children develop their play themes in a collectively constructed framework in which a multiplicity of perspectives shapes the play through a blending of voices rather than a consensus of opinions.

Reciprocal engagement in dialogue thus allows children to achieve 'mutual independence and recognition, and a degree of independence from adult control' (Carr *et al.*, 2010: 33) as they exercise their collective agency (Matusov, 2001, cited in Brennan, 2008) and co-construct meaning. Reciprocity develops and shifts over time as children develop a sense of belonging within the learning community and emerge as expert players. This process involves the acquirement of the competencies, or dispositions, to function in and contribute to the cultural activities of the community. Bronfenbrenner and Morris (1998) argue that these dispositions, which include agency, empathy, trust and curiosity, are the driving forces behind learning and development. Likewise, Carr *et al.* (2010) conceptualise the learning process as *dispositions in action* and identify these dispositions as 'reciprocity, resilience and imagination' (Carr *et al.*, 2010: 32).

The acquisition and application of dispositions within the learning community could thus be conceived as the process by which children move from novice to expert players. Expert players engage in experiences that move beyond play as a social experience towards the active co-construction and re-construction of meaning. Rogoff's (1994) model of learning is one of transformative participation, in which knowledge is not fixed but rather shifts and evolves in response to activities that take place within the learning community. Within this construct of learning, play becomes a reflexive process in which children critically reflect upon familiar experiences and explore alternative possibilities and ways of being (Duncan and Tarulli, 2003; Moran and John-Steiner, 2003). Hence, play is positioned not as a means of merely replicating cultural experiences but instead as a potentially transformative process in which children collectively re-construct roles, attitudes and relationships.

Play, resilience and risk

Carr *et al.* (2010) propose that resilience is a key learning disposition for young children. Drawing upon Ungar's (2004, cited in Carr *et al.*, 2010) social constructivist approach to resilience, they suggest that children build resilience through 'negotiating with others (people), the environments (places) and the resources (things) they need to position themselves as authoritative within adverse difficult or challenging circumstances' (Carr *et al.*, 2010: 29). As Claxton (2002) argues, the ability to be able to develop, sustain and persevere with an interest, in spite of distractions, underpins resilience. It would seem that play offers an important context for children to build resilience through the opportunities it presents for children to explore their environments and to 'develop a wide repertoire of responses to the situations they create' (Lester and Russell, 2010: 12). In this way, play can enable children to become aware of diverse possibilities (Cremin *et al.*, 2006), and to develop strategies and solutions for exploring and regulating risk (Sandseter, 2009). It is this capacity to explore multiple possibilities and to self-regulate risk that underpins the disposition of resilience and that thus enables children's active participation in their home and school communities.

Beyond observation: listening to children

The discussion so far has focused upon the limitations of interpreting children's play using only predetermined, developmental outcomes and has explored some alternative perspectives to enhance our understanding of play through the consideration of sociocultural contexts and the dispositions that underpin learning. The remainder of the chapter will discuss some examples from an empirical study that explored children's perspectives of play in an early years classroom. The examples form part of a larger study that also considered the perspectives of parents and practitioners, but in this section I will focus on the children's perspectives to show how their interpretations of play can make an important contribution to how we can develop a deeper understanding of play in our early years classrooms and settings.

The research was conceptualised within a sociocultural framework, which recognises that young children are active social agents who contribute to the construction of their lives (Prout, 2000). The emerging recognition of children's agency has been accompanied by a gradual shift in the field of childhood research from conceptualising children as relatively passive research objects towards their repositioning as active subjects within the research process (Christensen and James, 2000). These changes have been associated with an acknowledgement that, whilst constructs of childhood and children's lives have historically been structured by adult perspectives, there is a need to recognise children's voices as key to understanding aspects of their own lives (Mayall, 2000; Pascal and Bertram, 2009; Prout, 2000).

The research aimed to establish a holistic view of play within an English Foundation Stage unit by filming a range of 'joint attention episodes' (Bruner, 1995; Carr *et al.*, 2010) that took place during child-initiated play experiences over an eight-month period. The five key children who participated in the study were aged four and five years and were in their reception year of school. The approach used the filmed material as cues to elicit the children's perspectives of their play, and drew upon Tobin *et al.*'s (1989) and Tobin's (2009) seminal studies that used filmed material of everyday preschool events to explore the perspectives of early childhood practitioners across three countries. Tobin (2009: 261) describes this approach as 'video-cued multivocal ethnography' and, whilst the purposes and contexts for the research are different, Tobin's label is effective in describing the approach developed for this particular study of children's play. Hence, at the heart of this approach to researching and understanding play is an acknowledgement of the importance of developing a research design that enables the 'telling and re-telling of the same event from different perspectives' (Tobin *et al.*, 1989: 4).

A key priority for the study was to establish and sustain respectful and reciprocal relationships with the children who participated in the study. It was therefore essential to avoid an approach that trivialised participation whilst in reality only serving to reinforce differentials of power between children and adults. Flewitt's (2005) notions of consent were useful in shaping the approach taken to ensure that children's participation was ethical and respectful of their changing views of the research. Flewitt reminds us that initial consent can only be provisional, as 'the precise course to be taken by the research is unpredictable' (2005: 4). This was definitely the case with my study in which the methods were purposefully fluid and dynamic. I spent at least one day a week in the school, during which I participated in the life of the classroom alongside filming episodes of play and watching the filmed material with the children. I also visited the children at home and watched the films with their families. The study adopted an approach of 'slow listening' (Clark, 2011) that involved me in working alongside the children over the eight-month research period and developing methods to ensure their active participation throughout the duration of the study. For example, the video software adopted for the research was selected specifically for the potential it offered for children to take the lead role in deciding which play activities they watched and discussed. The films were viewed on a laptop to ensure a flexible approach that enabled the children to choose when, where and with whom they watched the films. The filmed material elicited a range of responses from the children. Sometimes children provided 'running commentaries' as they watched; on other occasions the films prompted conversations with friends and family members. Children also responded through non-verbal modes of communication that often proved to be powerful means of sharing their perspectives of play.

The child's voice: reflecting upon play motivations and meanings

The research focused upon 28 play vignettes, selected by the participating children, which acted as prompts for a total of 63 video-cued responses. The children's verbal and non-verbal responses to their play were recorded and analysed to identify four broad and interconnected themes: identity, possibility, reciprocity and resilience. Each theme embraced a number of sub-themes, but it is beyond the scope of this chapter to provide a detailed examination of each. The following section discusses some extracts from the analysed data that illustrate how the children's perspectives contributed to the identification of each theme.

Identity: play as a bridge between home and school cultures

The children in the study often talked about the connections between their play and their experiences at home. The notion that children draw upon familiar experiences in their play is not new. However, when viewed through the children's perspectives, this notion of play acquires new significance in relation to both the construction and the re-construction of identity within the classroom community.

Craig and the go-kart

Craig is in the block area with three other boys. A large open-framed storage basket has been overturned and the boys place large wooden blocks upon it. One child, Jack, crawls underneath the storage basket and uses a small brick to hammer against the side of the blocks. Craig shouts over to him 'no, don't do that, not there' and uses another brick to begin hammering. A girl from nursery, Casey, comes into the area and watches for a while before adding some more blocks to the top of the structure. Craig pauses his hammering and watches Casey, muttering 'yeah, OK' before continuing his own activity on the blocks. Soon he shouts out 'right tea break time, everybody stop' and the group of children put down their 'tools' that now become mugs from which they swig their tea. Jamie pulls a funny expression, which results in hoots of laughter and further face pulling. Craig runs over to the book area and picks up a large floor cushion, calling over to Jack to come and help him. The two sling the cushion over their shoulders and carry it over to the block area.

An initial reflection upon this observation would quickly identify that the children's play was focused upon using the blocks and other resources to make or fix 'something'. There would doubtless be opportunities to evidence Craig's progress towards the early learning goals. However, listening to Craig's perspectives of the play elicits a much deeper reflection of this episode in which his meanings and intentions become apparent. For example, the film prompted a conversation between Craig and his parents that demonstrates how the play serves as an important bridging activity between his home and classroom cultures. It emerged that Craig's dad, Paul, makes engine-powered go-karts in his garden workshop:

Yeah in terms of what he was doing there, what he says I suppose it comes from that [helping in the workshop]. We go off in a big van to get engines, and those sorts of things he was doing there. I ask him to help me unload the van at the end of the day.

(Paul, Craig's father)

It becomes clear that Craig and his father spend a lot of time engaged in a range of activities connected with making the go-karts. This is an important experience within Craig's life at home and it consequently forms a key element of his identity. Craig's play in the classroom acts as an important context for him to draw upon his funds of knowledge (Moll *et al.*, 1992) and his response enables us to understand that participation in this experience at home has enabled him to acquire significant technical knowledge that he brings to his play:

Craig: Look, I'm with Jack and Blake and Jamie. I'm making a go-kart.
Dad: Oh you're making one? Right.
Craig: Look, Jack put light in wrong place. You have to do it other way. You have to wire and hammer it through that way, look I'm showing him.

From a sociocultural perspective, the play serves as a cultural broker (Walker and Nocon, 2007) that contributes to Craig's sense of belonging within the classroom community. It enables him to participate in activities that carry cultural significance for him and to consequently build a positive sense of identity. In other words, Craig's play enables him to feel that 'it's OK to be me in this place'. As discussed earlier in the chapter, such a sense of belonging is essential for learning because it underpins children's effective participation within the classroom learning community.

It is sometimes argued that play serves to replicate the status quo of the real world by conforming to stereotypical roles and attitudes and hence marginalising or excluding certain children from particular play themes or roles (Grieshaber and McArdle, 2010). However, in this example Craig reflects upon a girl who joins in with the play. This event challenges his previous experiences associated with go-kart building: the world of his father's workroom is very much a male domain. Craig's friend pauses the film when Casey arrives:

Blake: Is that a girl?
Craig: Oh yeah, she's got a ponytail there. Rapunzel hair. Rapunzel's in the garage (the class have been reading *Rapunzel* at story time this week).

At home, Craig pauses the film at this point and muses over Casey's presence with his parents, saying to his mum, 'girls can work in garages'. This stimulates a conversation that enables Craig to reflect upon his play and to consider alternative possibilities: the presence of Casey challenges his experience to date, but perhaps girls can work in garages? We are reminded here of Rogoff's (1990) model of learning, in which both the individual and the cultural environment are transformed through the process of participation. When viewed through this lens, Craig's responses suggest that his views of gender have in a small but significant way been reframed through the play and his reflections upon the experience.

Possibility

The following example illustrates two elements of this theme: first, the exploration of possibilities through open-ended materials; and second, playing with ideas.

Dillon and the spaceship

Dillon and David have used large blocks and crates to build a large enclosure in a corner of the classroom. They have covered the floor with blankets and created seats at the front and back of the enclosure. Dillon uses a small wooden brick as a phone through which he is talking to David.

As they watch the film of their play, the two boys talk about their intentions:

Dillon: Ah, that was my game phone. And it can tell me about aliens and space monsters.

David: Ah yes, you said there was a bomb heading for the spaceship.

David: Here the engine had broken again (the two boys are bending over a corner of the enclosure).

Dillon: Yeah, we were fitting a new jet engine into it. And then it went fast with bombers even chasing it. We turned it back around and went bang bang bang. It went on a while and then the bombers, well they exploded.

Dillon's conversation with David reminds us of the multiple possibilities afforded by playing with open-ended materials. The children's perspectives reveal how they co-construct new meanings through their use of the bricks and blankets and use the resources to transform a corner of the room into a spaceship. Their running commentary was rich in expression – impossible to replicate in print – and reflects their involvement and immersion in the play. Clearly, these children feel confident in exercising their collective agency in relation to the utilisation of classroom spaces and materials. This has resonance with Cremin *et al.*'s (2006) notion of possibility thinking, which proposes that children's sense of ownership of the classroom environment is a prerequisite for creative learning. The 'spaceship' occupied a large area of the room and, when viewed through an adult's eyes, had the appearance of a rather large pile of bricks and fabric. Dillon and David are fortunate to belong to a class in which the practitioners value play, and there are important messages here for the reflective practitioner in relation to the availability and accessibility of open-ended materials and spaces.

Later in the play, Dillon moves more bricks into the spaceship to build a container. David and Dillon fetch plastic food from the home corner and throw it into the container. They periodically bend into the container, sniff and make 'being sick' noises. This is accompanied by hearty laughter from both boys.

Dillon reflects upon this aspect of his play as follows:

Dillon: We were pretending, David and me, that that was a bin and it was a bin that could make more food. But it makes smelly food (laughs).

Researcher: Wow, my bin at home can't do that!

Dillon: It's 'cause it's a spaceship bin.
Researcher: Oh, looks like you're covering it up.
Dillon: Yes, it's to keep the smelliness out of our spaceship.

Dillon's comments offer further insights into the notion of play as possibility thinking and the ways in which children subvert and 'play with' conventional behaviours through episodes of dizzy play (Kalliala, 2006). Play such as this can often be perceived to be of little value and is sometimes actively discouraged, or even seen as misbehaviour, in our classrooms. However, Corsaro (1997) suggests that the playfulness described by Dillon is an important element of children's participation within their peer cultures and hence their capacity to build and sustain relationships. Play as a participatory activity is perhaps sometimes 'taken as read' within our classrooms and not ascribed with particular importance. However, the relational aspects of play were significant for the children, and it is to the theme of reciprocity that the discussion will now turn.

Reciprocity

This theme focuses upon play as a context for relationships, friendships and the sense of togetherness (Van Oers and Hannikainen, 2001) associated with the co-construction of ideas and knowledge. All children in the study viewed these as key elements of play. The filmed episodes of play prompted the children to talk about their peers and, in some cases, to reflect upon the nature of friendship. Furthermore, the children's perspectives enable us to consider Wenger's (1998) notion of engagement within the learning community, whereby play is conceptualised as a collaborative process in which interests are sustained and developed as children participate in shared experiences.

The following example draws upon Lucy's reflections upon her play with water and guttering. The play proceeds as follows:

Lucy's explorations with water

Lucy fetches a box of brushes and takes them over to an area outside in which the practitioners have set up lengths of guttering set at an angle against a low wall. Lucy sits on the wall with her brushes for several minutes until Harry and Pippa appear from inside the classroom. The children begin to talk (inaudible on the film) and Pippa runs over to the tap and fills two buckets of water. Meanwhile, Harry and Lucy each place a brush at the top of a piece of guttering. Pippa returns with the water and the children pour the water into the guttering, causing the brushes to slide down and the water to overflow from the container at the bottom and rush onto the playground. There is much laughter and whooping from the children, and the actions are repeated several times, causing a small puddle to form at the bottom of the playground.

Lucy tells me that she was waiting for Harry and Pippa to begin the play, "cause they were inside working with a teacher'. It seems that this particular episode of play was conceived as a shared experience from the onset and that Lucy had no intention of beginning until her two friends could join her outside. Lucy and Harry continue to watch the play and provide a running commentary of their actions and intentions:

Harry: Lucy look, it's time for the brush to go. I dropped my brush, and then it went down [the gutter].

Researcher: Oh, in there?

Harry: Yes, it went zooming down.

Lucy: Yes, it went too far. It was actually his fault. He shouldn't have poured the water till I'd done it properly. Oh look, the water went all the way down, right down there [to the bottom of the playground]. Yeah, I liked that it went all the way down.

Harry: Yeah, I didn't know that was going to happen.

Lucy: Oh look, I was lifting it up [the gutter] so I could pour the water in properly then I called Pippa, I says, 'Pippa, can you get some more water, please?' We needed it you see for the brushes so I could do that bit.

The children's commentary suggests that their explorations with water are firmly embedded within a social context: it appears that their mutual engagement and shared interest sustain the play, even when there is some minor conflict over the 'rules of the game' that Lucy identifies above when she alludes to Harry being at fault! Furthermore, Lucy hints at a collaborative element when she explains Pippa's pivotal role in the proceedings: it is perhaps important to note that the children swapped roles later in the play, with Lucy ferrying the water and Pippa acting as the 'pourer'. As I watched the film with the children, I was fascinated by the fluidity of the play, which prompted me to ask if the children had played this particular game before:

Lucy: No, that's our first time. But we'll play it again now, we're gonna do it for well, seven weeks.

Harry: Yeah but next we'll tip the whole water out, won't we?

Lucy: Yeah, we're gonna get a lot of water so it goes down there and makes a puddle, no bigger than a puddle actually.

Harry: Yeah, shall we go and play it now, Lucy?

These brief exchanges between players are further evidence of the ways in which children co-construct ideas and consequently bring complexity to their play. The children provide a Zone of Proximal Development for one another in which their joint interest in the flow of water stimulates further play and exploration. Hence, what started as a relatively simple game becomes reframed as a more sophisticated investigation. These children are expert players who are able to engage in collective and collaborative experiences to propel their learning.

Resilience: play and challenge

Resilience is rather a broad theme that embraces a range of dispositions relating to the children's perspectives of play. The children presented insights into how they persist with challenging activities and also into how they manipulate the rules and routines of the classroom environment to fit in with their play priorities. However, the discussion will focus upon a key element of this theme that relates to play and risk.

Holly and the tree stumps

Holly and five other children are outside. They are playing a game in a circle of tree stumps set into the ground. The tree stumps range from 1 foot to 3 feet in height.

Holly explains the game as one in which 'you all jump off the big logs and then you all get back on again, you work your way through till we've all jumped.' The children sometimes wobble precariously as they await their turn to jump, and from an adult's perspective the game could appear too risky for comfort. We live in an increasingly risk-averse society and a corresponding emphasis upon risk assessment and safety within ECCE environments has reduced the opportunities for children to engage in play such as this (Little *et al.*, 2011; Sandseter, 2009). Many practitioners may understandably feel the need for an outright ban on risky physical play, but listening to Holly's perspective reminds us that we often underestimate children's ability to self-regulate their play.

For example, at one point a young child pedals a tricycle into the circle just as James is about to jump. James manages to avoid a collision with the younger child by jumping sideways. Holly pauses the film at this point and turns to James, who is also watching, to say: 'Oh look James, he put you off your jump there, didn't he. No bikes in the circle!' The practitioners confirmed that they had no involvement in the 'no bikes' rule and that the children had introduced it themselves to reduce the potential for accidents. Furthermore, Holly identified additional measures to manage the risk, as demonstrated by this extract taken from a conversation at Holly's home:

Holly:	Can we watch the jumping game?
Researcher:	What's the jumping game, Holly?
Holly:	You know, the one where we have to get on the logs and jump into the middle.
Maggie:	How high are these logs, Holls?
Holly:	Well. Very high. But don't worry, Mum, we can do it. And the little ones, well they jump off the little logs.

Holly's reassuring response to her mum's concern is a powerful example of her own understanding of the risks associated with her play. It appears that the children have developed effective practical measures to exercise their collective agency in risk management without the need for adult control. Experiencing risk is arguably a prerequisite for risk management (Sandseter, 2009) and consequently contributes to building resilience (Gill, 2007). Listening to the children's perspectives on risky play can enable practitioners to reflect upon the strategies that children have developed to manage risk. The boundaries and expectations for physical play thus become less associated with adult control and acquire a new emphasis upon negotiation and respect for children's capabilities.

Focused reflection point

- Before you read on to the next section, think about the key themes of identity, possibility, reciprocity and resilience in play as raised in this research. Can you interpret these for your own practice? What evidence of these have you seen in the children's play?
- Have you ever videoed children's play and then reflected on this when you have some time at the end of the day? What play episodes are occurring that you did not notice at first?

Implications for the reflective practitioner

This chapter began with a consideration of some challenges associated with play in our early years classrooms and settings. It was proposed that an emphasis upon predetermined outcomes and an associated focus upon school readiness have placed limitations on how practitioners understand, and consequently make provision for, play within early childhood education. Listening to children's perspectives on their play can offer alternative readings of play in which the focus shifts from externally imposed targets and goals towards the ever-changing co-construction of meanings, dispositions and identities within the context of the social world of the classroom. The children's responses remind us that play has the potential to be a rich meeting place of ideas in which children draw upon the knowledge and practices of their home and community as they engage in collaborative experiences. The individualised learning outcomes that currently dominate our interpretations of play appear rather grey and uniform in contrast.

I suggest that the observation-based practice that informs our current views of play could be enriched by a wider acknowledgement of the ways in which the perspectives of children and their families can contribute to professional understandings. Such perspectives help us to understand the complexities of children's play and to gain an appreciation of the complex social and cultural contexts within which it occurs. Furthermore, the children's perspectives explored within this chapter remind us that play can be an important context for children to participate in their classroom community and to experience a sense of togetherness and belonging. This requires the reflective practitioner to be mindful of the ever-changing social dynamics of the classroom and to adopt a reflexive approach to notions of power and inequality that impact upon children's playful experiences. Finally, the examples explored in this chapter exemplify some ways in which young children make use of resources and materials to develop and sustain their play. Now read the following focused reflection by Andy Burt to see how he made a difference to outdoor play for the children in his reception class.

Focused reflection point

■ Read the following case study by Andy Burt to see how he reflected on and altered his practice in the EYFS to see the depth of thinking and work involved.

■ Do you find the revelations about open-ended and child-initiated play opportunities in this case study fascinating?

■ What implications are there for your own practice?

What's going on? The challenge of making sense of open-ended play

Andy Burt

As Foundation Stage Leader at Fishergate Primary School from 2005 to 2011, I led a period of intense learning and reflection for both children and staff alike. During this time, the setting developed creative and reflective approaches to resourcing open-ended spaces, often breaking from the traditional areas of provision, and this journey is documented and explored in the text *Understanding Young Children's Learning Through Play* (Broadhead and Burt, 2012). Within this short text, I seek to provide a sense of the power that was evident in the children's increasingly complex use of resources and also to capture some of the challenges and rewards which lay ahead for the staff within the setting. I set out to provide a children's perspective by examining how the children were able to shape and change the resources in order to suit their own needs and ideas and a sense of how the power of this play led to further creative approaches. At a time when many EYFS practitioners continue to reflect upon the complex roles of the adult and the nature of resourcing in EYFS settings, this will provide a timely reminder of the power of open-ended play provision. For our purposes, we will focus on the development of the outdoor play provision at Fishergate and the impact that this had for two young children in particular as they used the resources to create, share and develop their own thinking in increasingly complex ways.

The outdoor area at Fishergate is a partitioned-off area of the larger school playground with a low fence around it. Children access the area throughout the day via a doorway linking it directly to the indoor area. The whole playground is divided by a high wall. For the early years team, this creates opportunities for the children to leave objects and constructions from one day to the next in order to continue and further develop their play. The area was developed greatly between 2005 and 2011 to include large chalkboards, a walk-in sand area, and a wide range of open-ended materials such as tarpaulins of different sizes, car and lorry tyres, large and small crates, wooden planks and a mass of containers and tubing. A variety of art and drawing materials such as paints, brushes and chalks were regularly available.

As these resources were explored and used by the children on a daily basis, staff commented positively on how engaged the children were becoming, and what also became evident was the number of children who were developing a new-found confidence when using the open-ended resources for their own needs. Children engaged closely with one another as they explored and created. On a daily basis, children would be seen to create large constructions and imaginative spaces for their play to continue. This play would evolve over days and also develop rapidly within a short period, often affected by the weather or simple changes to the environment such as puddles, ice or frost. There were many examples of collaborative learning and also powerful examples of the younger children learning as they observed the play of their older peers. The structure of the unit, with nursery and reception children accessing the resources together, meant that each year, ideas, themes and skills re-emerged. In this way, children were often seen to be building upon the ideas and themes of the most skilled children and becoming what we came to term 'master players' in their own right.

As the play became more complex, taking in a range of themes and developing quickly, even within any one session, this posed an increasing number of challenges for the early years team. More traditional methods of planning involving set activities linked to half-termly topics were soon shelved when they no longer reflected the vibrancy or complexity of the current practice. In order to respond and support effectively what they were seeing, the team had to try to unpick the many strands and points of reference within the play. The team became increasingly reflective, discussing key themes and developing ideas for enhancing the play on an ongoing basis. As can be seen in the following vignette, which was filmed, as a student teacher, Kat, engages with two boys at play, these themes were highly complex but provided a fascinating insight into the depth of learning that was taking place.

> Archie and Luke are playing together in the outdoor area. They have made a design by arranging cable reels and crates. A large plastic tube is balanced on one end on the reels. Luke goes inside and returns with a pan and some food. 'On a tea break we can eat one of these,' he says to Archie. Over a number of minutes, the play develops and conversation turns to the topic of telescopes. Archie begins arranging the resources in the design and looks for a few minutes at what was to become their 'telescope'. Archie explains to Kat about his visit to a telescope and how he 'went under it and I looked up through it'. Kat replies, 'Ah, so you want to look up through it' and she moves to the 'telescope' and asks, 'What will we see when we look through it? You might see some satellites' and is clearly thinking about what else might be seen and his past experience.
>
> Following this discussion, the boys set to work on painting their creation, accessing pots of paints and brushes from the indoor area. After a short period of painting, the boys can be seen moving two towers of three stacked crates across the outdoor area. Kat asks Archie where he wants them putting and she helps. Archie places them parallel and quite close together; he asks Kat to lift the tube into the gap between the crates so that the tube remains wedged with a gap above the ground. Once secured, the boys are able to lower themselves underneath the tube to look up. More minutes pass. Kat encourages the boys to think of other ways of supporting the tube and they run off to collect some tyres. As the tyres are added to the construction, guttering and a ramp are added and other children begin to fetch water to pour down it. A builders' tray is placed under the pieces of guttering at the

bottom of the ramp to collect the water. More water is added over a number of minutes and flows down the guttering into the tray. Kat asks Archie how full the collecting tray is. He stammers as he tries to find the words he wants: 'It's not too . . . it's not to the . . . it's not, it's not to the rim.' When he finds the final word he seems to be very pleased with himself, smiling as he looks at the tray of water. The play continues, but Archie is not interested in taking part any more; he is watching carefully as the other children are using his design.

FIGURE 10.1 Open-ended play with boxes.

It is clear from this short piece that the environment and its many possibilities had become a space where children could engage alone or with other children or adults. The familiarity with these possibilities empowered these young learners to create and recreate images, plans and memories. In this example, one of the boys had recently visited a telescope and his experiences and plans become key to this play.

The approaches displayed here require skilled thought and actions by both children and adults alike. The fascinating experience of unpacking the thought processes and motives behind the play often leads to more questions than answers. These questions, though, are extremely valuable for staff development in any setting which works in this way and promotes future planning, further debate and understanding of what has been observed. This intense and complex process of learning for both children and adults alike creates a powerful community of learners. At a time when our schools and settings are required to provide evidence of more clearly defined, measurable learning such as phonics tests, SATs tests and the EYFS profile the danger is that approaches such as those shown here are seen as too complex. As I hope to have shown here, however, the questions and mysteries that make open-ended and child-initiated play opportunities difficult to compartmentalise and measure are what make it fascinating. The playful process remains far more powerful and valuable than any measureable end product.

Summary of knowledge gained

After reading and reflecting on this chapter you should now be very aware:

- that young children engage in complex meanings in their play;
- that observing children's play can make a huge difference to practitioner understanding;
- that it is important for practitioners to reflect upon the social and cultural contexts for play within their classrooms and settings;
- that focusing upon children's dispositions regarding play can be more productive and exciting than emphasising predetermined developmental outcomes.

Challenges for the future

- To further deepen and develop your own understanding of the complexity of young children's play.
- To make time to listen, to watch, to reflect and to analyse young children's play.
- That you will effectively promote children's playful learning in your practice.

Further reading

Broadhead, P. and Burt, A. (2012) *Understanding Young Children's Learning through Play.* London: Routledge.

Brock, A., Jarvis, P. and Olusoga, Y. (2013) *Perspectives on Play: Learning for life.* Second edition. London: Routledge.

Papatheodorou, T. (ed.) (2012) *The Early Years Foundation Stage: Theory and practice.* London: Sage.

References

Adams, S., Alexander, E., Drummond, M.J. and Moyles, J. (2004) *Inside the Foundation Stage: Recreating the reception year. Final report.* London: Association of Teachers and Lecturers.

Anning, A. (1998) 'Appropriateness or effectiveness in the early childhood curriculum in the UK: some research evidence', *International Journal of Early Years Education,* 6(3): 299–314.

Avgitidou, S. (1997) 'Children's play: an investigation of children's co-construction of their world within early school settings', *Early Years,* 7(2): 6–10.

Avgitidou, S. (2001) 'Peer culture and friendship relationships as contexts for the development of young children's pro-social behaviour', *International Journal of Early Years Education,* 9(2): 145–52.

Brennan, C. (2008) 'Partners in play: how children organise their participation in sociodramatic play'. Doctoral thesis. Dublin Institute of Technology.

Broadhead, P. (2004) *Early Years Play and Learning: Developing social skills and cooperation.* London: Routledge.

Broadhead, P. (2006) 'Developing an understanding of young children's learning through play: the place of observation, interaction and reflection', *British Educational Research Journal*, 32(2): 191–207.

Broadhead, P. (2009) 'Conflict resolution and children's behaviour: observing and understanding social and cooperative play in early years educational settings', *Early Years*, 29(2): 105–18.

Broadhead, P. and Burt, A. (2012) *Understanding Young Children's Learning through Play.* London: Routledge.

Bronfenbrenner, U. and Morris, P.A. (1998) 'The ecology of developmental processes', in Damon, W. and Lerner, R.M. (eds) *Handbook of Child Psychology: Theoretical models of human development.* Fifth edition. New York, Wiley, pp. 993–1028.

Brooker, L. (2002) *Starting School: Young children learning cultures.* Buckingham: Open University Press.

Brooker, L. (2010) 'Learning to play, or playing to learn? Children's participation in the cultures of homes and settings', in Brooker, L. and Edwards, S. (eds) *Engaging Play.* Maidenhead: Open University Press, pp. 39–53.

Brooker, L. and Edwards, S. (2010) *Engaging Play.* Maidenhead: Open University Press.

Brooker, L. and Woodhead, M. (Eds) (2008) *Developing Positive Identities: Diversity and young children.* Milton Keynes: Open University with the support of the Bernard van Leer Foundation.

Bruner, J. (1995) 'From joint attention to meeting of minds: an introduction', foreword in Moore, C. and Dunham, P.J. (eds) *Joint Attention: ITS origins and role in development.* Hillsdale, NJ: Lawrence Erlbaum Associates, pp. 1–14.

Carr, M. and May, H. (2000) 'Te Whāriki: curriculum voices', in Penn, H. (ed.) *Early Childhood Services: Theory, policy and practice.* Buckingham: Open University Press.

Carr, M., Smith, A.B., Duncan, J., Jones, C., Lee, W. and Marshall, K. (2010) *Learning in the Making: Disposition and design in early education.* Rotterdam: Sense Publishers.

Christensen, P. and James, A. (eds) (2000) *Research with Children: Principles and practices.* London: Routledge Falmer.

Clark, A. (2011) 'Foreword', in Harcourt, D., Perry, B. and Waller, T. (eds) *Researching Young Children's Perspectives: Debating the ethics and dilemma of educational research with children.* London: Routledge.

Claxton, G. (2002) *Building Learning Power: Helping young people become better learners.* Bristol: TLO Limited.

Cobb-Moore, C., Danby, S. and Farrell, A.N. (2008). '"I told you so": justification used in disputes in young children's interactions in an early childhood classroom', *Discourse Studies*, 10(5): 595–614.

Cohen, L. (2009) 'The heteroglossic world of preschoolers' pretend play', *Contemporary Issues in Early Childhood*, 10(4): 331–42.

Corsaro, W. (1997) *The Sociology of Childhood.* London: Sage.

Corsaro, W. (2003) *We're Friends Right? Inside kids' culture.* Washington, DC: Joseph Henry Press.

Corsaro, W. (2005) 'Early childhood education, children's peer cultures, and the future of childhood', *European Early Childhood Education Research Journal*, 8(2): 89–102.

Cremin, T., Burnard, P. and Craft, A. (2006) 'Pedagogy and possibility thinking in the early years', *Journal of Thinking Skills and Creativity*, 1(2): 108–19.

Dahlberg, G., Moss, P. and Pence, A. (1999) *Beyond Quality in Early Childhood Education and Care: Postmodern perspectives.* London: Falmer Press.

Department for Education (2012) *Statutory Framework for the Early Years Foundation Stage*, Runcorn: DfE.

Duncan, R. and Tarulli, D. (2003) 'Play as the leading activity of the preschool period: Insights from Vygotsky, Leont'ev, and Bakhtin', *Early Education and Development*, 14(3): 272–92.

Dunn, J. (2004) *Children's Friendships: The beginnings of intimacy*. Malden, MA: Blackwell.

Early Education/Department for Education (2012) *Development Matters in the Early Years Foundation Stage*. London: Early Education.

Edwards, S. (2007) 'From developmental-constructivism to sociocultural theory and practice: an expansive analysis of teachers' professional learning in early childhood education', *Journal of Early Childhood Research*, 5(1): 83–106.

Faulkner, D. and Miell, D. (1993) 'Settling in to school: the importance of early friendships for the development of children's social understanding and communicative competence', *International Journal of Early Years Education*, 1(1): 23–45.

Fleer, M. (2005) 'Developmental fossils: unearthing the artifacts of early childhood education – the reification of child development', *Australian Journal of Early Childhood*, 30(2): 2–7.

Fleer, M. (2011) 'Conceptual play: foregrounding imagination and cognition during concept formation in early years education', *Contemporary Issues in Early Childhood*, 12(3): 224–40.

Flewitt, R. (2005) 'Conducting research with young children: some ethical considerations', *Early Child Development and Care*, 175(6): 553–65.

Gill, R. (2007) *Gender and the Media*. Cambridge: Polity Press.

Goouch, K. (2008) 'Understanding playful pedagogies, play narratives and play spaces', *Early Years*, 28(1): 93–102

Grieshaber, G. and McArdle, F. (2010) *The Trouble with Play*. Maidenhead: Open University Press.

Hedges, H. (2010) 'Whose goals and interests?' in Brooker, L. and Edwards, S. (eds) *Engaging Play*. Maidenhead: Open University Press, pp. 25–38.

Howes, C. (2011) 'Friendships in early childhood', in Rubin, K.H., Bukowski, W.M. and Laursen, B. (eds) *Handbook of Peer Interactions, Relationships and Groups*. New York: The Guilford Press, pp. 180–94.

Kalliala, M. (2006) *Play Culture in a Changing World*. Maidenhead: Open University Press.

Lester, S. and Russell, W. (2010) *Children's Right to Play: An examination of the importance of play in the lives of children worldwide*. Working Paper No. 57. The Hague, The Netherlands: Bernard van Leer Foundation.

Little, H., Wyver, S. and Gibson, F. (2011) 'The influence of play context and adult attitudes on young children's physical risk-taking during outdoor play', *European Early Childhood Education Research Journal*, 19(1): 113–31.

Löfdahl, A. (2010) 'Who gets to play? Peer groups, power and play in early childhood settings', in Brooker, L. and Edwards, S. (eds) *Engaging Play*. Maidenhead: Open University Press, pp. 122–35.

MacNaughton, G. (2005) *Doing Foucault in Early Childhood Studies: Applying poststructural ideas*. London: Routledge.

Mayall, B. (2000) 'Conversations with children: working with generational issues', in Christensen, P. and James, A. (eds) *Research with Children: Principles and practices*. London: Routledge Falmer.

Moll, L.C., Amanti, C., Neff, D. and Gonzalez, N. (1992) 'Funds of knowledge for teaching: a qualitative approach to connect households and classrooms', *Theory into Practice*, 31(2): 132–41.

Moran, S. and John-Steiner, V. (2003) 'Creativity in the making: Vygotsky's contemporary contribution to the dialectic of development and creativity', in Sawyer, R., John-Steiner, V., Sternberg, R.H., Nakamura, J. and Czickszentmihalyi, M. (eds) *Creativity and Development*. New York: Oxford University Press.

Moyles, J. and Worthington, M. (2011) *The Early Years Foundation Stage through the Daily Experiences of Children*. TACTYC Occasional Paper no. 1. TACTYC.

Moss, P. (2007) 'Bringing politics into the nursery: early childhood education as a democratic practice', *European Early Childhood Education Research Journal*, 15(1): 5–20.

Moss, P. (2012) 'Readiness, partnership, a meeting place? Some thoughts on the possible relationship between early childhood and compulsory school education', *FORUM*, 54(3): 355–68.

Moyles, J., Adams, S. and Musgrove, A. (2002) *SPEEL: Study of pedagogical effectiveness in early learning*. London: DfES Research Report 363.

Papatheodorou, T. and Potts, D. (2012) 'Pedagogy of early years', in Papatheodorou, T. (ed.) *The Early Years Foundation Stage: Theory and practice*. London: Sage.

Pascal, C. and Bertram, T. (2009) 'Listening to young citizens: the struggle to make real a participatory paradigm in research with young children', *European Early Childhood Education Research Journal*, 17(2): 249–62.

Piaget, J. (1936) *The Origins of Intelligence in Children*. New York: Norton.

Pramling Samuelsson, I. and Asplund Carlsson, M. (2008) 'The playing learning child: towards a pedagogy of early childhood', *Scandinavian Journal of Educational Research*, 52(6): 623–41.

Prout, A. (2000) 'Foreword', in Christensen, P. and James, A. (eds) *Research with Children: Principles and practices*. London: Routledge Falmer.

Rogers, S. (2010) 'Powerful pedagogies and playful resistance', in Brooker, L. and Edwards, S. (eds) *Engaging Play*. Maidenhead: Open University Press, pp. 152–65.

Rogers, S. (2011) *Rethinking Play and Pedagogy in Early Childhood Education: Concepts, contexts and cultures*. London: Routledge.

Rogers, S. and Evans, J. (2008) 'Rethinking role play in the reception class', *Educational Research*, 49(2): 153–67.

Rogoff, B. (1990) *Apprenticeships in Thinking: Cognitive development in social context*. New York: Oxford University Press.

Rogoff, B. (1994) 'Developing understanding of the idea of communities of learners', *Mind, Culture, and Activity*, 1(4): 209–29.

Sandseter, E.B.T. (2009) 'Characteristics of risky play', *Journal of Adventure and Outdoor Learning*, 9(1): 3–21.

Sawyer, R.K. (1997) *Pretend Play as Improvisation: Conversation in the preschool classroom*. Mahwah, NJ: Lawrence Erlbaum Associates.

Tobin, J. (2009) 'Moderated discussion', *Comparative Education Review*, 53(2): 259–83.

Tobin, J., Wu, D.Y.H. and Davidson, D. (1989) *Preschool in Three Cultures: Japan, China, and the United States*. New Haven, CT: Yale University Press.

Van Oers, B. and Hannikainen, M. (2001) 'Some thoughts about togetherness: an introduction', *International Journal of Early Years Education*, 9(2): 101–24.

Vygotsky, L.S. (1978) *Mind in Society*. Cambridge, MA: Harvard University Press.

Walker, D. and Nocon, H. (2007) 'Boundary-crossing competence: theoretical considerations and educational design', *Mind, Culture and Activity*, 14(3): 178–95.

Wenger, E. (1998) *Communities of Practice: Learning, meaning and identity*. Cambridge: Cambridge University Press.

Wheeler, E.J. (1994). 'Peer conflicts in the classroom: drawing implications from research', *Childhood Education*, 70(5): 296–9.

Whitebread, D. and Bingham, S. (2011) *School Readiness: A critical review of perspectives and evidence*. TACTYC Occasional Paper No. 2. TACTYC.

Wood, E. (2010) 'Reconceptualising the play–pedagogy relationship: from control to complexity', in Brooker, L. and Edwards, S. (eds) *Engaging Play*. Maidenhead: Open University Press.

11

Reflecting on school readiness

Avril Brock

School readiness seems to be high on the government agenda and this is a cause for concern for many early years practitioners, trainers, researchers and parents. The issue is not that children are not ready for early education; as can be seen in the previous chapters, early childhood care and education should go hand-in-hand right from the very early years. The issue raised in this chapter is how ECCE is provided for young children that are of an age to enter the formal school system. What is appropriate provision in terms of curriculum and pedagogy for the four- and five-year-olds entering English schools? This chapter and the next will critically reflect on these. This chapter examines the perspectives of policymakers, theorists, researchers and parents; the next chapter presents the perspectives of a reception class teacher who reflects on her quality provision.

Starting school

The majority of young children will commence reception class in school in the month of September as this single annual entry point for all is now mandatory. Yet how many parents know that the statutory school starting date is actually the term after children are five? It is possible to access information about the Schools Admission Policy on the Department for Education website. Parents are able to defer their child's start to later in the year; however, many are concerned about getting a place in their selected school. In March 2013 news headlines demonstrated there would be a distinct shortage of places from September 2013, which may concern many parents as to whether they will get a place for their child at the school of their choice. Parents' prime concern is that their child has a smooth, safe, secure, happy and confident transition into school (Foot *et al.*, 2002; Dockett and Perry, 2005) as well as achieving a good standard of early education. Many parents are very aware that young children learn best in a play-based environment, and probably have some understanding of the EYFS from their child's pre-school education. However, they may also think that their child will benefit from an early start to school as this is the strong message coming from the policymakers. Parents may think that delaying school entry could interfere with their child's friendships, transition and achievement; and furthermore, school attendance can greatly reduce the cost of childcare.

Focused reflection point

■ Reflect back and try to remember your own first days at school. Was the transition from home or nursery smooth for you? Do you remember playing or beginning to read? Compare your memories with those of a friend.

Young children and their families have the right that their chosen ECCE will meet each individual child's needs and promote successful, appropriate and enjoyable learning experiences. Some children may only be four years and a few weeks old on entering school and they will be in a class along with some children who are nearly a year older than they are. At this age a further year of physical, emotional, social and linguistic development can make a significant difference between children in their levels of capability on entering school. Reception teachers need to be fully aware of these differences, the maturation of the children, cultural expectations gained at home and the importance of a smooth and safe transition into school from the ECCE setting.

'School readiness' is a phrase about which most early years sector professionals feel uncomfortable. The early years is a distinct phase of education and should not merely be seen as a stepping stone to 'school' (National Union of Teachers (NUT), 2013: 2). Whitebread and Bingham (2011: 1) observe how there are tensions for ECCE practitioners that 'young children are being measured' against a 'deficit model', a set of inappropriate, one-size-fits-all standards of 'readiness for school'. They scrutinise the phrases of 'school readiness' or 'readiness' for school' that are used with a variety of connotations and find that there is 'a fundamental difference in conception of the purpose of early years education'. They argue 'whether, how and why' children should be 'made ready', stating that the 'significant question is not *whether* a child is ready to learn but *what* a child is ready to learn'. They state that the ability to sit still and take in information is important, but it is by no means the only, or the most effective, way of learning at any stage.

> The main reason that there is such widespread concern about the concept of school readiness in the field is that practitioners and parents understand through their first-hand experience and observations that children's development is very variable.
>
> (TACTYC, 2013)

Focused reflection point

■ How would you define the concept of school readiness? Compare your thoughts with those of a colleague or fellow student.

The full name of TACTYC is the Association for the Professional Development of Early Years Educators, an early years organisation that connects professionals who care deeply about the right of every child to access rich educational experiences in early years settings. The organisation presented their review on school readiness to the House of Commons in November 2012 and followed this with a meeting with Baroness Walmsley in February 2013. The organisation (TACTYC, 2013: 145) has concerns that the early learning goals (ELG) for literacy are set very high and that boys and summer-born children are most likely to find these difficult. Another of TACTYC's concerns is that the new ELG for mathematics has been raised to the level previously described for children in Key Stage 1. Furthermore, August-born children's achievement in the foundation stage profile is significantly lower relative to those born in September and this impacts on their perceptions of self-worth and influences their views on the value of schooling (TACTYC, 2013: 145). It is also argued by TACTYC that the phonics check is having a damaging top-down effect on the curriculum and therefore the morale of many children. Children's school readiness will be assessed at the end of the EYFS, in the final term of the reception year, when children are around the age of five years (Office of Qualifications and Examinations Regulation (Ofqual), 2013: 58). This will be through a newly configured early years foundation stage profile (EYFSP), which includes a new check of children's phonic decoding knowledge at the end of Year 1 in order to provide 'an even fuller picture of "school readiness"' (DfE, 2012: 112). This creates concerns for teachers in the early years, as many children are nearly fluent readers who do not rely on look and say strategies, but decode quickly and focus mainly on eliciting meaning from text. The overemphasis on specific 'desirable' skills for all children that are assessed at a national level regardless of each child's individual development and maturation or level of English language acquisition is worrying. A comparison to other countries internationally demonstrates how not all governments and cultures have the same emphasis.

All this is rather concerning because, as demonstrated in Chapters 10 and 12, young children require a safe, enhancing and supportive environment where they can learn through an informed pedagogy of play. If the focus is so emphasised on getting children 'school ready' what does this particularly mean for children in reception classes?

Four-year-olds in reception classes

The issue of school starting age in the UK continues to be contentious and a matter of concern for many early years practitioners and academics. The concerns about four-year-olds being educated in reception classes began 25 years ago through the National Foundation for Educational Research (NFER) funded research by Cleave and Brown (1987, 1989a, 1989b, 1991, 1992), which raised concerns about teaching methods and curriculum provision. These studies indicated the misgivings about 'the quality of educational experiences offered to 4 and 5-year-old children' and the 'limited evidence for the activity-based curriculum that has been recommended for this age group' (Aubrey, 2004: 633). Continuing research has still not provided any compelling evidence and it is a UK-based assumption that an early starting age is beneficial for children's later attainment or has lasting educational benefits (Sharp, 2002; Adams *et al.*, 2004; Rogers and Rose, 2007). Studies of educational achievement show that children in other European countries, where the statutory school starting age is six or seven, were performing better and actually eventually outstrip English children (Aubrey, 2004; Alexander, 2009; Rogers and Rose, 2007). Whilst an 'early start to education appears to be beneficial', if young children are 'placed in an environment that is not suited to their developmental needs', this can have 'potentially negative consequences' (Rogers and Rose, 2007: 47). Even though young children in England are being educated through the statutory EYFS, the foundations of which were clearly based on a pedagogy of play, the revised EYFS statutory framework seems to emphasise 'teaching and learning to ensure children's "school readiness"' (DfE, 2012: 1). This revised, simpler EYFS is mandatory for all early years providers on the early years register from September 2012, yet what sort of message does it transmit that independent schools are exempt? Rogers and Rose (2007: 47) suggest that the question should not be 'Are four-year-olds ready for school?' but 'Is the school ready for four-year-olds?'

It is rather concerning that the recent research by Moyles and Worthington (2011) found that there still seems to be a lack of understanding about pedagogy of play in some reception classes. This mirrors earlier research findings of Bennett *et al.* (1997), Dowling (2000), Adams *et al.* (2004) and Linklater (2006). Moyles and Worthington's (2011: 1) research observed children's experiences of the EYFS in eight classrooms in varied multicultural schools that had been judged good or above in Ofsted inspections. Whilst the teachers stated that observations of play and learning were of high importance, the researchers actually observed that children spent a third of the day in whole-class situations; a significant amount of time was spent on routine activities (assembly, registration etc.); and there was little evidence of teachers being involved in children's play. Moyles and Worthington stated that their findings mirrored those of the Association of Teachers and Lecturers (ATL) survey in 2004 by Adams *et al.*, which found that 'children experienced "impoverished learning" with little cognitive challenge or meaningfulness for the children' (Moyles and Worthington, 2011: 2). The teachers in the 2010 research largely spent time in managing resources and environment or supervising table activities that had been organised for specific learning outcomes. As in the 2004 survey, play seemed to be something that was left to the children's own devices, with very little teacher/child interaction in play. Moyles and Worthington (2011) found there was a lack of breadth in the curriculum delivery, with teachers using closed instructions, and it was the prescribed curriculum that informed planning and practice.

Focused reflection point

- What are your experiences of reception classes? Reflect on what you remember about practice you have seen.

The first days at school are so important!

A focus on early, didactic instruction is contrary to contemporary research into social, emotional and cognitive development which shows that children's emotional well-being and long-term educational achievement are empowered by their ability to become confident, capable, autonomous learners (Dowling, 2000; Whitebread and Coltman, 2008; Whitebread and Bingham, 2011).

> Deeper understandings of children's cognitive, metacognitive and motivational development, combined with the empirical evidence from research into the characteristics of high quality pre-school provision, enables the distillation of several key 'ingredients' required for an effective pedagogical model of learning and teaching in the early years.
>
> (Whitebread and Bingham, 2011: 3)

In September 2012, I heard a number of disturbing stories about young children's first days in school. Bradley (aged four years two months) trapped his finger on his first day at school in his reception class. This was rather upsetting for him and his mum, but was this as bad as receiving homework during this first week? He had to trace the letter 'a' and put it in a word. 'That's too hard. I can't do it!' cried Bradley, who is normally an enthusiastic, articulate and capable child. Mum was completing his reading homework book by writing what she had read to Bradley, not realising she was supposed to write what he had read himself. Unfortunately Mum must have somehow missed a school meeting and she had no knowledge about the school's policy on homework. She began to get really worried she was not doing things right and had not prepared Bradley for school effectively enough.

Rose and Rogers observed that

> student teachers of young children may be faced with cognitive and emotional dissonance between the content of university-based training on the one hand, which promotes a developmentally appropriate, play-based approach in keeping with the Early Years Foundation Stage, and the reality of pedagogical practice in early years settings on the other.
>
> (Rose and Rogers, 2012: 43)

This was brought home to the editor in October 2013 when PGCE students on their first teaching placement on their university course had been shocked to observe some similar events. Two weeks into her reception class at school Chloe's mum forgot to tick her reading record book, so she was kept in at playtime. Another four-year-old had not conformed in class and was punished by being kept in at playtime and made to read a book. It is hoped that these are exceptions to the norm for our four-year-olds in school, but in 2009 Brock also recorded examples provided by supportive concerned parents who had expressed reservations about the demands being placed on their young children:

> Jake had been so excited about going to school and joining his older brother Cameron. He loved school at first, but six months later he was crying that he couldn't do his writing, it was too hard to get it right. His mum said he set such high expectations for himself and he didn't like to fail.
>
> (Brock, 2009: 133)

What messages are being transmitted to young children about education in school, which should be beckoning young children in and providing success and an excitement for learning? As Anning and Edwards (1999) argue, children are unlikely to feel good about learning and to make academic progress if they are not happy and comfortable. 'School readiness should relate to attitudes and dispositions to learning and not specific targets being met such as phonic knowledge or the ability to operate in numbers up to twenty' (NUT, 2012). Most other countries do not commit their young children to 'formal schooling' until the age of six – what must they think about our educational practice, particularly if they hear stories such as these examples of poor practice? The OECD Starting Strong research (2006) suggests that a 'readiness for school' approach, focusing heavily on young children's cognitive development and the acquisition of specific knowledge, skills and dispositions, is poorly suited for their natural learning processes. 'In countries inheriting a social pedagogy tradition (Nordic and Central European countries), the kindergarten years are seen as a broad preparation for life and the foundation stage of lifelong learning' (NUT, 2012). The ATL does not believe in the concept of 'school readiness'; instead this professional organisation maintains that 'schools should be ready for children, not children ready for schools'; in Scandinavia children do not start school until the age of six or seven (ATL, 2013: 88) and there are clear objectives to forefront the development of children's personal, social and emotional education. Play-led pedagogy enables children to 'develop curiosity about learning, without being strait-jacketed by prescriptive formality' (ATL, 2013). As TACTYC argues, a shorter time in pre-school education may lead to a lack of coherence in young children's experiences:

> Countries with effective provision for early care and education keep children in pre-school for at least three years, which enables staff to provide a coherent programme focusing on the skills that underpin later more academic learning, and the building of secure relationships with families. In this country, early years education is disjointed, and is undermined by the loss of five year olds from nursery settings.
>
> (TACTYC, 2013: 3)

For children to be really 'school ready', they need to be confident emotionally and socially. A child's early years are an important stage of life in their own right and not just a time to get ready for school. In March 2013, the OECD report was welcomed in the UK because children were no longer at the bottom of the league tables for emotional resilience, as had been the case in 2006. However, the UK was now bottom for education. How is this possible when so much funding, policy development and training of teachers in the UK has occurred during the last two decades? For many early years academics the answer is quite simple – in the UK, particularly in England, we make unreasonable demands that *all* children have to meet the same outcomes and demands at a young age. Some young children find learning to read a struggle if they are not developmentally ready and their brain is not yet ready for abstract concepts (Early Childhood Forum (ECF), 2013: 57). If we turn children off education in the foundation stage, year 1 or year 2, then it will be so difficult to re-enthuse and energise their learning from then on in the education system. If children believe they are failing or that it is difficult to succeed in certain demands made by adults in the educational system, they will not become capable, confident learners. All this emphasis on school readiness rather than focusing on individual children's capabilities is rather worrying. Children are individuals with individual dispositions, abilities, attitudes and interests with different family and cultural experiences.

> Deeper understandings of children's cognitive, metacognitive and motivational development, combined with the empirical evidence from research into the characteristics of high quality pre-school provision, enables the distillation of several key 'ingredients' required for an effective pedagogical model of learning and teaching in the early years.
>
> (Whitebread and Bingham, 2011: 3)

The next section will help practitioners determine how to provide Whitebread and Bingham's effective pedagogical model of learning and teaching in the early years and to reflect on what is an appropriate curriculum and pedagogy for the children in their setting.

Curriculum and pedagogy

Curriculum and pedagogy are by no means simple concepts and effective educators will develop professional knowledge about them through building theories, values and beliefs (Brock, 2009). Pedagogy encompasses practice and the principles, theories, perceptions and challenges that inform and shape teaching and learning. Educators use their professional knowledge to mediate national policy frameworks and make informed choices about curriculum design and pedagogical approaches (Wood and Attfield, 2005). The quality of resources, practical experiences and the pedagogical decisions made by the educator all contribute to children's learning and development (Brock, 2009). Educators need to use a broad range of pedagogical skills and knowledge to ensure their provision facilitates children's learning needs and achievements (Bennett *et al.*,

1997; Turner-Bisset, 2001; Siraj-Blatchford *et al.*, 2002; Brock, 2009). Two New Labour government funded projects designed to explore effective pedagogy in the early years were commissioned in 2002. The 'Study of Pedagogical Effectiveness in Early Learning' (SPEEL) (Moyles *et al.*, 2002) brief was to investigate practitioners' perceptions and understanding of effective pedagogy. The components of effective pedagogy according to SPEEL comprise 129 statements within three areas: practice, principles and professional dimensions (Moyles *et al.*, 2002). The findings from this research emphasise that early years pedagogy is an extremely complex phenomenon acquired through training, experience and personal understanding (Brock, 2009). The research raised practitioners' awareness of the complexity of pedagogy and Moyles *et al.* (2002) argue that the respondents' articulation of, and reflection on, practice is key to improvement.

Focused reflection point

■ Did you realise that pedagogy was so complex?
■ What do you think are the key factors that form your own pedagogy for ECCE with the children with whom you work?

The 'Researching Effective Pedagogy in the Early Years (REPEY) study (Siraj-Blatchford *et al.*, 2002) was developed from the EPPE longitudinal research project. The findings of REPEY demonstrate that the most effective early years

FIGURE 11.1 Effective pedagogical strategies involve and enthuse children.

settings 'achieve a balance between the opportunities provided for children to benefit from teacher-initiated group work, and in the provision of freely chosen yet potentially instructive play activities' (Siraj-Blatchford and Sylva, 2004: 716). These research findings indicate that the more effective settings have well-qualified staff, who are able to match curriculum and pedagogy to children to promote cognitive challenges and sustained shared thinking (Siraj-Blatchford *et al.*, 2002). Siraj-Blatchford *et al.*'s (2002) pedagogical framework for early childhood education has four categories of professional knowledge: pedagogical content knowledge is the 'subject' knowledge and awareness of the child's level of learning; pedagogical interactions are face-to-face social or cognitive interactions; pedagogical framing is the provision and organisation of resources, space and routines surrounding teaching; and learning and pedagogical strategies are the social interactions and assessments that support learning (Brock, 2009). Siraj-Blatchford and Sylva (2004: 724) find that 'the higher the amount of good pedagogic practice, the greater was the effect on children's cognitive progress'.

Conclusion

Early years practitioners have to be knowledgeable about managing, delivering and transforming curriculum knowledge into practice through making ongoing decisions about each child's needs (MacNaughton, 2003). Kay (2012: 2) notes how elements of good practice change over time as new ideas, research and development bring new challenges. Practitioners need to be responsive to these and able to make judgements about quality as promoting good practice cannot be achieved by simply following guidelines (Kay, 2012: 9). The next chapter is concerned with what is appropriate, effective and desirable practice for children in their fourth and fifth year of age in a reception class. Tina's pedagogical decision-making and thinking are presented through her reflections on her provision. She justifies what is important for young children's learning in the final year of the EYFS before they enter KS1 and the demands of the National Curriculum.

Summary of knowledge gained

In this chapter you have learned:

- that school readiness is high on the government agenda and is mentioned in various policy documents;
- that the concept of school readiness can have different interpretations for parents, practitioners, the general public and policymakers;
- that developing your knowledge of pedagogy and curriculum into practice needs to account for young children's age, development, interests and previous experience;
- that we make different demands regarding school readiness at such a young age in the UK to those of most other countries in the world.

Challenges for the future

- Develop your knowledge and justify your provision of curriculum and pedagogy.
- Develop the three As of accountability, articulation and advocacy. This is really important if significant others challenge your beliefs about school readiness or if you are asked to provide practice that you think is inappropriate for the children with whom you work.
- Think about your continuing professional development and what training, courses or qualifications you need to develop in the near future.

Further reading

Beckley, P. (2013) *The New Early Years Foundation Stage: Changes, challenges and reflections.* Maidenhead: Open University Press/McGraw Hill.

Brock, A., Jarvis P. and Olusoga, Y. (2013) *Perspectives on Play: Learning for life.* Second edition. London: Routledge.

Pascal, C., Bertram, T., Delaney, S. and Nelson, C. (2013) *A Comparison of International Childcare Systems: Research report for the Department for Education.* Sheffield: Centre for Research in Early Childhood (CREC).

References

Adams, S., Alexander, E., Drummond, M.J. and Moyles, J. (2004) *Inside the Foundation Stage.* Report commissioned and published by the Association of Teachers and Lecturers. London: ATL.

Alexander, R. (2009) *Towards a New Primary Curriculum: A report from the Cambridge Primary Review. Part 2: The future.* Cambridge: University of Cambridge Faculty of Education.

Anning, A. and Edwards, A. (1999) *Promoting Children's Learning from Birth to Five.* Buckingham: Open University Press

Association of Teachers and Lecturers (ATL) (2013) *Foundation Years: Sure Start Children's Centres.* Written evidence submitted by ATL to House of Commons Education Committee. Retrieved 14 April 2014 from http://www.publications.parliament.uk/pa/cm201314/cmselect/cmeduc/writev/852/m19.htm.

Aubrey, C. (2004) 'Implementing the foundation stage in reception classes', *British Educational Research Journal*, 30(5): 633–56.

Bennett, N., Wood L. and Rogers S. (1997) *Teaching Through Play: Teachers' thinking and classroom practice.* Buckingham: Open University Press.

Brock, A. (2009) 'Curriculum and pedagogy of play: a multitude of perspectives?' Chapter 5 in Brock, A., Dodds, S., Jarvis, P. and Olusoga, Y. (eds) *Perspectives on Play: Learning for life.* London: Pearson Education.

Cleave, S. and Brown, S. (1989a) *Four Year Olds in School: Meeting their needs.* Slough: National Foundation for Educational Research.

Cleave, S. and Brown, S. (1989b) *Four Year Olds in School: Policy and practice.* Slough: National Foundation for Educational Research.

Cleave, S. and Brown, S. (1991) *Four Year Olds in School: Quality matters.* Slough: National Foundation for Educational Research.

Cleave, S. and Brown, S. (1992) *Early to School: Four year olds in infant classes.* London: Routledge.

Department of Children Schools and Families (DfCSF) (2008) *The Early Years Foundation Stage.* Nottingham: DfES Publications.

Department for Education (2012) *Statutory Framework for the Early Years Foundation Stage.* Runcorn: Department for Education.

Dockett, S. and Perry, B. (2005) 'Starting school in Australia is "a bit safer, a lot easier and more relaxing": issues for families and children from culturally and linguistically diverse backgrounds', *Early Years: An International Journal of Research and Development*, 25: 271– 81.

Dowling, M. (2000) *Young Children's Personal, Social and Emotional Development.* London: Paul Chapman Publishing.

Early Childhood Forum (ECF) (2013) *Written evidence submitted by Early Childhood Forum to House of Commons Education Committee Foundation Years: Sure Start Children's Centres.* Retrieved 14 April 2014 from http://www.publications.parliament.uk/pa/cm201213/cmselect/cmeduc/writev/surestart/contents.htm.

Foot, H., Howe, C., Cheyne, B., Terras, M. and Rattray, C. (2002) 'Parental participation in preschool provision', *International Journal of Early Years Education*, 10: 15–19.

Kay, J. (ed.) (2012) *Good Practice in the Early Years.* Third edition. London: Continuum.

Linklater, H. (2006) 'Listening to learn: children playing and talking about the reception year of early years education in the UK', *Early Years: An International Journal of Research and Development*, 26: 63–78.

MacNaughton, G. (2003) *Shaping Early Childhood: Learners, curriculum and contexts.* Maidenhead: Open University Press.

Moyles, J. and Worthington, M. (2011) *The Early Years Foundation Stage through the daily experiences of children*, TACTYC Occasional Paper no. 1.

Moyles, J., Adams, S. and Musgrove, A. (2002) *SPEEL: Study of pedagogical effectiveness in early learning.* DfES Research Brief and Report 363. London: DfES.

National Union of Teachers (NUT) (2013) *Written evidence submitted by the National Union of Teachers to House of Commons Education Committee Foundation Years: Sure Start Children's Centres.* Retrieved 14 April 2014 from http://www.publications.parliament.uk/pa/cm201213/cmselect/cmeduc/writev/surestart/contents.htm.

OECD (Organisation for Economic Cooperation and Development) (2006) *Starting Strong II: Early childhood education and care.* Paris: OECD Publications.

Office of Qualifications and Examinations Regulation (OFQUAL) (2013) *Written evidence submitted by OFQUAL to House of Commons Education Committee Foundation Years: Sure Start Children's Centres.* Retrieved 14 April 2014 from http://www.publications.parliament.uk/pa/cm201213/cmselect/cmeduc/writev/surestart/contents.htm.

Rogers, S. and Rose, J. (2007) 'Ready for reception? The advantages and disadvantages of single-point entry to school', *Early Years: Journal of International Research and Development*, 27(1): 47–63.

Rose, J. and Rogers, S. (2012) 'Principles under pressure: student teachers' perspectives on final teaching practice in early childhood classrooms', *International Journal of Early Years Education*, 20(1): 43–58.

Sharp, C. (2002) *School starting age: European policy and recent research.* Paper presented at the LGA Seminar 'When Should Our Children Start School', LGA Conference Centre, Smith Square, London, 1 November 2002.

Siraj-Blatchford, I. and Sylva, K. (2004) 'Researching pedagogy in English pre-schools', *British Educational Research Journal*, 30: 714–30.

Siraj-Blatchford, I., Sylva, K., Muttock, S., Gilden, R. and Bell, D. (2002) *Researching Effective Pedagogy in the Early Years.* London: Institute of Education.

TACTYC (Association for the Professional Development of Early Years Educators) (2013) *Written evidence submitted by TACTYC to House of Commons Education Committee Foundation Years: Sure Start Children's Centres.* Retrieved 14 April 2014 from http://www.publications. parliament.uk/pa/cm201213/cmselect/cmeduc/writev/surestart/contents.htm.

Turner-Bisset, R. (2001) *Expert Teaching: Knowledge and pedagogy to lead the profession.* London: David Fulton Publishers.

Whitebread, D. and Bingham, S. (2011) *School readiness.* TACTYC occasional paper no. 2. Retrieved 17 April 2014 from http://tactyc.org.uk/occasional-paper/occasional-paper2. pdf.

Whitebread, D. and Coltman, P. (eds) (2008) *Teaching and Learning in the Early Years.* Third edition. London: Routledge.

Wood, E. and Attfield, J. (2005) *Play, Learning and the Early Years Curriculum.* Second edition. London: Paul Chapman Publishing.

12

Capable, confident children

A reception class teacher's pedagogical reflections

Avril Brock and Tina Thornton

This chapter interconnects theory, research and policy with the professional thinking of an 'expert' reception teacher's practice. It has been written through a partnership between the editor and Tina Thornton, a reception class teacher in a Yorkshire rural infant and primary school. Tina was highly recommended by the school's Chair of Governors for her excellent practice and provision for early years education. Since 2008 she has been the reception class teacher at Scholes Primary School, Holmfirth and has recently gained a Master's degree. Tina's voice forms the basis of the chapter and we benefit from hearing about her journey of knowledge and her reflective processes as she disseminates her three As of early years reflective practice, 'accountability, articulation and advocacy', as introduced in Chapter 2. The chapter is structured around Tina's eight key aspects of her reception class provision and her thoughts are underpinned with reference to theory and research.

Reflecting on the journey to becoming a reception teacher

The quality of the educators' own knowledge, thinking and decision making is so important and, as Moyles (2001) argues, practitioners need to articulate the complexity of their pedagogy and be prepared to defend, justify and articulate this professional knowledge to varied audiences. Tina's fascination with play began when she became a parent and started reading books on play. Tina had entered into ECCE after having her children and, discovering the exciting world of play, she went to the library to read books on the subject. This had led her to help at a Mums and Toddlers, then to establishing a very successful pre-school playgroup and entering into partnership with a local school for twelve years. She became a teaching assistant and then gained her qualified teacher status on a graduate teaching programme, and after qualifying she applied for her present post as a reception class teacher. All this as a result of following her passion and continuing her journey of finding more and more about a pedagogy of play.

> *I've learnt lots and changed things over the years but one thing I won't change is my pedagogy of learning through play at this age. Absolutely 100 per cent! Play can be defined in different ways and there are lots of different perspectives. My Master's dissertation was on transition to Year 1 and I visited several schools and found that peoples' views are very different and interesting – 'Play is what children do when they misbehave'; 'Play is only when children choose to do what they want.' I think there are several layers of play. I interviewed some older children in school. They say they absolutely loved reception because all they did was play. I told them that they learnt to read and write in reception and they said, 'Oh, we thought we did that in Year 1.' How interesting is that! At first you'd think they didn't value it but when you reflect on it you realise the pedagogy had worked because it had been so fluid and they didn't realise they were learning and acquiring skills because it wasn't onerous for them! So that's what I try to achieve – them learning, enjoying it and challenging themselves. As long as I achieve good outcomes and I can justify my provision, then I am allowed to develop the pedagogy in the way I think appropriate. If someone told me you have to teach how I tell you then I would leave teaching. Honestly, I feel so strongly about it. I could not alter my ideology and not teach through pedagogy of play. I know what these children enjoy and how to challenge them and give them success. It's very child-led.*

This chapter is built upon Tina's thinking on her pedagogical decision-making processes and in doing so it enables you to follow her reflective processes on her practice in her reception class. The interconnection of theory, research and practice provides accountability and underpinning reasons for the development of appropriate provision. Tina has articulated her pedagogical framework for her reception class, and the complexity of the decisions that she and other ECCE practitioners make every day is evidenced. The foundations of Tina's practice are built on her beliefs in teaching through a pedagogy of play and this strongly underpins her teaching and learning provision. The following eight areas are key aspects of provision that Tina particularly emphasised:

1. classroom organisation;
2. EYFS framework;
3. capable thinkers, capable learners;
4. following children's interests;
5. outdoor provision;
6. teaching phonics;
7. managing children's needs: differentiation through teaching and inclusion;
8. planning.

Classroom layout and organisation

When Tina walked into Scholes School she immediately thought, 'This is the school for me. I want to work here.' However, her classroom had not been purpose-built for reception-aged children and the classroom layout required reorganisation to suit her pedagogical framing requirements in order to meet the children's learning.

> There was very little in here. I think it was built as a junior classroom and there were some issues with reception provision and with outdoor play. I started in September and in January, three days after Christmas, Ofsted came and said what would you do to improve provision and I said I would have a door there. The inspector said he would put this into his report and we therefore got a door in by March. It allowed us to have 'proper' free-flow play with children moving inside and outside. It allowed me to do what I wanted to do, which is basically indoor and outdoor provision with children choosing where they want to be and what they want to do. The adults are led by children's play, dropping into their learning but also directing play.
>
> When the children first arrive in school I get them to make a lot of noise and listen to it and then we do it outside. They get to understand that the four walls of a room hold the noise in and it is therefore too much to be loud inside but they can be outside. So we establish the rules.
>
> We all take turns to go outside and we are flexible according to how we feel. We all like to go outside and we all play; we don't just monitor and supervise. My teaching assistants job share and this means I have to be the key person as I am here all week, but having two TAs also means that we have three opinions and perspectives on children's achievements and we have three people to listen to children read. We do individual reading at this age because in guided reading the more confident children can override the less confident, who feel disempowered. They do guided reading in Year 1 when the children are socially and academically ready and do not get left behind. We do shared reading on topics books and finding things out.

FIGURE 12.1   Independent learning in the outside environment.

Reflective commentary

Tina is evidencing how Siraj-Blatchford's *et al.*'s (2002) pedagogical framing involves 'making informed decisions about the structure and content of the curriculum'. Tina demonstrates how she uses a 'wide range of pedagogical techniques and strategies, supporting through teaching, playing, observing and assessing' (Wood and Attfield, 2005: 138). She creates opportunities for children to learn and achieve in whole class, in small groups and in individual situations. Thinking about the principles related to one's beliefs and practice helps practitioners develop their own pedagogical values. In this way an enabling learning environment is provided that will allow children to be independent and pursue their own interests (Basford and Hodson, 2008).

'Early years settings are developed around the concept of "free flow" continuous play provision both indoors and outdoors', with classrooms organised into resource areas to promote choice and opportunity for children to have regular and sustained and independent access to resources (Rogers and Rose, 2007: 86). The provision of continuous provision should be both flexible and stimulating and enable both adults and children to follow their interests and needs (Thompson, 2012: 40). It involves providing suitable furniture, space and floor areas with accessible resources so that children can move around and play on the floor, at tables and outside. This pedagogical approach needs to be based on sound principles and a good understanding of play. Resources and activities should be added to enable children to further pursue their own areas of interest and engage in varied types of play. Knowledgeable, skilful and caring adults promote stimulating and effective learning environments and ensure there is a positive learning ethos. They need to acknowledge and value cultural diversity and equity and match provision to the dispositions and characteristics of the children with whom they work (Rogers and Rose, 2007: 86). First-hand experiences are essential to enable children to make sense of the world, explore, investigate and manipulate resources to find solutions to problems and develop deep understanding.

Tina's provision for her reception class reflects Ephgrave's (2011: 5–6) key principles, which include children feeling safe and confident so that they can explore and play independently. Both Tina and Ephgrave constantly review the provision and layout of their classrooms, inside and outside. Their children are able to select the resources and activities themselves and everything is accessible on a daily basis. Both teachers aim that children's interactions with adults are meaningful and valuable and, as Ephgrave asserts, 'interesting resources can inspire the most reluctant child' (2011: 25) and invite enthusiasm and co-operation with little persuasion. Garrick *et al.*'s (2010: 5) research sought children's experiences of the EYFS through eliciting the voices of the children themselves and found that young children have 'great interest in the rules, boundaries and routines of their settings . . . children were often keen to understand why particular rules and routines were needed'. Tina and Ephgrave have only a few ground rules established to enable the children to have free, safe exploration and to respect each other – they walk and talk indoors and take care of the class resources, inside and outside.

Focused reflection point

- Do you have similar principles for your room layout and organisation?
- If you could make changes what would they be?
- If you are on placement which is the area where you would like to make a difference to practice?

The early years foundation stage

The EYFS allows you to observe children, who they are what they can do. Each class has an iPad and I use mine to immediately record observations. These are then collated against the EYFS statements of attainment on the programme 2Buildaprofile from 2Simple. The 'Characteristics of Effective Learning' are new this year. I think these are brilliant and really should be what we attend to throughout primary school. We report on these to parents. We have them clearly signposted on a wall display outside the classroom so that parents can see what we are doing. I think they are superb; just listen to them:

- *Playing and exploring: engagement: finding out and exploring; playing with what they know; being willing to 'have a go';*
- *Active learning – motivation: being involved and concentrating; keeping trying; enjoying achieving what they set out to do;*
- *Creating and thinking critically: thinking: having their own ideas; making links; choosing ways to do things.*

The Prime Areas of learning and development are:

■ *Personal, social and emotional development: making relationships; self-confidence and self-awareness; managing feelings and behaviour;*
■ *Physical development: moving and handling; health and self-care;*
■ *Communication and language: listening and attention; understanding; speaking.*

The specific areas of learning and development are:

■ *Literacy: reading; writing;*
■ *Mathematics: number; shape, space and measure;*
■ *Understanding the world: people and communities; the world; technology;*
■ *Expressive arts and design: exploring and using media and materials; being imaginative.*

These commitments are so valuable – why would you just enable only young children to achieve them? Don't you think they are highly relevant and important for all children throughout early year and the KS1 and KS2 primary stages?
My advice is to get to know your children really, really well. The EYFS allows you to do that and that's what I love about it. You can interpret it to meet children's needs and so you get the best out of them. The NC is so set – there is less time to observe children – what they can do and who they are. I'm very lucky here as the head teacher allows me to deliver the EYFS through a play-based pedagogy in this way.

Reflective commentary

The EYFS should promote 'a secure foundation through learning and development opportunities which are planned around the needs and interests of each individual child' (DfE, 2012). The EYFS (DCSF, 2008; DfE, 2012) has been informed by the findings of the EPPE (2002) and REPEY (Siraj-Blatchford and Sylva, 2004) research which found that excellent settings provided both teacher-initiated group work and freely chosen yet potentially instructive play activities. Brooker *et al.*'s (2010: 90) research found that practitioners believed that the aims and intentions embodied in the EYFS (DCSF, 2008) statutory framework were fundamental to their practice; viewed as child-led and child-friendly; and confirm a holistic view of children's development and well-being seen to validate their professional beliefs welcomed as supportive. Practitioners found the EYFS to be manageable and it provided continuity. However Roberts-Holmes' (2012: 30) research suggests that, whilst the EYFS served to validate the existing child-led early years approach adopted by most schools, there was a pedagogic tension in reception classes between the child-led play-based EYFS approach and the knowledge-led National Curriculum. Tina has obviously defined her pedagogical approaches to deliver the EYFS in ways that meet both her values and beliefs and the children's learning needs. As Aubrey and Durmaz (2012: 59) observe, reception class teachers do not merely receive and implement policy expectations, but bring their own values and understandings to practice.

FIGURE 12.2   Characteristics of effective learning.

Focused reflection point

■   Are you able to define your pedagogical approaches to deliver the EYFS in ways that meet both your values and beliefs and the children's learning needs?

Capable thinkers, capable learners

Children are not often challenged enough – they are often spoon-fed as they get older. All children can achieve if they are given the right opportunities. I think it is underestimated what children can do. It's easy to do so. If I'm going to be honest I underestimated what they could do through play when I came into teaching. How manipulative you have to be – often when children have older siblings they can gain a low perception of their capabilities when they see they cannot achieve as well as they can. When a four-year-old says 'I'm rubbish at writing', where does he get that perception from? You can't force children to want to write. You have to work round the children and get them to see themselves as a mark maker first and then a writer. You have to get into their psyche.

We usually have an outdoor team group challenge every week. Last week I wanted them to make a working axle. All the resources are available for this outside – big plastic wheels, broomsticks – and the children work in mixed ability groups. They work in different ways and it's really interesting. A leader of the group always emerges and it will be different children and does not rely just on ability. These challenges are brilliant – the best thing ever to watch children and see their capabilities. I just challenge them to get on with it. Last week they had coloured cones and plastic hoops and they had to sort them. One group were just throwing them in whilst another group delegated a different colour to each child, so this group won. The children record their timing using the iPad and they understand how to use it to time the activity. Children can use the computers and are quite adept. They use a digital camera to photograph visible achievements and record their work. They remember who won the week before and why and adapt and apply their thinking to rise to the challenge. It does take up time but eventually they work it out – they think for themselves and they are not spoon-fed.

FIGURE 12.3   Tina at her most expressive.

Reflective commentary

Adult–child interaction is key in supporting children talking, thinking things through, rationalising their ideas and engaging in problem solving in intellectual ways. Scaffolding is one such pedagogy that encourages Siraj-Blatchford *et al.*'s (2002) 'sustained shared thinking' through appropriate interventions (Brock, 2009). Both educators and the children contribute to the learning process, with the adult monitoring interactions and thinking through the discursive processes. Whitebread and Coltman (2008) argue that 'when children are playing they are almost always problem-solving, or investigating, or engaging in various forms of self expression'. They believe that practitioners need to support children's confidence as learners so they feel in control in their environment. In this way they are able to 'take risks emotionally and intellectually', 'to persevere when they encounter difficulties' and so 'cope positively to setbacks and challenges' (Whitebread and Coltman, 2008: 17, 27, 28). They believe it is important to provide cognitive challenge through children being able to self-regulate play and work and develop their metacognition through planning, thinking and talking about what they are doing. Practitioners should consider where activities could be made more challenging and ask open-ended questions that require deeper thinking such as 'Why?', 'What would happen if . . .?' or 'What makes you say that?' Young children are definitely able to be Craft's (2012: 173) 'possibility thinkers' and 'skilful collaborators'. Many young children experience new technological ways of learning as digital technology permeates most homes. Wolfe and Flewitt (2010: 387) observe how children learn through 'collaborative multimodal dialogue' as they 'engage with a range of printed and digital literacy technologies at home and in nursery'. They believe that 'these experiences underpin metacognitive development and are crucial to children's abilities to act strategically in future situations' (Wolfe and Flewitt, 2010: 387). There is no doubt that children are able to be capable, confident learners if they are enabled to have rich play experiences where they can meet challenges, make decisions and enjoy what they are doing.

Focused reflection point

- How do you promote cognitive challenge and children's self-regulation?
- Monitor your questions throughout a morning session – do you ask more open than closed questions?

Following children's interests

We do lead from children's interests, but not totally. We will also include topics and ideas that I think they need to know about. I do not believe in pendulum swings of change of practice and not applying what is appropriate from different theories. You take the best. It's not appropriate to only work from children's interests because as they are only four and five these can be limited. They wouldn't suggest doing Diwali as it is not normally in their frame of reference living in this rural area. So I obviously make decisions. I work from their interests and I drop in all the extras. I've been doing it this way for three years now. I ask the children 'What do you want to learn about next half term?' and we have a vote and do a tally. We start from the role-play area and work from there. I can guarantee when they come back after Easter they will naturally start thinking about living things and this will move on to minibeasts. I've never known young children not be fascinated by minibeasts. They get fascinated by new life after winter. Our Chair of Governors, Cynthia, is making a bug hotel insect house with them using wooden pallets and natural resources.

We've just finished doing castles, because one child who had been to Skipton Castle enthused about it at show and tell. There was a lot of interest as some children had never been to a castle, so we decided to do castles and princesses. This led to history, which is so important to do, as young children's history is what they had for lunch! When we did the Easter story and I said Jesus lived a long time ago, before you were born, it was obvious they had very little understanding of what that meant. We looked at buildings and talked about glass; we made a large castle of cardboard; we had a medieval day with parents, baking sour dough and jousting with bikes and woggles; and we went to Tolson Museum. This then led to travel and visits and airports. A Year 2 class teacher might not find this focused, not being able to have the whole year planned and spontaneously following children's interests, but I love it. I look at the EYFS Development Matters, see what the children have to learn and work out how to do it through their interests. Young children don't compartmentalise their learning. The more open-minded you are the more children will be.

FIGURE 12.4   Now, children, what do we do next?

On Thursday we are having a pop-up planetarium arriving in school. Every class goes in one at a time – it's like being in the universe with planets and I think this will stimulate their next project. Last year a child brought in his small planetarium which stimulated a topic on the solar system. The children's responses and interest opened my eyes. Sometimes a topic doesn't work for long; sometimes only three weeks, not half a term. I would love to do child-initiated learning all the time and work as though a Reggio setting, but I have to live in the real world and in the English system I do not think it is possible as we have to achieve Development Matters. We are due an Ofsted soon and this external pressure inhibits how creative we could be. Jane and I would love to visit the schools in Finland and see how they operate.

Reflective commentary

Following children's interests is often not understood clearly by some observers of early years practice, and it is much more complex than it might appear. It is definitely not a laissez-faire approach, as can be seen in Tina's reflective thinking on her provision. In order to understand what is going on, an observer needs to discover the pedagogical decision-making processes that underpin effective practice. Basford and Hodson (2008: 12) advise that practitioners need to think about arranging the classroom spaces and choosing the learning materials with regard to what will 'enhance the learning environment to support children's' learning and help them make connections'. They propose a blend of:

- adult-led/directed activities involving adult working with a child or group;
- adult-initiated activities where the adult has provided a starting point with a specific learning objective in mind, but children's interests may lead to different outcomes;
- child-initiated activities where a child purses her own interest, selecting resources and activities independently and so takes responsibility for own her learning.

(Basford and Hodson, 2008: 12)

Wood (2010) reflects on the EPPE (2002) findings in her discussions of the pedagogical approaches of adult-led, child-initiated, free and structured play. In her view the EPPE findings can be 'open to misinterpretation in practice and raise questions about whose notions of instruction and whose plans are privileged'. Interventions can be inappropriate for children and their learning and decision making can be interrupted if adults are not in tune with the children's thinking, planning and enacting. Ephgrave (2011: 17) believes that practitioners should not plan ahead for young children as it is important to respond to their interest to gain the full value of their curiosity and engagement.

Payler (2009: 136) found that practitioners who prioritised specific educational objectives and predetermined learning outcomes often controlled the discourse and allowed little time for co-construction. She argues that practitioners should involve children's co-construction in their learning activities. Early years practitioners should reflect on:

- how the ethos and organisation of their settings may be influencing children's meaning making;
- the guidance strategies adults routinely use and why;
- whether these guidance strategies differ according to ethos of setting or for different groups of children according to their ability.

(Payler, 2009: 136)

It can be seen that many theorists, researchers and practitioners believe that a pedagogical framework of teaching through children's interest is both powerful and motivating, but it does require ongoing reflection on the effectiveness of teaching and how well the children respond.

Focused reflection point

- Are you able to follow children's interests?
- Do you do this all the time, some of the time or very rarely and why is this the case?

Outdoor provision

I arranged to have this canopy built and it is amazing! The children can go outside even when it's raining and whatever the weather (or nearly – this excess snow is limiting us at the moment!). Last year I had 18 boys and 12 girls and I would have gone insane without the outdoor provision, because boys in particular need it. I've always known this. I didn't want it to be exactly the same as inside, because you have more space and different options of larger resources. One trend was that outside should mirror inside and again, this is something I reflected on and questioned this advice – why? Some things work both inside and outside such as small world, whereas construction requires more space for the children to expand their creations that is available outside. Behaviour is better and the children evidence clearer thinking when they are outside because there is more space. I decided I didn't want 'toys' outside, I wanted open-ended provision. My husband got us some resources from a construction site – wooden construction, tubes, various guttering. He got a building site sign and the children have to sign in and out of the construction area and they are aware of health and safety.

I did buy wooden furniture suitable for early years which can adapt to different purposes and play activities. I bought mats to sit on and to put them in places where needed for safety. I like the children to assess the risks and decide themselves if they need mats to make things safe. I found an old table and we've pushed the legs into the ground so the children can use it as a stage to stand on or a table to paint on. We've had a digging area that the children started and we followed their interests through getting tools, creating a space, getting topsoil, pallets for a bug hotel. I will bury things in the soil for them to find. We had skeletons, which developed a counting activity to see how many they can find. The provision is open-ended and does not require a product and this enables us to do a lot of observations of what the children are achieving. Ninety per cent of our observations are done outside and you realise the children who have less observations are normally the girls who are reluctant to go outside, so they are directed outside. I do not believe the children can make all the decisions – they are only four and five and how do they know what experiences they are missing if they don't try? But I do respect it if they want to do something inside that they can't do outside.

FIGURE 12.5   Exploring outdoors.

Reflective commentary

According to Bilton (2010), the outdoor environment needs to be treated as you would the inside of a classroom, with activities and resources planned for position, access and purpose with continuous provision and versatile resources. However, Carruthers (2007: 172) reflects on Tina's mention of trends and poses the question: 'should the curriculum be the same outdoors as indoors?' Both observe that the outside is distinctly different from inside. Garrick *et al.*'s (2010: 33) research found that children 'appreciated free and continuous access to outdoor space' and Woonton (2006) firmly claims that if children are given a choice it is where they want to be most of the time. For many young children daily access to an outdoor environment impacts on their levels of well-being (Laevers, 1994) and they need different types of spaces to be quiet and thoughtful as well as adventurous and playful.

According to Parker (2008) the planning of the outdoor learning environment is a dynamic process that has to evolve over time . . . monitoring the play and learning, matching areas to potential development. She believes that 'children relish the grandeur of the problems they need to solve outdoors' (Parker 2008: 113) and she provides rich examples of children's imaginary and exploratory play as they transport resources of leaves, planks and blocks or save the planet as superheroes. Parker's ideas mirror Tina's knowledge and passion for outdoor learning. Children's outdoor play has the potential to support complex narrations as they become pirates on a ship bound for treasure; police officers writing a charge sheet about a robber; firefighters with hoses rescuing a baby from a building; Percy the park-keeper planting vegetables; or Hansel and Gretel escaping from the witch. In the outdoor environment children have more space to develop their imaginative activities based on their favourite television programmes, films or what is happening in the home environment. Conversations with parents, carers and grandparents about what is interesting the child at the present time can enable adults to support the interests, provide relevant resources, and ask challenging questions. (See the case study in the next section about superhero and weapon play for further discussions and ideas.)

> Through constructing the outdoor 'space' as a 'place' embedded with positive meanings, children may have had the opportunity to reconstruct themselves as strong, competent children rather than as 'underachieving' pupils.
> (Maynard et al., 2013: 212)

Maynard et al.'s (2013) research reinforced the importance of private spaces, personal spaces, social spaces and imaginary spaces in outdoor environments for young children. However, Waite (2010: 111, 2011: 65) believes that there is a decline in outdoor provision as many practitioners 'feel tensions through the government's drive for improving standards' and argues that opportunities to learn outside the classroom should be maintained throughout primary schooling. It can be seen that there are multiple benefits of promoting good quality outdoor play environments and the importance of this comes strongly through Tina's reflections.

Focused reflection point

- Are you happy with the outdoor provision in your setting?
- Do you have enough time, space, resources and support to provide what you really want for the children?

Phonics

Jane the Year 1 teacher and I are really interested in the method of teaching phonics. Over the last five years I have played around with it and we've been on lots of courses. We've developed a formula that really works; that's very interactive, fast, pacey and tactile. We do the same routine but the children do something different every day. We go through all the sounds; we introduce new sounds; we practise them, we work on it and apply it; then we think about if we've really learnt it. It's very quick so we continually assess to find out what needs revisiting and then reintroduce it in another way. We did follow the Letters and Sounds programme but then we realised that it was limiting what the children learnt. At first I thought whoever wrote this programme is really knowledgeable so must know better than me. Going on the MA was the one of the best things I ever did because it taught me to question and reflect and ask why do we do it like this? Is there a better way? My children are already doing several alternative graphemes and this morning we did 'ear; ere; eer'. I'm not saying they've all got it but they realise there are alternative spellings and they know how to apply them. So now when they are writing they ask 'which grapheme or which digraph do I use?' I've never considered this before; that they would be so capable. So the children's success with the phonics led me to think about challenge in other areas of provision.

One child, who couldn't even hold a pencil and thought he couldn't do anything, can now write well and is confident in reading. I don't yield to pressures from parents to give children a reading book too soon. The first books that are sent home are pictures only, to encourage speaking and understanding, and I tell parents their children will get a reading book when they can read. They need to be able to blend to read. I have had sight readers enter school but children need a strategy to help them learn new words so everyone does the phonics.

Reflective commentary

The recommendations of Jim Rose's *Independent Review of the Teaching of Early Reading* (Rose Review, 2006) led to the publication of *Letters and Sounds*; a 'high quality phonics resource which encapsulates the reading review recommendations, meets our published core criteria which define a high quality phonics programme, and takes account of the best practice seen in our most successful early years settings and schools' (DfES, 2007). There are many varied responses to the Rose Review. Chew (2006: 119), for example suggests that the review dealt fairly and clearly with important issues and provides the rationale for a literacy teaching approach, which is not only 'scientifically sound but also lively and stimulating for children'. In contrast, however, Rosen declares that by using synthetic phonics as a dominant method of teaching reading, children are deprived of 'a set of strategies with which to manage the vast amount of reading that doesn't fit the simplified system' (Rosen, 2006: 124). Wyse (2006: 126) questioned why such an important subject failed to fully exploit the research evidence because of alleged 'uncertainties'. He goes on to express his concern on the substantial emphasis on synthetic phonics and suggests that there is a danger that 'other equally important practices may not receive the full attention that they deserve' (Wyse, 2006: 127). In his review, Rose declared that:

> the introduction of phonic work should always be a matter for principled, professional judgement based on structured observations and assessments of children's capabilities.

> (Rose, 2006: 3)

However, his report has been taken and interpreted so that 'the phonics programme' has surreptitiously replaced 'principled, professional judgement'. Chew may have been optimistic in her interpretation of the report, but the actual implementation has produced the enforcement of a one-dimensional approach to the teaching of a multi-dimensional process. There are currently many programmes that have been developed to provide direct, explicit, systematic instruction in sound–symbol relationships to help children learn to read, especially those children who experience early difficulty in dealing with print. However, in order to provide the best experiences for children, this practitioner agrees with Torgesen and Mathes, who suggest that activities should be developmentally appropriate, fun and 'limited only by the creativity of teachers' (2006: 27).

This approach has also been reiterated by Rose in the *Independent Review of the Teaching of Early Reading*, when he advocated 'Quality First' phonic teaching through experiences that 'fired children's interest, often by engaging them in multi-sensory activities, drew upon a mix of stimulating resources, and made sure that they received praise for effort and achievement' (Rose, 2006: 16). Currently the DfE still promote best practice when phonic work is 'multi-sensory in order to capture their interest, sustain motivation and reinforce learning in imaginative and exciting ways' (DfE, 2013a).

There are many different factors involved in teaching children how to read, and it could be argued that no single method is applicable to all children on all occasions. However, it is equally important to consider all the methods and understand their possibilities and limitations. Phonics is important in learning to read, and though it is not the only important element, it needs to be given due care and consideration in order for it to meet the needs of every individual child.

Focused reflection point

■ Are you happy with the way you promote phonics in the early years? Discuss this with a colleague or fellow student.

Managing children's needs: differentiation and inclusion

The first term in school is all about transition. Three weeks is a general misconception. Children need skills to be happy, socialise, understand and feel safe and this can take until Christmas. By January they start to fly and to achieve really confidently. We now call differentiation 'managing children's needs'. We had a discussion in a staff meeting on planning and I decided I cannot do this as I differentiate all the time and I have a wide spread of children's ability. So after the meeting I reflected on what I actually do and wrote a paper that addresses how I differentiate through outcome, method, resources, communication time, questioning, vocabulary used and support.

For example 'managing children's needs' in physical development might be during a PE activity in the hall using large apparatus and focusing particularly on vaulting.

When a child jumps off a vault, outcome can be achieving a jump; method is the different ways of getting off the vault and how to improve this; vocabulary will be travel instead of move and vault instead of box; support will be personal finger to direct.

At some point in education someone has compartmentalised children and decided what average children at a certain age can achieve and if they can't they are low ability or SEN and if they are beyond this then they are Gifted and Talented. The programme of study (POS) is for the children who are middle ability and if they are above or below this then the teacher needs to do extra for the children below or beyond. Why bother with a POS – can't we teach all children what they can do when they can do it at the level they are at and then develop each individual from this? I understand that at a certain age the National Curriculum states that they need to know about Normans etc. and that it needs to be standardised so that everyone understands and can be accountable. But I had a child come in one year and was told he needed an Individual Education Plan and I refused to put one in place until I had worked with him and observed him. His preschool said he had been to a speech and language therapist and an occupational therapist and referred to the autism outreach service but nothing had been put in place. I said he will get the same opportunities as everybody else and if I need to do anything different I will give him an IEP. I observed him at school and his behaviour and language were both wonderful and one at a time he was discharged from all the support services. Some of the problem had been a lack of stimulation and low expectations. He requires challenges and high expectations to get him to achieve and this is particularly successful when he is outside and directing his own learning. In one phonics lesson he sat blankly with an empty expression, so I told him he would not be able to play on the bikes (something he really enjoyed) unless he concentrated on the phonics and he said 'oh right' and got on with the work. It was not lack of understanding or cognitive development that was preventing him from learning but his ability to 'switch off' so that he didn't have to comply.

Reflective commentary

Practitioners differentiate through supporting and adapting content, pedagogical approaches, resources, time and learning environment to meet individual needs. The use of ongoing observation and assessment and flexible grouping contributes to young children's success in learning. Practitioners scaffold learning through modelling through specific vocabulary and behaviour, or use support through adults, other children or resources. Differentiation may be by outcome or through setting different learning objectives. Medwell (2010b: 113) suggests that differentiation can occur through presentation, content, resources, grouping, task, support or time and that it is necessary for practitioners to determine what strategies are available and what works for individual children. Bearne (2010: 274) proposes that there is 'no clear consensus of what the term' differentiation implies and that there has been considerable debate about what it looks like in the classroom. She argues that there are 'many links between differentiation and inclusion, but while inclusion is largely concerned with equity in terms of individual rights and curriculum entitlement, differentiation focuses on the management of teaching and learning', including:

- identifying pupil's knowledge, experience, skills and learning preferences;
- planning for a variety of ways into learning;
- classroom organisation for learning;
- using resources;
- response to the outcomes of activities or units of work and assessment of achievement in order to plan for learning.

(Bearne, 2010: 276)

Once a practitioner has decided that a child might have Special Educational Needs (SEN) then she/he needs to follow the graduated approach in the SEN Code of Practice (DfES, 2001). Children are considered to be at the Early Action stage if practitioners are implementing extra or different help that is above and beyond the normal differentiation. Parents need to be informed and an Individual Education Plan or Play Plan needs to be written and shared with them (DfE, 2013b).

Focused reflection point

- If you have a concern about a child's individual needs and capabilities you will need to observe, assess and monitor these, then explore options, elicit advice and gain support. At the time of writing this chapter (April 2014) the government had been consulting on a new SEN Code of Practice and considering replacing SEN statements with 0 to 25 education, health and care plans.
- Do access the following web page to view the draft documents and keep a watch out for future developments: https://www.gov.uk/government/consultations/special-educational-needs-sen-code-of-practice-and-regulations.

Planning

My medium-term planning (MTP) is a list of the objectives they need to cover and they are quite wide to cover the SEN and the more able children. For continuous provision I plan through the activity and main objectives, but there are always more than one so I detail them and I write the focus of our observations and assessment. I love the characteristics of effective learning. They are on the wall so parents can see them and I can direct them to them so they can see what we are doing. All child-initiated activities should have elements of them, as should teacher-directed. We are getting to the stage now where we are concentrating on the children's writing, getting them to understand purpose as well as transcription. At the moment we are doing this through writing letters to the Easter Bunny. They again work in mixed ability groups and they learn to help each other. They understand about spelling and they independently soak up how to do things.

Reflective commentary

All teachers undertake short-term planning and will produce weekly and sometimes daily plans – a short-term plan is the tool for adapting the broad objectives of the medium-term plan (MTP) for the learning needs of the class. Medwell (2010a: 106) advises students that planning can be an onerous task during training, but it is such a valuable experience to enable understanding of provision and how to be accountable. She proposes that the 'cycle of planning, assessment, modification and more planning is the basis for children's learning. It is also the basis of yours!' (Medwell, 2010a: 106). Of course teachers get more experienced and knowledgeable about what they are doing, yet they still do the planning. It is a way of thinking things through to provide coherence, promote progression and to share with the head teacher, governors and Ofsted. It is very common in Key Stage 1 and 2 to find that planning is around a topic with particular subjects clearly labelled in sessions. 'The curriculum planning is to ensure a balanced curriculum, but the need for activities to make sense to the children is more important than the need for labels' (Medwell, 2010a: 98).

Garrick *et al.*'s (2010: 33) research found that whilst 'children's interests were often cited by practitioners as informing their planning', it was often difficult to find clear examples of children being aware of this. Garrick *et al.* (2010: 38) believe that the EYFS could give more emphasis to children's participation in planning activities, particularly as 'children have the right to express their views' and 'staff should recognise the expert contribution children can make'. Their research found that the best practice of 'children informing the planning, delivery and recording of the EYFS occurred where practitioners were able to respond to, negotiate and engage with children's interests sensitively'.

Through reading Tina's reflective thinking, it can be seen how her planning and assessments, her managing of children's needs and following their interests all interconnect in ensuring the children learn, achieve and become capable confident learners.

Focused reflection point

- Compare Tina's planning sheet (Table 12.1) to your own. What would you change?

Conclusion

This chapter has been structured around Tina's eight key aspects of her reception class provision, and her thoughts are underpinned with reference to theory and research. These eight aspects were determined through analysis of the issues she raised in an hour's interview, when Tina talked at length with great passion and enthusiasm for her teaching of young children. We could have determined further aspects of working with parents, assessment, boys' interests etc. but we hope

TABLE 12.1 Early years foundation stage long term planning 2012–2013

Early Years Foundation Stage Long Term Planning 2012–2013
Class: 1 Reception Teacher: Mrs Tina Thornton

1ST Half Term Topic:	Autumn Term	Spring Term	Summer Term
	Intake Assessments/All about me		
Personal, Social and Emotional Development	Class routines	SEAL – Going for goals/Saying no to bullying	SEAL – Relationships
	SEAL – New Beginnings	Chinese New Year (Sun 10th Feb – Snake)	RE: Unit FE – Remembering what is important to us
	Harvest Festival	RE: Unit FC – Special objects	
	RE: Units F – Holy places		
	FA – How to treat others		
Communication and Language/Literacy	See planning	See planning	See planning
Mathematics	See planning	See planning	See planning
Understanding the World (Science, Geography, History, ICT)	Our families, homes and routines	ICT: Using Computers: DB Primary – icons and symbols	ICT: Word Processing 2
	ITC: Intro to computers: IWB	Communication	Recording sounds
	Intro to digital photography		
Physical Development	Spatial awareness/self help skills	Fine motor skills	Games: Outdoor team games
	PE: Unit 1a: Ways of Travelling	PE: Using large apparatus	Dance: Everyday
	Dance (VS): Exploring rhythm	Dance (VS): Do then dance	
Expressive arts and design (Art, Music, D&T)	Self portraits/abstract portraits	Making things	Creating 3D minibeasts
	Music Express: JN to plan	Music Express: JN to plan	Music Express: JN to plan
2ND Half Term Topic:	Festivals/children's interests		Assessments
Personal, Social and Emotional Development	SEAL – Getting on and falling out	SEAL – Good to be me	SEAL – G: Changes
	Diwali (Hindu/Sikh) (Tues 13th November)	Easter Story	Learning journeys
	Hannuka (Jewish) (Sun 9th December)	RE: Unit FD – New Life	RE: Unit FF – Special places
	Christmas/nativity RE: Unit FB Celebrating Christmas		

TABLE 12.1 *Continued*

Early Years Foundation Stage Long Term Planning 2012–2013
Class: 1 Reception Teacher: Mrs Tina Thornton

	Autumn Term	Spring Term	Summer Term
Communication and Language/Literacy	See planning	See planning	See planning
Mathematics	See planning	See planning	See planning
Understanding the World (Science, Geography, History, ICT)	Bonfires & Fireworks	ICT: Word Processing 1	ICT: Assessment
	Autumn festivals as above	Programmable toys	Using Microsoft Photostory
	ICT: Using computers:		Using digital camera to record
	Paint programs		Video
	Using a microwave		
Physical Development	PE: Unit 1b: Ways of Balancing	PE: VS – Gymnastics/Activities leading to games	Games: Outdoor team games
	Dance (VS): Exploring moods & emotions	Dance (VS) Characters and Creatures	Sports day games practice
Expressive arts and design (Art, Music, D&T)	Christmas/Diwali cards, decorations etc.	Exploring different media	Observational drawing/painting
	Music Express: JN to plan	Music Express: JN to plan	Music Express: JN to plan

NOTE: Science topics of our bodies (inc. the senses), materials, living things and their environment and exploring and investigating are fit into themes as appropriate throughout the year.

that the eight aspects we chose have stimulated your interest and prompted you to reflect on aspects of your own practice. You might decide to choose different topics to address, but the challenge is to have a go at deciding your key interests and what you want to reflect on to further develop or improve!

Summary of knowledge gained

In this chapter you have learned that:

- the decisions made as a reception class teacher are complex and many; she/he needs to be accountable and articulate, able to advocate practice to parents, Ofsted, governors and other teachers;
- the quality of the reception class teacher's knowledge, thinking and decision making is important;
- she/he needs to develop a pedagogical framework to meet children's needs and to deliver the EYFS appropriately.

Challenges for the future

Having read this chapter ask yourself the following reflective questions adapted from Broadhead's (2009) research:

- Can you recall four or five instances when things went well in your classroom?
- Can you recall occasions or periods when you felt your practice had changed?
- Can you recall any times when you were experiencing difficulties in your classroom?

Further reading

- A really valuable book to support your practice is Ephgrave's *The Reception Year in Action* (2011), which provides a wealth of exciting activities from a year in her reception class. The children had a wonderful year of learning through pursuing their own interests, achieving highly and becoming confident, capable learners.
- The second edition of *Perspectives on Play: Learning for life* by Brock, Jarvis and Olusoga (Routledge, 2013) presents a range of perspectives on the importance of play.
- You could also read Goouch's book, *Towards Excellence in Early Years Education: Exploring narratives of experience* (Routledge, 2010), which presents the professional lives of two teachers of young children through examining the detail of encounter in their daily practice, demonstrating their playful pedagogy and intuitive practice and what it means to be an exceptional teacher.

References

Aubrey, C. and Durmaz, D. (2012) 'Policy-to-practice contexts for early childhood mathematics in England', *International Journal of Early Years Education*, 20(1): 59–77.

Basford, J. and Hodson, E. (eds) (2008) *Achieving QTS: Teaching Early Years Foundation Stage*. Exeter: Learning Matters.

Bearne, E. (2010) 'Providing for differentiation', Chapter 6.2 in Arthur, J. and Cremin, T. (eds) *Learning to Teach in the Primary School*. London: Routledge.

Bilton, H. (2010). *Outdoor Learning in the Early Years: Management and innovation*. Third edition. London: Routledge.

Broadhead, P. (2009) '"Insiders" and "outsiders" researching together to create new understandings and to shape policy and practice – is it all possible?' in Campbell, A. and Groundwater-Smith, S. (eds) *Connecting Inquiry and Professional Learning in Education: International perspective and practical solutions*. London: Routledge.

Brock, A. (2009) 'Playing in the early years: at liberty to play – not only legal but also statutory!' Chapter 5 in Brock, A., Dodds, S., Jarvis, P. and Olusoga, Y. (eds) *Perspectives on Play: Learning for life*. London: Pearson Education.

Brooker, E., Rogers, S., Ellis, D., Hallet, E. and Robert-Holmes, G. (2010) *Practitioners' experiences of the early years foundation stage*. Research Report DFE-RR029, London: DCSF.

Carruthers, E. (2007) 'Children's outdoor experiences: a sense of adventure?' in Moyles, J. (ed.) *Early Years Foundations: Meeting the challenge*. Maidenhead: Open University Press/McGraw Hill.

Chew, J., (2006) 'Getting phonics into perspective', in Lewis, M. and Ellis, S. (eds) *Phonics: Practice, research and policy*. London: Sage.

Craft, A. (2012) 'Childhood in a digital age: creative challenges for educational futures', *London Review of Education*, 10(2): 173–90.

Department of Children, Schools and Families (DCSF) (2008) *The Early Years Foundation Stage*. Nottingham: DfES Publications.

Department for Education (DfE) (2012) *Statutory Framework for the Early Years Foundation Stage*. Runcorn: Department for Education.

Department for Education (DfE) (2013a) *Draft Special Educational Needs (SEN) Code of Practice: For 0 to 25 years: Statutory guidance for organisations who work with and support children and young people with SEN*. DfE Reference: DFE-00205-2013. Runcorn: Department for Education. Retrieved 14 April 2014 from https://www.gov.uk/government/uploads/system/uploads/attachment_data/file/251839/Draft_SEN_Code_of_Practice_-_statutory_guidance.pdf.

Department for Education (DfE) (2013b) *The National Strategies: Best practice in early literacy and phonics*. Retrieved 14 April 2014 from http://www.teachfind.com/national-strategies/best-practice-early-literacy-and-phonics.

Department for Education and Skills (DfES) (2001) *Special Educational Needs Code of Practice*. London: DfES.

Department for Education and Skills (DfES) (2007) *Letters and Sounds*. London: DfES.

Early Education (2012) *Development Matters in the Early Years Foundation Stage (EYFS)*. London: Early Education.

Ephgrave, A. (2011) *The Reception Year in Action: A month-by-month guide to success in the classroom*. London: David Fulton/Routledge.

Garrick, R., Bath, C., Dunn, K., Maconochie, H., Willis, B. and Wolstenholme, C. (2010) *Children's Experiences of the Early Years Foundation Stage (EYFS)*. Sheffield Hallam University: Centre for Education and Inclusin Research.

Laevers, F. (1994) 'The innovative project: experiential education and the definition of quality in education', in Laevers, F. (ed.) *Defining and Assessing Quality in Early Childhood Education*. Leuven, Belgium: Studia Paedagogica Leuven (Leuven University Press).

Maynard, T., Waters, J. and Clement, J. (2013) 'Child-initiated learning, the outdoor environment and the "underachieving" child', *Early Years: An International Research Journal*, 33(3): 212–25.

Medwell, J. (2010a) 'Approaching long and medium term planning', Chapter 3.1 in Arthur, J. and Cremin, T. (eds) *Learning to Teach in the Primary School*. London: Routledge.

Medwell, J. (2010b) 'Approaching short term planning', Chapter 3.2 in Arthur, J. and Cremin, T. (eds) *Learning to Teach in the Primary School*. London: Routledge.

Moyles, J. (2001) 'Passion, paradox and professionalism in early years education', *Early Years: Journal of International Research and Development*, 21: 81–95.

Parker, C. (2008) '"This is the best day of my life and I'm not leaving here until it is time to go home!" The outdoor leaning environment', Chapter 5 in Whitebread, D. and Coltman, P. (eds) *Teaching and Learning in the Early Years*. Third edition. London: Routledge.

Payler, J. (2009) 'Co-construction and scaffolding: guidance strategies and children's meaning-making', Chapter 11 in Moyles, J. and Papatheodorou, T. (eds) *Learning Together in the Early Years: Exploring relational pedagogy*. London: Routledge, pp. 136–56.

Roberts-Holmes, G.P. (2012) 'Nursery and primary headteachers' experiences of the English early years foundation stage: "It's the bread and butter of our practice"', *International Journal of Early Years Education*, 20(1): 30–42.

Rogers, S. and Rose, J. (2007) 'Ready for reception? The advantages and disadvantages of single-point entry to school', *Early Years: Journal of International Research and Development*, 27(1): 47–63.

Rose, J. (2006) *The Independent Review of the Teaching of Early Reading*. London: DfES.

Rosen, M. (2006) 'Synthetic arguments', in Lewis, M. and Ellis, S. (eds) (2006) *Phonics: Practice, research and policy*. London: Sage.

Siraj-Blatchford, I. and Sylva, K. (2004) 'Researching pedagogy in English pre-schools', *British Educational Research Journal*, 30: 714–30.

Siraj-Blatchford, I., Sylva, K., Muttock, S., Gilden, R. and Bell, D. (2002) *Researching Effective Pedagogy in the Early Years*. London: Institute of Education.

Sylva, K., Siraj-Blatchford, I., Taggart, B., Sammons, P., Elliot, K. and Melhuish, E. (2002) *The Effective Provision of Preschool Education (EPPE) Project Summary of Findings*, DfES Research Brief. London: DfES and Institute of Education, University of London.

Thompson, P. (2012) 'Play in early years education', Chapter 1 in Kay, J. (ed.) *Good Practice in the Early Years*. Third edition. London: Continuum.

Torgesen, J.K. and Mathes, P.G. (2006) 'A basic guide to understanding, assessing, and teaching phonological awareness', in Savage, J.F. (ed.) *Sound It Out! Phonics in a comprehensive reading program*. Boston, MA: McGraw Hill.

Waite, S. (2010) 'Losing our way? The downward path for outdoor learning for children aged 2–11 years', *Journal of Adventure Education and Outdoor Learning*, 10(2): 111–26.

Waite, S. (2011) 'Teaching and learning outside the classroom: personal values, alternative pedagogies and standards', *Education 3–13: International Journal of Primary, Elementary and Early Years Education*, 39(1): 65–82.

Whitebread, D. and Coltman, P. (eds) (2008) *Teaching and Learning in the Early Years*. Third edition. London: Routledge.

Wolfe, S. and Flewitt, R. (2010) 'New technologies, new multimodal literacy practices and young children's metacognitive development', *Cambridge Journal of Education*, 40(4): 387–99.

Wood, E. (2010) 'Working with other adults in the classroom', Chapter 8.2 in Arthur, J. and Cremin, T. (eds) *Learning to Teach in the Primary School*. London: Routledge.

Wood, E. and Attfield, J. (2005) *Play, Learning and the Early Years Curriculum.* Second edition. London: Paul Chapman Publishing.

Woonton, M. (2006) 'Taking risks is vital for providing truly inclusive practice', *Early Years Educator,* 8(3): 23–5.

Wyse, D. (2006) 'Rose-tinted spectacles: synthetic phonics, research evidence and the teaching of reading', in Lewis, M. and Ellis, S. (eds) *Phonics: Practice, research and policy.* London: Sage.

13

Quality is in the eye of the beholder

Developing early years provision using child-led quality indicators

Jo Armistead

Recent debates about what represents high-quality effective early care and education reveal that this is a highly political area. Whilst there is consensus that all children benefit from a period of pre-school education before entering full-time school there is heated debate about what constitutes a relevant curriculum, the nature of the pedagogy and most recently the level and status of qualifications of early years practitioners. I acknowledge the complexity and the importance of the debate but I believe this will not be easily resolved. Meanwhile many thousands of children are attending hundreds of settings and I have chosen to sidestep the national level arguments and concentrate on the local level to consider how current practitioners can develop the quality of their provision from a service user perspective.

In this chapter I will discuss and argue for a way of viewing and developing quality early childhood education from the perspective of children. The chapter is written from a social constructionist viewpoint, which understands early years settings as spaces for children and communities of practice where children and adults both draw and create meaning from the place they share. Places from which unique and distinctive sub-cultures emerge, based on the contribution of children, practitioners and families. It will discuss how, by tapping into this as a resource, the setting can meet the needs of children with the aim of improving the quality of pre-school experiences for everyone involved.

Developing the quality of provision in this way is a reflective and reflexive process. It builds on existing practices of observation and assessment and working closely with children and families to understand children's interests and their learning, often documented as learning stories or journeys. From this rich knowledge of what matters to children, future practice is developed. This approach recognises children's agency within teaching and learning. It acknowledges that children have a critical awareness of the quality of their experiences in early education that they express verbally and non-verbally. I will argue that the skilled adults who work with young children can take responsibility for understanding children's perspectives on the quality of their experiences, and that they can (and do) develop provision to enhance children's learning accordingly. Unlike a universal curriculum framework, designed to ensure a parity of entitlement and minimum standards, child-led indicators of quality experiences are very locally defined, and have immediate relevance to all those taking part.

What do we mean by quality?

Quality is in the eye of the beholder and has multiple viewpoints (Farquhar *et al.*, 1994: 7), so that when early years practitioners reflect on the quality of their provision, it is likely that their thinking will be informed and influenced by one or more views on quality.

When *you* think about quality do you define it as:

- the effective implementation of the early years foundation stage *and* a good or excellent Ofsted grading?
- *or* parents' satisfaction with the education and care of their child?
- *or* children's happiness and enjoyment of their experiences and their progress?
- or perhaps you consider all of these.

In order to develop an argument for children's perspectives to be valued as a primary driver of quality within early years settings, this chapter will examine and critique these three broad perspectives on what represents quality in the early years by focusing on quality in relation to children's experiences.

Quality perceived as the effective implementation of the early years foundation stage

Quality, through the eye of Ofsted, relates to raising educational attainment and achievement. Any discussion of quality provision at setting level needs to acknowledge the accountability of settings to Ofsted through the inspection framework. Ofsted inspections set standards for measuring the quality of learning in early years settings against specified criteria. As part of the inspection process settings are required to self-evaluate to demonstrate the quality and effectiveness of their provision, using the early years self-evaluation form guidance (Ofsted, 2013). Self-evaluation is a reflective activity where practitioners consider how effectively they have met the criteria, identifying areas for improvement to develop their practice and raise outcomes for the children they work alongside. According to Cunningham and Raymont (online, 2008), who reviewed quality assurance practices for the *Cambridge Primary Review*, 'Research indicates that self-evaluation is one of the most promising ways of combining quality control with professional development.'

Settings are asked to report on children's experiences, in particular how well the early years provision meets the needs of the range of children who attend and how well they:

- promote children's learning and development;
- meet the needs of each child who attends your provision;
- help each child enjoy their learning and make progress towards the early learning goals.

(Ofsted, 2013: 7)

When considering the quality of their provision, early years practitioners are required to evaluate the effectiveness of their planning of the learning environment, including activities that help children 'to think critically, play and explore and be active and creative learners' and they must show evidence that they 'have high expectations for children and explain how they enthuse and motivate them' (Ofsted, 2013: 7). Raising overall attainment is a priority for government and settings need to make regular assessments of children's progress, against the norms for their age, with the expectation that they support children to maximise their personal achievements. Practitioners are required to meet the needs of all children, within a culture of inclusion, making learning 'enjoyable' and offering a 'challenge'. They must also work in partnership with children's parents and carers to promote children's learning.

An additional criterion that relates to children's experiences asks providers to evaluate and report on the contribution of the early years provision to children's well-being and how they help children:

- form appropriate bonds and secure emotional attachments with their carers;
- learn to behave well and develop good relationships with their peers;
- develop the characteristics of effective learning.

(Ofsted, 2013: 8)

In the context of their impact on supporting 'children's healthy development', practitioners are asked to reflect on the way their setting promotes secure attachments and how it offers practice that 'ensure(s) children are happy and enjoy what they doing' (Ofsted, 2013: 8). Emphasis is placed on children's behaviour, their ability to cooperate and to become independent. Practitioners need to monitor how well they 'encourage children to explore their surroundings and use their imagination' (Ofsted, 2013: 8) and how they facilitate talk and play amongst children and adults. They also need to consider how their practice enables children to understand 'the importance of physical exercise and a healthy diet' (Ofsted, 2013: 8).

Reflection on this section

Reflecting on the language and tone of the guidance, it appears to be promoting a generic Ofsted message in relation to current thinking about learning and applying this to the youngest learners. More relevant to this discussion, it also sets out the responsibility of practitioners towards young learners. Key phrases in relation to children's early learning are 'thinking critically', 'explore and be active and creative learners', with expectations that practitioners 'enthuse . . . and motivate' and 'challenge' children to 'make progress'. Notions related to well-being include 'appropriate bonds and secure . . . attachments', 'cooperation' and 'independence'. The message is simple and non-controvertible. I would argue that much of what is required of practitioners can now be viewed as self-evident because it represents an understanding of meeting young children's learning needs and values that have a long tradition (amongst many others, Isaacs, 1954; DfES, 1990; Abbott and Rodger, 1994). We may also find that it matches the expectations of children. And we might ask the question, 'Why wouldn't you do all these things?'

The early years foundation stage (EYFS) (DfE, 2012) is the fourth revision of a national early years quality framework in England since the short-lived *Looking at Children's Learning: Desirable Outcomes for Children's Learning on Entering Compulsory Education* (DfEE/SCAA, 1996). Each one has reflected the educational policy culture of the time. It is inevitable that within the 2013 Ofsted document we can detect current policy jargon, for example the requirement to 'challenge' children in their learning; and also current policy priorities, such as the requirement to 'promote talk', that reflect concerns over 'school readiness' and levels of language competence. We can see that, within the quality frameworks, some values stay the same, whilst others are targeted for particular attention depending on the culture and concerns of the time.

A final reflection on Ofsted's view of the quality of children's experiences is that the role of children in their learning is not acknowledged in the Ofsted process. There is an implied assumption that adults lead and direct learning, which many practitioners and all politicians would take for granted, but which should be open to question. However, the self-evaluation guidance prompts providers to report on the views of users of the setting, specifically asking providers for evidence of how you know and use children's views and ideas (Ofsted, 2013: 6). We can see from these four examples from recent Ofsted reports on day nursery settings that inspectors are responding to this requirement in relation to providers making 'improvements' in their settings:

> [T]hey have begun to complete the Ofsted self-evaluation form taking into account the views of children and parents, although this is yet to be fully embedded. Consequently, priorities for improvement are not yet precise and challenging, and realistic targets have not been set.
>
> (Day Nursery Ofsted Report, March 2013)

The nursery has a detailed and shared action plan, which takes account of the staff, parents' and children's contributions. This includes feedback from children's learning and the staff's training needs and prioritises areas to improve as a nursery.

(Day Nursery Ofsted Report, March 2013)

[S]elf-evaluation takes into account the views of staff, children and their parents. Views are sought through regular meetings and one-to-one conversations with staff, and children have opportunities to share their opinions through discussion and group time activities.

(Day Nursery Ofsted Report, April 2013)

They seek the views of parents and children through daily discussions and feedback forms. Team meetings enable practitioners to contribute to the self-evaluation process and their suggestions are considered when making changes. For example, a 'cosy corner' has been introduced to provide children with an area where they can relax.

(Day Nursery Ofsted Report, June 2013)

Whilst settings are completing self-evaluation and involving children in different ways, it is not clear from these reports exactly how children's views are being used to bring about 'improvement'. In the final example, a 'cosy corner' may have been introduced in response to children's contributions, but we can't be certain about this. We can say that Ofsted's view of children's participation within settings is restricted to a consultative approach, a passive rather than an active role. It is likely that the improvements referred to relate to the provision rather than practice with children. This is despite well-established methods for listening to children (Cousins, 1999; Clark and Moss, 2001) that demonstrate their expertise in their own lives and their learning. Later in the chapter we will consider the difference between asking for 'children's views and ideas' and understanding their perspectives on their learning.

Focused reflection point

- What do you do to raise the quality of learning and care in your setting and is it a continuous process that involves practitioners, children and parents?
- What do you think children have taught you about the quality of their experiences of learning and care?

Quality perceived as parents' satisfaction with the education and care of their child

Working in partnership with parents is another well-established principle of early education. Parents are recognised in the EYFS as 'children's first and enduring educators' (DfES, 2007). Settings working within the EYFS will use different strategies to engage with parents and carers to support children's learning and promote their well-being. The EYFS sets expectations that key persons in settings will share information formally and informally with parents, and will invite parents to contribute to their child's learning profile. Beyond this, many settings have developed ways to involve parents, not only organising parents' meetings and open mornings/days to discuss the curriculum and including parents in the development of children's learning stories (Carr, 2005; Carr and Lee, 2012), but also using social media to keep parents informed. In some nurseries Facebook and Twitter are used to offer daily or weekly updates. Within a phase of education where settings are in direct competition in an open childcare market, parental satisfaction is critical for survival. Two recent studies give us some idea of parents' expectations in relation to children's experiences in pre-schools and what they value about their child's setting.

A government survey (Smith *et al.*, 2010: 13) of parents' views of their childcare and early years provision found that 'parents . . . were most likely to choose a childcare provider because of the provider's reputation and concern with the care being given e.g. someone who was affectionate or well trained'. However, there was some variation in parents' reasons for choosing providers of different types. For example, parents were more likely to choose home-based childcare over other providers for reasons of trust and concern with the nature of care given; they often chose nursery schools and classes for the 'educational benefits', and playgroups 'so that the child could mix with other children' (Smith *et al.*, 2010: 13). Most parents of three- and four-year-olds prioritised the educational benefits that the childcare could provide, whilst parents of nought- to two-year-olds were 'more likely to mention trust, concern with care and so the child could mix' (Smith *et al.*, 2010: 13).

Virtually all parents of pre-school children stated that their provider helped their child develop academic skills, such as recognising letters, words, numbers or shapes. Parents thought that reception classes were more likely than other providers to develop academic skills. When looking at social skills encouraged by providers, for instance playing with other children or behaving well, parents believed that these were more likely to be encouraged in pre-school than in school.

In terms of working in partnership with parents, talking to staff was the most common way parents received feedback about their child's progress. It was suggested this was because 'pre-school children mainly attend early years settings that have an educational remit and are thereby expected to offer some formal progress reporting (like schools)' (Smith *et al.*, 2010: 13). Parents of pre-school children said that they spoke to providers about how their child was getting on and the activities that their child had been involved in.

Another small-scale study of transition from nursery to school (Shields, 2009), compared parents' experiences of their relationships with practitioners in pre-school and in reception class. All the parents in the study valued the quality of the relationship with their child's key person in their pre-school setting, and the free access to and closeness to the setting and the staff that they enjoyed at that time.

The study provides some insight into the perspective of the nursery practitioners who were interviewed about their view of working with parents. There is clear evidence of their commitment to this aspect of their work. Shields reports that they believed it was 'central to their role' and the 'biggest part of our role' (2009: 239). They believed they needed to understand the family and the children's interests in order to plan effectively for their learning. They felt that:

> Key workers recognise that good relationships with parents are central to what good practice 'looks like', rather than an add-on to their day-to-day work with children . . . providing daily feedback to parents about their child's day and sharing their enthusiasm for the children's learning.
>
> (Shields, 2009: 240)

The parents' response was equally enthusiastic. One parent commented that their child's key person was 'more like a friend than a teacher' and made nursery 'very homely for us to come. It wasn't just for children, it was for us as well' (Shields, 2009: 241). Another parent commented:

> They were very good at asking you what you wanted your child to work on . . . choosing one or two things and really thinking about that. When you're starting out and you really don't know that much about the development of your child, and they talk to you about what the categories are and what they're working on, it really helps you think through where she is.
>
> (Shields, 2009: 242–3)

Recent Ofsted early years inspection reports (Ofsted, 2013) endorse the importance of effective partnership with parents as a critical aspect of quality provision. Various strategies are mentioned that affect the quality of children's experiences, including:

- Parents receive clear information about the setting and the activities provided.
- Parents . . . contribute to their children's achievement records.
- Baseline assessments, which identify children's developmental starting points upon entry, are completed for all children. This allows a consistent approach in supporting children's needs between home and nursery.
- Parents feel welcomed by staff and have daily opportunities to speak with them and share information.
- The introduction of the parents' evening enabled them to discuss their children's progress and development with the key person, and this was well attended.

Reflection on this section

We can see a high level of agreement in the views and expectations of parents and practitioners. Parents' priorities are for their children to experience being with people they can trust, but they also recognise the importance of good levels of training and providers who are effective in the teaching of early literacy and numeracy skills. In addition, pre-school providers are perceived as helping to develop social skills – the settings provide the opportunity to mix with other children and to learn socially accepted behaviours.

We can also see that though parents value the quality of the relationships their children enjoy with staff in pre-schools, when children are closer to school age they start to consider the effect of the setting on their children's learning. The survey by Smith *et al.* suggests that parents want their children to acquire knowledge and that they share the widely held view that learning is a didactic process of acquiring knowledge imparted by adults. This view is also taken by the parents in Shields' study, for whom close working with their child's key person involved receiving advice and guidance about their child's learning in relation to the 'categories' of the EYFS. There is no doubt that the close relationship developed in partnership with parents is an important criterion of high-quality provision. Practitioners consider the partnership with parents to be the 'biggest' part of their work, and we might ask the question, 'Why wouldn't you work closely with parents?'

Before moving on to consider quality from children's perspectives, what appears to come across in parents' accounts is the unspoken dominance of the EYFS framework within an understanding of quality provision. Children's learning seems not to be valued for its own sake, but in reference to 'baseline assessment', 'activities' provided by adults, or acquiring early literacy and numeracy skills and good social behaviours. Right from the start there appears to be an assumption that children need adults to teach them necessary facts and skills. Children's own contributions to their learning are not acknowledged. That is disappointing as, in the course of writing this chapter, I have been lucky enough to talk to a six-year-old who was able to tell me that sea animals could not have featured in Noah's ark as they would have died out of water; and a two-year-old who told me snails like coming out in the rain; and an eleven-month-old who led his grandmother (me) through his night-time routine without words, guiding me very competently just by pointing and looking. It seems that the critical question to ask about children and our early education system is, 'Why do we unwittingly assume that young children know nothing of any importance?' The final section of the chapter will argue why children's perspectives are central to an understanding of quality provision.

Focused reflection point

- When you give feedback to parents do you identify the child's knowledge about their own life and their independent discoveries of their world?
- How do you respond to parents sharing their insights into their child's learning?

Quality perceived as children's happiness and enjoyment of their experiences and their awareness of their own progress

Over the past two decades an understanding of quality experiences through the eyes of children attending pre-school provision has been developed within both practice and research. A range of studies provide evidence of the competence of young children to participate in the life of their setting. Some of the impetus for research in this area comes from a children's rights agenda – in particular, the rights to be informed and to be consulted on matters that affect children. Article 12 of the United Nations Convention on the Rights of the Child gives children the right to speak out on matters that affect them (UNICEF, 2000).

A corresponding view that recognises the influence children have over their lives has emerged from sociological studies on childhood and the concept of children's social agency. Children are perceived as being active in the social construction of their lives, and those of others around them and the wider society. It perceives children as competent social actors within the social institution of childhood, which is explained as 'an actively negotiated set of relationships within which the early years of human life are constituted' (James and Prout, 1997: 7). Childhood is locally constructed and defined, creating many childhoods rather than one universal model. This is a view that can be understood when comparing one pre-school setting with another; whilst all operate under the same EYFS framework in England, each one is a unique social entity constructed as a result of the social interaction of the children, practitioners and parents, and the complex variables each of these social actors brings to it.

Children's participation in developing an understanding of quality early years provision

In one of the earliest studies to recognise young children's competence to make informed judgements about the quality of their childcare, in Denmark, Langsted (1994) found that five- and six-year-old children demonstrated strong and clear views on the differences between home and group care. They could comment on the different rules and accepted these differences and were able to express what they enjoyed about group care. They had a perception of care that was about children's issues, and not dependent upon the adults' agenda or understanding, though it was affected by these. Langsted concluded that 'it is an advantage to regard children as experts when it comes to their own lives to a far greater extent than has been the case until now' (1994: 42).

A later study involved three- and four-year-old children in the evaluation of their children's centre in London (Clark and Moss, 2001). The researchers developed a multi-method approach that was participative, treating children as experts in their own lives; it was reflexive, including parents, practitioners and children in reflecting on and interpreting data; it focused on children's lived experiences, rather than measures of their learning. Embedded in practice, it aimed to inform planning for children and possible changes in practice.

Children's place as stakeholders in the process of evaluation, alongside parents and practitioners, was made explicit as the purpose of this study. It used a mixed 'mosaic' methodology, including photographs taken by the children to reflect their views, as well as observations and conversations with children. The data generated provided the basis for identifying themes from the study that were the basis of what was perceived to be important to the sample of children in the study. These themes included those that were general and others that were specific to individual children. Children talked of friendships and the change of friends over time; they included adults amongst the people they liked; food and the kitchen and the cook formed another theme. Different activities were mentioned by children; children noted significant spaces and places that were important to them; they voiced concern over conflict between children, and spoke of adults 'tell(ing) people off'. Children expressed feelings about the past and the future, sharing memories of friends or adults who had left and anticipating moving on to school.

These studies generated authentic accounts of children's lived experiences within their pre-schools. They reveal what matters to young children when they are cared for outside their own homes. Their concerns can be recognised by those working with young children as typical of those observed in many pre-schools. A further study, which used Clark and Moss's multi-method 'mosaic' approach, aimed to understand quality experiences in pre-school from children's perspectives (Armistead, 2008). In this study nine main categories of 'quality experiences' emerged from analysing observations, conversations and photographs taken by children. The conversations were used as a method

FIGURE 13.1　A child's view.

to clarify understanding of the meaning children made of their experiences. They focused on explaining a photograph or a sequence of photographs. They also took place to discuss an earlier observation. Other conversations were incidental; chatting with children at lunch or snack time, or discussing a particular space or resource area within nursery. Nine categories emerged from initial analysis and these were refined further into themes (see Table 13.1).

TABLE 13.1 Categories and themes of quality experiences from the point of view of children

Category 1 Relationships

Theme: 1a Adults at my nursery are important

Theme: 1b Other children are important

Theme: 1c Sisters and brothers are important

Theme: 1d Mums and dads and carers are important

Category 2 Rules and routines

Theme: 2a The rules are important

Theme: 2b The routines are important

Category 3 Resources – places and provision

Theme: 3a Places and space outside and inside are important

Theme: 3b The different parts of nursery where I can find things to do are important

Category 4 Food at snack and meal times

Theme: 4a Lunch and snacks are important

Theme: 4b Eating together is important

Category 5 Children's emotions and feelings

Theme: 5a How I feel inside and how I feel about what happens in nursery are important

Theme: 5b Times when I am really enjoying myself are important

Category 6 Play

Theme: 6a Playing with other children and making good friends is important

Theme: 6b Playing and learning things is important

Category 7 Learning and knowing

Theme: 7a Learning and knowing about things and how to do things are important

Theme: 7b Knowing about and understanding other people is important

Category 8 Time

Theme: 8a The time I am in nursery is important

Theme: 8b The time taken for things to happen is important

Theme: 8c Time allowed to do things is important

Category 9 Control

Theme: 9a Being able to say or change what happens in nursery is important

Theme: 9b Not being able to change what happens is important

The categories represent aspects that affected the quality of children's experiences in their nursery setting. They are presented as an interpretation of the perspective of the children in the study and written in the language of children, rather than the jargon of education. They were refined into themes and sub-themes that provided more specific meaning to the categories. Examples of these are presented in Table 13.2 (Theme 1a).

The study aimed to provide evidence that children have a clear understanding of nursery life. They do not use the language of adults to evaluate their experience; however, they are able to make informed judgements about the effect of the experience. Table 13.2 (Theme 1a) provides some insight into the meaning they make of their relationship with adults, and their expectations of the interaction between adults and children. These are high standards to maintain and demand fairness, consistency, respect and kindness.

TABLE 13.2 Theme 1a: Adults at my nursery are important

Subthemes:

to look after me, to know me and to be kind and understand my feelings

to care for and to comfort me

to be fun to be with, to be fair and to understand and accept me as I am

to be there every day and to be the same every day towards me

to trust, respect and make me feel I can do things and be strong

to know about things and to share that with me and to tell me things to help me learn

to know and be known to me for a long time so that I feel happy with the adults who look after me

some grown-ups are more important to me than others and may be my key person

Tables 13.3 and 13.4 provide insights into the meanings children make of learning and their expectation of the learning process and the content of knowledge they will acquire. These require practitioners to be aware of children's interests and the acquisition of skills and understanding. In addition, they demand that practitioners value children's awareness of the process of learning. Practitioners should recognise that children are active and eager to learn, learning from each other, and within the family and community as well as at pre-school. Children expect high standards of practitioners' skills and relevant subject knowledge. Practitioners need to have an understanding of the complex interactions within pre-schools, between children, parents and practitioners to promote children's development across the seven areas of the EYFS.

TABLE 13.3 Theme 7a: Learning and knowing about things and how to do things are important

Subthemes:

I can learn from watching older children and younger children can watch me

I can learn and know about people and the world outside and link this to what happens or what I can find in nursery

I can learn and know about letters and books and reading; and letters and pens and writing; as well as knowing colours, numbers and counting and shapes, and weighing and measuring and things like that

I can learn to do sticking, cutting, drawing, writing, painting

I can learn to pedal a bike, to run, skip, jump and climb

I can learn to use the computer and other things like that

TABLE 13.4 Theme 7b: Knowing about nursery and understanding other people there is important

Subthemes:

knowing who the other children are and that they will help me

knowing who the practitioners are and that they will help me

knowing what is in nursery and where to find it

knowing how to ask other children if you can share the toys or to play with them

knowing what to do and how to do it and that you are allowed to do it

knowing the places and things that are not for children

Children don't talk in the language of Ofsted. However, it is clear that children expect to be 'challenged' in their learning; they 'enjoy' knowing things;

they 'think critically' and want to 'play and explore and be active and creative learners'. They expect to make progress and to develop the skills and knowledge of older children. As we saw earlier, these are the expectations of Ofsted.

Focused reflection point

- Are you aware of the 'expertise in their own lives' of the children you work with and their evaluation of their pre-school experience?
- Tables 13.1 to 13.4 are based on the views of one group of children attending pre-school. Do you feel they mirror the views of children you work with?

Involving children in developing an understanding of quality education and care

Young children's views were not formally sought in the evaluation of services until 2006 (Childcare Act, 2006). As we have seen, in current inspection reports their views are mediated through an adult conduit of consultation. A recent report by Coleyshaw *et al.* (2012) has analysed the impact of early years practitioners (EYPs) listening to children on the quality of early years settings. The report identified three 'stages of implementation' for children's perspectives in the settings they studied and compared the stages with a classification of children's participation and level of involvement identified by Shier (2001).

This model of stages of implementation is useful in helping to understand the graduated responses practitioners make to children's participation. Each stage reflects some interaction between children and practitioners, but only the co-construction stage allows children real influence in the setting.

In their conclusion the authors highlighted the implications of their research for effective practice. They include practitioners having the 'depth of understanding of children's perspectives to develop it as part of a setting's

TABLE 13.5 Stages of implementation

Children's perspectives stage	Characterisation	Compare to Shier (2001)
Choice	EYP's growing understanding of children's perspectives, focused on choice	Children listened to and supported to express their views
Consultation	EYP developing balanced, consultative approach to children's perspectives	Children's views taken into account
Co-construction	Embedded approach which encourages children to own and co-construct improvements in provision	Children involved in decision making and share power and responsibility

Source: Coleyshaw *et al.*, 2012: 21

overall pedagogical approach'. They recognised the importance of leadership to develop 'a common understanding of the children's perspectives amongst staff in order to ensure that it does not become tokenistic or contrived'. It is also felt that leaders need to have 'the capacity to deal with conflicts and tensions between children's, colleagues' and parents' views of quality provision' (Coleyshaw *et al.*, 2012: 25). Practitioners needed to be able to relate children's perspectives with the stages of the EYFS 'in order to create a phased programme that can support children in acquiring the required skills, understanding and attitudes, including the ability to be critical of the provision in their time at the setting' (Coleyshaw *et al.*, 2012: 25). However, this raises the question: is it necessary to teach children the skills of critical evaluation? As evidenced in earlier studies, children are able to make informed judgments about the provision they are in from an early age.

Perhaps, instead of developing a 'phased programme', we should consider the report's 'co-construction' stage, described as an 'embedded approach which encourages children to own and co-construct improvements in provision'. If we are seeking an approach to co-construct the meaning of quality provision with children in settings, methods already exist within current pre-school practices of assessment, using documentation, observations and conversations with children, in the creation of individual learning stories.

I suggest that a co-construction approach can serve several purposes if practitioners view the process and practice of creating learning stories as the basis of their understanding of quality learning and, by extension, quality provision in their setting. Planning for and assessing children's learning is not a separate process from other aspects of their work. Looked at from an evaluative perspective it can be seen to represent quality early childhood education and care. The process of documentation in the children's learning stories includes reflection on observations of preferences and interests, and skills and knowledge acquired, with photographs to reinforce this. There will be notes of discussions with parents, and contributions from parents, as well as the important contributions from the children themselves, reflecting on their learning. I suggest that all these are used as the basis for understanding quality from children's viewpoint.

A further example of co-constructed learning has been described by Anning (2004), writing about a project to develop an early years curriculum through methods of co-construction. It involved a group of practitioners from a range of pre-school settings who were brought together as a community of practice. The methodology required practitioners to collect extensive data of 'logs, field notes, accounts of conversations with colleagues and parents and children's drawings/paintings/models' (Anning, 2004: 63). Anning summarised the findings of the process of synthesising the experiences and understanding of parents and practitioners to create a curriculum model which, amongst other characteristics:

■ acknowledges the importance of the need for intimacy and emotional engagement in the quality of interactions between young learners and their teachers;

- exemplifies the importance of adults working diagnostically from the documented evidence of what children do rather than what policy-makers or politicians think they ought to do and know;
- places playful interactions between children and children and adults (parents and professionals) and children at the heart of effective teaching and learning;
- acknowledges the importance of the social and situated nature of learning; and where the construct of childhood underpinning the model is of active young learners connected to other children and to the adults in early learning settings.

(Anning, 2004: 67)

Whilst Anning's research was not directly focused on assessment practices, we can see parallel activities to those involved in creating and responding to individual learning stories as the impetus for teaching and learning. In addition, in Anning's summary some attributes of quality from children's perspectives identified previously can be identified, such as caring relationships between children and adults, and playful interactions.

In contrast to the assessment of children's learning though the Early Years Profile, as an outcome measure for quality in early years settings, it is more meaningful at setting level to aggregate the individual experiences of children's learning stories to form an understanding of quality through the contributions of all stakeholders. According to Carr *et al.* (2005), learning stories give voice to the child and reveal a previously disregarded perspective of learning that has proved very insightful. They highlight how learning stories rebalance the power relations between children and adults:

> After children are listened to, the power balance tips towards the child. Assessment practice . . . [can imply] that the adult has a pre-set agenda, in which case the power balance tips dramatically the other way – towards the adult. Assessment practices are usually associated with normalization, classification and categorization . . . If we redefine the purpose of assessment as being to notice, recognise and respond to competent and confident learners and communicators, then children's voices will have a large part to play in defining and communicating that learning.

(Carr *et al.*, 2005: 129–30)

In her influential study, Drummond described assessment as:

> a process that must enrich (children's) lives, their learning and development . . . and the way in which, in our everyday practice, we observe children's learning, strive to understand it, and then put our understanding to good use . . . Assessment is part of our daily practice in striving for quality.

(Drummond, 2003: 13)

Her comments add credence to the argument for the relationship between co-constructed assessment practices and quality to be recognised.

Focused reflection point

■ Where would you place your setting on Coleyshaw *et al.*'s stages of implementation of children's perspectives?

■ How do you use learning stories to inform an understanding of quality education within your setting?

Final reflection and discussion

The purpose of the final section of this chapter has been to argue that we should position children's perspectives, and the meaning made by young children of their experiences, as central to an understanding of quality in early years education and care. In order to develop this argument other perspectives were considered in relation to the quality of children's experiences. We have discussed how Ofsted requires settings to self-evaluate against criteria that reflect long-established values and principles of quality practice, developed over time. These relate to the actions of adults to ensure effective teaching and learning, and the well-being of children. Settings also need to report on how they have consulted children on their views and ideas, and how they have used these to bring about improvement in the setting. This acknowledges a basic competence in children that might relate to Coneyshaw *et al.*'s consultation stage. A co-constructive approach doesn't feature in the inspection framework, probably because Ofsted are not interested in the detail of children's experiences in any one setting. They are responsible for the regulation of the setting as a provider of funded early education and care, and they inspect the impact of the practitioners in providing this for children.

We have also seen that parents are concerned with both the quality of relationships and the level of expertise of practitioners in the settings they choose for their children. In Shields' study, both parents and staff placed a high value on working together to support children's learning and well-being. Parents rely on practitioners for guidance and advice on their child's development. Though they welcome contributing to their child's records, it is not clear from either of the studies if parents understand the role of children in their own learning or see their child as having an expert knowledge of their own lives. The notion of expertise is vested in the staff and the EYFS. They judge children's success as measured by their progress within this curriculum framework.

The place of the perspectives of Ofsted and of parents in an understanding of measuring quality is not contested. They are both important arbiters of what is good and desirable practice in early years settings. In recognition of this I posed the questions 'Why wouldn't you do all the things (Ofsted expects)?' and 'Why wouldn't you work closely with parents?' But a further question was asked – 'Why do we still unwittingly assume that children know nothing of any importance?' – which exposes the absence of children's perspectives in the development of quality education.

The final section of the chapter aims to provide evidence that children know much – perhaps *everything* – of what they *need to know* about the quality of their experiences in their pre-schools. Young children can make critical judgements about the activities, the people and the places where they learn and are cared for by adults. In order to translate these into indicators of quality from children's perspectives, children need to work with sympathetic adults, and together co-construct an understanding of their learning. This is an assessment process that involves reflection of all concerned on developing quality through a deep understanding of the social interactions within nursery, and the imaginative use of resources provided to promote learning. Children will influence other children; practitioners will influence children; the influence of parents and the home will be brought into the nursery. The point where this becomes a process of ongoing quality improvement is when the children influence the practitioners. Practitioners open themselves to deepen their knowledge and understanding of how children learn through reflection with colleagues, parents and, most importantly, children. They reflect on observations, conversations and other documentation to understand children's interests, activity and learning to create individual learning stories that represent children's perspectives on their experiences of learning in nursery (Carr and Lee, 2012). Many settings and practitioners are doing this already and are assessing and developing the quality of the provision they offer to children as well as their own pedagogy.

So how do we reconcile the various views on quality and work to develop a child-led quality indicators model within the Ofsted framework? Perhaps we need to consider the difference between Ofsted's requirement to ask '*for children's views and ideas*' and the process of '*understanding children's perspectives on their learning*'. We have seen from Ofsted reports that children's views and ideas appear to be elicited through a consultative process, and there is some evidence that children have an impact on cosmetic improvements to their setting. To move the level of children's participation forward within the Ofsted inspection framework, I suggest that when settings write their response to Ofsted's self-evaluation, they use the documentation of children's learning stories to present evidence of how children have influenced the development of pedagogy in the setting. In this way the power and dynamic of children's learning can be positioned within the Ofsted framework.

Summary of knowledge gained

- Children have clear views on what represents indicators of quality pre-school provision.
- Reflective practitioners can tap into children's expertise in their learning and care.
- Children, practitioners and families can share reflections and contribute to learning stories to record the progress and achievements of children over time.
- Settings can report these as 'children's views and ideas' to Ofsted, as part of their self-evaluation.

Challenges for the future

- Develop your practice to reflect a co-constructive approach to working with children.
- Deepen your understanding of children's awareness of and expertise in their own learning through observation, conversations and shared thinking.
- Co-construct quality indicators for your setting to reflect children's views.
- Provide evidence to Ofsted that children share power and influence in your setting.

Further reading

Anning, A. and Edwards, A. (2006) *Promoting Children's Learning from Birth to Five: Developing the new early years professional.* 2nd edition. Maidenhead: Open University Press.

Carr, M. and Lee, W. (2012) *Learning Stories: Constructing learner identities in early education.* London: Sage.

Isaacs, S. (1954) *The Educational Value of the Nursery School.* London: The British Association for Early Childhood Education.

Shier, H. (2001) 'Pathways to participation: openings, opportunities and obligations', *Children and Society,* 15: 107–117.

References

Abbott, L. and Rodger, R. (eds.) (1994) *Quality Education in the Early Years.* Buckingham: Open University Press.

Anning, A. (2004) 'The co-construction of an early childhood curriculum', in Anning, A., Cullen, J. and Fleer, M. (eds) *Early Childhood Education: Society and culture.* London: Sage, pp. 57–68.

Anning, A. and Edwards, A. (2006) *Promoting Children's Learning from Birth to Five: Developing the new early years professional.* 2nd edition. Maidenhead: Open University Press.

Armistead, J.L. (2008) 'A study of children's perspectives on the quality of their experiences in early years provision'. Unpublished PhD thesis, University of Northumbria.

Carr, M. (2005) 'The leading edge of learning: recognising children's self-making initiatives', *European Early Childhood Research Journal,* 13(2): 41–50.

Carr, M. and Lee, W. (2012) *Learning Stories: Constructing learner identities in early education.* London: Sage.

Carr, M., Jones, C. and Lee, W. (2005) 'Beyond listening: can assessment practice play a part?' in Clark, A., Kjorholt, A.T. and Moss, P. (eds) *Beyond Listening: Children's perspectives on early childhood services.* Bristol: The Policy Press, pp. 129–50.

Clark, A. and Moss, P. (2001) *Listening to Young Children: The mosaic approach.* London: National Children's Bureau.

Cousins, J. (1999) *Listening to Four Year Olds: How they can help us plan their education and care.* London: National Early Years Network.

Coleyshaw, L., Whitmarsh, J., Jopling, M. and Hadfield, M. (2012) *Listening to Children's*

Perspectives: Improving the quality of provision in early years settings. Part of the Longitudinal Study of Early Years Professional Status. Department For Education Research Report
RR239b. Retrieved 17 April 2014 from https://www.gov.uk/government/uploads/
system/uploads/attachment_data/file/183412/DfE-RR239b_report.pdf.

Cunningham, P. and Raymont, P. (2008) *Quality Assurance in English Primary Education*
(Primary Review Research Briefings 4/3). Retrieved 17 April 2014 from http://www.
primaryreview.org.uk/Downloads/Int_Reps/7.Governance-finance-reform/RS_4-3_
briefing_Quality_assurance_080229.pdf

Department for Education (DfE) (2012) *The Statutory Framework for the Early Years Foundation Stage: Setting the standards for learning, development and care for children from birth to five.*
Runcorn: Department for Education.

Department for Education and Employment (DfEE)/School Curriculum Assessment Authority (SCAA) (1996) *Looking at Children's Learning: Desirable outcomes for children's learning on
entering compulsory education.* London: DfEE/SCAA.

Department for Education and Science (DfES) (1990) *Starting with Quality: The report of the
committee of inquiry into the quality of the educational experience offered to 3- and 4-year-
olds* (Rumbold Report). London: HMSO. Retrieved 17 April 2014 from http://www.
educationengland.org.uk/documents/rumbold.

Department for Education and Skills (DfES) (2007) *The Early Years Foundation Stage: Setting the
standards for learning, development and care for children from birth to five.* London: DfES.

Drummond, M.J. (2003) *Assessing Children's Learning.* Second edition. London: Davis Fulton.

Farquhar, S.E., Smith, A.B. and Crooks, T.J. (1991) *Quality is in the Eye of the Beholder: The
nature of early centre quality.* Research Report No.2 to the Ministry of Education. Dunedin,
New Zealand: University of Otago. Retrieved 17 April 2014 from: http://files.eric.ed.gov/
fulltext/ED341504.pdf.

Great Britain. *Childcare Act 2006*: Elizabeth II. London: The Stationery Office.

Isaacs, S. (1954) *The Educational Value of the Nursery School.* London: The British Association for
Early Childhood Education.

James, A. and Prout, A. (1997) *Constructing and Reconstructing Childhood.* Second edition. London: Falmer.

Langsted, O. (1994) 'Looking at quality from the child's perspective', in Moss, P. and Pence, A.
(eds) *Valuing Quality in Early Childhood Services: New approaches to defining quality.* London:
Paul Chapman Publishing, pp. 28–42.

Ofsted (2013) *Early Years Self-Evaluation Form Guidance* (online). Retrieved 17 April 2014 from
http://www.ofsted.gov.uk/resources/early-years-online-self-evaluation-form-sef-and-
guidance-for-providers-delivering-early-years-founda.

Shields, P. (2009) 'School doesn't feel as much of a partnership': parents' perceptions of their
children's transition from nursery school to Reception class. *Early Years: An International
Journal of Research and Development*, 29(3): 237–48.

Shier, H. (2001) 'Pathways to participation: openings, opportunities and obligations', *Children
and Society*, 15: 107–17.

Smith, R., Poole, E., Perry, J., Wollny, I., Reeves, A., Coshall, C., d'Souza, J. and Bryson, C.
(2010) *Childcare and Early Years Survey of Parents 2009.* Department For Education Research
Report RR054.

United Nations Children's Fund (UNICEF) (2000) *The UN Convention on the Rights of the Child.*
London: UNICEF.

Case studies of contemporary issues

At different times during your practice you may need to explore any of the issues raised in this section, which is a key element of this handbook as it presents a range of issues that you may commonly encounter. Some of these you might never find a need to address, whilst others you will meet at varying times during your career. These 'case studies' have been written by a range of ECCE practitioners – some are experienced professionals who provide information drawing on their professional knowledge and experience, whereas other writers are at the beginning of their careers and have written them as part of acquiring an ECCE qualification. The case studies reflect on issues that interest the writers and they present their research, experience and reflective thinking. The case studies aim to develop your knowledge and understanding and invite you to revisit the different issues as and when they might arise in your professional career. In this case you may need to engage in further reflection and deeper thinking through discussion with others, reading further theory and research, accessing relevant informative websites or visits to other settings.

The pattern of each child's life experiences can differ considerably and there is no such concept as the 'average' or 'normal' child, as the variables are too many and too complex. Smith (2009) asks 'to what extent there is a constant core to childhood, whether it is located in the child or in the social processes, which conceptualise and classify the distinctive features of childhood, and how, when identified, these can be balanced with those aspects which are variable and reflect wider social diversities' (Smith in Brock, 2011: 7). How do we develop key aspects of young children's learning and development? What is important about outdoor play, acquiring knowledge of phonics, or using IT? Some children have to cope with serious incidents that affect themselves and their families. How do we, as ECCE practitioners, support young children and their families and help them develop resilience through individual critical incidences that may affect them, such as bereavement, mental health issues or safeguarding?

In order to address some of the critical questions and issues this part of the book has been organised into three sections, in which each issue is considered in a 'case study', a phrase used in its broadest sense, encompassing actual case studies; real or created scenarios; examples of reflective practice; and reflective thinking and writing on an issue. They will not necessarily give the 'right' solutions because each situation, each child, each family and each practitioner is different and will have different experiences and demands, and this is where reflection comes into its own. It is only through interacting with concepts, situations and issues, through debating advantages, problems and possible outcomes with oneself, colleagues, critical friends, research and theory (depending on the complexity and the level of the issue) that you will then feel comfortable that you have undertaken appropriate interaction and reflection. You may not necessarily get the most opportune outcome (because that might be debatable from someone else's perspective) but you will have attempted to arrive at the correct outcome.

Section 1: What's it like for a child?

Why are my friends so important? Avril Brock

What's it like for a black child in the classroom? Gina Houston

Why are my stories so important to me? Avril Brock

Adyta – the silent period, as experienced by young bilingual learners. Caroline Bligh

What is it like for a child living with violence? Naomi Lewis

What is it like for a bereaved child? Avril Brock

Section 2: How can I develop my professional knowledge and practice?

How can I cater for children's individuality? Rachel Sparks Linfield

How do I develop children's understanding of the concept of time? Lyndsey Shipley

Communication using new technologies – the tip of the iceberg. Alix Coughlin

What should I do about young children's gun play? Rachel Marshall, Nicola Milton, Paula Render and Jennifer Smith

Reflecting on the process of learning how to teach reading using systematic synthetic phonics. Bev Keen

How do I observe and assess children's capabilities? Avril Brock

Section 3: Widening reflective professional knowledge: what do I need to know about this issue and why is it important?

Dealing with racist incidents. Gina Houston

How can an early years setting support the mental health of young children and why is this important? Lucy Akroyd

How to support asylum and refugee children in early years education. Rebecca Wood

Does bullying really happen in early years? Melanie Henderson

Children with parents in prison. Avril Brock

Reference

Brock, A. (2011) 'The child in context: policy and provision', Chapter 1 in Brock, A. and Rankin, C. (eds) *Professionalism in the Early Years Interdisciplinary Team: Supporting young children and their families*. London: Continuum.

What's it like for a child?

Why are my friends so important?

Avril Brock

James is my best friend – he's my cousin. Oscar Morris, Giles Munro, Jason Smith, Emily Paxton, Charlene Jennings, Winston Bussey are my best friends at nursery. I play Mike the Knight with them. I like horses – they're my favourite.

(Oscar aged 2 years 9 months)

Certainly there is much to be gained by observing children and taking note of their friendships, who they work and play with most effectively and enjoyably and how this makes a difference to each child's emotional well-being. Oscar could recognise his friends in day-care before he was one and he talked about and named his friends from the age of two. How important is this notion of young children's friendships for early years practitioners – is it a relevant issue

FIGURE cs.1 Best of friends on a mission.

that should be taken account of in educational provision? A teacher of six-year-old children was quite dismissive about the importance of friends for children and believed that the children in her class were too young to form friendships! Is this really true – what was her definition of friendship? What is your view? This case study argues that friends are incredibly important to young children and they can develop both their desire for friends and concept about friendship from a very young age.

The UK Children's Society *Good Childhood Inquiry* (2007) gathered evidence from almost 3,000 sources, including 1,200 children. 'Friendship' was the first of the six themes, along with family, health, learning, lifestyles and values, and the findings identified that from the age of two years onwards, friendship is very important for children, both for their social and emotional development and for their sense of well-being (Brock, 2011 in Brock and Rankin). This independent inquiry found that:

> Adults often underestimate the importance of friendship for children, and how friends help them to adjust to school, the arrival of new siblings and the experience of being bullied . . . being separated from friends is often a deeply unhappy experience for children and can result in poorer mental health.
>
> (Children's Society, 2007)

The IPSOS MORI UNICEF (2011) research on child well-being, inequality and materialism asked children 'What makes you happy?' and found the answers to be spending time with people they love (friends, family and pets), being outdoors and doing fun activities, and that problems at home, fights with friends, being bullied, and being bored and stuck indoors make children unhappy.

Young children's friendships are formed through family connections or in ECCE settings. Young children do talk about the importance of playing with their friends and they develop a sense of identity and belonging through sharing experiences as they play. Three is the age when most children's social skills get better and real friends start to be possible, and friendly children have an early advantage. 'Children who create new, imaginative and amusing versions of games or who are good humoured and funny should have no trouble making friends' and 'the average three-year-old can find up to 400 things to laugh at every day' (Livingstone, 2004: 284). Yet not all children have learnt to negotiate relationships and establish friendships and the school playground can be a socially isolating environment (Ledger *et al.*, 2000). Parents can be concerned about children's transition into school regarding whether they will establish friendships and be accepted (Fabian, 2002).

Friendship lies at the heart of a happy, fulfilled life. Research suggests that the complex skills of friendship have their roots in the early years, when children encounter a wider social circle and establish relationships with peers that are mediated by their parents/carers. Habits of behaviour and understanding established in these earliest friendships form the pattern for relationships in adult life (Slater and Bremner, 2003: 326). Children are social animals and they gain:

- support through their friends and the groups they encounter in family groups and in the ECCE setting;
- self-esteem mirrored through significant others;
- shared preferences, likes and experiences creating bonds of friendship;
- enhanced emotional intelligence through being with significant others;
- feelings of safety when there is shared thinking;
- shared understandings and knowledge that improve the quality of life experiences;
- shared laughter, humour and fun that promotes emotional well-being and reduces stress levels;
- re-experiencing and reflection on enjoyable or problem experiences through reminiscing with a friend.

The EYFS (DfE, 2012) provides information about the stages of social development and what practitioners should be observing – such as that babies between 8 and 10 months show pleasure at seeing their friends and will offer toys; at 12 to 18 months they will begin to share but also fight over toys, for space and for attention; by three they will engage in pretend play together and engage in co-operative play, problem solving and role reversal.

> It is at this stage where children learn the power to hurt each other by ignoring another and pretending the other does not exist. By the age of five, children should have all of the basics of friendships. This stage marks the beginning of the give-and-take of reciprocal play and the ability to solve conflicts with each other.
>
> (Emery and Huitt, 2002: 6)

Judy Dunn is perhaps the most significant researcher into children's friendships and in her research (2004) she argues that our understanding of a child's development can be greatly enhanced by studying children's friendships, as friendship can greatly influence a child's behaviour. She believes it is valuable for practitioners and parents to develop their own understandings to help manage children's friendships at different developmental stages and to help children who might have friendship difficulties. However, Dunn believed that children were not able to discuss friendship effectively. Her research focused on observations of children, whereas Olusoga and Brock's (2005) research elicited the voices of children themselves in three different early years settings (inner city, suburban and village) to gain their perceptions of friendship. Amar, a boy puppet, was the stimulus for this and small groups of children were informed that Amar had never been to the school/nursery before and he needed to make friends. The children were asked for advice about how Amar could make friends.

Most children talked about mixed-gender friendships, though they always identified friends of the same gender first in their lists. They identified aspects of friendship that included security and socialising, play experiences and work activities, humour and closeness: 'Friends don't hurt you', 'Friends colour and work hard' and 'Friends play nice, no pushing or pulling'. 'Dylan's always been my best friend. He says funny things.' They also identified some grown-ups as being their friends because 'I like Granny cos she plays what we want to play' and 'My mummy's my friend cos she buys me nice things.' Olusoga and Brock's (2005) findings indicated that:

- children as young as three can identify and list their friends;
- four-year-olds can give reasons why they like their friends;
- between four and five years they can discuss their friendships at some length and why a friendship is important to them, and are aware of the friendships of others.

Much of the children's talk on friendship centred on their reflections on their pretend and fantasy play (*Star Wars*, Peter Pan and Spiderman), games (hide and seek, catch me, invisibility) and role-play areas (construction, picnics, jungle).

In the research one child stood out as being isolated in a setting, seeming rather anxious and speaking abruptly. His interactions with other children were often unsuccessful and he seemed to be in need of constant adult reassurance and often asked for adult intervention during outdoor play. In his interview, he wanted to be identified as having best friends 'cos I want someone to play with me so I won't be on my own.' The absence of a friend was found to be problematic for many children in Peters' (2003: 52) research and she found that the 'presence of friendships appeared to go a long way towards establishing a positive experience of school'. It is therefore important that practitioners in ECCE, and particularly in schools, recognise that how they group children in their work and play activities, how they organise the seating and how they use circle time and promote Social and Emotional Aspects of Development (SEAD) can make a difference to emotional intelligence and also educational achievement. Children will be more likely to achieve if they feel happy and supported by their friends, as well as by their key-worker or teacher. Buysse *et al.*'s (2003) research in 18 inclusive settings found that the 25 teachers and 20 early childhood special educators did not normally employ classroom-wide interventions to guide children's interactions with peers. These educators allowed children to form friendships on their own and provided free choice activity periods, and Buysse *et al.* (2003: 496) believe this could imply that teachers do not fully understand (as didn't the teacher mentioned at the beginning of this study) the importance of their role in helping young children form and maintain friendships with their classmates, and may view active encouragement of a developing friendship as 'interference'. They suggest eleven strategies that educators could use to promote friendship between children:

1. allow friends to exclude others from their play;
2. comment on friends' play;
3. invite two children to play together;
4. arrange for two children to play together outside of class;
5. provide special materials or activities to encourage children to play together;
6. arrange for a child to be close to a friend;

7. speak or interpret for a child so the friend can understand;
8. provide enough free choice time for the friends to play together;
9. let children form friendships on their own;
10. provide suggestions to solve problems or resolve conflict between friends;
11. allow friends to play off on their own.

(Buysse *et al.*, 2003: 494)

It is evident that practitioners need to ensure that children know how to establish friendships and that no child feels left out. Reflecting on the issues raised and empowering children in this way can make a significant difference to their lifelong learning and the development of emotional intelligence.

Reflective challenges

- What would you do if you saw a child on his/her own?
- Give reasons as to why you would take the course of action you've decided.
- What have been the results of your intervention or non-intervention?
- What are your beliefs now about children's friendship?

References

Brock, A. (2011) 'The child in context: policy and provision', Chapter 1 in Brock, A. and Rankin, C. (2011) *Professionalism in the Early Years Interdisciplinary Team: Supporting young children and their families*. London: Continuum.

Buysse, V., Sparkman, K.L. and Wesley, P.W. (2003) 'Communities of practice: connecting what we know with what we do', *Exceptional Children*, 69(3): 263–77.

The Children's Society (2007) *Good Childhood Inquiry*. London: The Children's Society.

Department for Education (DfE) (2012) *Statutory Framework for the Early Years Foundation Stage 2012*. Runcorn: DfE. Retrieved 15 April 2014 from https://www.education.gov.uk/publications/standard/AllPublications/Page1/DFE-00023-2012.

Dunn, J. (2004) *Children's Friendships: The beginnings of intimacy*. Oxford: Blackwell.

Emery, C. and Huitt, W. (2002) 'An introduction to the development of friendships', *Educational Psychology Interactive*. Valdosta, GA: Valdosta State University. Retrieved 15 April 2014 from http://teach.valdosta.edu/whuitt/brilstar/chapters/friendships.doc.

Fabian, H. (2002) *Children Starting School*. London: David Fulton Publishers.

IPSOS MORI UNICEF (2011) *Children's Well-Being in UK, Sweden and Spain: The role of inequality and materialism*. IPSOS MORI Social Research Institute.

Ledger, A., Smith, B. and Rich, P. (2000) 'Friendships over the transition from early childhood centre to school', *International Journal of Early Years Education*, 8(1): 57–69.

Livingstone, T. (2004) *Child of Our Time*. London, Bantam Press

Olusoga, Y. and Brock, A. (2005) *Who's your friend? Conversations around friendship in the foundation stage*. Paper presented at EECERA 15th Annual Conference, Dublin.

Peters, S. (2003) '"I didn't expect that I would get tons of friends . . . more each day": children's experiences of friendship during the transition to school', *Early Years*, 23(1): 45–53.

Slater, A. and Bremner, G. (2003) *An Introduction to Developmental Psychology*. Oxford: Blackwell.

What's it like for a black child in the classroom?

Gina Houston

This case study is taken from a research project which was aimed at understanding the experiences of black children from their own standpoints as they began their statutory education in reception classes. The qualitative study used direct observation over a period of six weeks in each school, to 'hear the voices' of the young black girls and boys (Clark and Moss, 2008). The study used a Critical Race Theory (CRT) framework which recognises that racism is endemic in society and is bound to impact on black children either covertly, overtly or both (Delgado and Stefancic, 2001; Dixson and Rousseau, 2006). The CRT approach supports the view that it is imperative to hear the voices of the black community when understanding racism in society (Zamudio *et al.*, 2011). The case study below is an opportunity to hear a little of what one black child's 'voice' is saying as she finds her new identity away from home.

> *Donna is a four-year-old black British girl of Jamaican heritage attending a reception class in a school where the other pupils are predominantly of Asian heritage. Her 'best friend' is Sumira, with whom she spends most of her time during the day. Sumira's family are from Sri Lanka. The three reception class practitioners are white European. One morning, Donna decides to make a picture using photos of children from some magazines, which have been displayed in the creative art area. She looks through the magazines and selects a picture of a young white girl, with long blond straight hair, cuts around the figure and sticks it onto her piece of paper. She continues to do this for another ten minutes, discussing the pictures with her friend Sumira as they look through the pages of the magazine, commenting on how 'nice' the girls look in their fairy and princess costumes. She takes her finished collage to show the practitioner. It is of four girls that she has cut out and arranged on the paper, all of whom have the same long, straight blond hair. The practitioner comments on her 'lovely picture', remarking on her good cutting-out skills. Donna then goes into the 'café' role play area and makes 'patties' alone with the playdough, while Sumira 'reads' to the practitioner in the adjoining literacy area of the classroom.*
>
> *A few days later, while sharing a photo book with the researcher and a group of four children, Donna mentions that a boy in the playground during lunch time had*

commented on her hair saying, 'that's the stupid hair ever heard'. She says that this upset her and that he 'shouldn't have said that'. When asked, Donna said that she hadn't told anybody about the comment. That afternoon, Donna asks the researcher to twist her two bunches for her into long strands. She then sits in a group session flicking her strands from side to side. On another occasion, a practitioner enters the classroom, touches Donna's hair, which is in two bunches that day, and says to her, 'my daughter's got a doll with hair like this'. Donna makes no comment and moves away from the practitioner. Often when sitting in the whole-class group carpet sessions, Donna will feel the long, straight hair of the Asian children sitting nearest to her. However, when Donna's peers feel her hair she gets angry and complains to the practitioner. Shortly after these events, Donna's mother tells the researcher during an interview for the research project that she was very angry with Donna the previous evening because she had cut 'large chunks' out of her hair. She had not mentioned this to the practitioners in Donna's class as she 'hadn't had the chance' to do so.

This case study shows how a black child is finding her identity outside the home, in which it is likely that she has been valued for her appearance, especially in regards to her hair which is thick and long. She is beginning to understand that not everyone feels that her kind of hair is beautiful. This is apparent from the comments and reactions of others in the classroom and to the images of what characterises desirable hair in the resources around her.

There are two occasions where Donna shows her feelings verbally regarding interactions with other children about her hair. The first is that she is upset about the negative comments made in the playground by a boy. The second is when she shows a practitioner she is angry by asking her to tell another child to stop touching her hair. When feelings are shown verbally in this way it is easier for the practitioner to identify issues and address the situations to support Donna to understand her own reactions and the actions of others. Other examples in the case study are much more difficult to identify as they represent incidents where the practitioner is not so aware of the emotions derived from Donna's experiences as they are not verbalised. If the opportunity had been there for the parent to inform the practitioner that Donna had cut her hair at home, this would have been an alert for understanding that Donna's classroom experiences were negatively affecting her feelings about her hair and her identity. The two overt examples above may then have added to a more holistic understanding of the need for the practitioner to address this.

Reflective challenge

- For the reflective practitioner it is essential to understand the range of experiences, in context with racism in society, which may impact on the black child as a consequence of an event which is initially perceived as unimportant.
- The reflective practitioner should give time to discuss the feelings and opinions of the children in the class in order to support their emotional and personal development as this can impact on their attitudes to school throughout their education.

> ■ The reflective practitioner should find ways of gaining support to feel confi-
> dent in raising these issues with the children and to understand their personal
> attitudes and the terminology they are confident to use before discussion
> with the children.

Research with older black children in the primary and secondary phases has
shown that disaffection with school begins with their early experiences of covert as well as overt racism, personal and institutional racism (Brooker, 2002;
Richardson, 2007). Donna was able to relate how she felt about the negative
comments directed to her in the playground through the use of a photo book to
raise discussion about being black as well as being unique in appearance, such
as skin colour and hair texture.

The fact that Donna chose the pictures of white girls with long blond hair
for her collage has implications for the resources that are provided in the classroom. Black children are bombarded with images on television, DVDs and in
publications of whiteness as being the norm and most desirable in society, with
relatively few alternatives. Practitioners should be aware of this and ensure that
differences are discussed as valuable in society and not patronised as Donna
was when the practitioner admired her hair in relation to a doll. Many times
practitioners have been heard to admire a black girl's hair when it is plaited
in elaborate cane rows as opposed to the 'afro' style or bunches which Donna
often wears and which was seen by the boys in the playground as 'stupid'.
Magazines representing black people are easily obtainable from newsagents
or from parents to address the imbalance in classrooms. Resources can be used
to raise discussion with the class about attitudes to differences in appearance.
It was easy to for Donna to use her home experiences to support her learning
when the resources provided were non-didactic, such as when she made pat-
ties with playdough while exploring shape, size and pattern. Not all resources
can reflect all children's home experiences that they bring to school with them
but opportunities should be afforded through unstructured opportunities for
expression. A variety of material and paper patterns common across cultures
may have been more appropriate for developing cutting skills than the Euro-
centric magazines provided in the classroom for Donna and Sumira, which
reinforced stereotypes of what was acceptable and 'nice' in their thinking.

What should the reflective early years practitioner do to support black children in the classroom?

- ■ Be aware that racism is evident in society and how this may impact on black
  children's experiences both in and out of school.
- ■ Use formal training opportunities and informal discussion with colleagues
  about racism in society and how this has affected their own attitudes to race
  and understanding of cultural diversity.

- Understand the impact of 'whiteness' which may predominate as the norm in the school and how this may affect their practice and priorities in the classroom.
- During observations of black children, keep in mind that their experiences are affected by racism differently than those of the white children in the class.
- During observations of children in the class keep in mind that they may have internalised negative attitudes to those different from themselves.
- Do not ignore the children's 'voices' and provide opportunities to discuss attitudes to race as they occur either individually or in groups.
- Ensure that time is taken during the day to give parents and carers an opportunity to approach practitioners to discuss important events that have happened at home and to understand the experiences of children outside school as well as to discuss significant events concerning their child in school.
- Be knowledgeable about the ethnicity and unique cultural experiences of each child in the class and use these as a starting point to support each individual child's learning and development. A child with an African heritage often has a very different experience at home than a child with a Caribbean heritage and they are too often seen as being black without differentiation.
- Provide open-ended resources that children can use flexibly and independently to reflect their experiences from home and the community to scaffold their learning across the curriculum.

Theoretical framework

Most early years practitioners support the view that the child is a unique being with their differences to be respected equally (DfCSF, 2008). However, Donna's classroom experiences as a black child can be further illuminated through the framework of Critical Race Theory (CRT). The use of narrative and listening to what the black child says about her/his own experience is an important tenet in CRT. This is proposed as an alternative to the majoritarian white voice, which usually dominates their educational experiences and masks their experiences of being black in a 'white' institution.

The CRT framework also emphasises the psychological effects of racism on the black community and how this can start from a very young age. The perpetual racial microaggressions which are felt at many levels by black people from childhood in an endemically racist society such as Britain are explained by Sue:

> Countless examples of microaggressions are delivered daily without the awareness of perpetrators. And while these actions may appear harmless or innocent in nature, they are nevertheless detrimental to recipients because they result in harmful psychological consequences and create disparities. Microaggressions sap the spiritual energies of recipients, lead to low self-esteem, and deplete or divert energy for adaptive functioning and

problem solving . . . But it is important to note that microaggressions are not only confined to their individual psychological effects. They affect the quality of life and standard of living for marginalized groups in our society. Microaggressions have the secondary but devastating effect of denying equal access and opportunity in education, employment, and health care. While seemingly minimal in nature, the harm they produce operates on a systemic and macro level.

(Sue 2010: 15–16)

These covert and overt racial microaggressions, such as those directed to Donna through comments about her hair, should be acknowledged as a reality in our classrooms, and all children must be supported to understand these microaggressions and their relationship to them as well as how to deal with them as they interact in society.

Whiteness is another important concept in CRT, which places the responsibility on the white community to understand the predominance of white attitudes as a priority in education. This is manifest through curriculum resources and content as well as through school policy, practice and ethos (Gillborn, 2009). A recognition of a need by white practitioners to understand other viewpoints and cultural norms, as well as racism, which is historically embedded in British society, is essential when considering the experiences offered to black children in their education.

Reflection and discussion points

- How far do your observations hear the unique 'voice' of the black child and are you aware of all children's attitudes to race and difference during observation?
- How can your practitioner team begin to discuss issues of race and racism in the early years classroom and support each other while developing a 'no blame culture'? (Lane, 2009).
- Do your resources and does your classroom organisation give children enough time and opportunity to use their home experiences to extend their learning?
- How can you facilitate communication with parents to understand the experiences of black children?

References

Brooker, L. (2002) *Starting School: Young children learning cultures*. Buckingham: Open University Press.

Clark, A. and Moss, P. (2008) *Listening to Young Children: The mosaic approach*. London: National Children's Bureau.

Delgado, R. and Stefancic, J. (2001) *Critical Race Theory: An introduction*. New York: New York University Press.

Department for Children, Schools and Families (DfCSF) (2008) *The Early Years Foundation Stage, Statutory Framework*. Nottingham: DfCSF.

Dixson, A. and Rousseau, C.K. (eds) (2006) *Critical Race Theory in Education*. London: Routledge.

Gillborn, D. (2009) 'Education policy as an act of white supremacy', in Taylor, E., Gillborn, D. and Ladson-Billings, G. (eds) *Foundations of Critical Race Theory in Education*. London: Routledge.

Lane, J. (2009) *Young Children and Racial Equality*. London: National Children's Bureau.

Richardson, B. (2007) *Tell It Like It Is: How our schools fail black children*. London: Bookmark Publications.

Sue, D.W. (2010) *Microaggressions in Everyday Life*. Hoboken, NJ: Wiley.

Zamudio, M., Russell, C., Rios, F. and Bridgeman, J. (2011) *Critical Race Theory Matters: Education and ideology*. London: Routledge.

Why are my stories so important to me?

Avril Brock

We have always known that reading stories is a worthwhile activity to do with children, but there is much more to story (Wells, 2010). Stories in the mind (storying) is one of the most fundamental means of making meaning. We all make up stories, making our lives meaningful and interesting through the telling of stories and relating events. Children have a natural impulse to tell stories as a means of making connections between what they are learning and what they already know (Wells, 2010). Do you enable children to tell their own stories and do you listen to what they say? As a reflective practitioner you should be able to understand many of the connections that children are making and build on these to further develop their metacognition about story and enhance their language development.

FIGURE cs.2   Oscar and James story sharing.

James's story

James:	This is a book about a bunny rabbit, Little Rabbit Foo Foo. I'm trying to read this granddad. Don't laugh granddad. So this is about Little Rabbit Foo Foo. Do you want to listen about Little Rabbit Foo Foo?
Granddad:	Riding through the forest
James:	Scooping up all the mouses . . .
Granddad:	Scooping up all the mice.
	[James and his Granddad speak together]
James:	. . . and bopping them on the heads.
Granddad:	I'll turn you into a . . .
James:	Granddad, it says I'll turn you into a Goonie. It says Little Rabbit Foo Foo. It's got a fairy on it. Little Rabbit Foo Foo riding through the forest and bopping them on the heads. Down came the good fairy and said Little Rabbit Foo Foo stop frightening the mouses. I don't like your attitude.

Oscar's story

Eeyore was very lonely and all on his own. And he was not very kind to people. He was bad nice cos that's what it's about. The end! It's not a very good story though. Only one person wrote. Eeyore was naughty as his friends wasn't there. He killed himself!

James and Oscar have been listening to stories since they were two months old. They are not only avid story listeners, they are now storytellers at three years old and each has their own bookshelves as well as a library of books at Grandma's house. Oscar and James's favourite stories at age three-and-a-half include:

We're Going on a Bear Hunt
Once Upon a Time
Room on the Broom
Charlie Cook's Favourite Book
Where the Wild Things Are
Not now Bernard
A Walk Through the Woods
Peace at Last
The Little Mouse, The Red Ripe Strawberry and The Big Hungry Bear
Little Rabbit Foo Foo

Experience of stories promotes language development, develops understanding of the world and the people in it, and enriches imagination. Children love to listen to, and to read, stories they like over and over again. They enjoy familiar themes unchanging and the same ending always occurring. They can pay attention to words after they have discovered what happens (Meek, 1991). They use the prediction, sequencing, repetition and text illustration correlation promoted in stories.

Bilingual stories enhance development in their first language as well as in English. Stories are so important for early language development as they promote:

- varied linguistic structures;
- vocabulary and rich description;
- organisation of thought processes;
- complex narrative sequences;
- pace, mood, atmosphere, suspense, anticipation;
- intonation, gestures, paralinguistics;
- plots, characters, events, places, problems;
- emotions, morals, moods and the words to express these;
- semantics, syntax and grapho-phonemics for early reading skills;
- enjoying language for its own sake; and
- enjoying the story itself!

(adapted from Brock and Rankin, 2008)

Observing children's story-play provides windows into children's minds, and analysis of their story discourse provides insights into language and learning and you can see their metacognition in action through reflecting on their story repertoires, meaning making, knowledge about language and decision making. Practitioners should:

- match the language of stories to activities and experiences;
- promote specific vocabulary from story through opportunities to use, repeat, understand and consolidate;
- contextualise learning through play, first-hand and active experiences around story;
- interest, excite and get the children actively involved in talking and doing;
- create an atmosphere of fun where children want to participate;
- use practical resources, visual support and other children;
- story tell as well as read stories so children have to develop their own images;
- use magnet boards, laminated figures, finger puppets;
- provide storysacks or builders' trays with small world resources of a story;
- create role-play areas with a story as theme for children to enact stories.

(adapted from Brock and Power, 2006)

'We are failing too many boys in the enjoyment of reading,' declared Michael Morpurgo, the children's author in June 2012 when English primary schools brought in the new compulsory Phonics Screening Check. The findings of the National Literacy Trust's report (Clark, 2012) into boys' reading revealed that boys were falling behind in reading and that attitudes to reading between boys and girls are widening even further. This report demonstrated that many schools in the UK were concerned about boys' reading, and 60,000 boys were not reaching the required levels of reading at 11 and were performing less well and expressing less enthusiasm for reading than many of their international peers. Morpurgo believes that children have to be motivated to want to learn to read and it should not be just a taught skill. He suggests that enjoyment of story should be part of every day in primary schools, devoted to the simple enjoyment of reading and writing; that there should be regular visits from storytellers, theatre groups, poets and writers; that fathers and grandfathers, mothers and grandmothers should enter settings and schools to tell and read stories; and that libraries, access to books and the encouragement of the habit of reading should be paramount for educators.

Using story as a vehicle for delivering pedagogy and curriculum can reconceptualise and support the ECE practitioner's role through promoting playful contexts rich in language. Educators need to be able to provide quality, appropriate play provision for young children through a pedagogy of play. Yet there is a rhetoric about play that does not always match reality, possibly due to tensions inherent in a work/play dichotomy (Wood, 2010). Story-play can bridge these tensions! A pedagogy of story-play can reconceptualise the educator's role through facilitating coherent planning. Promoting play around story can provide adults with a framework that enables co-construction in narratives, imaginative conversations, shared sustained thinking and problem-solving contexts. It also facilitates parents' involvement in their children's learning, as everyone understands stories!

Reflective challenge points

- Do you have your own collection of books?
- Do you practice storying and storytelling as well as story reading?
- Think about analysing story for linguistic features.
- Think about contextualising, planning and resourcing for a specific story.
- Enable children to create their own story repertoires.
- Introduce parents to a pedagogy of story-play.

References

Brock, A. and Power, M. (2006) 'Promoting learning in the early years', Chapter 2 in *Promoting Learning for Bilingual Pupils 3–11: Opening doors to success*. London: Paul Chapman Publishing/Sage.

Brock, A. and Rankin, C. (2008) *Communication, Language and Literacy from Birth to Five*. London: Sage.

Clark, C. (2012) *Boys' Reading Commission 2012: A review of existing research conducted to underpin the Commission*. London: National Literacy Trust. Retrieved 15 April 2014 from http://www.literacytrust.org.uk/assets/0001/4047/BRC-_Research_overview_-_Final.pdf.

Meek, M. (1991) *How Texts Teach What Readers Learn*. Stroud: Thimble Press.

Morpurgo, M. (2012) 'We are failing too many boys in the enjoyment of reading', *The Guardian*, 12 July. Retrieved 15 April 2014 from http://www.theguardian.com/teacher-network/teacher-blog/2012/jul/02/michael-morpurgo-boys-reading?

Wells, G. (2010) *The Meaning Makers*. London: Hodder & Stoughton.

Wood, E. (2010) 'Developing integrated pedagogical approaches to play and learning', in Broadhead, P., Howard, J. and Wood, E. (eds) *Play and Learning in the Early Years: From research to practice*. London: Sage, pp. 9–26.

Adyta – the silent period, as experienced by young bilingual learners

Caroline Bligh

This reflective case study stems from a three-year ethnographic study (Bligh, 2011) which examined the emergent stage of learning English as an additional language – the silent period, as experienced by young bilingual learners. The silent period, in this reflection, refers to the initial stage in emergent acquisition of English as an additional language, when, on entering an early years setting in England, the language of discourse and instruction (English) is not understood. Not every young bilingual learner encounters a silent period like Adyta, because not every child invests many of their hours, days, weeks and years in an environment where their mother tongue is disregarded (Bligh, 2011).

'Adyta' first attended his local pre-school playgroup aged three-and-a-half years. Adyta's mother tongue was Punjabi, as from birth Adyta made sense of his world (Conteh, 2007; Mills, 2004) through Punjabi – the language through which his mother and close family members had communicated with him from birth.

I observed Adyta's participation from when he started attending the pre-school playgroup, in reception class and Year 1. Adyta, who presented as a confident, fun-loving boy at home (recorded from his home visit), remained almost silent in the pre-school setting. I had initially presumed that he would communicate in spoken English because both he and his parents were born in England and his parents were articulate Punjabi/English speakers. However, as is customary in many South Asian communities, the paternal grandmother, 'Jasmit', lived with Adyta's parents. According to Adyta's mother, her mother-in-law kept the Punjabi tongue alive and active within the family. Although Adyta's parents could and would speak English in alternative situations, out of respect to Adyta's grandmother, family members spoke Punjabi in her presence.

Studies by Cummins (2000), Baker (2000) and Skutnabb-Kangas (2000) demonstrate the value of maintaining the mother tongue for a child's continued success in learning and development. Speaking Punjabi together inevitably bound Adyta's family members collectively, as in Jean Mills' (2004) study of women and families of Pakistani heritage which articulates the inevitable binding between the mother tongue and the maintenance of cultural identity as follows.

As both of Adyta's parents worked full-time (Adyta's father worked for a property company and his mother worked in a large department store), Adyta's grandmother was his main carer and educator during weekdays between 8.00 a.m. and 5.30 p.m. Adyta's mother (who collected Adyta from pre-school occasionally) encouraged Adyta to refer to Nicole (the play-school leader) as 'Auntie'. According to Dasgupta's (1993) study, many families in the Bay area of India (South Asia) commonly adopt the 'Western' term 'auntie' as an expression of intimacy towards significant others, and pass this practice on to their children. The following two vignettes demonstrate Adyta negotiating his learning trajectory through the silent period.

Vignette 1

Thunder, lightning and torrential rain has started, and the children run inside. Nicole decides to suspend the outside activities and tells the children that she is going to put the television on. When the children have 'settled down' in the carpet area, Nicole and her two assistants move away from the carpet area as they start to tidy the morning's activities away. Adyta is sitting on the carpet with all the other children watching a humorous children's DVD. Some of the other children have started to move into smaller groupings on the carpet and are chatting informally . . . Adyta's eyes circle the television monitor . . . There is loud laughter from the other children as a humorous incident occurs on the screen . . . Adyta opens his eyes wide and stares in surprise at the rest of the children, turning his head around in both directions. There is a pause and then Adyta copies the other children laughing and he laughs really loudly . . . Adyta doesn't realise at first when the rest of the children have stopped laughing. Adyta suddenly turns his head and looks in all directions; he lowers his head a little, looks at his fingers and stops laughing. This same pattern of attempting to 'join in' with the other children's behaviour patterns continues throughout the fifteen-minute episode shown on the television.

(Adyta observed in pre-school, 19 February 2008)

The pause (before Adyta laughs) represented Adyta's realisation (through hearing laughter) that something had happened. Adyta did not join in with the laughter until he could see and hear that all the children were laughing. He then copied the laughter and contributed to this shared endeavour by laughing really loudly, until he heard and observed that the laughing had ceased. Adyta then stopped laughing. Although he wanted to participate he did so peripherally and fractionally.

Revisiting Vygotsky's (1986) understandings of children's learning, Adyta was attempting to connect on an interpersonal level with the other children through the practice of laughing. Gregory's (2008: 19) notion of connecting as 'learning between individuals within or between social or cultural contexts . . . provides the foundation for intercultural learning as children learn to learn in a new language in school.' In order to negotiate his participation more centrally within the early years setting, Adyta transformed his language and narrative style, relationships and learning styles appropriate to the observed practice. However, there was no active mediation apparent from the practitioners in either guiding his transformation as he moved through one language and cultural experience to the next, or in assisting negotiation through his levels of participation.

Adyta mediated his learning through observation of others, listening to the indigenous language and copying the practices – simultaneously. Similarly to Samia in Drury's (2007) research, Adyta absorbed 'the everyday language . . . [and the] routines and expectations' of the early years setting. The synthesising of practices (Kenner, 2004) was presented as fluid, overlapping and intersecting pathways which mediated Adyta's increasing participation.

Vignette 2

> Adyta looks at Nicole, who is telling a story to children in the story corner. Adyta continues to eat his fruit whilst watching Nicole. He appears to be concentrating hard . . . He continues sitting at the table for ten minutes whilst eating fruit. His eyes are scanning the room . . . Tyrone passes and Adyta 'catches' him with his eyes. He smiles at Tyrone and points to some fruit on the floor and giggles. Tyrone looks back at Adyta and then walks straight ahead to sit with the other children. Adyta turns his head around to look at Nicole. He watches the actions of the other children, who are copying Nicole's demonstration of how to make a phone call.
>
> (Adyta observed in pre-school, 19 February 2008)

Adopting Rogoff's (2003) sociocultural interpretations, Adyta was an apprentice to participation within the story-telling session. However, he also chose to be situated legitimately on the periphery of practice (the snack table), where he looked out and listened in on the activities of more central members. Adyta fractionally increased participation by drawing Tyrone (unsuccessfully) into engagement in practice. This attempt towards a shared endeavour failed, but demonstrates how important a peripheral location is for children like Adyta. Not only could he negotiate participation with Tyrone, but he could also observe silently throughout from a 'safe' distance, using 'observation and imitation as a legitimate means to gain peripheral membership of a community' (Lave and Wenger, 1991: 95).

The vignette samples revealed the complex struggle that exists for young bilingual learners like Adyta when attempting to mediate negotiation on the peripheries of converging communities of practice. Despite the demands put upon them, young children like Adyta silently attempt to carve their own paths to success in the face of the dominant monolingual discourse (Sharrock, 1997). Gee and Green (1998: 147) defined this agentive action as 'changing patterns of participation in specific social practices within communities of practice'.

This case study serves to highlight that young children like Adyta need their alternative contributions to learning to be recognised and valued. Silence may be the only agentive action that an emergent bilingual learner can access when unable to make meaning with others through their silenced mother tongue. The intention of this case study is to challenge the reflective practitioners' thinking. On encountering young children like Adyta, the reflective practitioner may now reconsider their initial evaluations of such children's silent contributions. Providing secure and safe spaces for such children to silently participate not only nurtures an inclusive learning environment, but is also the first and most important step in the mediation of learning for children who might otherwise feel alienated from the early years community of practice.

Reflective challenge points

- Consider your initial evaluations of such children's silent contributions.
- Do you respect children's right to be silent?
- Do you provide safe, secure places for children to have time out?

References

Baker, C. (2000) *A Parents' and Teachers' Guide to Bilingualism*. Second edition. Clevedon: Multilingual Matters.

Bligh, C. (2011) 'The silent experiences of young bilingual learners: a small-scale sociocultural study into the silent period'. Unpublished thesis, Centre for Research in Education and Educational Technology: Open University.

Conteh, J. (2007) 'Bilingualism in mainstream primary classrooms in England', in Hua, Z., Seedhouse, P., Wei, L. and Cook, V. (eds) *Language Learning and Teaching as Social Interaction*. London: Palgrave Macmillan, pp. 185–98.

Cummins, J. (2000) *Language Power and Pedagogy: Bilingual children in the crossfire*. Clevedon: Multilingual Matters.

Dasgupta, P. (1993) *The Otherness of English: India's auntie tongue syndrome*. New Delhi: Sage.

Drury R. (2007) *Young Bilingual Learners at Home and School: Researching multilingual voices*. Stoke-on-Trent: Trentham Books.

Gee, J. and Green, J. (1998) Discourse analysis, learning and social practice: a methodological study', *Review of Research in Education*, 23: 119–69.

Gregory, E. (2008) *Learning to Read in a New Language*. London: Sage.

Kenner, C. (2004) *Becoming Biliterate: Young children learning different writing systems*. Stoke-on-Trent: Trentham Books.

Lave, J. and Wenger, E. (1991) *Situated Learning: Legitimate peripheral participation*. Cambridge: Cambridge University Press.

Mills, J. (2004) 'Mothers and mother tongue: perspectives on self-construction by mothers of Pakistani heritage', in Pavlenko, A. and Blackledge, A. (eds) *Negotiation of Identities in Multilingual Contexts.* Clevedon: Multilingual Matters, pp. 34–67.

Rogoff, B. (2003) *The Cultural Nature of Human Development.* New York: Oxford University Press.

Sharrock, W. (1997) *The Philosophy of Social Research.* Third edition. Reading, MA: Addison Wesley.

Skutnabb-Kangas, T. (2000) *Linguistic Genocide in Education – or worldwide diversity and human rights?* Mahwah, NJ: Lawrence Erlbaum Associates.

Vygotsky, L. (1986) 'Thought and language', in *Thought and Language,* ed. and trans. Kozulin, A. Cambridge, MA: MIT Press (original work published 1934).

What is it like for a child living with violence?

Naomi Lewis

'Do you know what?' The little boy standing in front of me began with the phrase so typical of young children before they give you a glimpse into their minds. He leaned in towards me to use a quiet voice. *'Last night my dad pulled my mum's hair and kicked her and me and my brothers all jumped on him to get him off.'* He was smiling, but it was an uncertain smile as he looked to see how I would respond. I was a student teacher on my first teaching placement, and this child was one of the quiet stars of the class, always polite and attentive; his words shocked me and left me uncertain as to how to respond. I decided I needed to explore the degree to which domestic violence is a critical issue for children and therefore for schools, and the best ways for practitioners to help children living with this frightening reality.

Some of the biggest victims of domestic violence are the smallest.

(UNICEF, 2004)

Research shows that domestic violence is a reality for women globally (UNICEF, 2004). Violence contained within the familial environment is characterised by control, where one partner is 'kept under control', dehumanised, belittled and aggressively or emotionally dominated by the other (Romito, 2008: 17). In one year in Britain figures show that 32,017 women and 22,500 children sought protection in a refuge (Seager, 2003 in Romito, 2008). However, any statistics such as these belie the full scale of the problem, as domestic violence remains under-reported, a taboo subject in the worldwide community. More recent evidence would suggest there has been a gross underestimation of the problem, as Sussex Police reported that in one day alone 50 reports of domestic abuse were made following their Twitter campaign (BBC News Kent, 2012). In 2006 the United Nations General Secretary conducted a vast global investigation into violence against children. In his report he identified the 'private sphere' of the home as 'the most challenging context for eliminating and responding to violence' (UN, 2006: 12). When children are present in homes where domestic violence occurs, they are either direct victims themselves as research indicates (Romito, 2008) or indirectly through witnessing acts of brutality committed against the caregivers in the home.

The Children's Society report into what constitutes 'A Good Childhood' emphasised how the family unit should be a child's first experience of being immersed in a loving, supportive structure (Layard, 2009). If this were the case universally then the non-statutory early years guidance, *Development Matters*, which states that education settings must encourage positive relationships that are 'warm and loving, and foster a sense of belonging' (Early Education, 2012: 2) would be a natural continuation of a child's equally enabling home environment. The reality, however, is that many young children begin in an early years setting with damaged understanding of relationships, where the adults in their life are inconsistent in their interactions and emotionally absent because of stress or fear. In particular younger children are the most vulnerable to being exposed to domestic violence as 'studies show that domestic violence is more prevalent in homes with younger children than those with older children' (UNICEF, 2004: 3). Another study found similar results in a sample of 2,751 child witnesses of abuse, where children less than six years old constituted the biggest proportion (Willis *et al.*, 2010). This indicates that family violence is a critical issue for early years practitioners and teachers, with one study suggesting that in every class of 25 pupils, at least one child will witness domestic abuse at home (Meltzer *et al.*, 2009, cited in Ellis, 2012). Children who live in an environment where domestic abuse is a daily occurrence will be significantly affected by the repetition or variety of abuse in its many physical or psychological incarnations. Young children who cannot remove themselves from being physically present during an episode of domestic violence or who stay because they are reliant on the mother for protection are exposed to abuse which can have a measurable detrimental impact on their cognitive and emotional development.

Failure to thrive: developmental impact on children

The EYFS Statutory Framework highlights that providers are responsible for safeguarding children in their setting and must be 'alert to any issues of concern' (DfE, 2012: 13). Research has identified a whole plethora of other developmental delays that originate from a child's exposure to early violence, such as lower reading ability (UNICEF, 2004), speech problems, disturbed sleep patterns, headaches, poor concentration (Mullender *et al.*, 2002), and an inappropriate use of socialisation (Ellis, 2012). Another immediate indicator of problems in a child's home life is sporadic attendance or beginning in a new setting halfway through the year, as families in crisis may move regularly to avoid detection. Where children demonstrate strange behaviours around food, such as hoarding or eating particularly fast, this may relate to the fear and tensions they have come to associate with mealtimes in their own homes, which can be particularly volatile occasions in violent households.

Identifying changes in children's general dispositions relies on practitioners knowing their children as individuals, so that they can spot deviations from normal behaviour. In Byrne and Taylor's research, they interviewed a sample of teachers who specified two common, opposite changes in pupils, either becoming 'quiet and withdrawn' or 'loud and aggressive' (2007: 185) or 'difficulties sitting still, hyper-vigilance and poor concentration' (2007: 187). However, children may not outwardly display any physical symptoms of abuse such as bruises or cognitive or emotional complications. Some children possess amazing resilience that comes to light only once teachers or social workers are made aware of their exceptional circumstances. Groves and Gerwick (2006) define resilience as 'children's ability to function adequately despite considerable adversity' (quoted in Willis *et al.*, 2010: 553). A primary teacher colleague recalled one little girl who *'always looked sad behind her eyes'*, but it was only when she unexpectedly disclosed to the school nurse during a routine health assessment that the full extent of her difficult home life was related.

Disclosures from children (and parents) can confirm what may have been suspected in a setting. It would be a mistake to assume that disclosures come primarily from older children who can articulate their anxiety; as the opening vignette demonstrates, children as young as four use their vocabulary to express incidents that are playing on their mind. A disclosure may not express blame or communicate a sense of victimhood but as in the original case may rather reveal the child searching for meaning or affirmation that this is normal behaviour between adults. For young children especially, who align bad behaviour with physical punishment, this cause-and-effect dichotomy does not neatly align with the roles of mummy and daddy operating in tandem (McGee, 2000).

> When he was about five he started asking things like, 'Why did Daddy hit you, Mummy?' . . . 'Why did Daddy always want to hurt you, Mummy?' I said I don't know, Daddy has problems . . . He [the child] would then be very comforting and tell me how much he loves me.
>
> (McGee, 2000: 80)

Procedures to protect

Once a disclosure has been made the setting's safeguarding policy will be followed. The three imperatives as outlined by the London Safeguarding Board are: to protect the children; to support the mother in ensuring her and her children's safety; and to address the abusive partner's behaviour (2013). These active measures will more than likely fall under the jurisdiction of social services, whereas the setting's role – through the named safeguarding staff member – will be to provide evidence, a number of disclosures or other symptoms that either prompt social services investigations or corroborate their own suspicions. Initial disclosures are taken immediately to the senior safeguarding staff member who contacts Duty and Assessment – the safeguarding board particular to that local authority. Multi-agency working is a facet of domestic violence cases. The Children and Family Court Advisory and Support Service (CAFCASS) comes into settings to carry out assessments and counselling with children when there are disputes over custody or access. A setting's safeguarding procedure applies to all children regardless of heritage and culture. If a child does disclose, whilst the normal routines of investigation will be followed, staff must be sensitive to the interplay of shame in the community that could lead to women and their children being ostracised, so specialist support or refuges may need to be involved to support the family.

The EYFS statutory guidance states that practitioners must respond to possible abuse 'at the earliest opportunity' and in 'a timely and appropriate way' (DfE, 2012: 14). This seems to imply that practitioners must use their professional judgement and knowledge of a child in deciding how best to approach either the child or the parent. Whilst very young children may not have the language to communicate their stress, playing alongside such children may be equally revealing as to their emotional state. It has been documented that through play children act out incidents from their home life, often in an attempt to come to terms with traumatic incidents that have imprinted on their minds (Brock *et al.*, 2009). For children who do possess the communicative capabilities, the London Safeguarding Board advises the use of a framing question such as: 'We know that many mums and dads have arguments, does that ever happen in your family?' (2013). Such a question does not dictate an answer and allows children the opportunity to unburden themselves. Whilst this may be viewed by some practitioners as intrusive and unnecessary, advice from child survivors of domestic abuse to other children emphasises the importance of finding someone to talk to. The children urge others experiencing domestic violence to talk to someone who can make them feel good, reassure them it is not their fault and ensure they are not overwhelmed by the situation (Mullender *et al.*, 2002). If teachers feel they are incapable of fulfilling this role for their pupils then that in itself would raise issues of neglect of professional duty.

There is no panacea for child victims of domestic violence and the bleak reality can be sending them back to those troubled homes every day. Each child and circumstance will present practitioners with a unique dilemma, but by having knowledge of the safeguarding procedure an immediate response can be taken even if it feels inadequate. Willis *et al.* (2010) qualify the need for good role models, not just powerful teachers who extend the trajectory of control that begins in the children's home lives. As for many children from violent homes, school is a refuge itself from the chaos and conflict, where they can be children.

My research on this issue has illustrated that there is not one standardised answer I could have given to the little boy in my class. Domestic violence is a vast and dehumanising issue where relentless aggression can chip away at our humanity and, for children, their fragile understandings of human interactions and safety are particularly vulnerable. It is critical that the practitioner has a holistic knowledge of her children and is seen as a trusted adult in whom they could confide. One girl's account vividly attributes the restorative power alternative experiences can have:

> When I look back I think I was saved by the memory of my early years with my grandparents. I remembered the lessons I learned from them . . . Consequentially, I was able to observe my own miserable home life and know that things could be different.
>
> (Craven, 2012: 83)

This affirms that children are able to recognise that violence is not the only lifestyle when they are included in other nurturing environments and relationships. Whilst ensuring they follow every safeguarding guideline, settings can also create daily warm and caring interactions that value and empower the child in a sphere beyond that of the home.

Reflective challenges

- Are you surprised by the statistics and issues raised in this case study?
- Have you ever experienced anything like the example given at the beginning of the chapter?
- Do you know what to do if a child discloses to you?

References

BBC News Kent (2012) *New Sussex domestic violence campaign.* Online. Retrieved 15 April 2014 from http://www.bbc.co.uk/news/uk-england-kent-20736192.

Brock, A., Dodds, S., Jarvis, P. and Olusoga, Y. (2009). *Perspectives on Play: Learning for life.* Harlow: Pearson Longman.

Byrne, D. and Taylor, B. (2007) 'Children at risk from domestic violence and their educational attainment: perspectives of education welfare officers, social workers and teachers', *Child Care in Practice,* 13(3): 185–201.

Craven, P. (2012) *Freedom's Flowers: The effects of domestic abuse on children.* Marston Gate: Amazon.

Department for Education (2012) *Statutory Framework for the Early Years Foundation Stage.* Runcorn: DfE.

Early Education (2012) *Development Matters in the Early Years Foundation Stage (EYFS).* London: Early Education.

Ellis, G. (2012) 'The impact on teachers of supporting children exposed to domestic abuse', *Educational and Child Psychology,* 29(4).

Layard, R. (2009) *A Good Childhood: Searching for values in a competitive age.* London: Penguin.

London Safeguarding Board (2013) *London Child Protection Procedures.* Retrieved 15 April 2014 from http://www.londonscb.gov.uk/procedures.

McGee, C. (2000) 'Children's and mothers' experiences of support and protection following domestic violence', in Hanmer, J. (ed.) *Home Truths about Domestic Violence: Feminist influences on policy and practice – a reader.* London: Routledge.

Mullender, A., Hague, G., Imam, U., Kelly, L., Malos, E. and Regan, L. (2002) *Children's Perspectives on Domestic Violence.* London: Sage.

Romito, P. (2008) *A Deafening Silence: Hidden violence against women and children.* Bristol: Policy Press.

UNICEF (2004) *Behind Closed Doors: The impact of domestic violence on children* (online) Retrieved 15 April 2014 from http://www.unicef.org/protection/files/BehindClosedDoors.pdf.

United Nations (2006) *Report on Violence against Children* (online). Retrieved 15 April 2014 from www.unicef.org/violencestudy/reports/SG_violencestudy_en.pdf.

Willis, D., Hawkins, J., Pearce, C.W., Phalen. J., Keet, M. and Singer, C. (2010) 'Children who witness violence: what services do they need to heal?', *Issues in Mental Health Nursing,* 31(9): 552–60.

What is it like for a bereaved child?

Avril Brock

Sophie Brysdon's had her hair cut. I preferred it long. I like mine long, but Mum says I'll catch nits if I don't have it tied back. Our Joshua didn't have any hair left – not even eyelashes. If he'd have had nits they'd have had nowhere to hide. But I don't think nits like hospitals anyway. Our Joshua was in Mrs Morton's class, in the Juniors. I saw Mrs Morton in the playground this morning. I couldn't tell if she was cross with me – or cross with our Joshua because he won't be coming back to school after all. She just had a funny look on her face. Sophie Brysdon keeps scratching her neck. I bet she's cold without her hair there. Or perhaps the nits were frightened by the scissors and they're still running away. Eeeurgh! Miss Copperfield will be listening to me read soon, but I know there's new words in this book and 'sound it out' just doesn't work when there's too many letters. Our Joshua sometimes told me the new words at breakfast. Sometimes he was mean at breakfast though and pretended the Weetabix was all gone, so I'd have to have eggs. I hate eggs. But he always found the Weetabix again if I got really upset . . . It was Easter when Joshua stopped coming to school. I was in Mrs Johnson's class then . . . We did autumn pictures with real leaves yesterday. Mrs Pemberton puts our pictures on the wall – but only when they're very good. My picture of Joshua when he was dead wasn't good enough. Mrs Pemberton said it looked like someone asleep and when I said it was Joshua she looked so sad I knew it was a rubbish picture. Sophie Brysdon's finished reading to Miss Copperfield now. My turn soon . . . Oh. My throat hurts and my chin feels wobbly again. If I blink really fast it stops. Bethany Price called me a cry-baby yesterday. She said her Nana died ages before Joshua and it's not sad at all because now she's a star in the sky and she looks after Bethany all the time. I know that's rubbish because Joshua told me about stars. And anyway, it is more sadder when your big brother dies than when your Nana dies because your big brother lives in your house all the time and has a room and lots of things – but you only see your Nana sometimes. Actually, most of the time I just pretend Josh is at home being poorly – and that's why there's just me coming to school. Like when I was in Mrs Johnson's class last year. Blink, Lizzie, blink . . Mummy and Dad are always tired and there's no one to play with anymore. My throat hurts. My tummy hurts too. Maybe I'll be ill like Josh. I don't care. I don't care even if I die.

It must be easier than living. Oh no, big splodgy tear on my paper. Hope Bethany Price can't see.

This case study is an extract from *Lizzie's Story*: the mundane and the tragic randomly intermingle in the thoughts of a bereaved six-year-old written by Potts, who used this fictionalised narrative with her research participants to provide a child's 'voice' based on her experiences of 'working with children of that age when in a professional counselling role at a children's hospice' (Potts, 2013: 8).

Why did my mum die when I was a baby? Why did my daddy marry my new mummy? Why can't grandma and granddad live with us? Why do they have to go home now? Why doesn't Joe and Tom live with Uncle Simon and Aunty Jackie? Did Mummy and Aunty Jackie live near their cousins when they were little? Why is Mia's skin a different colour to her mummy? Why are families so complexicated?
(Brock, 2011)

Madeleine was aged six at the time of this dialogue and her challenging questions confounded me as her step-grandma. Philosophical discussions such as these had commenced from when Madeleine was three years old. Her mother had been diagnosed with breast cancer during the pregnancy and the family was bereaved by the time Madeleine reached 16 months of age. From a very early age Madeleine would talk about death, age, illness, relationships and friendship. She had a photo of her birth mother in her bedroom and albums with photographs throughout her early years, which were particularly perused when her baby brother was born so she could make comparisons.

These 'case studies' indicate the long-term impact of bereavement and the nature of a young child's thinking and reasoning about complex issues that affect them. Parents, carers and educators often feel uneasy and unprepared in dealing with children's experiences of death and in how to respond to children's curiosity about death. Bereavement is our experience of grief when someone we care about has died (Royal College of Psychiatrists, 2009). The impact on a child who is bereaved can include sadness, depression, anger, a loss of certainty in seeing the world as a safe place, and feelings of isolation. These emotions can have a temporary impact on children's ability to concentrate and can create difficulties in learning which consequently may cause emotional and behavioural difficulties and a decline in educational performance. The long-term impact of childhood bereavement researched by the Child Wellbeing Research Centre in 2011 produced some staggering statistics:

Every 22 minutes a child in Britain is bereaved of a parent, which equates to 24,000 new children each year learning to live with a powerful range of confusing and conflicting emotions. Bottled up, these emotions can have damaging consequences in later life for the individual, their family and society as a whole.
(Parsons, 2011: 2)

Akerman and Statham's (2011) literature review on childhood bereavement provides a brief overview of educational and psychological outcomes for children and young people bereaved of a parent or sibling, and the effectiveness of services provided for this group. They found that whilst most children do experience some negative impact on psychological well-being in the short term, for the majority these difficulties do not persist or require specialist intervention. However, evidence of impact on educational attainment is generally lacking, as it is on long-term outcomes. Parsons (2011) found that there was more likely to be impact on boys' education than on girls and that this could affect their educational achievements and aspirations. Boys are less likely to talk with peers about a parent's death and were less comfortable in sharing their feelings (Dopp and Cain, 2012: 48).

The need for this to be a reflective critical issue has been justified through students' contributions and valuing of the 'topic', as they have provided many examples of personal experiences encountered during their practice in schools.

- A five-year-old announcing his dad had died – the school knew nothing of this as the father had been estranged from the family.
- A five-year-old was not told her mother had died until the afternoon of the funeral, when she was told to say goodbye to her.
- Lack of attention paid to a young child whose father had died from drug abuse.
- A head teacher died suddenly while a student was on teaching practice and the whole school grieved and the psychological services/counselling team was brought in to support both staff and children.

Reflective challenge points

What do you, as an early years practitioner, need to know about and do if any similar situation occurs in your setting?

- First acknowledge that grief is a natural response to bereavement but that young children may manifest this grief in different ways – sadness, withdrawal, inappropriate or different behaviour to normal.
- Provide consistency, tenderness; support; personal time and space.
- Check if the setting has a policy and ask for support from colleagues.
- Arrange a parent/staff meeting to meet the needs of the child and support parent(s) when a significant member of the family (parent or sibling) has died.
- Find out about charities such as Winston's Wish and Child Bereavement UK for support and resources.
- Determine whether the local authority provides counselling support for families and practitioners where necessary.
- Promote positive peer relationships and support through circle time and SEAL resources.
- Use empathy dolls to promote sympathy and understanding.
- Be watchful for any teasing of children.

Children's beliefs about death

Each child has a unique concept of death developed through previous experience, emotional development, media such as cartoons, films, video games, books and television, and quite often through the death of a pet. Children are very interested and curious about death and their common repetitive questions include:

■ What happens when someone dies?
■ How do dead people eat?
■ Which star is Grandma?

There is a strong connection between death concepts and overall cognitive development and children's understanding of what causes death changes as they grow older:

■ Magical – 'I wished he was dead and now he is.'
■ Naive – 'You die from eating a dirty bug.'
■ Moral – 'My Daddy died because I was a bad child.'
■ Scientific, rational – 'You die when your body wears out or when you get an incurable disease.'

A classic study by Nagy (1948) of almost 400 Hungarian children aged three to ten conducted interviews with children and collected their pictures. Her research revealed that a concept of death requires development through three stages.

■ Stage 1 (3 to 5 years) – children believed that death involved a continuation of life, but at a reduced level of activity and experiences resembling sleep. Of greatest concern was the fear of separation, not necessarily the fear of dying or being dead.
■ During Stage 2 (5 to 9 years) children progressed to an understanding that death is final and irreversible.
■ Stage 3 (age 9 and older) reflected the mature components of death.

Abdulmaali's (2010) research on the concept of death in pre-school Muslim children in Iran showed that the children believed:

■ they go to sleep;
■ they go to the sky and stand next to angels and god;
■ they get destroyed;
■ they take a trip underground;
■ they will be recovered and revive again.

Research by Slaughter (2005) demonstrated that children first conceptualise death as a biological event around age five or six years, at the same time that they begin to construct a biological model of how the human body functions to maintain 'life'. Her account of children's developing biological knowledge has implications for practitioners who may be called on to communicate about death with young children. Slaughter and Griffiths' (2007) study about the developmental acquisition of a concept of death with 90 children between four and eight showed that fostering a mature understanding of death as a biological event was associated with lower levels of fear and anxiety. Slaughter (2005: 184) advises asking open-ended questions to get a feel for the child's understanding of basic biology – the human body, life and death. She suggests young children will need simple explanations that death means that life stops: the deceased cannot eat, breathe or move and will not return. They may need this repeating as they try to come to terms with this very difficult concept. Children who have been bereaved will require a lot of support. They will need much reassurance that they are loved and safe and that everything is going to be all right.

However, it is too simplistic to view just age as the determining factor with regard to death concepts. Children who have experienced a parent's death, who are dying themselves, or who have witnessed violent, traumatic death will perceive death in an adult-like manner at a much earlier age than children who have not had such experiences. These children can gain a mature concept of death at an earlier age.

Reflection challenge points

- What are the causes of death and are some more traumatic than others?
- Think about illness; accidents; old age; victims of crime; experience of war as service families or as refugees and asylum seekers.
- Think about euphemisms – do adults' misconceptions and euphemisms confuse children – e.g. passed away; gone away; gone to sleep.
- What do you need to know about a child's family and community's beliefs, religion and culture in how they deal with death?
- How do you deal with your own cultural beliefs and experiences?

Further reading

Arnold, C. and the Pen Green Team (2010) 'Cara: trying to make sense of a death in her family', Chapter 8 in *Understanding Schemas and Emotion in Early Childhood*. London: Sage.

Griffiths, R. (2007) 'Coping with bereavement', Chapter 7 in Moyles, J. (ed.) *Early Years Foundations: Meeting the challenges*. Maidenhead: Open University Press/McGraw Hill.

Resources and support

- Winston's Wish – childhood bereavement charity – information for schools and professionals when supporting a bereaved child, such as *Muddles, Puddles & Sunshine* activity book to help when someone has died (www. winstonswish.org.uk).
- Child Bereavement UK supports families at such difficult times and aims to limit the potential for psychological problems in the longer term. They believe it is crucial that all professionals are able to recognise and respond appropriately to bereaved families' varied emotional needs (www. childbereavement.org.uk).
- Memory Box – to keep special items in.

References

Abdulmaali, K. (2010) *The concept of death in preschool children*. Paper presented at EECERA conference, Birmingham, 5–8 September.

Akerman, R. and Statham, J. (2011) *Childhood Bereavement: A rapid literature review*. London: Childhood Wellbeing Research Centre.

Brock, A. (2011) 'The child in context: policy and provision', Chapter 1 in Brock, A. and Rankin, C. (eds) *Professionalism in the Early Years Interdisciplinary Team: Supporting young children and their families*. London: Continuum.

Dopp, A.R. and Cain, A.C. (2012) 'The role of peer relationships in parental bereavement', *Death Studies*, 36: 41–60.

Nagy, M. (1948) 'The child's view of death', in Feifel, H. (ed.) (1959) *The Meaning of Death*. New York: McGraw-Hill.

Parsons, S. (2011) *Long-Term Impact of Childhood Bereavement: Preliminary analysis of the 1970 British Cohort Study (BCS70)*. London: Child Wellbeing Research Centre.

Potts, S. (2013) 'Least said, soonest mended? Responses of primary school teachers to the perceived support needs of bereaved children', *Journal of Early Childhood Research*, 11: 95–107.

Royal College of Pyschiatrists (2009) *Bereavement: Key facts*. Retrieved 15 April 2014 from http://www.rcpsych.ac.uk/healthadvice/problemsdisorders/bereavementkeyfacts.aspx.

Slaughter, V. (2005) 'Young children's understanding of death', *Australian Psychologist*, 40(3): 179–86.

Slaughter, V. and Griffiths, M. (2007) 'Death understanding and fear of death in young children', *Clinical Child Psychology and Psychiatry*, 12(4): 525–35.

How can I develop my professional knowledge and practice?

How can I cater for children's individuality?

Rachel Sparks Linfield

When Lucy, aged four years and three days, first joined my reception class I quickly realised that she was extremely independent and observant with a strong desire to help. Three examples stand out from her first year in school:

An early morning during the first week when a friend had difficulty putting on his indoor shoes and Lucy tried to assist. Lucy's method was to lay Stan on his back, grab his ankle and slam the shoe against the foot. Lucy tried this approach several times but not unsurprisingly the shoe would not go on. After failing to help, Lucy approached me with the shoe: 'Here you go, Mrs Linfield, I think this one needs you.' I put on the shoe and quietly wiped a tear from Stan's eye. Lucy looked on in interest at my shoe techniques and then said, 'Actually I think it would be better for you if Stan learnt to do it himself.'

The lunchtime when I put out materials for a surprise creative card-making activity. After lunch I returned to find my classroom had been cleared. On collecting the class from the playground Lucy explained that after lunch she had found the classroom in 'a real mess' so had wanted to surprise me and clear it up. I still smile at the irony of the two 'surprises', one which then did not happen.

The school inspection when Lucy peeped at the inspector's observation notes for a phonics activity and realised the satisfactory box had been ticked. 'Oh, is that what you thought?' she asked. 'I thought it was the "out-something" word (Lucy meant "outstanding"). Perhaps if you'd been in with us last week you'd have known more about what we were on about.' The inspector later changed his report.

A principle that should guide early years settings is that 'every child is a **unique child**, who is constantly learning and can be resilient, capable, confident and self-assured' (Department for Education, 2012). Lucy in the examples above typifies this principle. She demonstrated surprising maturity and an ease in speaking with adults. Yet, when more is known about Lucy's home background, her social skills and desire to please are less surprising. Lucy's parents were divorced and never spoke to each other. Lucy spent half the week with her mother and soon to be stepfather, and the second half with her father and nanny. Wednesdays were changeover days. These were the occasions when Lucy needed to ensure she had all she required for the coming half-week. Throughout the year, Lucy successfully managed her own school needs such as remembering to bring in her book bag, costumes for plays, and ingredients for cooking. She also always asked for two letters for school events. Lucy's independence and ability to take responsibility, not only for herself, but also to ensure each parent knew what they needed to know, showed many traits that one would associate with a child of greater age and was a surprise to me as her class teacher. On reflection, however, it high-lighted the need to not limit what we might expect from a child. As Thomas, when discussing children's competence (cited in Waller, 2005) argues, 'children often turn out to be more capable and sophisticated than they are given credit for.'

Throughout her reception year Lucy made a great impression on me. She frequently managed to make astute comments that helped me to focus on what I did and, at times, question my own practice. She was correct when she com-mented that it would be better to teach Stan how to put on his shoes than take the quicker route of doing it for him. Her view that the inspector needed knowl-edge of the phonics sessions in the previous week to understand the value of the session he observed showed her awareness of the development of knowl-edge over time. Yet, at times, her comments could appear blunt and over famil-iar. Her manner raised questions as to when an adult should intervene. This is echoed within the SPEEL study which concluded, when considering the aspect of knowing when and how to intervene in children's learning, that 'it became clear that practitioners found this aspect challenging' (Moyles *et al.*, 2002: 131). Indeed, throughout the year there was a fine balance between helping Lucy to follow the routines of the early years setting and allowing her to follow her own train of thought.

In recent years the importance of child-initiated activity has been recognised, and the benefits that may follow from allowing children to engage in their own areas of interest. It has been shown that child-initiated learning can ensure that 'children feel they have ownership of their learning and in the direction (with guidance) in which they want the learning to develop' (Lambert, 2012). Whilst Lucy's independent personality lent itself easily to initiating activities for both herself and her peers she also, as the year progressed, required support in accepting that sometimes she needed to participate in adult-led sessions and that her way was not always the only option!

Reflection challenge points

- How would you have reacted to Lucy within the three examples?
- How can we enable children to develop their unique dispositions?
- To what extent is child-initiated learning a feature of your early years practice?
- How can practitioners help children to express critical opinions with sensitivity, in socially acceptable ways?

Resources and support

Featherstone, S. (2008) *Like Bees, Not Butterflies: Child-initiated learning in the early years.* Lutterworth: Featherstone Education Ltd.

Hodgman, L. (2011) *Enabling Environments in the Early Years.* London: Practical Pre-School.

Lindon, J. (2010) *Positive Relationships: Child-initiated learning.* London: Practical Pre-School.

References

Department for Education (2012) *Statutory Framework for the Early Years Foundation Stage.* London: Department for Education.

Lambert, S. (2012) 'Inclusion and "educating" the whole child', in Beckley, P. (ed.) *Learning in Early Childhood.* London: Sage.

Moyles, J., Adams, S. and Musgrove, A. (2002) *SPEEL Study of Pedagogical Effectiveness in Early Learning.* London: Department for Education and Skills.

Waller, T. (2005) *An Introduction to Early Childhood.* London: Paul Chapman Publishing.

How do I develop children's understanding of the concept of time?

Lyndsey Shipley

The EYFS area of learning for mathematical development in Development Matters (DfE, 2012) states that practitioners should enable children to use everyday language to share their thinking about size, weight, capacity, position, distance, time and money. Getting young children to understand the concept of time can be difficult, as their present or being 'now' is more important (Montague-Smith, 2002). Montague-Smith (2002) believes that the priority for time is for children to understand concepts of every day. By the term 'every day' Montague-Smith (2002) means that current and present is what children need to understand, Fortunately the new EYFS (DfE, 2012) states that children need to grasp the verbal stages about time concepts first through language rather than the starting point of reading the time on a clock as proposed at an earlier time in the National Curriculum (DfEE, 1999). Children do not understand the reality of time so they will recollect events differently (Williams and Goodman, 2000) and a more in-depth understanding of time through hours and minutes is difficult to justify within early years practice (Hurst and Joseph, 2003).

Hurst and Joseph (2003) suggest that understanding time procedures can develop through play by ordering events and this can be achieved by putting visual image cards in order. Barker (1998) states that using play techniques will increase the understanding of time, as children will have a visual image of the events and interaction strategies. Haylock and Cockburn (1997) describe the experience of a child playing happily for an hour feeling the time has gone fast, but when a child is bored, an hour may seem a lot longer. Therefore the concept of time according to the clock has no real meaning and specific time on a clock is meaningless until children have understood the wider time scales such as months, weeks and days (Montague-Smith, 2002). Children interpret a number of years, for example ten years, as 'forever' (Haylock and Cockburn, 1997).

The teaching objectives for 'time' are hard to identify within early years as there are no specific strategies for teaching 'time'. In the conversations that I had with the teachers and nursery nurses, it was clear to see that they understood the basic concept of teaching the children time. This was linked to the early stages of time and how this was developed. Talking to one colleague made me realise that as time progressed from day to night, that was a way to explain stages of time to the children. As a series of days led onto weeks, months and years etc., it combined with significant events to produce a development of history. This is a broad way of explaining the development of time to the children without too much in-depth analysis. Atkinson (1960) writes about the same process that the teachers described, giving me a clear understanding of how the broad approach of early years teaching is important in order to develop and further the understanding of smaller time scales such as minutes and hours later. Coward (1997) agrees with Atkinson and relates to the progression of time through teaching historical stages and development, and you will have seen how Tina Thornton in Chapter 12 also works in this way with the children in her reception class.

To begin to understand the concepts of a day children are encouraged to count in 'sleeps' (as my mother did with me). Hunting et al. (2012) described this as a 'fundamental pattern' which children can understand in the run-up to significant dates. Children begin to realise time development through going to bed and waking up to begin a new stage. According to Williams and Goodman (2000), children understand that a stage evolves by linking to science. A chick hatches from an egg and over a period the chicken grows into a hen. However, they do not understand the specific time the process takes, but they do understand that it does not happen straight away. By linking to the cycle of life the children see that everything develops through stages, meaning 'time' increases and does not just happen in one stage (Martin, 2001).

Sequencing events may become clearer as children can relate better to significant events (Pound and Lee, 2011). Most children know their personal significant events, such as religious celebrations and birthdays, because their parents become more enthusiastic as the celebration gets closer. They will then know about Christmas and understand New Year. Children know about these through adult influences and they can begin to piece together the sequence of events, for example, by knowing that Bonfire Night follows Halloween; teachers can then present the stages of what happens next. A child may say that 'It is my sister's birthday before Christmas', knowing in the time scale that their sister's birthday comes before Christmas. This links to the use of time connectives in language to understand what comes first (TES, 2012). According to Haylock and Cockburn (1997) and Barker (1998), children first need to grasp that events happen in a particular order. Looking at a sequence of events allows children to see that there are different times when things happen. They then move on to look at their daily routine and begin to understand that things happen at different times of the day.

To begin with, children believe that time is something that happens over a long stretch. However, when they have a structured routine they begin to see that even a day has stages as well. Haylock and Cockburn (1997) believe this is because the word 'time' has a broad meaning and has no specific scale; children become confused about how long one period of time actually is. Within the EYFS (DfE, 2012) teaching time is done through speaking activities, in order for children to meet learning objectives, and profile points such as 'recalling past events' and 'ordering events' (DfE, 2012).

The progression from early years is developing what the children already know. Practitioners also continue to develop knowledge in order to increase their understanding. According to Vygotsky (1978), building on the children's knowledge allows the children to have a clearer understanding of the concepts they are learning (cited in McLeod, 2012). The teacher will work in classroom settings talking to the children about different sections of the day and they will begin to use set times in order to describe this. They will look at specific times of the day that do not change within their routine – for example, dinner time is at twelve o'clock. Progressing by describing what the clock looks like at this point (both hands on the twelve), the children get a clearer idea of the 'time and time' concept. Feilker (1997) believes this indirect way of teaching allows children to begin showing curiosity about learning. However, this could give early misconceptions of how to read time as the two hands are on the same number, not giving each hand a specific 'job' (hour and minute hand). Introducing these steps allows children to discover new terminology. Hunting *et al.* (2012) believe this is a good progression idea in early mathematics as children move directly on to a new topic with a prior understanding. According to Cotton (2010), Haylock and Cockburn (1997), Suggate *et al.* (2000) and others there are many misinterpretations of the clock as so many children do not recognise the numbers on the clock and the terminology used.

The next step is telling the time. Cotton (2010) states how many children often tell the time using the digital clock (even if reading an analogue clock) as more children are used to seeing digital clocks and time being expressed as 'three forty-five' rather than 'quarter to four' due to the development in technology. Suggate *et al.* (2000) disagree with Cotton (2010), and they believe that children have to have an understanding of the analogue clock before the digital clock. Koshy *et al.* (2000) describe one issue of time that most children would expect, and that is for the clock to have a metric configuration and therefore have one hundred minutes in an hour. Suggate *et al.* (2000) agree with this misunderstanding and also develop the idea further that there is no clear concept of time functions for a child. The clock consists of twelve hours; however, there are twenty-four hours in a day, each hour is sixty minutes and there are seven twenty-four hours within a week. There are fifty-two weeks and also three-hundred-and-sixty-five-and-a-quarter days in a year. This has no clear pattern for children as their numbers are used mainly with whole numbers in groups of ten, therefore the concept of a singular transaction in time can confuse children from the start. Suggate *et al.* (2000) describe this as an awkward process for children to master; however, most children do grasp the concept eventually.

From the research it is clear to see that the earlier stages of education have a wider view of 'time'. For example, the younger children discuss the big scale of years, months and significant events whereas the older children look at smaller time scales such as clocks, hours and minutes. My research shows that children have to have a clear understanding of the concept of time in order to grasp the specific time scale. The misconceptions I have outlined can only be solved by further understanding and pedagogy within the area through the use of visual aids and exercises.

Reflective challenge points

- Do you now think you have a better understanding of the concept of time as perceived by young children?
- How would you teach the concept of time to children of different ages?
- How will you deal with children's misconceptions?

References

Atkinson, R.J.C. (1960) *Stonehenge*. London: Hamish Hamilton Ltd.

Barker, S. (1998) *Maths through Play*. London: MacDonald & Co.

Cotton, T. (2010) *Understanding and Teaching Mathematics*. Harlow: Pearson Education.

Coward, B. (1997) *Social Change and Continuity*. Harlow: Pearson Education.

DfE (2012) *Early Years Foundation Stage*. Runcorn: Department for Education.

DfEE (1999) *The National Curriculum*. London: Department for Education and Employment.

Feilker, D. (1997) 'Some notes on mental mathematics', *Mathematics Teaching* 160, Derby: Association of Teachers of Mathematics.

Haylock, D. and Cockburn, A. (1997) *Understanding Mathematics in the Lower Primary Years*. London: Paul Chapman.

Hunting, R., Mousley, J. and Perry, B. (2012) *Young Children Learning Mathematics: A guide for educators and families*. Camberwell, Australia: ACER Press.

Hurst, V. and Joseph, J. (2003) *Supporting Early Learning: The way forward*. Second edition. Buckingham: Open University Press.

Koshy, V., Ernest, P. and Casey, R. (2000) *Mathematics for Primary Teachers*. London: Routledge.

Martin, D. (2001) *Constructing Early Childhood Science*. Albany, NY: Thompson Learning.

McLeod, S. (2012) 'Zone of proximal development' (internet), *Simply Psychology*. Retrieved 15 April 2014 from http://www.simplypsychology.org/Zone-of-Proximal-Development.html.

Montague-Smith, A. (2002) *Mathematics in Nursery Education*. London, Cromwell Press.

Pound, L. and Lee, T. (2011) *Teaching Mathematics Creatively* (Learning to Teach in the Primary School Series). London: Routledge.

Suggate, J., Davis, A. and Goulding, M. (2000) *Mathematical Knowledge for Primary Teachers*. Second edition. London: David Fulton Publishers.

TES (2012) 'Time connectives' (internet), *TES Connect*. Retrieved 15 April 2014 from http://www.tes.co.uk/teaching-resource/Time-Connectives-6303362/.

Williams, S. and Goodman, S. (2000) *Helping Young Children with Maths*. London: Hodder Education.

Communication using new technologies – the tip of the iceberg

Alix Coughlin

Early years practitioners are educating 'Generation M', so named for the central role media has in young children's lives (Roberts *et al.*, 2005, in Birdi, 2012). From a very young age children are exposed to the new technologies around them – photographed from birth on digital cameras and phones, their images posted on the internet or in digital photo frames; computers, laptops and tablets are present as they sit with their parents; using video-calling to communicate with family, often in different countries; questions answered at the touch of a screen. Consider all the new words that have entered the English language in the last few years – Google, Skype, e-reader, tweeting, texting, blogging, hashtags, trolling, even lols (Chatfield, 2013) – that will become part of a child's vocabulary without their needing any of it explaining. It is no wonder that media has such an important role in their lives. And for those practitioners who have been born into Generation Z (Emelo, 2013) and are already reliant on technology it will be just another part of practice, but what about the 'digital immigrants' (Prensky, 2001), those practitioners who are less confident or scared by the amount of new technologies they are supposed to use and to teach children to use? How will they gain the necessary knowledge and skills to meet the early learning goal of children being able to 'select and use technology for particular purposes' (Standards and Testing Agency, 2012)?

The market for 'educational apps' is growing rapidly, but does that mean that a setting should purchase tablets and a whole set of apps, and feel that they have met the early years foundation stage (EYFS) requirements? There have been calls for early years educators to 'reflect and build upon young children's experience' of new and digital technologies (Burnett, 2010: 1), while the new EYFS includes a separate aspect for 'technology' rather than Information and Communication Technology (ICT) and it is mentioned specifically as part of the Characteristics of Effective Learning. However, the rapid growth in technology has not been matched by practitioners' understanding of appropriate ways of using new technologies (Brooker, 2003). Research has shown that early years practitioners have a limited or restricted view of what is meant by ICT, with most viewing it as computers and software (Hale, 2008, in Ingleby, 2012). Pedagogical practices and training has only prepared practitioners in using ICT for their own purposes. Chen and Chang (2006, in Burnett, 2010) discuss the lack of confidence among the early years workforce and whether practitioners have enough skill and knowledge to implement the necessary standards. This lack of confidence can lead to a reliance on single desktop computers and didactic software (Brooker, 2003). Some practitioners may argue against the inclusion of new technologies at an early age, citing developmentally appropriate practices as a reason to keep screens out of the early years setting (technology in early childhood, 2013), but there are also compelling reasons as to why technology should be embraced and included in the early years.

Arguments against the use of technology include discussions around the nature of childhood itself, the belief that children should indulge in 'natural', healthy and developmentally appropriate play, as well as concerns about very young children's safety and well-being if using online content. Other concerns include the extent to which young children can engage critically with these new technologies and whether there is any purpose to their use or whether technology is seen as a toy rather than a tool. There is also, as Plowman and McPake (2013) found, a wide variance in access to technologies, both in homes and in settings and schools. Many practitioners have reservations about ICT being used to keep children busy, as a reward or motivating tool or to simply practise skills, rather than as a tool for enquiry, investigation and exploring (Cook, 2004, cited in Ingleby, 2012).

However, studies of children's interactions with digital texts highlight the playfulness, agency and creativity used when engaging with them (Burnett, 2010) and indeed, the Characteristics of Effective Learning encourage finding out and exploring, and being willing to have a go (Moylett and Stewart, 2012), so practitioners should be using their professional skills to encourage children to explore and make links on their own. Highly qualified and knowledgeable practitioners would use their skills to help children engage with any new toy, game, experience or activity in an interactive and developmentally appropriate way, and in a way that is relevant to each individual child – why should this change because the new activity is using technology? Worries about the impact of technology should be 'mediated by teachers' use of the same developmentally appropriate principles and practices that guide the use of print materials and all other learning tools and content for young children' (NAEYC, 2012: 4). The NAEYC statement also includes comments about limitations on the use of technology, pointing out that it is not a substitute for other types of learning but that 'when used intentionally and appropriately, technology and interactive media are effective tools to support learning and development' (NAEYC, 2012: 4).

With the introduction of the new National Curriculum from 2014, in which ICT is replaced by 'Computing' (DfE, 2013), children from as young as five are going to be learning about and using computer programs and computer languages. The move is away from the use of technology, to what it does as a tool to be manipulated and used. Simply being able to use technology is no longer going to be enough: children need to know how it works and to make it work for them. Practitioners are going to need to prepare themselves and the children in their care for a very new world.

So where does this leave technology in the early years? Brooker (2003) points towards the fact that the lack of specific guidelines in the early years, unlike the National Curriculum, leads to more exciting, adventurous and exploratory use of technology. Plus the child-centred and child-led approach to learning in the early years leads to a broader use of technology, especially taking the Characteristics of Effective Learning into account. Practitioners should feel able to use their imagination and creativity to explore ways of introducing and encouraging young children to learn about technology in a way that will prepare them for further school life. Practitioners need to be taking control of their own professional development and using the many sources of information available to further their own knowledge and recognise the possibilities of blogging, connecting with other professionals on Twitter and Pinterest, using apps and tools to make life easier for themselves and stretching the possibilities of what technology can mean in the early years.

> Don't be afraid of technology, or think it is has nothing to offer young children. They have been born into the digital world and encouraging them to make use of this technology will ensure that they develop confidence in making it work for them.
>
> (Kennington, n.d.)

Reflective challenge points: ten ideas on increasing the use of technology in the early years

1. Make each child a 'mini-me' – photograph each child in a pose in front of a white sheet, involve the children in downloading to the computer, printing, laminating and cutting out the figures, then use for the children to illustrate their own stories, playing with the characters wherever they want.
2. Take an iPad on school trips to take photos, then use it as a tool to remind children of details once back in the setting, using the zoom facility to focus on interest points, e.g. photos of birds' feathers, buildings, patterns.
3. Use an app, for example Puppet Pals, for children to make and tell their own story, with their own characters and recording their own voices. These can be saved and shown to parents and other children. Example from Davyhulme Primary School: http://davyhulme.primaryblogger.co.uk/2013/07/05/.
4. Using a microphone, such as the Easi-Speak MP3 recorder, or a recording app on a phone or tablet, such as Audio Memos, children can interview each other, record songs and tell their own stories which can be saved and shared with parents and each other.
5. Blogging, quad-blogging and eTwinning – all devices for showing the children that they are part of a wider community of early years, and that their opinions, views and interests have value. Children are generally interested in other children, no matter where they are in the world: http://quadblogging.

net/quadblogging-with-4-year-olds/; http://www.etwinning.net/en/pub/index.htm.

6. Have a technology 'loose parts' role-play area; fill it with old phones, old computers, keyboards, parts of computers that can be looked at, old cameras, tills, typewriters, torches with batteries and without, anything with buttons to press, tape player, robots, moving toys, old toys, real tools, kitchen tools that move, cardboard boxes, and ask a lot of 'What happens if . . .?' and 'What can you do with . . . ?' questions. Use the book *Welcome to Your Awesome Robot* by Viviane Schwarz (London: Flying Eye Books) as a stimulus to lots of imaginative play.

7. For your own professional development join Twitter, Pinterest and Tumblr and share your ideas with other professionals and learn from them. There is a lot of technology going on in early years settings and practitioners, leaders and policymakers are using social media to find each other and develop ideas. Some suggestions: @NurseryWorld, @earlyyearsontap, @ey_athome, @TESEarlyYears, @community_play, @FoundationYears, @NCrNE, @EYEearlyEd, @blamehound, @MeninEarlyYears, @PACEYchildcare, @TeacherROAR.

8. Use purpose-made and suitable apps and websites, and try to avoid generic American-accented voices. Nosy Crow make story-telling apps that use children's voices, are interactive and look beautiful. Find websites that read books aloud, such as The British Council, or apps that can be engaged with and changed rather than being static: the Ladybird Me Books are a good example.

9. Use available free technology – Vine on Twitter makes seven-second looping videos incredibly easily; it only records when the screen is touched. Children love to see themselves on film or to make a film, or do a snapshot of a day, or film stages in an activity as they build their robot.

10. Make life easier for yourself and use purpose-made programs to record learning journeys and profiles, for example 2Simple's 2Build a Profile or Look@Me.

References

Birdi, B. (2012) 'The changing shape of reading: the 21st century challenge', in Rankin, C. and Brock, A. (eds) *Library Services for Children and Young People: Challenges and opportunities in the digital age*. London: Facet Publishing.

Brooker, L. (2003) 'Integrating new technologies in UK classrooms: lessons for teachers from early years practitioners', *Childhood Education*, 79(5): 261–7.

Burnett, C. (2010) 'Technology and literacy in early childhood educational settings: a review of research', *Journal of Early Childhood Literacy*, 10(3): 247–70.

Chatfield, T. (2013) 'The 10 best words the internet has given English', *The Guardian*, 17 April 17 (online). Retrieved 15 April 2014 from: http://www.theguardian.com/books/2013/apr/17/tom-chatfield-top-10-internet-neologisms.

DfE (2013) *Consultation on Computing and Disapplication of the Current National Curriculum* (online). Retrieved 15 April 2014 from: http://www.education.gov.uk/schools/teachingandlearning/curriculum/nationalcurriculum2014/a00224578/consultation.

Emelo, R. (2013) *Forget Gen Y. Get ready for Gen Z, ASTD*, 21 June (online). Retrieved 15 April

2014 from http://www.astd.org/Publications/Blogs/Human-Capital-Blog/2013/06/Forget-Gen-Y-Get-Ready-for-Gen-Z.

Ingleby, E. (2012) 'How can you survive in the world if you can't use a computer? Exploring the vocational education and training needs of early years practitioners in England', *Journal of Vocational and Educational Training*, 64(4): 475–90.

Kennington, L. (n.d.) *Children and technology (Learning together series)*, BAECE (online). Retrieved 15 April 2014 from: http://www.early-education.org.uk/sites/default/files/publications/Young%20children%20and%20technology%20%2813%29.pdf.

Moylett, H. and Stewart, N. (2012) *Development Matters in the Early Years Foundation Stage*. London: BAECE.

NAEYC (2012) *Technology and Interactive Media as Tools in Early Childhood Programs Serving Children Through Birth to Age 8*. NAEYC (online). Retrieved 15 April 2014 from www.naeyc.org/files/naeyc/file/positions/PS_technology_WEB2.pdf.

Plowman, L. and McPake, J. (2013) 'Seven myths about young children and technology', *Childhood Education*, 89(1): 27–33.

Prensky, M. (2001) 'Digital natives, digital immigrants'. *On the Horizon*, 9(5): 1–13.

Standards and Testing Agency (2012) *EYFS Profile Exemplification for the Level of Learning and Development Expected at the End of the EYFS*. Coventry: STA.

technologyinearlychildhood (2013) 'Is it really OK to put technology in an early childhood classroom?' *Technology in Early Childhood* (blog), 21 February 21 (online). Retrieved 15 April 2014 from http://technologyinearlychildhood.com/tag/developmentally-appropriate/.

What should I do about young children's gun play?

Rachel Marshall, Nicola Milton, Paula Render and Jennifer Smith

Case study scenario: a small group of children are pretending to play with guns

Practitioner 1: What's going on over here, boys? Do we play like this in school?

The children freeze and stop what they are doing.

No we don't, now go and play nicely in the sand or do a nice painting. *(Not giving the children a chance to answer)*

Practitioner 2: Why did you ask them to stop playing?

Practitioner 1: Well, they were shooting each other and we don't play with guns here!

Practitioner 2: But why not?

Practitioner 1: Well, there's a zero tolerance policy.

Practitioner 2: There isn't actually a government or school policy. It's just what we've always done but maybe we need to re-think our practice.

Practitioner 1: Really, well there should be one! Allowing aggressive play just promotes violence. And what about children that have witnessed violence, like the refugee children who have come from war-torn countries. Aggressive play, particularly guns, could be disturbing for them and for children who witness violence at home.

Practitioner 2: That is certainly something we need to consider and monitor closely but role-play can allow children to come to terms with things they have witnessed and make sense of the world they live in. If we make sure they know that it doesn't have to be that way and let them act out their experiences, we'll have a better idea of how to support them.

Practitioner 1:   Well I don't agree at all, I think children get hurt if we let them play like that.

Practitioner 2:   Of course we need to establish ground rules and if they're getting too boisterous we need to step in, but if they are allowed to play they are more likely to understand the boundaries and rules they need to adhere to so that no one gets hurt. Banning gun play doesn't stop them, it just encourages them to be deceitful.

Child 1:   Let's play outside.

Child 2:   Yeah, the teacher won't see us out there.

Child 1:   Why am I allowed to watch telly and see lots of my favourite superheroes shooting baddies and saving the day?

Child 2:   I know. I love *Transformers* and *Ben 10*. I only want to play like them. Transformers have massive guns and shoot the baddies.

Child 1:   So if it's so bad for us to play with guns and pretend to shoot and beat up the baddies, does that mean my daddy is bad for being in the army and using real guns?

Child 2:   And does it mean that my big brother is bad because I've seen him play computer games that have loads of guns in?

Practitioner 1:   Well, I blame the media and video games; even those children who haven't witnessed violence see it every day on the TV!

Practitioner 2:   And nothing is going to change that, so the best we can do is support them to make sense of what they see.

Practitioner 1:   Why are boys so obsessed with aggressive play; why can't they be more like the girls?

Practitioner 2:   Although generally boys are more interested in this type of play, some girls will join in given half a chance. Maybe they are just more willing to conform to the adult rules than the boys. Our boys aren't doing as well as the girls either, so we need to raise their attainment, so why don't we try a different approach?

Practitioner 1:   OK, I take your point . . . so how can I more effectively support their learning?

Practitioner 2:   I found this book, *We Don't Play With Guns Here* really helpful; it helped me look at things from a different perspective and see how this sort of play can support social skills and imagination.

This script case study, based on an excerpt from Holland (2003: 1–2), also draws on research undertaken by Brown (2007), Browne (2004), Fabian and Dunlop in Moyles (2010); Bauer and Dettore (1997), Levin and Carlsson-Paige (2006), Carlsson-Paige (2007) and DCSF (2007).

FIGURE cs.3   Superhero play.

Focused reflection point

- Why is superhero gun play a critical issue for practitioners?
- How do we reflect on this issue and take account of the different perspectives and factors that influence our thinking and practice?

Children of the 1950s would later remember with genuine fondness the sunny moments of play out of sight of grownups. Keaton (2010) observes that men, and sometimes women, even those who identified themselves as anti-war during the Vietnam years, often recall the war play, war scenarios and war toys of their childhood with a special fondness.

> With our guidance and some encouragement, children can use alternative avenues of expression to work on war play-related themes in ways that will help them bring their own ideas and creativity into the process.
>
> (Levin and Carlsson-Paige, 2006: 4)

Practitioners need to remember that children do not understand violence like adults do. Children are intrigued by the powers superheroes possess (Bauer and Dettore, 1997). We can allow children to draw, story-tell or write about superhero play and offer open-ended toys and resources to enable them to engage in imaginative play.

Through their play children experiment with the kind of person they can become. Superheroes are always good. They do the right thing in every circumstance.

(Greenberg, 1995, cited in Bauer and Dettore, 2006: 18)

Boys are sometimes depicted in adverts as more aggressive, active and instrumental to actions than girls are.

(Hoyer and MacInnis, 2008)

Boys are more likely to be involved in aggressive play than girls and are given different toys by their parents because of this (Valkenburg, 2004). This is due to the way boys are portrayed on television. Ross would agree, saying that 'there is a presence of aggression or violence in the adverts aimed at boys' (Ross, 2012). A study undertaken in a classroom in Sheffield showed that girls will join in with superhero and gun play if given the opportunity:

In order for girls to take more active roles in heroic play, teachers need to ensure that they create the conditions in which this can happen. Girls need to feel safe and be given the permission and space to explore these roles.

(Marsh, 2000)

At the end of this case study is a focus plan for physical development based on television's *Ben 10* superhero that might provide an interesting activity to positively channel young children's interest in superheroes.

Focused reflection point

- What are your perspectives on this case study?
- Why not discuss issues raised with a colleague?
- What are children doing when they are involved in war and superhero play?
- How can practitioners support this in a school setting with thirty children and keep them safe?

References

Bauer, K. and Dettore, E. (1997) 'Superhero play: what's a teacher to do?' *Early Childhood Education Journal*, 25(1): 17–21.

Brown, J. (2007) 'Time, space and gender: understanding 'problem' behaviour in young children', *Children and Society*, 21: 98–110.

Browne, N. (2004) *Gender Equity in the Early Years*. Maidenhead: McGraw-Hill Education.

Carlsson-Paige, N. (2007) 'War play: balancing children's needs and adults' concerns', in New, R. and Cochran, M. (eds) *Early Childhood Education: An International Encyclopedia*. Westport, CN: Prager. Retrieved 15 April 2014 from http://www.nancycarlsson-paige.org/articles1.html.

Department for Children, Schools and Families (DCSF) (2007) *Statutory Framework for the Early Years Foundation Stage*. London: DCSF.

Holland, P. (2003) *We Don't Play With Guns Here: War, weapon and superhero play in the early years*. Maidenhead: Open University Press.

Hoyer, W. and MacInnis, D. (2008) *Consumer Behavior*. Mason, OH: South-Western Cengage Learning.

Keaton, A.F. (2010) 'Backyard desperadoes: American attitudes concerning toy guns in the early Cold War era', *The Journal of American Culture*, 33(3): 183–96.

Levin, D.E. and Carlsson-Paige, N. (2006) *The War Play Dilemma: What every parent and teacher needs to know*. New York: Teachers College Press.

Marsh, J. (2000) '"But I want to fly too!": girls and superhero play in the infant classroom', *Gender and Education*, 12(2): 209–20.

Moyles, J. (2010) *The Excellence of Play*. Third edition. Maidenhead: Open University Press.

Ross, K. (2012) *The Handbook of Gender, Sex and Media*. Malden, MA: Wiley-Blackwell.

Valkenburg, P. (2004) *Children's Responses to the Screen: A media psychological approach*. Mahwah, NJ: Lawrence Erlbaum.

Focus plan for Physical Development Activity – Ben 10 Superhero

---

Learning intentions
To copy and explore movement ideas and respond imaginatively to a range of stimuli.
To move confidently using gesture and changes of movement, direction, speed and level.

Physical development

- To show awareness of space, of themselves and others.
- To move with confidence, imagination and in safety.

Cross curricular links: creative development

To use imagination in music, dance.
To match movements to music.

Resources
CD player, *Ben 10* theme song or superman theme.

How the activity will be carried out
Ensure the children are changed for PE appropriately. All jewellery removed and hair slides etc. Walk sensibly in to the hall. Warm up with children finding a safe space and reiterate the need to avoid being close to apparatus and other children.

Introduction: warm up

Teacher led – copying body actions (Discuss what superheroes need to wear. Encourage the children to get dressed as a superhero as follows)

- Put on mask (move head round circular movements)
- Put on cape (swing arms out, up high and down low)
- Put on belt (arms circled around body)
- Put on boots (bend knees touch toes and stretch hands from toes to knees)
- Fly slowly (arm out and travel around hall slowly)

Adult led: main activity

Introduce Ben 10 as a character not at all like the other superheroes we have met in our topic. The children probably know more about this that you do so let them show you their movements and encourage them to make their own movements to some of the other aliens from the Omnitrix. Benjamin 'Ben' Tennyson, also known as 'Ben 10', is the main character in the *Ben 10* series. When he is 10 years old he finds a powerful watch-like alien device, the Omnitrix, which fastens onto his wrist and gives him the incredible power and ability to transform into super-powered aliens. Unable to remove or destroy it, he uses his new powers and abilities to become a superhero. Today we are going to explore some of these aliens.

Big Chill	The **Big Chill** has wings and antennae that can fold up into a cloak with which he can become invisible or fly. It can provide superhuman strength and release freezing vapour. While his cloak can freeze objects, Big Chill also makes Ben capable of withstanding extreme heat. Explore folding the wings like a cloak, fly around the hall but when teacher shouts freeze stay in your shape for 5 seconds.
Swampfire	**Swampfire** ability also allows him to alter his own body, such as tunnelling or growing his feet to root him into the ground. Explore tunnelling actions using arms and legs to burrow, low shapes, grow feet by stretching out arms and legs then make a shape that can root you to the ground.
Spider monkey	**Spider monkey** is an alien with four arms, four eyes and two legs. He is a six-limbed monkey-like alien, with four green eyes, hairy body, and a line coming out from his Omnitrix symbol to his back. He has superhuman agility and, like a spider, can stick to walls, spin webs that he can swing from or create spider web from his tail. Encourage children to split into groups of two and make a spider monkey between them. Discuss the variety of shapes and the different levels and space that is used.
Goop	**Goop** is a shape-shifting, self-regenerating green blob that weighs 200 pounds. Goop is able to change the shape of his body at will. Encourage the children to make their own Goop shape using their bodies. Discuss the variety of shapes and the different levels and space that is used.
Humungousaur	**Humungousaur** is very tall, and can grow taller and larger at force. He has great super strength and a thick layer of skin which provides vast resistance to injury. Encourage the children to explore making their body a different shape and size.

Plenary

Finally, ask the children to make their own alien using many parts of their body and then choose some children to describe their alien, what features it has and how it travels and what its powers are. Play *Ben 10* theme tune and encourage children to dance freely to the music. Give praise and positive feedback.

Questions to ask/Language to use

What shapes have you made with your body? What are your legs/arms/hands/feet doing? How can you make it bigger/smaller/longer/shorter? What others do you know? How would that one move? Can we all do this movement? Can you do it slower, faster, higher, lower? What is next? Can you match your movements to the music?

Differentiation

Encourage children to join in and move in a well-defined area with lots of praise and support. This will help to keep them safe and refrain from bumping into other children or equipment.

Extension

Talk with children about the different aliens and their movements and how it makes them feel. Let the children 'invent' some new moves and teach them to the rest of the class.

Observation and assessment

Teacher observations, photographs, movements and control, also responses to open-ended questions.

Look, listen and note

- Child's ability to copy teacher-led movements during warm up and movement sequence.
- Child's ability to use own ideas to add creatively to the movements.
- Child's ability to choose appropriate movements to fit range of stimuli.

Can the children

- Describe and comment on my own and others' actions.
- Copy, repeat and explore simple skills and actions with basic control and coordination.
- Move with control and vary how they use the space.
- Talk about how to exercise safely and say how their body feels during an activity.

Reflecting on the process of learning how to teach reading using systematic synthetic phonics

Bev Keen

The Rose Review (2006) recommended the 'Simple View of Reading' as the most effective approach for teaching young children to read. This approach separates the process of reading into two elements, decoding and comprehension, which children need to develop to become fluent, confident readers. Within this context, the Rose Review recommended systematic synthetic phonics as the most efficient approach to teaching the skills children need to decode. This review formed the basis initially of the New Labour Government, and more recently the Coalition Government's policies on teaching early reading (Jolliffe *et al.*, 2012). However, as this reflection by an early years trainee teacher on a QTS course shows, the process of learning to teach young children to read can appear far from simple:

> In the beginning, a lack of knowledge made the language of phonics seem beyond comprehension. So many irregular words appeared to be popping up, and I wondered how I have got through my entire education without hearing them. It was also daunting that my KS1 pupils appeared to know more than me!

As a confident adult reader, why can the teaching of systematic synthetic phonics appear so difficult initially?

Spear-Swerling and Brucker (2005: 267) suggest that 'the knowledge base required for teaching beginning reading skills effectively . . . is extensive'. English language can be harder to learn to read than many other languages, such as German or Finnish, which have less complex orthography (Ziegler and Goswami, 2005, cited in Hall, 2006). This is due to English having an advanced code where there are around 44 phonemes (the smallest unit of sound) but only 26 letters (Waugh *et al.*, 2013). In order to represent all the phonemes the English language uses single letters and combinations of letters to create the graphemes (written representation of a sound) such as the digraphs /ai/ /ee/ or the trigraphs such as /ear/ /ure/. This is further complicated because some phonemes such as /ae/ can be represented by several combinations of letters such as /ay/ /ai/ /a/ /a-e/. Similarly there are several graphemes which are pronounced in more than one way, for example /ea/ is pronounced differently in 'stream' and 'bread'.

Within the 2012 Teachers' Standards, there is a requirement that teachers are able to 'demonstrate a clear understanding of systematic synthetic phonics' when teaching early reading (DfE, 2012: 7). However Spear-Swerling and Brucker's (2004: 333) research with trainee teachers demonstrated although a person may be a confident, fluent reader, this specialist knowledge base 'is not an automatic consequence of adult literacy'. This is reflected in these comments from early years trainee teachers, who were discussing their initial impressions of using a systematic synthetic approach to teaching phonics:

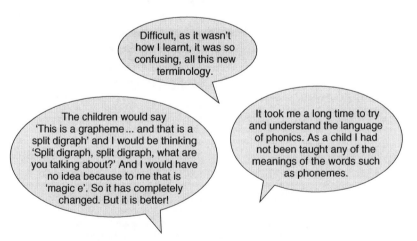

A key element for systematic synthetic phonics is the need to be able to explicitly articulate personal subject knowledge using terminology which may have changed since you were taught it as a child, for example 'magic e' to 'split digraph' to explain /ai/ in the word 'bake'. Similarly. most adults would be able to confidently pronounce the /ai/ digraph in 'train' as an internalised decision, yet if explicitly asked to name another eight ways of writing the /ai/ phoneme, would find this a more difficult task even though they would be able to read words confidently containing those alternative /ai/ graphemes. This mismatch between the internalised knowledge adults apply when reading, which then needs to be explicitly articulated when teaching early reading and phonics, can create apprehension and sense of insecurity, especially for trainee teachers.

Supporting the development of confidence and competency in teaching early reading and phonics

Chard (2004: 182) identified that teachers need to develop:

- specific domain knowledge about the teaching of reading;
- general understanding of how to teach different types of knowledge, skills, concepts and strategies effectively.

These elements were also identified by a group of trainee early years teachers when discussing their experiences about developing an understanding of how to teach early reading and phonics (Keen, 2013). They identified a range of experiences which particularly impacted on their confidence and competency during their ITE course. At the end of the first year of their training the importance of developing their personal subject knowledge and also their understanding of the pedagogy of teaching early reading and phonics were identified as key stages in their development. Fisher (2010: 2) suggests that 'attaching high visibility to phonics is a way of building students' confidence'. The students also identified that it was also important to have opportunities to link this theory to practice through:

- activities such as observing experienced teachers teaching discrete phonics;
- having opportunities to plan sequences of discrete phonics sessions to develop an understanding of the stages of progression;
- planning opportunities for dialogic book talk during guided reading sessions;
- opportunities to discuss children's progress with experienced practitioners;
- opportunities to observe and discuss practice across different age ranges, through observing phonics in a reception, a Year 1 and a Year 2 class within the same school;
- hearing a range of children across the 4–7 age range to enable them to develop an understanding of the progression in early reading skills.

This emphasis changed as the trainee teachers became more confident in their subject knowledge. By the end of their training they were reflecting on different aspects of early reading, such as applying their subject knowledge when discussing individual children's progression in both decoding and comprehension. They also reflected on the effect of the results of their teaching reading with these children. A key element of these reflections was the relationship between the key aspects of their approach to early years teaching and the teaching of early reading and systematic synthetic phonics. This relationship, for some of the trainee teachers, had created dilemmas about how to incorporate the structure of discrete phonics sessions into an ethos of planning from children's interests, or how to address the four-part phonics session (DfE, 2007) using a play-based pedagogy. Several of the trainee teachers reflected with concern on the increased focus during their placement on decoding non-words, in preparation for the DfE Year 1 phonics testing, whilst emphasising their personal belief that early reading should encourage the children to read for meaning. This demonstrated that they reflected on their experiences across several teaching placements and that they were able to articulate their personal positions on teaching early reading and phonics. This evidenced their knowledge, autonomy, skills and values and demonstrated the developing sense of their own professionalism (Brock, 2013).

There was a clear sense that these trainee teachers, as NQTs, would be entering the teaching profession with a sense of their personal professional position on the teaching of early reading and systematic phonics. This cycle will then potentially begin again, as they bring their 'prior knowledge' (from their ITE

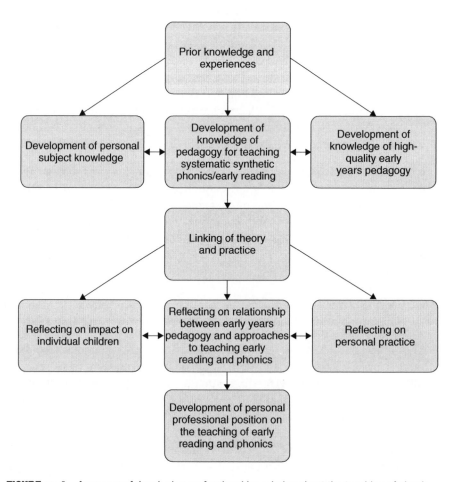

FIGURE cs.4 A process of developing professional knowledge about the teaching of phonics.

course) to the context of their first teaching post. These processes, developed through a combination of experiences, will have different emphasis depending on the stage of development, whether in the process of training as a teacher or as a more experienced teacher changing age ranges or during the introduction of a new teaching approach or scheme. Figure cs.4 represents the series of related experiences highlighted by the trainee teachers as important experiences in developing their understanding of the teaching of early reading, including systematic synthetic phonics.

Reflective challenge points

- What is your confidence level regarding the subject knowledge of teaching phonics?
- Reflect on this case study and on Tina's discussion on phonics in Chapter 12.
- How would you support a trainee development of teaching phonics effectively?

References

Brock, A. (2013) 'Building a model of early years professionalism from practitioners' perspectives', *Journal of Early Childhood Research*, 11(1): 27–45.

Chard, D. (2004) 'Towards a science of professional development in early reading instruction', *Exceptionality: A Special Education Journal*, 12(3): 175–92.

Department for Education (DfE) (2012) *Teachers' Standards*. Runcorn: Department of Education. Retrieved 16 April 2014 from http://www.education.gov.uk/schools/teachingandlearning/reviewofstandards/a00205581/teachers-standards1-sep-2012.

Department for Education and Skills (DfES) (2007) *Letters and Sounds: Principles and practice of high quality phonics*. Nottingham: DfES.

Fisher, R. (2010) 'The pedagogical context of synthetic phonics', in *Report of the UCET Synthetic Phonics and the Teaching of Early Reading Seminar*. London: UCET.

Hall, K. (2006) 'How children learn to read and how phonics helps', Chapter 1 in Lewis, M. and Ellis, S. (eds) *Phonics: Practice, research and policy*. London: Paul Chapman Publishing.

Jolliffe, W., Waugh, D. and Cass, A. (2012) *Teaching Systematic Synthetic Phonics in Primary Schools*. London: Sage/Learning Matters.

Keen, B. (2013) *Aspects of the teaching of early reading, including systematic synthetic phonics, within the context of an Initial Teacher Training course in England*. Paper presented to European Early Childhood Education and Research Association (EECERA) 23rd conference, *Values, Culture and Contexts*, Tallinn, Estonia, 29 August–1 September 2013.

Rose, J. (2006) *Independent Review of the Teaching of Early Reading*. Nottingham: DfES Publications.

Spear-Swerling, L. and Brucker, P. (2004) 'Preparing novice teachers to develop basic reading and spelling skills in children', *Annals of Dyslexia*, 54(2): 332–64.

Spear-Swerling, L. and Brucker, P. (2005) 'Teachers' literacy-related knowledge and self-perceptions in relation to preparation and experience', *Annals of Dyslexia*, 55(2): 266–96.

Waugh, D., Warner, R. and Waugh, R. (2013) *Teaching Grammar, Punctuation and Spelling in Primary Schools*. London: Sage/Learning Matters.

How do I observe and assess children's capabilities?

Avril Brock

This case study examines how to reflect on children's capabilities through observing children and compiling purposeful assessments for children's profiles, the EYFS, the foundation stage profile (FSP), for documenting learning journeys or for understanding children's levels of involvement. These three perspectives from three different professionals reflecting on assessing young children's capabilities demonstrate that they are keen to do a good job, but they have different demands on their role and time and sometimes also a different understanding of what it is best to do, and how, to meet the children's needs and the statutory expectations. Coping with change can be difficult and it is not just lack of knowledge that is the problem, but often time to assimilate and accommodate new thinking and practice.

Jade – Level 3 practitioner

I find the new EYFS assessments difficult to do; they don't seem to be as easy as before, they seem to be harder. I wish they hadn't changed. We used to know them by heart. What are the new ten points to remember? It's difficult to work to the changed statements and time to learn them is hard to find. It's more difficult to transfer observations now. We have to clean each room every night; washing has to be washed and dried and folded away; we have to wash up after breakfast and snacks. Every time a child has a drink we have to wash the cups. All these activities mean that at least one member of staff is not actively working and playing with the children, so actually making time to think through and record observations is difficult. I will ask Shazia when she comes into the setting, what a specific aspect of a child's behaviour or learning means in terms of the EYFS statements.

Claudia – owner manager of an ECCE setting

Some of my staff are finding the new EYFS assessments difficult to do as the wording has changed within the progression statements. There are some new standards, but mostly they have made the original statements broader and less specific. It's not a problem with the number and reasoning and some of the literacy ones, but those such as the new standard of thinking creatively are less tangible. The children have now got to be assessed in the three areas of emerging, expected and exceeded and the staff need to understand what these mean. None of our children will be on exceeding as they leave us before they are near five. It isn't really difficult; they just need to change their thinking a little. The children now have to be assessed on capabilities at 12 to 24 months, 24 to 36, 36 to 48 and 48 to 60, which is no bad thing. For instance it is better for many children such as summer-born boys, as it now shows what they are achieving at a specific age rather than failing to achieve at the end of an academic year. I get the staff to organise assessment activities so they can observe children's acquisition of numbers and sounds.

Shazia – early years teacher attached to a setting

I am finding the new EYFS assessments easy to do now I have the technology. I use an iPad so I can do observations spontaneously, quickly and directly into the system. Of course it is more difficult for practitioners in many private settings. Young children need constant supervision that caters for their care needs which have priority over educational achievements. However, it is valuable for these practitioners to have good practice modelled and see how valuable observations are that come from young children's independent learning and play activities. Of course I have years of experience to draw on and understand about the value of observing. It is really good when a qualified early years teacher is attached to a setting.

Chapters 10, 12 and 13 provide interesting and valuable insights into how to listen to children purposefully and have evidenced how listening to children is necessary to acquire a true picture of their capabilities and to document these to create learning journeys to be read by other practitioners and parents or the foundation stage profile assessments. Clark and Moss (2001) developed the mosaic approach to gain deeper understanding of children's perspectives on their early childhood settings. Mosaic is a multi-method approach and includes talking, listening and observing children, as well as using children's own photographs, tours and maps to develop a holistic perspective on children's views. Mosaic is a valuable approach to use in assessing children's understanding, skills, attitudes and achievements. Using Laever's (2005) levels of engagement and well-being can be a useful way of examining one's practice through reflecting on how children are involved in your provision.

Learning journeys

Perspectives on reflection in the processes of assessing children's learning are influenced by the theories and practices from Reggio Emilia: 'the concept of reflective practice is about a rigorous process of meaning making, a continuous process of constructing theories about the world, testing them through dialogue and listening then reconstructing those theories' (Moss, 2008: xii). Carr (2001) shows that learning journeys or learning stories are a holistic way to document teaching, learning and assessment of young children's achievements, which includes reflecting on children's dispositions and interest. Children's learning journeys are so exciting for all concerned – children, parents and staff. Surely parents keep these for ever, as they can be a superb record of the early years. The detail of what children do and say and what they are interested in are not meant to be brief snapshots but to evidence the depth of thinking that children do. The use of photographs in the documentation can bring it alive, as you can see so much in a photo observation, and when detail and analysis is added through the written word, meaning and understanding are developed for the reader. Carr (2001) talks about magic moments of learning and says that it is important to reflect on children's dispositions to learning.

Involving parents and children

It is important to be careful in your assessments and think about the impact they have on children and parents when they are taken home and read. It is not best practice to hand out reports, assessments or learning journeys on the final day of a term when parents cannot respond or ask questions. Assessments should always include the involvement of both children and parents in order for them to be meaningful and worthwhile.

Reflect on the following true experiences of two parents that occurred in July 2013. What do you think is wrong with them? What would you do about it if it happened in your setting?

Parent perspective 1

Jessica is an only child and whilst she is capable, confident and articulate at home, she is normally quiet and unassuming away from home and at nursery. Jessica's mum was extremely worried when she read the nursery's end-of-year report that she received on collecting Jessica on the final day of the summer term. The nursery had assessed Jessica's achievements according to the three aspects of emerging, expected and exceeded in the areas of learning in the EYFS. The nursery had decided to use symbols to demonstrate this. It was a shock for Jessica's mum to see that the nursery had used a minus sign against many of the statements for personal, social and emotional development. This did not send a message of emerging for this child, who is articulate at home, but strongly indicated that she was not achieving at all in these areas.

Parent perspective 2

I think it is great that Ava's reception class implements a programme of learning along the aims of the Reggio approach that follows children's individual interests. However, the children's experiences in the reception class seemed to vary greatly according to which teacher or teaching assistant was their key worker/group leader.

Ava's group had worked on the topic of trains all year. When Ava's mother and her best friend's mother were comparing the learning journey profile books of their children they found they were identical except for some changes of names.

Reflective practitioners

Practitioners require both insight and knowledge about children when observing and assessing their capabilities and it is valuable to have 'the ability to be a humble interpreter reflecting upon children's statements' (Paige-Smith and Craft, 2008: 53). Recognising how important our interactions with children are and reflecting on these interactions is integrally bound into a reflective approach to practice (Wood, 2008). Remember Schön's 'professional artistry' discussed in Chapter 1 and draw on all aspects of your knowledge and experience to help you improve your provision through developing meaningful assessments.

Reflective challenge points

- How do you observe and assess children's learning and achievements?
- Would you consider using Clark and Moss's (2001) mosaic approach?
- Read about and reflect on Laever's (2005) levels of involvement.
- Have you ever compiled a learning journey or learning story for children?

References

Carr, M. (2001) *Assessment in Early Childhood Settings: Learning stories.* London: Paul Chapman Publishing.

Clark, A. and Moss, P. (2001) *Listening to Young Children: The mosaic approach.* London: National Children's Bureau for the Joseph Rowntree Foundation.

Laevers, F. (2005) *Well-Being and Involvement in Care Settings: A process-oriented self-evaluation instrument.* Leuven, The Netherlands: Kind & Gezin and Research Centre for Experiential Education, Leuven University.

Moss, P. (2008) 'Foreword', in Paige-Smith, A. and Craft, A. (2008) *Developing Reflective Practice in the Early Years.* Maidenhead: Open University Press/McGraw Hill.

Paige-Smith, A. and Craft, A. (2008) 'How does reflective practice inform working with children?' Chapter 3 in Paige-Smith, A. and Craft, C. (eds) *Developing Reflective Practice in the Early Years.* Maidenhead: Open University Press/McGraw Hill.

Wood, E. (2008) 'Listening to young children: multiple voices, meanings and understandings', Chapter 7 in Paige-Smith, A. and Craft, C. (eds) *Developing Reflective Practice in the Early Years.* Maidenhead: Open University Press/McGraw Hill.

Widening reflective professional knowledge

What do I need to know about this issue and why is it important?

Dealing with racist incidents

Gina Houston

Since the Race Relations Amendment Act 2000 came into force, it has been a legal requirement for all institutions in the public sector, including early years provision, to report racist incidents. For many practitioners in early years settings this identified a new concept in their understanding of young children and that they are not exempt from the effects of living in a racist society. Some early years practitioners find the recognition of racism in young children a difficult concept when the traditional pedagogical approach is to nurture young children through supporting their individual growth and development while viewing them as innocent and to be protected (Brown, 1998: 53; MacNaughton, 2003: 17).

The following case study gives an example, from a research project, of a racist incident and how this was addressed by the adults present in the classroom.

Case study

Children in a reception class are lining up to leave the classroom for lunch. The children in the class are predominantly black with an African or African Caribbean heritage. There are two white children in the class. The nursery nurse, Sita, is Asian and the teacher, Christina, is white. The white researcher and Sita are present in the classroom. The researcher is observing the children in the line and notices a black boy, Obi, crying. He sees the researcher looking at him and calls out in a loud voice that a white child, Jason, two children in front of him in the queue, has called him 'chocolate face'. Sita is busy attending to a child and is not apparently aware of the incident. The researcher feels that she has no option but to deal with the situation immediately as Obi is extremely distressed. The other children who are lining up are aware of the situation and some are laughing with Jason. Initially she comforts Obi and tells him that people can be very unkind and make ridiculous comments that are not true. She then turns to Jason and asks him why he has made a comment like that which has upset Obi so much. He stops laughing, shrugs his shoulders and is unwilling to speak further about the incident. At that moment, the children are called into the dining hall by a support worker who comes to the classroom door. The researcher approaches Sita when the children have left the room and asks if she heard the comment. She replies that she had heard but dismisses the incident by saying that 'nothing was meant by it' and that Jason was just repeating the words on a television advert that was currently on television for a chocolate bar. During the lunch period the researcher asks the teacher if she heard about the incident from the nursery nurse. She said that she was 'aware of it', knew that 'this was happening' and 'must do something about it'. Her statement implied that this was not the first incident in the classroom of racist name-calling and that she had not yet addressed it. The researcher did not observe any action on that or subsequent days.

As is legally required, at the time of this incident there was a specific policy in the school on dealing with racist incidents. The policy clearly outlined different kinds of racism that staff should be aware of, both covert and overt, direct and indirect. When the head teacher was asked by the researcher what she thought of as a racist incident, she gave an indirect example of when a child was rude about another child's packed lunch because it contained food from a culture different to his own. All staff had been previously informed of the content of the policy, and the legal requirement to report any such incident in writing to the senior managers. Minimal training and support had been given for analysing what was meant by a racist incident. The recent Single Equality Act 2010 has unified all previous equality legislation, resulting in the outcome that, since 2011, there is no longer a legal requirement to report racist incidents in schools, but this was not so at the time of the incident.

The case study shows that Sita did not consider the incident to be racist and that she believed Jason was harmlessly repeating what he had heard in a television advertisement. This raises an important issue of what is perceived as acceptable in society through the exposure given in the various forms of the media. Because the advert in question used this terminology it was not thought by Sita to be insulting or damaging. She thought it acceptable to see Jason's comment as funny, as did the other children in the classroom line, ignoring the pain felt by Obi which was shown through his tears. This example of the use of terminology on television is an example of how society, and the media in this case, is organised from the majoritarian perspective of whiteness, which does not take into account the underlying implications of racism and the effects on the black population. Obi gave an alternative meaning to the term, from his home and community experiences of being black in a predominantly white society, and interpreted it as being negative and insulting.

The case study also shows how these incidents of racism can occur in the classroom with no warning. The unexpectedness of the remark meant that the researcher was unprepared to discuss this effectively with the children. Because of the classroom routines the situation was not dealt with immediately, which was necessary to provide meaningful support for the black child and to discuss with the white child the implications of the remark and his own attitudes to race. The practitioners did not feel able to address the incident with the children as there were no strategies in place to do this and they had not adequately thought about the issues surrounding the incident previously so as to understand their own feelings and attitudes. This highlights the need for both external and internal training as well as ongoing discussion, to understand issues of racism, the different forms this can take and the implications for classroom practice.

As a result of the practitioners not addressing the incident, Obi and the other children in the class may internalise the lack of emphasis given by practitioners to supporting an important element of black children's experiences and the implications for their socialisation into institutional practices (Katz, 1996). It also reinforces the majoritarian whiteness as being the superior power in the school. This hierarchy based on race can then marginalise black pupils as well as having an effect on their capability to learn and develop.

In Critical Race Theory, when applied to education, the marginalisation of black pupils through the institutional practices of the school being based primarily on white, generally middle-class norms of society can create a psychological double consciousness (Goran, 2007; Gillborn, 2008). This term can be interpreted as black pupils learning to behave in a way that is contradictory to that of their identity outside, in the home and community. Searls (1997: 161) sees double consciousness as a series of 'tensions' which are to be 'perpetually negotiated'. This then creates a new inferiorly perceived identity which can be psychologically damaging to young children (Delgado, 2000).

As Wilson (1978) explains, attending school for the first time:

> for the black child is often a schizoid process. They are alienated abruptly from their culture and must maintain a precarious psychic balance between a black and white world, belonging to neither. The school requires the child to think, feel and behave in ways quite different from everyday life outside school. To the children, white middle class, institutional demands may seem unreasonable, unjust and unnecessary.
>
> (Wilson, 1978: 185–6)

This pressure felt by black pupils can often lead to disaffection with education and can cause them to underachieve. Ignoring racist language and incidents is one way in which this marginalisation can occur. In the case study, Sita and the other black children who were in the classroom line and laughing at the comment made by their white peer were colluding with the ideology of the majoritarian white society by accepting racist language, although perhaps unaware of the implications of this.

Reflection and discussion points

- Considering the recent change in the law through the Equalities Act 2010, do you still think it is necessary to record incidents of racism when they occur in the setting; and if so, why is this important?

- Are you aware of the national and local equality and anti-racist policy and legislation and the implications for practice in your early years settings?
- Can you find any examples of how racism is covertly reproduced in the media to children in programmes that they might watch or children's magazines that they might read?
- Are you ready to deal with incidents of racism in your classroom as soon as they arise? If not, how can you be better prepared?
- What strategies could you use to address racism in the classroom to support black children and attempt to avoid any incidents of racism occurring?

Further reading

Banks, J.A. (2001) *Cultural Diversity and Education*. Boston, MA: Allyn and Bacon.

Connolly, P. (2002) *Too Young to Notice: The Cultural and Political Awareness of 3–6 Year Olds in Northern Ireland*. Belfast: Community Relations Council.

Graham, M. (2001) 'The mis-education of black children in the British education system', in Majors, R. (ed.) *Educating our Black Children*. London: Routledge Falmer.

Preston, J. (2007) *Whiteness and Class in Education*. London: Springer.

References

Brown, B. (1998) *Unlearning Discrimination in the Early Years*. Stoke-on-Trent: Trentham Books.

Delgado, R. (2000) 'A tort action for racial insults, epithets and name-calling', in Delgado, R. and Stefancic, J. (eds) *Critical Race Theory: The cutting edge*. Philadephia, PA: Temple University Press.

Gillborn, D. (2008) *Racism and Education: Coincidence or conspiracy?* London: Routledge.

Goran, G. (2007) *Towards Bi-cultural Competence: Beyond black and white*. Stoke-on-Trent: Trentham Books.

Katz, I. (1996) *The Construction of Racial Identity in Children of Mixed Parentage*. London: Jessica Kingsley Publishers.

MacNaughton, G. (2003) *Shaping Early Childhood*. Maidenhead: Open University Press.

Searls, S. (1997) 'Race, schooling and double consciousness', in Giroux, H. and Shannon, P. (eds) *Education and Cultural Studies*. London: Routledge.

Wilson, A. (1978) *The Developmental Psychology of the Black Child*. New York: Africana Research Publications.

How can an early years setting support the mental health of young children and why is this important?

Lucy Akroyd

Mental health has been described as a state of overall well-being (World Health Organization, 2013). 'Well-being' is the term referred to in the majority of policy concerning practice within the early years since the publication of the *Every Child Matters* Green Paper (2003) and the succeeding Children Act (DfES, 2004). Although several different meanings of well-being have been established (Ereaut and Whiting, 2008) it is commonly based on 'a holistic understanding of their needs and their psychological/emotional needs' (Montgomery *et al.*, 2003: 2) and is regularly used alongside the notion of personal, social and emotional development (PSED). Would you have thought that this topic really has relevance for the early years reflective practitioner working with young children? It is when you realise that one in ten children suffer from a mental health disorder!

A mentally healthy child should be able to

> develop psychologically, emotionally, intellectually and spiritually; initiate, develop and sustain mutually satisfying personal relationships; use and enjoy solitude; become aware of others and empathise with them; play and learn; develop a sense of right and wrong; and resolve (face) problems and setbacks and learn from them.
>
> (DES, 2001: 1)

Poor mental health can mean a variety of problems for children. Green *et al.* (2005) divided mental health disorders into four categories: emotional, such as anxiety, depression and low self-confidence; social, which includes aggressive behaviour; hyperkinetic, referring to lack of concentration or acting restlessly; and less common disorders, such as schizophrenia.

Key factors within the child themselves, their family and the community that can put a child at greater risk of having mental health difficulties include the child having 'specific learning difficulties, communication difficulties or specific developmental delays', living with 'overt parental conflict, family breakdown or . . . inconsistent or unclear discipline' and experiencing 'socio-economic disadvantage, homelessness or discrimination' within the community (DfEE 2001: 3). These factors are supported by evidence from the National Statistics which shows that in 2004 the prevalence of mental disorders was much higher in children who experienced one of the risk factors outlined above (Green *et al.*, 2005). Most of these factors are not uncommon experiences for many children in the UK, which may have some link to the finding that one in ten children suffer from a mental health disorder such as those listed above (Green *et al.*, 2005).

Implications for the early years

A child who is, or who is at risk of being, mentally unhealthy will be suffering, so therefore all those who come into contact with that child have responsibility to support the child and work with the family. The emotional and behavioural problems that mental health disorders can cause, such as anxiety, aggression or hyperactivity for example, can act as a barrier to learning, leading to 'difficulties at school, difficulties with peer relationships and poor school attainment' (Sure Start 2004: 3). Green *et al.* (2005) also found that children with emotional disorders were twice as likely as other children to have a special educational need (SEN) and 52 per cent of those with conduct disorders were considered by teachers to have SEN, which shows that these children will be in real need of extra support from their early years setting.

By the time a child is five years old damage to their mental health may already have occurred, therefore supporting their mental health from as early as birth should be a priority (Balbernie, 2001). Early intervention is a valuable approach, but prevention as a method could be seen as essential. Emde suggested that the reason the issue of mental health in babies is only very rarely referred to in policy and practice is because 'it is often painful and difficult to recognise and address mental health problems in infants and young children' (2001: 23). Perhaps it is for this reason that early years settings and the policies that they follow often use different terminology, such as 'well-being' or 'personal, social and emotional development', to refer to mental health. However, the use of different terminology may be confusing or could be misinterpreted and make multi-agency working difficult as medical professionals, early years professionals, teachers and social workers all use different terms to describe mental health disorders. In addition to this, if they are able to describe how they feel, children will use different terminology to these professionals, and their parents would also be likely to use different words to describe their child's health.

How can an early years setting support the mental health of young children?

Early years settings work with the child, parents and any other agencies that might be involved to establish and agree on the individual difficulties child has, in order for all to work together to improve them successfully. Funding to support children as soon as any mental health problems arise has been introduced by the DfE (2011) – the 'Early Intervention Grant: early intervention and preventative services for children, young people and families' includes funding for Sure Start children's centres (HM Government, 2011: 40). The Early Intervention Grant (EIG) replaced a number of centrally directed grants to support services for children, young people and families and is targeted to respond to local needs:

- Sure Start children's centres;
- free early education places for disadvantaged two-year-olds;
- short breaks for disabled children;
- targeted support for vulnerable young people;
- targeted mental health in schools;
- targeted support for families with multiple problems.

(DfE, 2012a)

The Targeted Mental Health in Schools (TaMHS) (DCSF, 2008) project provides useful advice on how to support and improve children's mental health by tackling problems quickly through whole-school, multi-agency support of the family as well as the child. This programme promotes social and emotional skills being taught as part of the curriculum, and both teachers and parents are given extra training and guidance on how to support their children. This is an advantage as both parents and teachers of those children at risk of, or with, mental health problems become more confident and help recognition of any other children who may be at risk. Settings should have in place specific interventions for any children with 'early signs of social and emotional difficulties' (DCSF 2008: 13). These interventions could include group sessions delivered by a trained specialist which focus on individual problems, with parenting sessions running parallel to these (DCSF, 2008). Children who do not show these early signs, but do live with some of the 'risk factors' discussed earlier, are also supported by this approach.

Early years settings within schools should also use the Social and Emotional Aspects of Learning (SEAL) resources. The SEAL resources refer to five key skills, as set out by Goleman (1995), which can help a child to build resilience and stay mentally healthy: 'self-awareness, self-regulation (managing feelings), motivation, empathy, and social skills'. The fact that a young child would be unlikely to grasp the meaning of each of these skills is taken into account in this approach, as settings are advised to promote the skills indirectly, practising and consolidating them through focused pedagogy.

Every Child Matters (DfES, 2003) and the early years foundation stage Aspects of Personal, Social and Emotional Development (DfE, 2012b) indirectly address supporting young children's mental health. Each of the five *Every Child Matters* outcomes is still relevant:

- Be healthy: mentally and emotionally healthy;
- Stay safe: safe from maltreatment, neglect, violence and sexual exploitation, safe from bullying and discrimination (*all these are established risk factors for poor mental health*);
- Enjoy and achieve: ready for school, attend and enjoy school, achieve personal and social development and enjoy recreation;
- Make a positive contribution: develop self-confidence and successfully deal with significant life changes and challenges;
- Achieve economic well-being: engage in further education, employment or training on leaving school.

By focusing on the significance of each outcome, early years settings should be able to support each child by ensuring they are fulfilling, or are on target to fulfil, each one. If practitioners recognise the relevance of the EYFS Aspects of Personal, Social and Emotional Development (DfE, 2012b) in relation to the child's mental health, they may realise the areas of a child's development, behaviour and understanding which might need to be supported:

- dispositions and attitudes;
- self-confidence and self-esteem;
- making relationships;
- behaviour and self-control;
- self-care and a sense of community.

Building good relationships with children's parents will support the parent–child relationship and help improve the child's mental health. One method used in the programme is the combination of 'behaviourally oriented group parent training' and individual sessions which has been shown to 'improve the quality of the mother–child relationship, which accounts for over 40% of the reduction of the child's difficulties' (Sure Start, 2004: 5). Offering support to help solve individual family problems, such as a financial crisis or parents' relationship difficulties, which are factors that have the risk of damaging the child's mental health, can also make a difference (Sure Start, 2004).

To conclude, it is the responsibility of early years settings to support the mental health of young children as 'emotional well-being and good mental health are crucial for every aspect of a child's life, now and in the future' (DSCF, 2007: 33). Those who work within the setting need to ensure that all children get the best start in life.

Reflective challenge points

The key areas to address are to:

- offer early intervention in order to tackle problems before they have a serious effect on children's mental health;
- remove stigma and unfamiliarity of the fact that young children can have mental health problems in order for professionals and parents to be comfortable with and capable of supporting their children effectively;
- work in partnership with other agencies, parents and the children themselves to agree on how best to support the child;
- support the mental health of young children through working with parents to uphold a positive relationship with their child and to reduce any other risk factors within the home;
- provide young children with an environment that offers the resources, routines and opportunities which can provide for the child's basic needs and leave them free to develop their essential personal, social and emotional skills.

References

Balbernie, R. (2001) 'Circuits and circumstances: the neurobiological consequences of early relationship experiences and how they shape later behaviour', *Journal of Child Psychotherapy*, 27(3): 237–55.

Department for Children, Schools and Families (DCSF) (2007) *The Children's Plan: Building brighter futures*. London: The Stationery Office.

Department for Children, School and Families (DCSF) (2008) *Targeted Mental Health in Schools Project: Using the evidence to inform your approach: a practical guide for headteachers and commissioners*. Nottingham: DCSF Publications.

Department for Education (DfE) (2011) 'Government sets out reform of early learning and children's centres' (internet). Retrieved 16 April 2014 from: http://www.education.gov.uk/childrenandyoungpeople/earlylearningandchildcare/a00191829/government-sets-out-reform-of-early-learning-and-childrens-centres.

Department for Education (DfE) (2012a) *Early Intervention Grant FAQs* (internet). Retrieved 16 April 2014 from www.education.gov.uk/childrenandyoungpeople/earlylearningandchildcare/delivery/funding/a0070357/eig-faqs.

Department for Education (DfE) (2012b) *Statutory Framework for the Early Years Foundation Stage (EYFS)*. Runcorn: Department for Education.

Department for Education and Employment (DfEE) (2001) *Promoting Children's Mental Health within Early Years and School Settings*. Nottingham: DfEE.

Department for Education and Skills (DfES) (2003) *Every Child Matters*. London: The Stationery Office.

Department for Education and Skills (DfES) (2004) *The Children Act 2004*. London: The Stationery Office.

Emde, R.N. (2001) 'Infant mental health challenges for Early Head Start: understanding context and overcoming avoidance', *Zero to Three*, 22(1): 21–4.

Ereaut, G. and Whiting, R. (2008) *What Do We Mean by 'Wellbeing'? And why might it matter?* London: DCSF.

Goleman, D. (1995). *Emotional Intelligence.* New York: Bantam Books.

Green, H., McGinnity, A., Meltzer, H., Ford, T. and Goodman, R. (2005) *Mental Health of Children and Young People in Great Britain, 2004.* London: Palgrave Macmillan.

HM Government (2011) *No Health Without Mental Health: A cross-government mental health outcomes strategy for people of all ages.* London: The Stationary Office.

Montgomery, H., Burr, R. and Woodhead, M. (2003) *Changing Childhoods: Local and global.* Chichester: Wiley.

Sure Start (2004) *Early Years Foundation Stage (EYFS) Resources: Children's mental health promotion.* Nottingham: DfES Publications. Retrieved 16 April 2014 from www.teachfind.com/national-strategies/early-years-foundation-stage-eyfs-resources-childrens-mental-health-promotion.

World Health Organisation (2014) *Mental Health: Strengthening our response.* Fact sheet No. 220. Updated April 2014. Retrieved 16 April 2014 from http://www.who.int/mediacentre/factsheets/fs220/en.

How to support asylum and refugee children in early years education

Rebecca Wood

'Refugees are ordinary people to whom extraordinary things have happened' (Olusoga, 2008: 240). In 2011, there were 19,804 applications for asylum in the UK (Refugee Council, 2012). A person who has refugee status refers to someone who 'owing to a well-founded fear of being persecuted for reasons of race, religion, nationality, membership of a particular social group or political opinion' has fled from his or her home country or is unable to return to it (Rutter, 2003: 4). An asylum seeker is defined as 'a person who has crossed an international border in search of safety, and refugee status, in another country' (Rutter, 2003: 4). Refugee families have proportionally more children under the age of five than the general population (Olusoga, 2008: 236) and this creates increasing challenges and importance for practitioners who work in ECCE. It is therefore imperative that practitioners meet the needs of very young children of refugee status and background, as they are in the same critical periods as other children of their age with an added pressure of experiencing a new environment, culture and ECCE setting.

When refugee children move to the UK, they bring not only inquisitive thoughts and wonders about their new world, but also trauma, worries and confusion. These children are entering ECCE settings and schools where there is often little prior knowledge of supporting their needs or the languages spoken (Hoot, 2011). The NSPCC policy (2008) for refugee or asylum-seeking children states that these children should receive the same protection and welfare as that afforded to other children – they should grow up with their family and not be separated from parents against their will, unless it is in the child's best interest. Every child has the right to an education, the right to an identity, and the right to enjoy her culture (UNHCR, 1994). As a refugee child it is common for one or more of these rights to be taken away and it is therefore the duty of a practitioner to ensure that rights are reinstated.

Refugee and asylum-seeking children face far greater danger to their health and well-being than the average child (UNHCR, 1994). They are subject to sudden and/or violent emergencies, disruption to the structure of their family and community, and shortages of resources. Parental distress and anxiety may also have an effect on the child's well-being, as it can seriously disrupt the normal and emotional development of the children. The asylum application process is known to be time-consuming and stressful for those involved, and this alone may have a negative effect on children's behaviour, mood and educational factors.

It is common for refugee children in ECCE to lose their cultural identity and they may develop low self-worth as they can be overwhelmed with the need to 'fit in'. It is imperative that a child's first language is encouraged as it is 'often the first thing to be lost and a vital part' of a child's identity (UNHCR, 1994). All refugee children will have very different life experiences to one another, and it is their right to embrace these if they choose to; some of these, however, may be quite traumatic, and children may be sensitive when discussing or thinking about these experiences.

An advantage of receiving refugee or asylum-seeking children in early years education is that they have the freedom to play; and this play is vital for the healthy development of these children. Play experiences can help children to cope with the experiences they have had, and can relax them and relieve tensions which may be at home; this process is crucial to their development and their ability to cope and learn to function within the new community (UNHCR, 1994). It is valuable if these children can explore their surroundings without an adult attempting to talk to them or 'at them' and for practitioners to observe and look for any signs of development issues.

It is important for children to use their first language in their play and work to develop their first and additional language, knowledge and understanding and self-identity. Children need to know that the teachers and practitioners value and respect their first language and their culture. This could be done by teachers giving the refugee children opportunities to develop their first language and to share it with the class and by the practitioners learning some words in the child's first language. Value and respect could also be shown by the school embracing multiculturalism, celebrating festivals, tasting different foods, discussing religion; this could be of the refugee child in question or a range which aren't necessarily celebrated in the classroom or school.

All settings should make sure they have a refugee or asylum-seeker policy in place, and before a child begins the school, they should ensure that there is a person with designated responsibility for refugees (Rutter, 2003). This policy should then be translated into the home language of the refugee child starting the school and given to parents. It should include the setting's views about what they expect from the individual child, their parents and also the race and discrimination policies; this is so the parents or family of the child do not feel alone if anything should happen to them when in school. It gives the family reassurance over what is tolerated within the school and what is not; that the setting does not agree with or tolerate racism and that it promotes cultural diversity.

Practitioners need to be especially critical of labels attached to children, and to understand the implications of labelling these children as refugees. For example, these labels can often change the school's and local authority's views on refugee children. In addition to these labels, how teachers talk about refugee and asylum-seeking children is incredibly important; the stereotypes which are given in the classroom can stay with the children for the rest of their lives.

Practitioners can build up their knowledge of refugee children in general and then specifically when they enter the setting. They need to provide support for social and emotional development, cultural identity and promoting meaningful family and home partnerships. Promoting a sense of belonging can enable families to participate more within the setting and the child will then be able to make progress in her education. This may require practitioners to step outside their role in regards to supporting and creating contacts with those who can also provide help, as not all problems can be solved by the same professional.

Reflective challenge points

- This 'case study' has introduced some key factors that you need to know about – what are these?
- Do you know where to access further knowledge if the need arises?
- How will you get support for yourself as a reflective practitioner and for the children with whom you work?

References

Hoot, J.L. (2011) 'Working with very young refugee children in our schools: implications for the world's teachers', *Procedia: Social and Behavioural Sciences*, 15: 1751–5.

National Society for the Prevention of Cruelty to Children (NSPCC) (2008) 'NSPCC policy summary: children who are asylum seekers or refugees (online). Retrieved 16 April 2014 from http://combattrafficking.eu/sites/default/files/NSPCC-Asylum%20Seeking%20Children.pdf.

Olusoga, Y. (2008) 'Educating refugee children: a class teacher's perspective', in Jones, P., Moss, D., Tomlinson, P. and Welch, S. (eds) *Childhood: Services and provision for children*. Harlow: Pearson Education Limited, pp. 236–44.

Refugee Council (2012) *Asylum Statistics, May 2012* (online). Retrieved 16 April 2014 from http://www.refugeecouncil.org.uk/assets/0001/5800/Asylum_Statistics__May_2012.pdf.

Rutter, J. (2003) *Supporting Refugee Children in 21st Century Britain: a compendium of essential information*. Stoke-on-Trent: Trentham Books.

United Nations High Commissioner for Refugees (UNHCR) (1994) *Refugee Children: Guidelines on protection and care*. Geneva: UNHCR. Retrieved 16 April 2014 from http://www.unicef.org/violencestudy/pdf/refugee_children_guidelines_on_protection_and_care.pdf.

Does bullying really happen in early years?

Melanie Henderson

> Assessing bullying in preschool children is a difficult process for researchers mainly due to the restrictions underpinning the implementation, at such a young age, of some of the well-known measurement techniques that are considered appropriate and employed for estimating bullying in older age groups.
>
> (Vlachou *et al.*, 2011: 332)

Not only is it not realistic to collect evidence through the normal avenues of questionnaires, but it is also difficult for practitioners to differentiate bullying from everyday conflicts. Lee (2006) examines how a group of primary school teachers define bullying, finding that factors of function, culture and context might influence their definition. There seemed to be little consensus about practitioners' personal understanding of bullying and Lee's conclusion is that professionals and other staff in an institution should generate a shared understanding, which can be called upon when resolving bullying issues (Lee, 2006: 61). Sule Tepetas *et al.*'s research (2010) found preschool teachers' opinions on bullying behaviours were defined as mostly physical violence and disobedience and did not account for verbal and psychological aspects.

Sullivan (2000: 14) states that the different types of bullying are physical, including hitting, nipping, biting, pushing, spitting, scratching and hair-pulling; verbal, including name-calling, teasing, threats, racist remarks, sexually suggestive language, spiteful remarks and spreading false rumours; and non-verbal, including pulling mean faces, making rude gestures, manipulating/ruining friendships, ignoring or isolation. Cyber bullying in early years children is probably scarce (Kidscape, 2005); however, there is evidence of eight and nine-year-old children being affected in the UK (Cross *et al.*, 2012). The children and young people in Childline's (2013) research described bullying as:

- being called names;
- being put down or humiliated;

- being teased;
- being pushed or pulled about;
- having money and other possessions taken or messed about with;
- having rumours spread about you;
- being ignored and left out;
- being hit, kicked or physically hurt;
- being threatened or intimidated.

Homophobic bullying

More than two in five primary school teachers (44 per cent) have witnessed children being subjected to homophobic bullying such as name-calling and harassment in their schools, regardless of their sexual orientation (Guasp, 2009: 5). The word 'gay' is used by young children, even though they probably do not understand what it means. Children as young as four years are experiencing homophobic bullying as a result of their parents being lesbian or gay (Guasp, 2012: 3). Very young children with gay or lesbian parents don't see their families as being different from other peoples' families. However, they experience other children being mean, and face intrusive questions and judgements about their parents and upbringing (Guasp, 2012: 3). I witnessed the following incident on placement in a challenging Foundation Stage Unit (FSU) environment.

Vignette 1: evidence of homophobic bullying

The Foundation Stage Year 2 pupils (FS2s) were told to line up at the classroom door for lunch. There was a scuffle between two boys to get to the front of the queue. The teacher went to intervene, by which time one boy was sobbing and the other had reached his destination. The class teacher approached the sobbing child whose response was '****** says I am a faggot and faggots can't go at the front of the queue!' There was a visual exchange of shock between the teacher and myself, and then we took control of the situation. I comforted the sobbing child and later escorted him to lunch when he was calm. The remaining cohort of children went to lunch with a lunchtime assistant who arrived just at the right time. The teacher took the other boy to see the KS1 coordinator, who immediately reported the incident to the head teacher. I was requested to attend the meeting with the head teacher having witnessed the event. The head teacher made jokes, was sarcastic and said we were overreacting. However, the matter was eventually formally recorded and action was taken. The parents of the children involved were informed.

Reflection

What surprised me most was that both of the children involved knew the word 'faggot' was meant to cause hurt or be an insult at the ages of four and five respectively. More concerning was that other adults in the room (apart from the teacher and myself) didn't know what the offending word meant. The KS1 coordinator was also unfamiliar with the term when the child was presented to her to deal with the incident! Finally, the manner in which the matter was dealt with by senior management perturbed me. As a result I have sought guidance to ensure I am prepared in the event of this type of incident occurring again.

Children with special educational needs

These children are two to three more times at risk of being bullied and are more likely to bully. Their disabilities make them easy targets and they tend to be less well integrated in their setting. Children with behavioural problems are very susceptible to becoming victims (Sullivan, 2000: 12). A recent study by Zablotsky *et al.* (2012) supports this statement. They conclude that children with developmental disabilities are at increased risk of involvement in bullying, and children with autism spectrum disorders (ASD) may be at particular risk because of challenges with social skills and difficulty maintaining friendships. They identified children with Asperger's to be most at risk of being bullied in comparison to other ASDs. As a parent of a KS1 age child with SEN including mild Asperger's reflecting on my experiences to date, I am in full agreement with the report. They state that a positive school climate may protect children with ASDs from being bullied, which I have found to be true. It also helps protect the child from being made a scapegoat for bullying when complaints regarding incidents which have occurred are misinterpreted as bullying by the complainant and their families. The reliance on school staff to manage bullying situations is paramount; however, the next section shows that the pupils don't always cause the bullying.

The effects of bullying

The effects of bullying or 'unjustified aggression' on young children can include psychosomatic symptoms such as headaches and stomach aches, and psychological illnesses such as depression and anxiety (Alsaker, 2012: 3). Children may also display separation anxiety such as excessive clinging to parents or school refusal (Cowie *et al.*, 2004: 5). In slightly older primary school age children loss of appetite, sleep disturbance, skin problems, bed-wetting and tearfulness are just some of the other symptoms of stress reported on by Fekkes *et al.* (2004: 21). They also reported that some of the above symptoms were common in the bullies and not just the victims, which links back to the reasons as to why children display unjustified aggression and bullying behaviour initially. The effects on the victims of bullying can be life-damaging, but the effects can also be catastrophic for the families and carers and may even ripple outwards to affect the victim's friends, their peer groups and the school community. Adults can be responsible for bullying in classroom and EYFS settings and this can be due to inexperience, but also other factors such as stress.

Vignette 2: FSU staff under stress

The pressure on highly experienced early years teachers from senior management untrained in this area was observed directly during a recent school placement at an FSU. Pressures to implement strict timetables and teaching pedagogies more suited to KS1/KS2 resulted in stressful and inappropriate practices. The staff also contributed to the challenging classroom environment by treating pupils with disdain, sarcasm or put-downs, hence providing negative role modelling for other impressionable young pupils to emulate. An explanation for the applied pressure and resulting situation was offered. The pending Ofsted inspection and the implementation of the new EYFS curriculum were the reasons given.

Reflection

My reflection was: would Ofsted draw the same conclusions regarding the practices seen? Would they consider the application of 'school readiness' (DfE, 2012b: 2) was being applied excessively to pupils who had only had their third birthdays in the previous summer months! The negative role modelling by staff concerned me most. I observed certain pupils' inappropriate behaviour worsening as the negative experiences from the FSU staff became more frequent as the stress levels increased. The EYFS framework sets out practices for developing positive behaviour and focuses on inclusion and working in partnership with parents to support all children's needs. The most recent curriculum in 2012 has personal, social and emotional development as a prime area of learning. The EYFS also prioritises the development of knowledge of other communities and learning about diversity, though as a specific area (DfE, 2012a). The National Strategies SEAL programme (DfCFS, 2008) is also a valuable resource to use in the EYFS.

Reflective challenge points

- What are your thoughts after reading and reflecting on this case study?
- Have you ever needed to deal with a bullying incident in an early years setting?
- Do you feel prepared? Do you know what to do and who to go to for support and advice?

References

Alsaker, F.D. (2003) *Bullies and Their Victims: Bullying among children – and how to deal with them.* Bern: Hans Huber.

Childline (2013) *Bullying* (online). Retrieved 16 April 2014 from http://www.childline.org.uk/explore/bullying/pages/bullying.aspx.

Cowie, H., Boardman, C., Dawkins, J. and Jennifer, D. (2004) *Emotional Health and Well-Being: A practical guide for schools.* London: Sage.

Cross, E-J., Piggin, R., Douglas, T., Vonkaenel-Flatt, J. and O'Brien, J. (2012) *Virtual Violence II: Part II: Primary-aged children's experience of Cyberbullying.* London: Beat Bullying. Retrieved 16 April 2014 from http://archive.beatbullying.org/pdfs/Virtual-Violence-Report-II-FINAL.pdf.

Department for Children, Schools and Families (DfCSF) (2008) *The National Strategies: Social and Emotional Aspects of Development (SEAL): Guidance for practitioners working in the Early Years Foundation Stage.* Nottingham: DSCF Publications.

Department for Education (DfE) (2012a) *School Readiness at Age 5.* Runcorn: DfE, Department for Data, Research and Statistics. Retrieved 16 April 2014 from http://www.education.gov.uk/researchandstatistics/statistics/keystatistics/b00221154/school-readiness-at-age-5.

Department for Education (DfE) (2012b) *Statutory Framework for the Early Years Foundation Stage.* Runcorn: DfE.

Fekkes, M., Pijpers, F.I.M. and Verloove-Vanhorick, S.P. (2004) 'Bullying behaviour and associations with psychosomatic complaints and depression in victims', *The Journal of Pediatrics*, 144(1): 17–22.

Guasp, A. (2009) *Homophobic Bullying in Britain's Schools: The school report.* London: Stonewall. Retrieved 16 April 2014 from http://www.stonewall.org.uk/documents/school_report_2012(2).pdf

Kidscape (2005) *Anti-Bullying Policy for Schools: Some guidelines.* London: Kidscape.

Lee, C. (2006) 'Exploring teachers' definitions of bullying', *Emotional and Behavioural Difficulties*, 11(1): 61–75.

Sule Tepetas, G., Akgun, E. and Akbaba Altun, S. (2010) 'Identifying preschool teachers' opinion about peer bullying', *Procedia: Social and Behavioural Sciences*, 2: 1675–79.

Sullivan, K. (2000) *The Anti-Bullying Handbook.* Auckland, New Zealand: Oxford University Press.

Vlachou, M., Andreou, E., Botsoglou, K. and Didaskalou, E. (2011) 'Bully/victim problems among preschool children: a review of current research', *Evidence: Education Psychology Review*, 23: 329–58.

Zablotsky, B., Bradshaw, C.P., Anderson, C. and Law, P. (2012) 'Involvement in bullying among children with autism spectrum disorders: parents' perspectives on the influence of school factors', *Behavioural Disorders*, 37(3): 179–91.

Children with parents in prison

Avril Brock

I miss my Dad so much. When I feel lonely I listen to my CD and hearing his voice makes me feel better.

(Jake, aged 7 – Storybook Dads, Keeping Families
Together in Brock, 2011)

Every year more children are separated from a parent by prison than by divorce. In 2013, more than 200,000 children had a parent in prison in England and Wales. This is two-and-a-half times the number of those in care and more than six times the number of those on the child protection register. Around 2,500 women prisoners are mothers and one-third of these are lone parents, which makes prison particularly traumatic (Hunter, 2008). This is particularly the case as they may be more than 50 or 100 miles away from home, making family visiting problematic. Half of incarcerated parents do not receive any visits from their children (Seymour and Hairston, 2001). Seven per cent of UK children will experience their parents' imprisonment before they leave school and a quarter of men in young offenders' institutes are, or are shortly to become, fathers (Walsh, 2013).

Children with parents in prison are at a greater risk of depression and anxiety, have behaviour problems, and experience a range of powerful emotions such as fear, anger, sadness, loneliness, guilt, frustration and low self-esteem; and they will be very upset. Barnardo's advise that it is important to allow young children to express their emotions in a controlled way, as they may bottle things up or act withdrawn. Barnardo's is a key charity that supports prisoners' families (download the *Supporting Prisoners' Families* report (Clewit and Glover, 2009) from the Barnardo's website at www.barnardos.org.uk/children_of_prisoners). They demonstrate the devastating effect on a family left behind to cope when a parent goes to prison. Often the parent in prison cannot see the impact on their family. The report *Every Night You Cry: The realities of having a parent in prison* (Glover, 2009) can also be downloaded and this report reflects on the poor outcomes of children with a parent in prison. It calls for better identification of children affected, and more timely intervention, as too many local authorities are failing to address their needs.

A parent in prison may have strong emotions of guilt, frustration, anger and regret, particularly if they have young children. The amount of information a young child is given about the situation will differ according to their age and ability to understand the situation. Barnardo's affirms how difficult this can be and advises that it is important to go at a slow pace to give them time to think and understand (Clewit and Glover, 2009). Young children will need plenty of reassurance and will often be more clingy than normal. If a child has been asked to keep the situation a secret from their friends or teacher, this may put them under a lot of pressure, and they could end up feeling rather miserable. It is so valuable if the setting is informed and so understands the situation, and practitioners are able to be supportive. Clearly, ECE practitioners will have an important role as they are such significant people in young children's lives. When a parent is in prison, they will need to be a constant, reliable and trusted person who is there for the child.

Dibb (2001) led research for the Federation of Prisoners' Families Support Group project, which aimed to raise awareness in schools about issues for children when they have a parent in prison. She advises that educators require confidence to address children's needs through effective resources, training and policy to develop a whole-school approach.

> Having discovered that we had at least three children who had a father in prison we realised that we had work to do. We would need to build on our knowledge of loss and separation to move more fully to understand the complex range of issues facing families, especially their children, who had a loved one in prison. We encouraged the parent to talk about ways in which we could actively support the family and assured them that authorised absence would be given to ensure family visiting. One six-year-old boy wanted his friends to believe that 'Dad's in the army', a little girl in nursery repeatedly told her teacher that 'Dad is at training camp'. In both these situations we talked to the mothers and explored with them their own concerns about mentioning the word prison – they expressed real relief at being able to discuss their home situation openly and honestly. We helped them think of ways to introduce the prison concept gradually and positively. In both cases the behaviour of each child affected showed a marked improvement as the child relaxed into an understanding that 'it's all right, my teacher knows and I can talk to him/her about it'.
>
> (Pauling and Lipman, in Dibb, 2001)

School and ECCE settings will be an anchor point for children in difficult, troubling times in their young lives, and ECEs need to be aware how to provide supportive, sensitive environments that are non-judgmental, dealing with information confidentially, developing trust with families and working inter-professionally with appropriate agencies. Children of prisoners can face multiple barriers to educational achievement. They may experience poverty, mental health problems or poor housing. They may have to move house and change location, which means their education will be disrupted. They may lose friends, be far away from family support systems or experience bullying. Visiting a prison to see their father or mother will be in a very unfamiliar environment and can often be very distressing for young children. Children of imprisoned parents are often described as the forgotten victims of imprisonment: 'someone should ask me what it is like for me. Nobody had ever asked what I think about it, how it has affected me, not until now' (Brown *et al.*, 2010).

Advice for practitioners

- Be a constant sensitive support for the child.
- Listen to children and make individual time for them to talk to you.
- Use books and stories to support children's knowledge and empathy.
- Talk to the parents if possible.
- Never speak badly of the parent in prison.
- Be careful about making generalisations and never be judgmental.

Support and resources

There are several supportive organisations such as the Offender's Families Helpline (www.offendersfamilieshelpline.org), and Action for Prisoners' Families (APF) (www.prisonersfamilies.org.uk) also has lots of advice. i-HOP (Information Hub on Offenders' families with children for Professionals; www.i-hop.org.uk) is a service that supports all professionals in working with children and families of offenders. It is commissioned by the Department for Education and is run by Barnardo's in partnership with POPS (Partners of Prisoners and Families Support Group). Action for Prisoners' Families has produced story books to help children come to terms with their experiences, namely *Finding Dad*, *Danny's Mum* and *Tommy's Dad*. *Homeward Bound* is a DVD that acts out the experiences, thoughts and fears of a family where the father is due for release from prison. See also the Social Care Institute of Excellence (SCIE) website 'Children of prisoners – maintaining family ties' (www.scie.org.uk/publications/guides/guide22/contacts.asp) and the Family Lives website 'How to cope if a parent goes to prison' (http://familylives.org.uk/advice/your-family/parenting/how-to-cope-if-a-parent-goes-to-prison).

References

Brock, A. (2011) 'The child in context: policy and provision', Chapter 1 in Brock, A. and Rankin, C. (eds) *Professionalism in the Early Years Interdisciplinary Team: Supporting young children and their families*. London: Continuum.

Brown, K., Dibb, L., Shenton, F. and Elson, N. (2010) *No One's Ever Asked Me: Young people with a prisoner in the family*. London: Federation of Prisoners' Families Support Groups.

Clewit, N. and Glover, J. (2009) *Supporting Prisoners' Families: How Barnardo's works to improve outcomes for children with a parent in prison*. Ilford: Barnardo's. Retrieved 16 April 2014 from http://www.barnardos.org.uk/supporting_prisoners_families.pdf.

Dibb, L. (ed) (2001) *'I didn't think anyone could understand, Miss': Supporting prisoners' children in school.* London: Federation of Prisoners' Families Support Groups.

Glover, J. (2009) *Every Night You Cry: The realities of having a parent in prison.* Ilford: Barnardo's. Retrieved 16 April 2014 from http://www.barnardos.org.uk/everynightyoucry_briefing_final_double.pdf.

Hunter, M. (2008) 'Parents in prison: don't judge the children', *Learning Support*, 20. Bishops Castle: Brightday Publishing.

Seymour, C. and Hairston, C. F. (2001) *Children with Parents in Prison: Child welfare policy, program, and practice issues.* Piscataway, NJ: Transaction Publishers.

Walsh, C. (2013) 'Family matters to young fathers in prison', *The Guardian*, 23 July. Retrieved 16 April 2014 from http://www.theguardian.com/society/2013/jul/23/family-important-young-fathers-prison.

Continuing professional development and action research on reflective practice

This part of the book is aimed at continuing professional development, deepening reflective thinking and undertaking action research on promoting effective reflective practice.

Chapter 14: Deepening reflection even further

Avril Brock

This chapter aims to ensure that you see reflective writing as both meaningful and valuable and to support the deepening of reflective thinking processes through introducing and exploring a range of reflective writing activities. It explores activities that enable a deepening of critical reflection and draws on the reflective writing of students studying for a Master's degree.

Chapter 15: On reflection: examining undergraduate reflective practice across two higher education (HE) sector endorsed foundation degrees (FDs) and BA (Hons) programmes within a further education (FE) provision

Helen Rowe

Chapter 16: Does the use of reflective practice enhance early years foundation degree students' personal and professional development?

Nicola Firth

Helen Rowe and Nicola Firth studied the MA Early Years and MA Childhood Studies respectively at LeedsMet University and, inspired by the focus of reflective practice in the PPRP module, they both decided to make it a focus for their Major Independent Study (MIS/dissertation). At the time of studying they worked in further/higher education with students on foundation and top-up degrees in early years and in business and management. Their interest in reflection was an inherent part of their professional roles and they were keen to further develop their own understanding through undertaking research projects with the students with whom they worked or had worked.

Both studies were to become action research projects as they aimed to improve their teaching, with the development of course provision in the area of reflective practice. Both these chapters are extracts from Helen and Nicola's MIS, which were 15,000 words, but you should get a good impression of both the content of their research on reflective practice as well as how to undertake an action research study.

Action research is important for postgraduate students and practitioner researchers in ECCE, for those who want to evaluate their provision, teaching, or any change or new policy development initiatives. It is often undertaken for a dissertation as part of gaining a higher qualification, but can be undertaken in a practical way without writing it up for an external audience. Helen and Nicola present their interest, impetus and purpose for their studies and demonstrate the research processes undertaken. On reading each of these two chapters, you will be able to see how they both evidence the relevant theoretical backgrounds to underpin and justify their studies; which methodological strategies they use; and how they present their data and analyse their findings. They each draw conclusions relevant to their professional role and critically review the impact of their study in order to make improvements to their teaching.

These final chapters not only demonstrate further thinking about critical reflective practice, but also provide an insight into how to deepen critical reflection through writing activities and how to complete a successful action research study.

14

Deepening reflection even further

Avril Brock

This chapter aims to ensure that you see reflective writing as both meaningful and valuable and to support the deepening of reflective thinking processes through introducing and exploring a range of reflective writing activities. It explores activities that enable a deepening of critical reflection through compiling a CPD portfolio, creative metaphoring, five-minute writing exercises to share with critical friends, writing an autobiography, timelines and creating digital paperchases to document personal and professional successes. As part of students' study on a childhood and early years course, they had to enrol on a personal, professional reflective practice (PPRP) module. My research has been inspired by the students' work and their evaluations, which have included such comments as 'valuable and interesting' and even 'life-changing and cathartic'. Their comments, interspersed in the second half of this chapter, were made through their participating in my research, which occurred after they had completed the module. The chapter presents the theory underpinning the writing processes, and the students' and practitioners' opinions of how these reflective activities have worked for them. At the beginning of the PPRP module Sakinah, Gail and Alix did not believe that the module would be particularly beneficial for them.

I didn't have a clue as to what it was all about until I read a bit on it and then we went on to discuss it in class. Gail

I was fairly cynical about the whole thing, having covered a little of reflective writing in my teaching on a foundation degree, I don't think I had thought about reflective practice or even distinguished between the writing and practice, i.e. my teaching. I wasn't sure what I would get out of the module. I had already started my MA as I began in January and had already written two assignments, and thought I'd done quite well in them without the need for reflective writing, or 'navel gazing' as my husband called it! Alix

Deepening reflective thinking and practice

Reflective practice can get disconnected with the theory or philosophy that originally underpinned it, so in order to combat this dissonance and to deepen thinking, this section attempts to get you to appreciate reflective practice through relating it to both personal and professional practice. In this way you should be persuaded to engage in critical investigation through exploring different activities at different levels. It is important to hear other student/practitioner perspectives, as well as academics' perspectives gained through reading theory, to engage in debate and to build on each other's ideas. West (2010: 67) believes reflective practice should be holistic and build critical insights into self and others through enabling engagement with autobiographical dimensions of professional interactions. Fook (2010) promotes critical reflection in small groups, over several sessions, in which each participant presents a piece of practice for critical reflection in two stages – a reflective awareness stage and a linking with practice stage. Both West's and Fook's strategies aim to change practice through reflecting on fundamental assumptions and questioning taken-for-granted norms in working contexts. As Bolton (2005: 1) says, the nature of reflective practice can be 'politically and socially disruptive: it lays open to question anything taken for granted'.

In my teaching on undergraduate and postgraduate courses my aim is that students examine their personal style, academic study and professional performance through a process of reflective thinking and practice. I provide opportunities for participants to develop, test and enhance professional approaches to study and to reflect on professional roles, duties and responsibilities. Informal seminar discussions and debates, workshop sessions, individual writing tasks, and personal and group presentations are promoted to encourage independent reflection. Collegiate support enables the group to seek collective remedies and solutions to professional issues and engaging in a variety of writing exercises facilitates reflection on these.

> It was when I started the writing process that I realised I had issues which needed dealing with. Issues which were directing some of my current actions and drive, and preventing me from moving on. Sakinah

> All tasks were useful in different ways, and encourage critical thinking, for example in exploring conflict at work made me realise that I could have acted differently, which I have thought about many times since doing that exercise. Amanda

> I think the act of writing down not only focuses the mind, but for me was cathartic too. I think the different writing exercises will have reached more people. Elizabeth

The writing activities included diaries, autobiographies, timelines, digital portfolios and critical incident reflections, and in this way the group engaged in a reflective synopsis of personal and professional development that contributed to a portfolio of analytical reflections. Using a range of reflective writing and thinking devices is a more effective way of encouraging reflective practice than focusing on one method such as journaling or reflective cycles.

> *The writing exercises within the PPRP module enabled deep reflective thinking and facilitated exploration of a variety of modes of reflection which were both insightful and enlightening. The freedom to express myself and the scope to be creative was motivating and inspiring for me, both as a teacher and as a learner.* Helen

> *I 'loved' the creative ways in which we were taught different ways to reflect, i.e. Timelines, Life in Pictures, Autobiography . . . They made me consider how I have become the person I am today and how my values and beliefs have been shaped by past experiences.* Nicola

The engagement in varied reflective writing activities facilitated students' interest, diversity and inclination. It enabled varied levels of professional and academic experience and the aim was to address the concerns raised at the beginning of the chapter – to promote meaningful reflective practice that is undertaken willingly and purposefully and not just to tick the assessment box! The next section details the theory, purpose and value of compiling a portfolio to produce a variety of examples of reflective writing.

Creating a portfolio

A portfolio can be described as a file or folder (paper, electronic or multimedia) that contains a collection of writings, papers, documentation of work practice, observations, blogs, artefacts, photographs or displays. The objective of Goodfellow's (2004: 66) learning portfolios was that they would be a way of mapping and self-discovery for her students, so they could be encouraged to engage with, reflect on and analyse their professional practices and gain a sense of self-empowerment and professional autonomy through the process. In her view portfolios can:

- demonstrate, display and highlight aspects of one's own practice in relation to those practices that are valued by the profession;
- provide analytical and interpretative records of reflection on practices and so enhance the skills of critical thinking;
- identify professional growth and establish a basis for furthering one's own professional development;
- document the purposefulness of one's work as a professional.

(Goodfellow, 2004: 71–2)

Elbaz-Luwisch's (2010) participants also created a portfolio or suitcase of reflective activities. Her research focused on promoting autobiographical writing and professional development to determine if graduate study in education could sustain teachers in their work. Her respondents saw 'professional learning as entailing the expansion of their repertoire of professional knowledge and skills' (Elbaz-Luwisch, 2010: 307). The creation of the portfolio strengthened her participants' reflective processes, enabled them to integrate theory and practice, and promoted inquiry into and clarification of their personal stories. There are five key purposes of keeping a reflective portfolio:

- to celebrate;
- to keep a record of personal experiences;
- to ensure understanding of practice;
- as a means to demonstrate developing competence;
- as a way of making sense of working life.

(Ghaye, 2007: 159)

I decided that a professional academic learning portfolio of reflective writings to promote engagement in meaningful *reflectioning* would be what I would ask my students to do for their assessment on their higher degree course. The word count was to be the equivalent of 4,000 words – equivalent because it is problematic to count words of a PowerPoint, autobiography, timeline or even a poem, when a word count might not represent the work undertaken in such a reflective, creative study piece. The students were able to select which of the reflective writing activities they wished to pursue and submit in the portfolio. This allowed for their personal interests and learning styles and would therefore be purposeful for their personal, professional role. This was crucial for the portfolios to be successful: it was not meant to be a tick box exercise; the aim was to engage in reflective processes and so deepen the individual's *reflectioning*. All the activities could be undertaken as personal or professional reflections and often these were not distinct from each other. Personal and professional thinking and practice are often interconnected, as each influences the other as our values, beliefs and practice are developed through experiences from home, study and work.

> *After completing the module my understanding of reflection deepened. I already understood its benefits in terms of improving practice but didn't realise that there were so many different ways of reflecting (such as the use of logs, timelines, digital stories, autobiographies etc.). These are all methods that I now use with my students to engage them at a level that they can easily be absorbed in. Jackie*

> *Developing this portfolio helped me to think about events in my past and my personal and professional learning journey. Capturing my story and sharing it with my peers helped me to make meaning of the critical decisions I have made in both my professional and personal life. Developing the portfolio helped to clarify my values as well as enhancing my capacity to reflect on learning. Sharon*

Content for the portfolio could include any combination of the following reflective writing pieces:

- academic thinking
- action planning

- autobiographical writing
- continuing professional development
- critical incidents
- diary
- digital paperchase
- illustrative life pattern
- journaling
- Johari window
- mapping creatively
- metaphors
- narratives
- observations
- personal/professional timelines
- poetry
- reflection on one's profession, professionalism, professional life, ideology
- reflective writing piece
- ten-minute writing activities and reflecting on streams of consciousness
- time management
- work evaluations.

Some examples of these writing activities are now presented in more detail, outlining the purpose of the writing activity and justifying their development through theory, research and students' own reflections on the process.

Focused reflection point

Why not have a go at writing a reflective diary for a week? You could reflect on the whole of each day or select a particular aspect of each day. See Appendix 2 for an example of a week's reflective diary.

Autobiographical writing

Writing an autobiography can be a route into writing as it can create a realisation of the varied impacts of personal life and professional development. It has now become the custom for qualitative researchers to include some autobiographical details, in recognition that their 'selves' – 'their personal histories, beliefs and values' – are all bound up in the study in some way' (Woods 1999: 55). Gregory *et al.* (2005: ix) argue for personal commitment and a 'legitimisation of self within a study' as 'by making visible the lives of people whose stories are not normally told, it gives voice to all of us who are nothing special.'

It is my strong belief as a tutor that it is important to form secure 'study' relationships with students and practitioners, so that they view me as a critical friend and mentor, rather than as someone who just assesses their work. It is important to make people feel comfortable and relaxed so that they can trial ideas and enter into debates with others. In promoting this context of academic interaction it was therefore important to model the activities and in doing so to share and provide examples from my own personal and professional experiences. This definitely enabled the building of a community of learners and colleagues – a process just as important in a workplace environment. This is established through showing empathy; sharing appropriate personal examples and supporting others' self-esteem through having an interest in and respect for others as individuals. Discovering cultural and professional differences should enable the creation of a supportive working or study environment and help build the interconnection between personal/professional and personal lives. This knowledge and interconnection of different professionalities and roles in ECCE can be seen in Brock and Rankin (2011). In the university environment I needed to model my reflective processes and professional development through writing my autobiography, compiling a personal/professional timeline and creating my digital paperchase (see Appendices at the end of the book).

> I was very interested in autobiographical work but this was new to me. At the time of the module I was fascinated; I knew I would come back to this and I did. I read about autobiographical writing long after the module had finished and it influenced my belief that academic study affects us holistically. Sarah

> Autobiographical writing was good – just a chance to write about yourself and your life which doesn't happen very often! Women particularly don't seem to get much of a chance to think about themselves, I find that as a wife, mother and teacher, my personal thoughts and opinions come last and don't count – it was nice to have a bit of 'me' time. Alix

> This was time-consuming; however, it did give perspective; awareness of the lack of constraint over what I included was useful. Re-reading this and reflecting deeply about why events occurred and why I included them or how I felt about them encouraged real critical thought. Helen

As Eraut (2000) informs us, personal biography is a useful starting point to document our unconscious reflections and to realise what is part of our intuitive and tacit knowledge. My autobiography commenced at the age of five with a visit to the library with my father and the beginning of a love for reading which, I strongly believe, greatly influenced my future career and ongoing professional development, which at the moment is the writing of this book! I have included an extract of my own and a student's autobiography (see Appendices).

Focused reflection point

■ Have a go at writing about an interesting or particularly relevant point in your life history. Of course it would take far too long to write all your autobiography, so be selective about a particular moment in time. Then why not share it with a friend or member of your family?

Digital paperchase

Reflecting on oneself in a digital paperchase of personal, professional achievements and experiences can enable articulation of vision and promote professional growth. Records and reflections can be saved and educational vision statements created. 'By capturing the learning journey, reflecting on its meaning over time, sharing the learning with others' it is possible to develop new insights and understandings (Hartnell-Young and Morriss, 2007: 26). Personal mastery often begins with knowing and understanding yourself – lifelong learners are said to be reflective, self-directed, active investigators, problem solvers and effective communicators.

> A thoughtful reflection is like a dialogue that creates links between past, present and future and theory and practice, vision, values and actions.
> (Hartnell-Young and Morriss, 2007: 36).

Maxine Alterio (2006a) observes that most of us have stories that illustrate our professional practice, and we can use these in constructive ways to grow as individuals. She prompts us to peel away the layers of these stories, working with our insights to critically examine what we do. Through narrative imagination, we can reach new and meaningful understandings and can bring about stimulating and productive reflective practice and positive change. Alterio (2006a) suggests that narrative-based experiences can create new knowledge, integrate subjective and objective aspects of learning and constructively alter our views of ourselves. They can enable us to critically examine the political and social context in which we work and live and offer insights to bring about thoughts and images to practice. Narrative accounts about shared professional and personal experiences that are processed reflectively are invariably underpinned by facts and evidence. They also contain narrative imagination and make empathy possible through forming creative and meaningful connections at multiple levels and in diverse ways.

On a staff development day at university, I was inspired by Maxine Alterio's (2006b) presentation on digital paperchases. So much so that I compiled my own that very evening and I have used it each year with students and have now inspired many practitioners to compile their own. The evening I compiled my digital paperchase I collected my certificates – birth, marriage, divorce, school and university; photos of family, weddings and grandchildren; and scanned images of my book covers and PhD thesis. This made me think about my personal and professional accomplishment, both small and large. The creation of a digital paperchase was not just valuable for the personal satisfaction and creativity, but also in the sharing of it with others.

The students found listening to other people's presentation of their paperchases to be really interesting and a great way to get to know each other, share interests and empathise with feelings. The group found they had some really important things in common they could share. Some found it difficult to create one at first or were nervous, but the fact that others had taken the time to share was really facilitating.

> *This was one of the most exciting methods of reflecting as it challenged both ICT skills as well as story-telling ability. It was a privilege to share with peers and provided an extra dimension to reflecting collaboratively. It again allowed for higher levels of creativity which I believe makes reflecting more real, alive and appealing. Helen*

> *I loved doing the digital timeline autobiography – really interesting to see patterns and influences from my past, and give me a bit of confidence that I haven't ended up on the MA by chance, and showed what is important to me. Alix*

The students produced and presented their digital paperchases in varied ways according to their interest and individuality. One student used humour as a theme; another moving house; one chose her desert island discs as a way of pinpointing personal and professional life experiences; and one international student drew on the places she had lived. They visited families to get pictures and a student from the USA got her mother to send her journal. We travelled around Leeds and West Yorkshire, throughout the UK and globally to Ghana, the USA, China and the Philippines. We appreciated the vast diversity of the groups in age, culture, language, experience and professional knowledge.

> *Although photography is an important hobby I chose not to use photos. I think because I didn't feel comfortable to do so. Rather than produce a standard autobiography I decided to do something different and produced my own desert island disc with links to all my favourite songs (learning a new technical skill along the way). This was great as I had often thought about which songs I would choose, but of course it still took hours to decide on which tracks – even though most of the artists were definites. Jane*

> *I really didn't want to do this when it was first suggested. I watched other people's presentations of their digital timelines and realised that I didn't want to share so much of myself in the same way they had. But, by seeing the varying degrees in which each person was contributing, I realised that I could do it my way. I would make it entertaining and would share only the things I really wanted to. It ended up being, again, quite safe in its content in that I didn't expose myself beyond where I was comfortable, but I found a way of enjoying talking about positives in my life. I could use a style of writing to tell some of my 'story' so as not to feel too exposed. I found that I rely on humour a lot – I attempt to amuse the reader. I really enjoy that, but have a tendency to self-deprecate in the process. Pavla*

Pavla's paperchase can be seen in the Appendices, along with mine. These should provide the reader with concrete examples of a digital paperchase that reflects on the stories and occurrences of our professional and personal lives and how these intertwine to make us knowledgeable and interesting people. This was the case for every single participant in this exercise – we were all very interested in each other and found common interests and experiences. There is no doubt that this free sharing of personal and professional self with colleagues, when in a positive listening environment, can enhance collegiate support and create empathetic working relationships. Sharon and Fay presented their digital paperchases in the same session and I wrote the following observations on their presentations regarding the themes I thought could be derived from their work and what their interests were.

> *Sharon emphasised the connection between personal and professional interconnections and I think it was there in Fay's as well. Both demonstrated resilience – at quite different times in their lives. Family was obviously very important to both of them. Children were very significant for them, both family and in their professional role. They both obviously think having fun and enjoying what you do is crucial and passing this enjoyment onto others is key. Teamwork and leadership were themes for Sharon, as was decision making and ideology of early years curriculum and pedagogy. Friendship was very important for Fay. They both reflected on education at different points in their lives – I was really interested in Fay's points about GCSE choices which mirrored what happened to me probably 30-plus years earlier – this could raise interesting critiques on how education and policy decisions do or do not meet individual needs. Understanding own capabilities and celebrating achievements came across through both presentations. Continuing professional development and thinking about future professional roles and job opportunities was evidenced – both had complex reasoning as to why and what they have decided to study. Both, I think, enjoy the study process. For Sharon it was obviously rather a cathartic exercise. Hope my reflections will be useful to all of you – if you choose to do a digital portfolio, autobiography, timeline etc. Some themes will be generic to most of you but some will be very specific to yourself. Avril*

There were some common themes across the presentations as well as there being topics specific to individuals. Using narrative in creative ways such as creating digital paperchases can promote knowledge about practitioners' diverse personal and professional experiences. Through interconnecting storytelling with reflective learning processes, professional practice can therefore be informed and developed (McDrury and Alterio, 2004).

Focused reflection point

- Have a go at creating your own digital paperchase – there are examples of two in the appendices. You should find it a really rewarding exercise.

Personal/professional timelines

Timelines are a succinct, efficient and accessible way of demonstrating personal and professional information. A timeline offers an overview of significant achievements, of changing events and situations that can be seen at a glance. It can encapsulate personal history in a short time as it is normally limited to one line or to short entries.

This was a useful reflective tool as it was easy and quick. It was effective for visual learners and it can be used as a prompt for discussion between peers. It also forces separation of personal and professional or at least consideration of how these two aspects of one's life interact. Helen

I always thought I hadn't achieved much but after reflecting on my timeline, I realised there was a lot to be thankful for. Gail

As Miles and Huberman (1994: 110) observe, 'life is chronology – we live in a flow of events'. In completing a timeline you should consider significant events, people and feelings as well as significant achievements. Themes could include:

- personal themes of childhood, family, primary/secondary education, relationships, moving house/city;
- professional themes of qualifications, university, employment, CPD, promotion/changes in role;
- significant milestones such as voluntary work, illness, passing a driving test;
- interests such as religion, politics, travel, holidays, hobbies, sport and leisure.

Timelines can be an interesting reflective process as they demonstrate change and development across personal and professional lives. When compiling a timeline you will discover:

- what you consider to be important;
- what has influenced you;
- what you remembered as being significant.

The acquired value from Personal Professional Timeline was the fact that it showed me, very clearly, all that I had achieved both professionally and personally. I hadn't realised I had accomplished that much until I saw it clearly through my writing. The effect it then went on to have on me, was in making me less harsh on myself in thinking I had not achieved as much as my peers or friends. It enabled me to humbly beat my drums. Sakinah

The timelines undertaken with participants in my research demonstrated that the following themes and patterns emerged: family, relationships, location, roles, education; qualification, continuing professional development, courses and training.

My timeline made me really think about my life and the journey I had taken, which did provoke many emotions, some good some negative. Amanda

This was very useful; to use chronology within personal and professional changes helped me to reflect on important life events and see how they were interlinked.

Whether these were correlations or causal was another point of reflection. Jackie

Most students composed them in a linear diagram but timelines can be a list of events or composed as a database. Doing a timeline can be an end in itself and as Amanda and Jackie indicate they can be a springboard into reflective thinking on different aspects of one's personal, professional lives.

Focused reflection point

■ Have a go at creating your own timeline – there are examples of two timelines in the Appendices. You should find this to be another really rewarding exercise.

Metaphors

Metaphors are ways of expressing ideas and they can help people to communicate complexity and shared thinking of these ideas. Lakoff and Johnson (1980: 118) propose that metaphors are compactors of information that capture richness and continuity of experiences through succinct illustrations. Metaphors can provide the vividness of an experience through evoking shared mental images for the listener that reflect the speaker's intentions; for example, theories could be perceived as buildings with thousands of rooms and long, winding corridors. In study metaphors 'can be highly effective in enabling learners to create mental representations of complex or abstract concepts' (Dean, 2009: 1), as well as being valuable when reflecting on provision and practice. Fook and Gardner (2007: ix) provide metaphors of the process of reflective experiences that it could be 'exciting walks; dark alleys; bright lights; shadowy mazes; exciting doorways and thorny bushes'. Bolton (2005: 125) suggests that using metaphors enables hidden meanings to be perceived and abstractions, memories and ideas to be expressed. They can also be useful to explore difficult issues or personal feelings and enable you to perceive your identity and feelings at different points of time in your personal and professional lives. I had never heard of the 'elephant in the room' until recently, but now it seems to be a very commonplace metaphor to use in the workplace!

I now have an appreciation and awareness of professional, political and social metaphors and the power that metaphors add to meaning making. Metaphors act as a frame through which we can perceive, understand and feel. Sharon

I am not sure how I came to use metaphors in my teaching, but I found them to be an innovative way of getting the students to reflect in different ways and to share their ideas. I collected and laminated about 40 pictures and photographs that could represent experiences and actions connected to reflection and so stimulate some creative and non-pressurised thinking. The images on the cards were of people, patterns and cartoons and were collected on postcards, photographs, adverts from magazines and newspapers and from museums and shops.

This was perhaps the most challenging of the reflective tools as the concept of a metaphor was not straightforward. However, once this was grasped metaphors did encourage a more creative stance to reflecting. It became apparent that for some learners on the programme metaphor use was undertaken without their appreciating the significance from a reflective perspective. Helen

The metaphor exercise was really helpful. Again, it is a way to distance yourself from being too exposed. I was aware that I really wanted to go through all my 'traumas' in my life (not that there are many and not that they are particularly severe) with other people, but that I didn't want to come across as someone who is falling apart at the seams. Pavla

These metaphorical images were what the students starting the course played around with and shared with the rest of the group. They did not know each other and they came from varied professional roles, backgrounds and cultures. The cards became an empowering and integrating experience and an active way of getting to know other people. They elicited comparisons of journeys, struggles, isolation, achievement, excitement, work, friendship, strangeness etc. They enabled the group to easily reflect on their thoughts. Select a few of these ideas and see if you can create a metaphor that relates to your experiences or aligns to your thinking. It is a fun thing to do and really does start you thinking in a reflective way.

Focused reflection point

■ Do any of the following images resonate with your feelings at this moment in time?

■ Read though the list and see what meanings or metaphors you can imagine from these examples that might reflect how you are feeling about study, essay writing, tackling a qualification, working with a colleague, starting a new job or liaising with parents.

TABLE 14.1 Some examples of images and metaphors

a dense forest	a butterfly emerging from a chrysalis	four babies in a bed with the caption 'need more space'	a large waterfall with a small boat beneath	a climber standing on a rock jutting out of a mountain	a person standing at the top of a staircase
a woman playing chess with a robot	a woman huddled in the rain covering her face	a bus stuck at the top of a cliff whilst two walkers struggle upwards	a highland cow waiting for a call by a phone box	the inner workings of a machine	men sat on a girder above a US city
a large warehouse of small objects	multicoloured junk	an isolated person in a crowd of people	a geyser erupting	circular patterns in sand dunes	a rocket aiming for the stars

Ten-minute writing task

A decade ago Winch and Ingram observed that writing in one's own hand was a very 'different process to sitting at a computer, as thoughts move energetically, emotionally from body, to mind, to pen, to page, in the imperfect scrawl that is part of who we are as individuals' (2004: 235). However, this is less the case since many of us now constantly work on laptops, tablets, phones and other platforms. Nevertheless, I requested my students to select from one of the following suggestions and write for ten minutes, to see if this would enable them to write freely and easily in a flow of immediate consciousness:

- breakfast time
- an interesting occurrence today
- journey to university
- what you would rather be doing at the moment
- an important friendship.

Although a little nervous, they all got on with the task – after all, ten minutes wasn't such a long time – how difficult could it be? They all produced some writing and then I asked them to share it with a neighbour. This again was nerve-wracking but it turned out to be so empowering, as people really enjoyed reading what others had done and many were praised for the interesting way they wrote. We had people writing seriously, humorously, factually and fictionally, and in essay, narrative, poetic and informative styles.

> The ten-minute writing activity was another effective collaborative reflective tool and it promoted high levels of reflection. It was quite intense and focused and perhaps suited some learners more than others. More reflective learners and those perhaps challenged by writing quickly would find this more difficult than others. It could perhaps be adapted to suit others, by encouraging the creation of a picture, spider diagram perhaps. Helen

> Again I enjoyed this because it stimulated a really interesting conversation and it was quite amazing how much reflection could be stimulated from such a short piece of writing. Jane

Dye (2011: 218) advocates thinking about a learning experience in any context and writing it as a piece of autobiographical text. It may begin with 'What I hoped to achieve was . . .', 'I learned how to . . .' or 'I learned that . . .' in order to facilitate the writing process. Other quick writing activities could take the form of:

- stories or poems;
- musings and reflections on why, what, when, how;
- descriptions;
- evaluations or assessments of practice;
- philosophising or examining ethical processes;

- fictional dialogues or monologues with others;
- diagrams;
- extended metaphors;
- letters;
- fantasy;
- cartoons or sketches;
- journalism.

Focused reflection point

- Why not try writing in some of these different ways? Free-flow writing can just be for oneself and enable you to reflect and think things through, explore professional values which underlie practice, examine new issues and probably connect the personal and professional elements. It can really facilitate your creative thinking without using too much time.

Johari window

I experimented using the Johari window on the PPRP module with the practitioners. The Johari window was created by Luft and Ingham (1955) in the United States as a cognitive psychological tool to help people understand their interpersonal communication and relationships. It looks like a window, as shown in Figure 14.1, and it is a tool to enable people to develop their self-awareness. There are several graphical images of the Johari window – I have created the model below with the aim of making it personal and meaningful for you.

Handy (1990: 65) describes the Johari window as four rooms in which a person controls the size of the rooms and holds the key to each:

Room 1 – public space self and others see
Room 2 – how others see of which the individual is unaware

1. Open – known to self What I know about myself I know that others know this too	3. Blind/unseen – not known to self This may be apparent to others but not to me
2. Hidden to self I know this about myself but I choose not to let others know or see	4. Unknown to self and others There may be things about me that are not obvious or known by me or others yet

FIGURE 14.1 The Johari window.

Room 3 – hidden room of the subconscious or potential, of which no one is aware at present

Room 4 – private room not shared with others.

The students were asked to think of themselves in the four rooms and to reflect on how they see themselves and how others might see them. Luft and Ingham (1955) used 56 adjectives (as shown in Table 14.2) as possible descriptions of the participant. However, I did not provide these, but requested my participants to use their own ideas. The students then exchanged their thoughts with another participant and they then shared what they wanted with the larger group. They were very positive about each other and it became a very empowering group exercise:

I have used this in supervision before and found it a useful tool when identifying different perceptions of the same behaviour. Jane

This was quite complex though it did promote the concept of 'others'. Helen

TABLE 14.2 Johari window adjectives

able	dependable	intelligent	patient	sensible
accepting	dignified	introverted	powerful	sentimental
adaptable	energetic	kind	proud	shy
bold	extroverted	knowledgeable	quiet	silly
brave	friendly	logical	reflective	smart
calm	giving	loving	relaxed	spontaneous
caring	happy	mature	religious	sympathetic
cheerful	helpful	modest	responsive	tense
clever	idealistic	nervous	searching	trustworthy
complex	independent	observant	self-assertive	warm
confident	ingenious	organized	self-conscious	wise
				witty

Focused reflection point

■ There are numerous examples of lists of adjectives that can be used in a Johari window exercise produced in many different ways more interesting than my unadorned list. Enter the phrase 'Johari window adjectives' into a search engine and see what you can find and then decide which appeals most to you.

The Johari window is a valuable tool to use in a setting to explore personal professional relationships. However, whilst it has the potential to promote 'openness, self reflection and communication about personal feelings by team members', it also has the 'potential for leaving people feeling very vulnerable' (Allen, 2012: 145). Allen used the Johari window to enable her team in a children's centre, as a 'constructivist practice based on reciprocal understanding' in a continuous interpersonal group experience (2012: 145). Opening the Johari window requires trust and risk-taking amongst participants. It can lead to greater trust, and Allen found that the team became more engaged in deep-level thinking about roles and the group articulated some sensitive and enlightening personal reflections.

Conclusion

Paige-Smith and Craft (2008: 16) advise that practitioners should be aware that it can be a long journey to change and implement reflective practice and that it is important to start creating the research to do this. It will involve more than just thinking about practice – how we see it and feel about it as well as how we understand about it. Essentially, in reflective practice we become researchers looking at our own work in order to develop and improve it (Craft and Paige Smith, 2011). Chapters 1, 2, 3 and this chapter should have set you well on your way in this process of researching your own practice through engaging in ongoing reflection. Participating in writing activities to deepen the reflective process is so important to enhance personal professional development. This is what a sample of the participants in the research stated:

> *Professionally I have utilised several of the reflective writing techniques which I believe have enhanced the delivery of the PPD modules within a foundation degree programme. I have instigated the use of collaborative reflection and led discussions with peers about how reflective writing is assessed. I feel strongly that reflection is a life skill and that once the process has been demystified for learners then it is a vital aid to learning and developing thinking skills. Personally I have explored the development of reflective writing and its use across two foundation degree subjects as part of my Master's dissertation. I recognised that reflection is a key element of many qualifications, yet it can be undertaken with such varying degrees of success which suggested that the delivery of the theory as well as the practice can be improved. Helen*

> *I have always been quite good at reflection, but this module has taken me to another level. I question myself more which I see as a positive, as I am always trying to improve, this is more so in my professional life, but it does cross over to my personal life as well. Amanda*

> *It has helped make me a better teacher and pass that knowledge on to my students, it has helped me teach on the BA in Young Children's Learning and Development and to encourage my students to think critically about their actions and decisions in their job. The module I teach is linking theory to practice, and thinking critically has been invaluable in helping the students to make the links between their practice and why they do it, and in helping them to reflect on their methods of working with*

young children. Many of them have changed their practice or challenged existing practice because of being reflective practitioners and thinking critically about what they do. Alix

You have heard the voices of a range of practitioners who undertook further professional development of which deepening the reflective processes was a key dimension. Hopefully this may have proved to you that engaging in reflective writing activities is not only beneficial for professionals, but can also be interesting and enjoyable too.

Summary of knowledge gained

After reading and reflecting on this chapter you should now be very aware that:

- to support the deepening of reflective thinking processes it is useful to participate in a range of reflective writing activities;
- reflective writing should be meaningful and valuable for your professional role;
- engaging in these activities and discussing your work with a critical friend, colleague or fellow student really enriches your reflective thinking and can be a really enjoyable experience.

Challenges for the future

- At this point there is just one main obvious challenge for the future – keep deepening your reflective thinking and practice. It is an ongoing process as new issues will definitely keep arising!

Further reading

Bradbury, H., Frost, N., Kilminster, S. and Zukas, M. (eds.) (2010) *Beyond Reflective Practice: New approaches to professional lifelong learning*. London: Routledge.

Hartnell-Young, E. and Morriss, M. (2007) *Digital Portfolios: Powerful tools for promoting professional growth and reflection*. London: Corwin Press.

McGregor, D. and Cartwright, L. (2011) *Developing Reflective Practice: A guide for beginning teachers*. Maidenhead: Open University Press.

References

Allen, G. (2012) 'Effective leadership. Effective learning. It's all about relationships', Chapter 8 in Arnold, C. (ed.) *Improving Your Reflective Practice through Stories of Practitioner Research*. London: Routledge.

Alterio, M.G. (2006a) 'Using story to enhance learning and teaching practices', a keynote address presented at the Assessment, Learning and Teaching Conference, Leeds Metropolitan University, Leeds, England, September 2006.

Alterio, M.G. (2006b) 'Interactive storytelling: a creative and reflective learning approach', a presentation delivered at Leeds Metropolitan University's Staff Development Festival, Harrogate, England, September 2006.

Arnold, C. (ed.) (2012) *Improving Your Reflective Practice through Stories of Practitioner Research.* London: Routledge.

Bolton, G. (2005) *Reflective Practice: Writing and professional development.* Second edition. London: Paul Chapman Publishing.

Brock, A. and Rankin, C. (2011) *Professionalism in the Early Years Interdisciplinary Team: Supporting young children and their families.* London: Continuum.

Craft, A. and Paige Smith, A. (2011) 'What does it mean to reflect on our practice?' Chapter 1 in Paige-Smith, A. and Craft, A. (eds) *Developing Reflective Practice in the Early Years.* Second edition. Maidenhead: Open University Press/McGraw Hill.

Dean, L. (2009) 'A critical look at the use of metaphors in the development of electronic learning resources', *Assessment, Learning and Teaching Journal*, 6. Leeds Metropolitan University.

Dye, V. (2011) 'Reflection, reflection, reflection. I'm thinking all the time, why do I need a theory or model of reflection?' Chapter 13 in McGregor, D. and Cartwright, L. (eds) *Developing Reflective Practice: A guide for beginning teachers.* Maidenhead: Open University Press.

Elbaz-Luwisch, F. (2010) 'Writing and professional learning: the uses of autobiography in graduate studies in education', *Teachers and Teaching*, 16(3): 307–27.

Eraut, M. (2000) 'Non-formal learning and tacit knowledge in professional work', *British Journal of Educational Psychology*, 70: 113–36.

Fook, J. (2010) 'Beyond reflective practice: reworking the "critical" in critical reflection', in Bradbury, H., Frost, N., Kilminster, S. and Zukas, M. (eds.) *Beyond Reflective Practice: New approaches to professional lifelong learning.* London: Routledge.

Fook, J. and Gardner, F. (2007) *Practising Critical Reflection: A resource handbook.* Maidenhead: Open University Press.

Ghaye, T. (2007) 'Is reflective practice ethical? The case of the reflective portfolio', *Reflective Practice*, 8(2): 151–62

Goodfellow, J. (2004) 'Documenting professional practice through the use of a professional portfolio', *Early Years: An International Journal of Research and Development*, 23: 63–74.

Gregory, E., Conteh, J., Kearney, C. and Mor-Sommerfeld, A. (2005) *On Writing Educational Ethnographies: The art of collusion.* Stoke-on-Trent: Trentham Books.

Handy, C. (1990) *Inside Organisations.* London: BBC Books.

Hartnell-Young, E. and Morriss, M. (2007) *Digital Portfolios: Powerful tools for promoting professional growth and reflection.* London: Corwin Press.

Lakoff, G. and Johnson, M. (1980) *Metaphors We Live By.* Chicago: University of Chicago Press.

Luft, J. and Ingham, H. (1955) *The Johari Window: A graphic model for interpersonal relations.* Berkeley, CA: University of California Western Training Lab.

McDrury, J. and Alterio, M.G. (2004) *Learning through Storytelling in Higher Education: Using reflection and experience to improve learning.* London: Routledge Falmer.

Miles, M.B. and Huberman, M. (1994) *Qualitative Data Analysis: An expanded sourcebook.* Thousand Oaks, CA: Sage.

Paige-Smith, A. and Craft, A. (2008) *Developing Reflective Practice in the Early Years.* Maidenhead: Open University Press.

West, L. (2010) 'Really reflexive practice: auto/biographical research and struggles for a critical reflexivity', Chapter 5 in Bradbury, H., Frost, N., Kilminster, S. and Zukas, M. (eds) *Beyond Reflective Practice: New approaches to professional lifelong learning.* London: Routledge.

Winch, A. and Ingram, H. (2004) 'Activating learning through the lifetime navigator: a tool for reflection', *International Journal of Contemporary Hospitality Management*, 16(4): 231–6.

Woods, P. (1999) *Successful Writing for Qualitative Researchers.* London: Routledge.

15

On reflection

Examining undergraduate reflective practice across two higher education (HE) sector endorsed foundation degrees (FDs) and BA (Hons) programmes within a further education (FE) provision

Helen Rowe

As a tutor with 13 years' experience, I was interested in examining students' perceptions of reflective practice, in particular their views about preferred reflective styles and how they are asked to reflect within assessments. I was keen to establish whether the students felt supported in developing their reflective skills, if they had developed gradually over the programme of their study and if a more collaborative approach to assessment could enhance this area of learning. My research was with students on Foundation Degree and Bachelor Arts (Hons) Top-Up in Young Children's Learning and Development (YCLD) and Business and Management (B&M) Personal and Professional Development (PPD) modules. Approximately 80 YCLD students and 40 B&M students at varying stages in their academic study (first to third year) attending the same further education institution were invited to participate. By comparing findings between students of the two programmes, I was able to investigate whether there were any differences in approach and attitudes to reflective practice. According to Bottle (2007), early years practitioners in the UK are less sure of their own practice compared to practitioners from other countries, and a key way to develop confidence and practice is to encourage practitioners to reflect. My aim was to develop the early years practice of the participants, which in turn would benefit children.

> Teachers must join the culture of researchers if a new level of educational rigor and quality is ever to be achieved.
>
> (Kincheloe, 2003: 8)

The study

This non-experimental, small-scale research sought to understand students' perceptions and views of reflective practice, as well as their ability to reflect, so requiring a qualitative approach. Through questionnaires, semi-structured interviews and a small action research project, the findings of the research were triangulated and therefore resulted in greater validity. The research was participatory as this, according to Kellet (2010), results in knowledge being produced rather than gathered. Another issue relating to participatory research is reflexivity, of the researcher as well as the participants, and it is important to acknowledge that the students had a degree of influence not only over their responses but also on the direction of the interviews. This is significant as the researcher intends to use the findings to improve delivery of teaching for the students. Their voice and control is therefore a vital element of making this research meaningful. Indeed Christensen and James (2009: 6) state that reflexivity is 'widely regarded as a methodological necessity in research'.

The questionnaire aimed to identify information about the participants, their views on reflective practice and the assessment tools, their current understanding of reflection and the level of support they have received in developing reflective practice. One participant per cohort from both programmes was chosen randomly from those agreeing to be interviewed (eight in total). This flexible approach to data collection is facilitated when the interviewer decides the direction of the interview beforehand, and encourages the interviewee to explain in greater depth and respond to prompts, if necessary. The action research took place at the end of the interview, where interviewees were able to discuss with the interviewer a short piece of reflective work, chosen by the interviewee. The purpose of this exercise was to introduce the participant to collaborative assessment of their reflection using Hubbs and Brand's matrix (2010). Hubbs and Brand devised this model to provide a structure for collaborative conversation and common reflective language, as they believed that this will not only facilitate assessment of qualitative writing but will also enable tutors to teach more effectively reflective skills.

The students then provided feedback on their views, about the appropriateness of using an assessment matrix to assess, as well as the benefits or drawbacks to investigating collaboratively with a tutor. There are many benefits of action research such as it leading to the instigation of change or integration of theory and practice, known as praxis (Hohmann and Wickett, 2010). Yet at the same time the decisions about what to examine, and the temptation to look at issues that have the greatest impact or facilitate raising standards, can result in the research being less theoretical or biased from the outset.

TABLE 15.1 Hubbs and Brand matrix

	A	B	C	D	E
1	Acquiring facts/data	Acquiring new information (e.g., principles and concepts)	Engaging in a reflective journal process	Expressing in a self-focused but not self-disclosing manner	Elaborating a factual biography
2	Recognizing that one's profession is influenced by legal, moral, and ethical guidelines	Organizing facts and data into new information	Identifying one's own values, thoughts, and beliefs on an issue	Using new information as a building block for examining one's values, beliefs, and attitudes	Acknowledging a physical, behavioural, or personal feature that causes embarrassment or shame
3	Understanding ethical guidelines	Analyzing events, principles, and concepts, and working toward applying relevant theories to explain events or behaviour	Identifying one's own values, thoughts, and beliefs	Testing how new information integrates with one's existing value system	Acknowledging that one's beliefs and values may significantly deviate from others
4	Understanding the importance of theories, models, and frameworks	Acknowledging the influence of power and power issues in the relationship	Examining issues, even those that conflict with one's own value system	Reassessing (reformulating) one's own value and belief system in light of new information	Celebrating one's uniqueness as a person and as a professional
5	Using new information as a building block for re-conceptualizing a principle	Analyzing the observed event and applying relevant theories to explain it	Analyzing own attitudes toward those different from himself/herself (cultural, age, political, educational, gender, socioeconomic, etc.)	Connecting new learning with personal growth and development	Demonstrating open attitudes toward those who are different from one's self
6	Generalizing elementary concepts into overarching principles	Applying a rational analysis to a conflicting issue or moral dilemma	Assessing the impact of one's own values, thoughts, and beliefs on his/her identity/practice	Accepting how values, thoughts, and beliefs impact one's ability to work appropriately with clients	Demonstrating a genuine self-acceptance as well as an acceptance of others

Source: Hubbs and Brand, 2010: 67

The data was coded and analysed to identify patterns and themes through an inductive approach where the themes were strongly linked to the data which then drives the analysis. Braun and Clarke (2006) remind us that the researcher plays an active role in the identification of themes as well as the reporting on them, as they do not just passively emerge from the data. Involving the Business and Management students in the study hopefully resulted in a more inductive approach to identification of themes. The sample size was 120 part-time students; 35 Business and Management (B&M); and 85 Young Children's Learning and Development (YCLD). The B&M sample was smaller as there were only two cohorts of students compared to six cohorts of YCLD. The numbers of returns were 69 from 120 (57.5 per cent).

Value of reflective skills

The questionnaire findings indicated that 91.3 per cent of all respondents felt that reflective skills are a valuable tool: 88.9 per cent of the B&M students and 91.7 per cent of YCLD (see Figure 15.1).

There did not appear to be any notable differences in the respondents' views of reflective practice between the different programmes of study. The three respondents who strongly disagreed that reflective practice is valuable were all from the YCLD programme and the findings indicated that the age or gender of the students did not appear to impact upon their views of reflective practice. The reflective logs were the most popular form of reflective tool for the whole sample, followed by reflective essay. Critical incident and spider diagrams were the third and fourth most popular with the respondents.

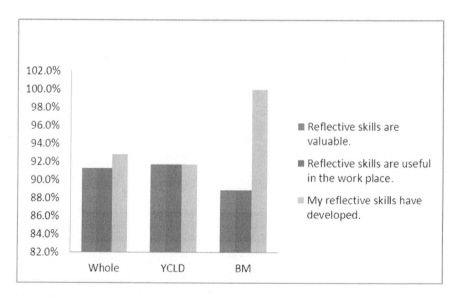

FIGURE 15.1 Sample's views on reflective skills.

Students' definitions of reflective practice

On the questionnaire respondents were asked to define reflective practice and their views are encompassed in the following six themes:

1. reflection is looking back;
2. reflection is a tool to improve practice or make changes and solve problems;
3. reflection involves different perspectives – involving others' views, opinions and the importance of considering the impact of an event on others when reflecting;
4. reflection involves feelings;
5. reflective practice requires awareness of personal development, learning and future training;
6. reflection requires critical appraisal and evaluation and should involve critical thinking.

Examples of reflective writing

The interviewees found that written examples of reflection were really helpful, and being able to see these provided more detail as they illustrated the theory. One interviewee described how he thought that terminology linked to reflection was off-putting and suggested it might be beneficial to students if a tutor could demonstrate the reflective thinking stages by asking students to work through an incident together:

> It brings out their natural ability. You let people do it first . . . they get it right . . . then you tell them what they have done . . . then they can relate to it.

This mirrored views of Russell (2005) who, when researching whether reflective practice can be taught, explained that he wanted experience, not just talking to introduce the process.

Writing reflections down

References were made by several interviewees about the significance of recording thoughts and reflections and some extolled the virtues of using reflective logs and a diary.

> I think that everybody reflects, but doesn't necessarily write them down and reference them.

> I like the structure of the reflective logs . . . it helps to write things down and really look at them.

> The fact that you can actually go back to it . . . I think if I have written it down I remember it.

Reflective logs

Analysis of the interviews showed differing views about the use of structured reflective logs. Whilst some students found them beneficial, others felt they were too prescriptive and preferred a freer, more creative way to express reflections.

I like the structure of reflective logs.

I quite like doing the reflective logs . . . I think because they are structured more and I struggle personally with structuring an essay.

Others commented that the use of structured logs was possibly inhibitive or a model they were expected to follow in order to gain marks from the assessor.

You write to the model because you know that it is going to be assessed . . . sometimes it's a struggle trying to dissect your thoughts and . . . put them in the right subheading.

Yes that's why I liked the [reflective] summaries because I like writing like that. It is difficult to get started, because it is not as prescriptive as other essays, but it gives freedom to write.

Subjectivity of tutors

When asked about their experiences of assessment of their reflective writing, the majority of these interviewees made positive comments. However, some students did acknowledge that there are issues surrounding subjectivity.

Tutors have a responsibility to be able to gauge whether or not actually that is reflective.

Because everybody assesses differently, because everybody's perception of reflection is different.

This respondent then suggested that presentations could be a way to assess reflection but felt that there were possible problems with this method of assessment:

Because you are putting across what you think people want to hear, you do not know what each person is looking for.

Considering 'others' when writing reflectively

Some interviewees commented that reflections should incorporate 'otherness': either the impact of an event on others or the need to acknowledge others' views or attitudes.

You are looking at others' opinions . . . so you may be looking at how it affects staff or children, other people involved, look at it from others' points of view.

It might have some impact on other people, so it might be about trying to understand how other people might have thought, how other people were influenced, by your decision making or your actions.

Reflecting collaboratively

Several respondents referred to reflection in the workplace as a team activity, and for one individual this was a preferable way to reflect.

Where I work my colleagues are reflectors: in staff meetings we look at what had previously been brought up. Definitely at work I am talking to colleagues about it. I feel confident talking with them because they know what reflective practice is really about.

We have an EYP [early years professional] and she has made us look at ourselves very deeply and evaluate what we are doing and improve it . . . We sit down together . . .

Some interviewees suggested that it was not always easy to do it collaboratively and that this could create significant challenges.

It's always good to share the positives but . . . perhaps if things haven't gone very well and you reflect on them and it's not down to you . . . That's quite difficult, sharing that reflection with others.

Uses of reflective practice

The interviewees provided examples of using reflective practice and gave many different scenarios and explanations referring to both positive and negative aspects.

I like to know when I have done a good job. It's reflecting on things you have done well . . . on the other hand it's good to reflect on things when they haven't gone so well. I tend to reflect on the opposite ends of the scale.

Reflection as an entrepreneurial opportunity

Some interviewees saw reflection as an opportunity for creativity or entrepreneurialism. A similar comment was made by Moon (1999), who thought that creative thoughts or insights can emerge from writing journals.

Makes you think and then leads you to different directions . . . it opened up an avenue of learning from experience . . . it opened up avenues of research.

I found that writing about these things helped me to realise that 'OK, you cannot change it, but I can maybe tweak it a little'.

However, some interviewees held less influential positions and for them reflecting could be frustrating if it is only used as an agent or mechanism for change.

Beliefs and attitudes/the affective domain

Emotional intelligence (Goleman, 1996) involves self-awareness, empathy, self-motivation and altruism. For many respondents to both the questionnaire and interview, reflective practice was a process involving looking at an event, thinking about what happened, why, and what could be done differently. Others considered that reflection also included thinking about the feelings, attitudes and beliefs of those involved. A complex reflection would be one which involved talking about feelings and emotions.

It gives you chance to evaluate your own beliefs.

It makes you think about what you believe and you can explain what you feel . . . more thoroughly.

Describing simple and complex reflective practice

Some of the interviewees commented on the inclusion of theory in more complex reflections and felt that a more in-depth reflection would consider others' views and opinions as well as the impact on them. They referred to a simple reflection as one which was descriptive and could be basic and short. In their opinions both complex and simple reflections could involve personal feelings.

Teaching and assessing reflective practice and skill

All of the interviewees gave positive comments when asked about teaching of reflective practice. This positivity could have been affected by the relationship which existed between the interviewees and tutor; however, two interviewees were unknown to the tutor. Mantle (2010) found that students who demonstrated positive emotion in interviews matured in their ability to reflect. The responses indicated that some individuals found reflecting inspirational, motivating and exciting, whereas others found the process challenging and difficult. This accords with Brookfield's (1997) view that critical thinking is emotive and can lead to anxiety and fearfulness as well as feelings of joy, relief and liberation.

Action research findings

In addition to the questionnaires and interviews, three respondents were asked to volunteer in a short discussion about a piece of reflective writing and the use of an assessment matrix devised by Hubbs and Brand (2005). After this discussion the sample completed a questionnaire indicating whether such an assessment grid was useful and if collaborative assessment was beneficial. They were asked again what words and phrases they now associated with reflection. All three students 'strongly agreed' that the Hubbs and Brand assessment matrix would be a useful tool when examining reflective practice and that collaborative assessment was beneficial when looking at whether this discussion and use of the assessment matrix had altered the words and phrases they associated with reflection. Figure 15.2 shows that there were some differences, though no significant changes in perception.

Discussion

As stated earlier, reflective practice is a frequently used technique for adult learners and is being linked with professionalism across many disciplines. According to Brock (2010), reflecting on reflections involves individuals in reflecting upon their theoretical, practical and personal knowledge, which leads to enhanced understanding and generation of professional knowledge. Reflective practice is recognised as a key attribute in many professions and Cole (2008), when exploring attributes and practices for qualified teacher status, referred to the need for self-criticism and collaboration as well as creativity. In fact, to obtain qualified teacher status (QTS) individuals must pass certain 'Q' standards and Q7 states that the teacher must be able to 'reflect on and improve

TABLE 15.2 Action research table showing interviewee word associations before and after using the Hubbs and Brand matrix

Respondent	Words associated with reflective practice <u>before</u> looking at the Hubbs and Brand grid (from interview data)	Words associated with reflective practice <u>after</u> looking at the Hubbs and Brand grid (from interview data)	Level of study and programme
1	Change, stability, adapting, progress, innovation, creativity, creative thinking, critical thinking, positive experiences	Deeper understanding, purpose, effective and challenging one's own position in order to improve things for others as well as for oneself	Level 6 YCLD
2	Describing, action planning and making changes	(the same)	Level 4 B&M
3	Feelings, putting feelings down in words, and I think really as well as research it gives you the opportunity to start looking at other areas . . . problem solving	Problem solving, broadening awareness, direction, structure	Level 4 YCLD

practice' (Mantle, 2010). Of the questionnaire respondents, 91.3 per cent either 'agreed' or 'strongly agreed' that reflective practice is valuable and useful in the workplace. The interview findings reinforced this view as 75 per cent gave very positive responses when asked for their view of reflective practice. Two of the interviewees agreed that reflective practice is valuable and useful; however, they both claimed to dislike it and explained that they found it difficult. An explanation for their feelings could be similar to that proposed by Ghaye and Ghaye (1998), who said that too much emphasis on reflection can result in fear of failure and negatively affect students' development. The level of study or programme did not appear to affect the students' views about the significance of reflective practice from the questionnaire findings. When asked if their skills in reflective practice had developed over the course of their programme, 92.8 per cent either 'agreed' or 'strongly agreed' that they had. There is the possibility that these results were biased by the relationship that existed between the researcher and respondents.

Reflective logs were the most preferred, critical incidents the second most popular and reflective essays third. Reflective logs were used either 'occasionally' or 'often' by 95.7 per cent of the whole sample and reflective essays by 97.1 per cent. Other methods of reflecting such as autobiography, digital storytelling and a montage of articles were less familiar to both sets of respondents. One explanation could be that tutors are only exposing students to more traditional methods such as reflective logs and essays.

Conclusion

The researcher's background is in early years and, as such, that is where her knowledge and expertise lies, rather than in Business and Management. It was the intention that this research would lead to enhancements in the teaching and learning of reflective practice in an FE establishment across both disciplines. Reflective practice is an integral part of both the programmes of study and definitely a growing aspect of professional roles and responsibilities in many fields. Within the early years workforce there have been many changes and much reform, some of which has focused on making services more accountable for improvements in children's outcomes (DCSF, 2010). Reflective practitioners will be responsible for leading these improvements, and developing their reflexivity will be paramount in ensuring the quality of early years provision. Reflective practice is given similar credence by the Training and Development Agency (TDA), who set out ten attributes that teachers must have in order to achieve qualified teacher status (QTS). One of these professional attributes is to 'Reflect on and improve their practice, and take responsibility for identifying and meeting their developmental needs' (Cole, 2008: 143).

Brownlee *et al.* (2007), when researching childcare workers' beliefs about childcare quality and professional training, found that staff practice and beliefs are strongly influenced by level of qualification and quality of training, which in turn reflect societal and political contexts. The researcher does not know if similar developments have taken place in the workplace sectors of the B&M programme but suspects that the recent recession and organisational restructuring may result in many industries implementing change that requires the workforce to increase its professionalism. Evans (2002), when referring to Hoyle's 'professionality continuum', stated that it was an increased capacity for reflection, which facilitated the move from 'restricted professional' to 'extended professional'.

A growing responsibility of FE providers is business enterprise and working with business partners to provide skilled employees for the local communities. The power relationships that therefore exist between those that create and deliver qualification and training and the recipients must be explored and assumptions identified when individuals deconstruct their knowledge through critical reflection (Fook, 2002).

As a tutor, there is always the worry that knowledge is only transferred to students rather than transformed. This is of great concern, as these respondents are mature learners, who may be of the traditional opinion or assumption that technical knowledge and knowledge gained from formal education is most regarded, and knowledge gained every day is less important. If this were the case, then it is a possible explanation for the attitudes and views of some of the respondents who found reflecting challenging. Critical reflection challenges this assumption as it embraces concrete experiences as food for learning (Fook and Askeland, 2007). Personally this research has strengthened my belief that a major responsibility of educators has to be to develop independent learners who are able to undertake transformational learning acting on their own values, beliefs and meanings.

References

Bottle, G. (2007) 'Leadership in the early years', Chapter 12 in Nurse, A.D. (ed.) *The New Early Years Professional*. London: Routledge, pp. 153–65.

Braun, V. and Clarke, V. (2006) 'Using thematic analysis in psychology', *Qualitative Research in Psychology*, 3: 77–101.

Brock, A. (2010) 'The nature of practitioners' reflection on their reflections about play', Chapter 3 in Moyles, J. (ed.) *Thinking About Play: Developing a reflective approach*. Maidenhead: McGraw Hill/Open University Press.

Brookfield, S. (1997) *Developing Critical Thinking: Challenging adults to explore alternative ways of thinking and acting*. Buckingham: Open University Press.

Brownlee, J.M., Berthelsen, D.C. and Segaran, N. (2007) 'Childcare workers and centre directors' beliefs about infant childcare quality and professional training', *Early Child Development and Care*, 179(4): 453–75.

Christensen, P. and James, A. (2009) *Research with Children: Perspectives and practices*. Second edition. London: Routledge.

Cole, M. (ed.) (2008) *Professional Attributes and Practice: Meeting the QTS standards*. London: Routledge.

Department for Children, Schools and Families (DCSF) (2010) *Breaking the Link between Disadvantage and Low Achievement in the Early Years: Everyone's business*. Nottingham: DCSF.

Evans, L. (2002) *Reflective Practice in Educational Research*. London: Continuum.

Fook, J. (2002) *Critical Theory and Practice*. London: Sage.

Fook, J. and Askeland, G.A. (2007) 'Challenges of critical reflection: nothing ventured, nothing gained', *Social Work Education*, 26(5): 520–33.

Ghaye, T. and Ghaye, K. (1998) *Teaching and Learning through Critical Reflective Practice*. London: David Fulton.

Goleman (1996) *Emotional Intelligence: Why it can matter more than IQ*. London: Bloomsbury.

Hohmann, U. and Wickett, K. (2010) 'Action research', Chapter 16 in Parker-Rees, R., Leeson, C., Willan, J. and Savage, J. (eds) *Early Childhood Studies*. Third edition. Exeter: Learning Matters.

Hubbs, D. and Brand, C.F. (2005) 'The paper mirror: understanding reflective journaling', *Journal of Experiential Learning*, 28(1): 60–71.

Hubbs, D. and Brand, C.F. (2010) 'Learning from the inside out: A method for analysing reflective journals in the college classroom', *Journal of Experiential Education*, 33(1): 56–71.

Kellet, M. (2010) *Rethinking Children and Research*. London: Continuum.

Kincheloe, J.L. (2003) *Teachers as Researchers: Qualitative inquiry as a path to empowerment*. Second edition. London: Routledge Falmer.

Mantle, M. (2010) 'An exploration of the maturation of PGCE student teachers' ability to reflect, using a range of reflective strategies to identify possible stages of development', *Research in Education*, 83: 26–35.

Moon, J. (1999) *Learning Journals*. London: Kogan Page.

Russell, T. (2005) 'Can reflective practice be taught?' *Reflective Practice*, 6(2): 199–204.

16

Does the use of reflective practice enhance early years foundation degree students' personal and professional development?

Nicola Firth

As Socrates claimed, 'the unexamined life is not worth living' (Moncur, 2010), and if reflection was to have boundaries it could be argued that life may not be fully examined and reflection would not be effective in terms of both personal and professional practice. This is where the impetus for writing this major independent study comes from my own experiences and how reflection has developed my personal and professional development, particularly over the past decade.

During studying for the Personal, Professional and Reflective Practice module on the MA Childhood Studies course, it became clear that I had a real focus and passion for the subject matter of reflection and how it can impact on and enhance personal and professional development. My job role for the past five years has seen me progress into teaching on higher education programmes and leading teams within a college environment. This has been predominantly foundation degree students, progressing to a BA Top-Up and on to early years professional status. The students have been what would be classed as non-traditional higher education students: mature students working within an early years environment. A thread running through the foundation degree programmes is reflective practice. Many of my students have found the concept of reflection difficult to comprehend and lack understanding of how reflective practice can enhance development. They often see it as a 'chore' rather than something to embrace and develop. As McFarland and Saunders (2009) suggest, reflection, setting goals and self-evaluation are tools to assist in guiding oneself. Nevertheless, Potter and Hodgson (2007) argue that there is a lack of research on reflective practice in relation to early years work, but with the early years professional status role comes the requirement to be able to reflect on practice and skills, and this is seen as being a crucial element (Johnson, 2010).

There are various aspects of reflection, one of them being emotion. Both personally and professionally, reflection has taken me to many emotional levels including high emotions both happy and sad. Moon (2006) considers that there are three myths to the reflective process, one of which is that emotion is very much a central process to reflective practice. A study conducted by Alterio (2004) would support the notion that reflection can trigger emotions: 'Like an onion – good for you but sometimes makes you cry.' This could suggest that people worry about the process of reflection, as it is going to open up emotions that they had 'locked away' and attempted to forget about.

The emotional aspect of how studying has impacted on students' families and feelings of resentment and guilt, for example, was explored throughout the study. Only one of my students on the FD has been male and my sample group are all female, married, have children and work either on a part-time or full-time basis in early years settings and primary schools. Daniels (2010) acknowledges that more mature women are returning to learning; however, their everyday lives and experiences are often misunderstood and this can create problems for female learners. This is a view supported by Gouthro (2009), who argues that women's homeplace knowledge and roles are normally unrecognised by educational institutions and in turn this affects their learning requirements.

For these reasons I have chosen to research the subject matter of reflective practice in this study and how or if non-traditional higher education early years students who have completed or are in the process of completing their studies feel that reflection has enhanced their personal and professional development.

Background to the study

The Leitch Review of Skills stated that there has been a long-standing policy concern in the United Kingdom with regard to the level of qualifications in the workforce, which was seen as inferior to that in other countries (Leitch, 2006). The foundation degree qualification was designed with the intention in mind to 'equip people with skills for tomorrow's jobs' (HEFCE, 2000: 5) and make a valuable contribution to the concept of lifelong learning (Greenbank, 2010). Foundation degree programmes are designed in unison by universities, colleges and employers with a strong focus on work related learning (Directgov, 2009). The emphasis on work-related learning and personal and professional development is a thread running through foundation degrees and, as Directgov (2009) states, 'foundation degrees offer a route into higher education for people of all ages and backgrounds . . . with a particular area of work in mind'.

Professionalism within the early years field has become a central concern to policymakers, early years practitioners, parents and others who are working with children (Osgood, 2010). This is a view supported by the Children's Workforce Development Council (CWDC, 2011a, 2011b, 2011c), who state that the early years professional demonstrates excellence in their personal practice. The CWD endorsed foundation degrees in the early years sector, therefore giving the higher education qualification a professional status. Osgood (2010) suggests that a key aspect of the reform agenda is to structure a hierarchy to establish a graduate-led profession within the early years workforce.

Foundation degrees for early years practitioners recruited high numbers of students. The New Labour Government made it mandatory that all early years settings must have an early years professional qualified to graduate level by 2010 for children's centres (Potter, 2007) and 2015 for private and voluntary settings (CWDC, 2010). The role was created as part of a key strategy by the Labour Government in order to improve the quality of early years care and education in England (Johnson, 2010).

Work-based practice is embedded into 50 per cent of the foundation degree model and this is underpinned by the investigation and acknowledgement of the students' understanding (O'Keefe and Tait, 2004; Edmond, 2010). Edmond (2010) discusses how the combination of work-based learning and academic study contribute widely to professional development, though argues that this distinctive contribution often goes unrecognised. There also has to be acknowledgement of responsibility from the student for their own learning and a commitment to their personal and professional development (Bagnall, 2006). Reflective practice is also a theme that runs throughout and is embedded into work-based practice, which Potter and Hodgson (2007) assert should be a core requirement not only in higher education qualifications but also in initial early years training. Professional reflection is seen as an underpinning requirement for quality services in the early years sector (Hughes and Menmuir, 2002; Sylva *et al.*, 2004) whilst incorporating the importance of depth of knowledge (Fawcett and Calder, 1998). It must be recognised that fostering reflection requires much more than just 'telling people to reflect and then simply hoping for the best' (Russell, 2005).

There are various ways in which a practitioner may choose to reflect in order to document their thoughts and ideas, such as journals, storytelling, digital portfolios and mind-mapping. Holly (1989) asserts that professional journals allow the individual to clarify ideas and experiences. However, surely this is also the case for personal journals and thought processes. It is also deemed vital to reflect in the written form and not only the verbal, as this form can be forgotten; reflective writers will adapt stages and find their own way of writing, often in a creative reflective manner (Bolton, 2010).

The study

This study is based on qualitative research using semi-structured interviews with seven participants: five students and two lecturers. The aim was to gain access to my participants' 'real' thoughts and opinions and so enhance my understanding of the issues faced by participants studying on a Foundation Degree in Early Years. All of the participants had completed the Foundation

Degree in Early Years and were either continuing or had completed a Bachelor of Arts (BA) Top-Up Degree or a BA Top-Up Degree with Early Years Professional Status. I chose participants who were at different stages in their studies, as this was an essential part of my study in order to analyse if this made any difference to the participants' understanding and thoughts of the subject matter. The participants were also employed in early years settings in primary schools, nurseries and a children's centre and one was a self-employed childminder. As the research progressed, it became clear that it was not only the views of students that were important but also the views of those who teach in the post-compulsory education sector, and so I interviewed two of my colleagues who teach on the Foundation Degree of Young Children's Learning and Development.

Methodology

I was interested in exploring how reflective practice enhanced personal and professional development for those studying on a Foundation Degree in Early Years programme. Denscombe (2010) asserts that there is no 'single pathway' in undertaking good research and the chosen strategy will greatly depend on the particular research project being undertaken. DiCicco-Bloom and Crabtree (2006) explain semi-structured interviews as being a guided conversation during which time the interviewer elicits information about the meaning of behaviour, interactions and rituals. This method was chosen as my preferred approach because I felt that it would give me access to my participants' 'real' thoughts and opinions about how or if reflective practice had enhanced their personal and professional development. Punch (2009) suggests that the interview approach I had chosen is an effective method in view of the fact that the interviewer can access their participants' perceptions, meanings and constructions of reality. I also gathered biographical details of the participants that would offer a more in-depth and richer picture of the individuals in the group (Sagan, 2008).

My aim was that the study would be an action research project, as action research allows the researcher to gain a better understanding of everyday practice in order to then actually alter things (Denscombe, 2010). Through undertaking this study I hope to change practice in the classroom and allow students to develop reflective, personal and professional skills whilst understanding the barriers they come up against on a daily basis. It was important that the research was reliable and valid; reliability can be measured by consistency over a period of time and validity can be measured by the quality aspect of the research (Punch, 2009). I adhered to Leeds Metropolitan University's Research Ethics Policy (2012) throughout the research. One factor that I needed to consider was that I had been known to the five original participants as their tutor. I no longer taught any of them at the time of the research; however, the teacher–student relationship needed to be considered.

Analysis

To assist me in analysing and evaluating the data I needed to attempt to find common themes that were evident from the interviews and key subject matter included in the literature review. Noting patterns and themes promotes tactics for generating meaning and is the primary tactic in a logical chain (Punch, 2009). The key themes that emerged from the analysis processes are:

- understanding of reflective practice;
- time and place for study;
- emotions;
- development of personal and professional skills;
- career development.

Understanding of reflective practice

I wanted to gauge the participants' understanding of reflective practice prior to starting their Foundation Degree in Early Years. I asked the participants: 'When you first started your Foundation Degree in Early Years, did you understand the concept of reflective practice and did you see it being worthwhile?'

> To be honest at first I didn't, and when we had to do, when we had to write reflective, like reflective diaries they were called, I was very descriptive and it took me quite a long time to understand, to understand why we were doing it. Since doing my BA I recognise that I am a reflective early years practitioner and I feel this very important in my role, because I am of the opinion that there's always areas to improve, you can always do better, the only way you can do that is through reflecting. Leanne

All the participants stated that by the end of the foundation degree or when moving on to the BA Top-Up they did understand the concept of reflective practice and saw it as being worthwhile. They felt that their skills of reflection had developed throughout their studies.

Time and place for study

Finding quality time to study can be difficult in reality, particularly for students who have dependent children. It can prove to be problematic to manage time and family needs, and there may be barriers to meeting their educational goals there and the development of personal and professional growth.

> I'd been at home, stay at home mum and my husband works away a lot, he can work away for three to four nights a week and everything in the house was done, you know, everything ran smoothly and then I got a job and things did start to change ... instead of being there all the time I was upstairs on my computer every weekend. My husband would have to take the children out. Leanne

After school we would go to Play Palace and Claire (daughter) would go and play with children her own age and I knew she was safe and interacting . . . and I could just sit with a cup of coffee, sprawl out with my books, there were no distractions . . . and that was my time, my two hours and bizarrely it worked. Gina

Study time was my lunch hour at work . . . Do an hour's worth of studying, reading and then go back into my job . . . I would finish my job, come home, see to my family and all the rest of it and even got my husband trained so I could put him to bed with the kids at nine o'clock. He loved it. The house was quiet and I would go upstairs to the study. Karen

Each participant found time and places to reflect and study and it was interesting in seeing how their families had coped with their studies and the emotional aspect this had on the participants.

Emotions

Throughout the interviews it became apparent that the participants had indeed experienced various positive and negative emotions such as guilt, frustration, resentment and happiness, not only generated by reflective practice but also through the time taken for study.

I felt frustrated because I still feel like I have got a lot of work to do on reflections . . . but that is something I just have to work on . . . I have to be more critical, yes more critical. Karen

Leanne reflected that she found writing assessments an emotional strain:

I do my research and I'd go upstairs into my office and I'd be, you know, trying to write the essays and I found that really, really hard, it didn't come natural to me and I really did have to work at it and yeah it was emotional and you have that stress as you're doing it. There's loads of times that I'd be there and have my head in my hands, 'I can't do this, I can't do this'.

Leanne also related to feelings of guilt on a personal level:

Last week doing my BA my husband did actually say, 'Leanne, this has really affected our family, hasn't it?' and I said 'Yeah, don't make me feel guilty' because I have felt guilty. I've not felt like I've been a good mum. Have I done the right thing? But then reflecting on it I think, well yes I have done, because I've been happier because I've been studying and I've gained all this new confidence, I think it has benefited us. All of us.

As Michelle moved into the BA in Childhood Studies course she had a baby daughter, Rachael, and it was clear that this had altered Michelle's priorities about studying and family life:

Rachael made me kind of resent my studies because it was time I was missing with her. But what I had to do and it was a very strong thing that came over me, once I'd kind of got over the emotions of having Rachael because obviously your hormones are all up and down. Once my hormones settled, I found myself thinking this is for her. I'm now doing this for her. I'm bettering myself so that potentially I've got more career opportunities so I can look after her . . . Simple as that and suddenly the degree took on a whole new meaning and it was suddenly like, do you know what, I'm doing this.

Eileen, who is the oldest participant, described feeling guilty towards her father who lives on his own:

'You never come and see me, you're always working' and he would moan and groan but from my own daughters and my husband I had no feelings of guilt.

Emotions such as frustration, guilt and resentment were all described by the participants. They discussed the various barriers and emotions they had experienced, but nevertheless they all successfully achieved their foundation degrees and went on to further study.

Development of personal and professional skills

The participants talked about the impact of reflection and how it had enhanced their personal and professional development and really developed their confidence.

I really did lack confidence but through you know the support of the tutors and reflecting and yeah my confidence has really, really grown and in a way now that I've come out of studying, as in I've finished my BA, I am scared if anything, I don't want to lose that confidence. Leanne

It [the foundation degree] has given me a lot more confidence both personal and professional. I wouldn't have gone into rooms or even training courses, I would have felt really strange whereas now I am quite happy to go anywhere. Eileen

Eileen is now considering setting up her own pre-school setting. All of the participants agreed that their personal and professional skills had developed during their studies and declared that reflective practice had been a worthwhile tool to use in order to further develop their own skills.

Career development

I needed to leave and I needed to . . . I mean I don't like change as well, change is a big thing for me, but I just felt I had to resign and get a new post and I do believe that that is because of my study. I don't think if I hadn't have done my studying and reflecting, I think I would probably still be there doing the same job and I just learnt so much through studying. Leanne

Each participant believed that their career options had changed through studying the foundation degree and all were considering moving into a different type of job role that involved working with children. All five of the participants were considering career options for the future that did not seem to be an option prior to commencing on the course. This suggests that studying at a higher level and reflecting on the past and moving forwards has had a strong impact on their professional development.

Findings

A significant discovery was the barriers which non-traditional female students are faced with, particularly on a personal level for me, as I found that the students were experiencing the same types of barriers as I had while studying for my Master's degree. As Schuller *et al.* (1999) and Hughes and Menmuir (2002) suggest, studying in part-time education can be combined with work, family commitments and domestic chores, but it has to be acknowledged that it can sometimes be difficult. The participants discussed these as being barriers but did in fact overcome them, not always to the liking of other family members. This discovery will assist me in further supporting my own students through understanding their needs and being in a position where I can empathise with their positions not only in the college and working environment but also in their personal lives.

The discovery of barriers that impacted on the participants' learning included the emotional aspects to studying at higher education level becoming clearer. Many of the emotions such as guilt, frustration and resentment all carry with them a strong element of negativity; however, as Eastaugh (1998, cited in Bolton, 2010: 37) suggests, emotions can bring with them understanding. It is evident that whatever emotions the participants felt they still did not allow themselves to become too drawn into the negative thought process and again continued with their studies. An element of confidence may have had a bearing on the participants' dealing with their emotions and feelings; each participant discussed how their confidence had developed during their studies and through the use of reflective practice. Bolton (2010) proposes that through effective reflective practice, practitioners analyse their roles in both social and professional contexts and in turn this encourages action. It can be argued that confidence would be required to have the self-assurance to undertake action required.

The participants resoundingly agreed that reflective practice and studying for the degree had enhanced their personal and professional development. This was evidenced through the dialogue that emerged through the interviews. The participants have continued on their journey of lifelong learning. It is, however, distressing having to report that none of the participants are actually recognised for their graduate status in the settings where they are employed, with the exception of Michelle, who is self-employed but again does not get recognition from any other body such as the local authority.

Conclusion

A study carried out by Ranns *et al.* (2011) found that early years settings that employed an early years professional (EYP) made significant improvements in the quality of care for pre-school children in comparison to settings that did not have an EYP. It is worrying that the Coalition Government has removed New Labour's requirement of having an early years professional in every early years setting by 2015 (Early Education, 2011).

Although the findings in this study are based on a relatively small sample of practitioners, I believe that the quality of the dialogue during the interviews has provided a meaningful and thought-provoking collection of data.

However, I would make two recommendations that would develop and further enhance the study:

1. Undertake further research on the barriers that are faced by non-traditional female higher education students in order for educational institutions to recognise and meet the needs of this group.
2. Develop lecturers'/tutors' understanding of and engagement with reflective practice so that they can embrace the power of reflection and encourage students to reflect in a manner that is suitable for purpose and further develop practice.

References

Alterio, M. (2004) 'Collaborative journaling as a professional development tool', *Journal of Further and Higher Education*, 28(3): 321–32.

Bagnall, R. (2006) 'Lifelong learning and the limits of tolerance', *International Journal of Lifelong Education*, 25(3): 257–70.

Bolton, G. (2010) *Reflective Practice: Writing and professional development*. London: Sage.

Children's Workforce Development Council (CWDC) (2010) *Government Aims for Early Years*. Retrieved 26 March 2011 from http://www.cwdcouncil.org.uk/eyps/government-aims.

Children's Workforce Development Council (CWDC) (2011a) *Early Years Professional Status*. Retrieved 14 May 2011 from http://www.cwdcouncil.org.uk/eyps.

Children's Workforce Development Council (CWDC) (2011b) *Funding for EYPS*. Retrieved 25 July 2011 from http://www.cwdcouncil.org.uk/eyps/suitability/funding.

Children's Workforce Development Council (CWDC) (2011c) *Information for Training Providers*. Retrieved 25 July 2011 from http://www.cwdcouncil.org.uk/qualifications/recent-qualifications/foundation-degrees/training-provider.

Daniels, J. (2010) 'Women learners and their virtual handbags: invisible experiences and every-day contexts in vocational education', *International Journal of Lifelong Education*, 29(1): 77–91.

Denscombe, M. (2010) *The Good Research Guide: For small scale social research projects*. Fourth edition. Maidenhead: Open University Press.

Eastaugh, A. (1998) 'The pursuit of self knowledge through a study of myself as a member of a group of co-tutoring facilitators', unpublished MA dissertation.

Edmond, N. (2010) 'The role of HE in professional development: some reflections on a foundation degree for teaching assistants', *Teaching in Higher Education*, 15(3): 311–22.

Fawcett, M. and Calder, P. (1998) 'Early childhood studies degrees', in Abbott, L. and Pugh, G. (eds) *Training to Work in the Early Years*. Buckingham: Open University Press.

Gouthro, P. (2009) 'Neoliberalism, lifelong learning, and the homeplace: problematizing the boundaries of "public" and "private" to explore women's learning experiences', *Studies in Continuing Education*, 31(2): 157–72.

Greenbank, P. (2010) 'Foundation degrees: a case for greater institutional autonomy?', *Perspectives*, 14(2): 56–61.

Higher Education Funding Council for England (HEFCE) (2000) *Invitation: Foundation degree prospectus*. London: HEFCE.

Holly, M. (1989) *Perspectives on Teacher Professional Development*. London: Falmer Press.

Hughes, A. and Menmuir, J. (2002) 'Being a student on a part-time early years degree', *Early Years: International Journal of Research and Development*, 22(2): 147–61.

Johnson, L. (2010) *Positive and Trusting Relationships with Children in Early Years Settings*. Exeter: Learning Matters.

Leeds Metropolitan Univeristy (2012) *Research Ethics Policy*. Leeds: Leeds Metropolitan University. Retrieved 17 April 2014 from https://www.leedsmet.ac.uk/about/files/Research_Ethics_Policy_2012.pdf.

Leitch, S. (2006) *Prosperity for All in the Global Economy: World class skills* (Final Report of the Leitch Review of Skills). Norwich: HMSO.

McFarland, L. and Saunders, R. (2009) 'Reflective practice and self-evaluation in learning positive guidance: experiences of early childhood practicum students', *Early Childhood Education Journal*, 36: 505–11.

Moncur, M. (2010) 'Quotations by author: Socrates'. *The Quotations Page*. Retrieved 2 January 2010 from http://www.quotationspage.com/author.php?author=Socrates.

Moon, J. (2006) *Learning Journals*. Second edition. London: Routledge.

O'Keefe, J. and Tait, K. (2004) 'An examination of the UK early years foundation degree and the evolution of senior practitioners: enhancing work-based practice by engaging in reflective and critical thinking', *International Journal of Early Years Education*, 12(1): 25–41.

Osgood, J. (2010) 'Reconstructing professionalism in ECEC: the case for the critically reflective emotional professional', *Early Years: International Journal of Research and Development*, 30(2): 119–33.

Potter, C. (2007) 'Developments in UK early years policy and practice: can they improve outcomes for disadvantaged children?', *International Journal of Early Years Education*, 15(2): 171–80.

Potter, C. and Hodgson, S. (2007) 'Nursery nurses reflect: Sure Start training to enhance adult child interaction', *Reflective Practice*, 8(4): 497–509.

Punch, K. (2009) *Introduction to Research Methods in Education*. London: Sage.

Ranns, H., Mathers, S., Moody, A., Karemaker, A., Graham, J., Sylva, K. and Siraj-Blatchford, I. (2011) *Evaluation of the Graduate Leader Fund: Evaluation overview*. Research Report DFE-RR144d. London: Department for Education.

Russell, T. (2005) 'Can reflective practice be taught?', *Reflective Practice*, 6(2): 199–204.

Sagan, O. (2008) 'The loneliness of the long-anxious learner: mental illness, narrative biography and learning to write', *Psychodynamic Practice*, 14(1): 43–58.

Schuller, T., Raffe, D., Morgan-Klein, B. and Clark, I. (1999) *Part-Time Higher Education: Policy, practice and experience*. London: Jessica Kingsley Publishers.

Sylva, K., Melhuish, E., Sammons, P., Siraj-Blatchford, I. and Taggart, B. (2004) *The Effective Provision of Pre-School Education (EPPE) Project: Technical Paper 12 – The final report*. London: DfES/Institute of Education, University of London.

Appendices

Appendix 1: Avril Brock's autobiography extract

Appendix 2: Reflective diary on the Personal and
Professional Reflective Practice module

Mobalanle Cole

Appendix 3: Avril Brock's timeline

Appendix 4: Mobalanle's timeline

Appendix 5: Avril Brock's digital paperchase

Appendix 6: Pavla's paperchase

1

Avril Brock's autobiography extract
A personal preamble – a CPD autobiography (written April 2000 as I commenced my PhD)

CPD has worked for me – at least it has so far – we'll have to see how this PhD progresses!

As I have thought back over my professional developmental experiences I have decided that I must begin when I learnt to read. I come from a family of readers. My father at the age of eighty-one still reads a book a day, albeit in large print and normally about crime or mystery. I have asked teachers on my inservice courses if they can remember learning to read. Some of them may remember a certain reading scheme, but few remember the process unless it had been problematic for them. This is also true of me. I don't remember learning to read, except for the big red lorry going up the hill. (Gay Way, I think.) I do remember being enthralled by *The Magic Wishing Tree* – Enid Blyton of course! I began to read Enid's vast range of stories and then gravitated towards C.S. Lewis; Laura Ingalls Wilder; Mary Norton and hundreds of other authors.

Therefore you can see that I have always loved to read and I really believe that this all-consuming interest has made the difference to my personal and professional ability. The library was a rich resource and a haven for me. A place that has offered delights since my father took me when I was four years old. I used to read avidly, often one book a day, from the age of seven onwards. The reading would continue into the late evening. To escape detection by parents, who would object to late nights on a weekday evening, I needed a torch to light under the bedclothes to help the reading process. Radio Luxembourg provided accompaniment in the background. English Literature became my favourite subject at school – I'd even come top in an examination one year. (I'm not sure who was more surprised – me or the teachers!) However, English Literature was not a subject the school would offer at O level – they preferred you to specialise in the sciences or in modern foreign languages.

Somehow education in school could not compete with the education that the outside world had to offer. I had not particularly enjoyed my private education and began to truant at the age of fifteen, as new extra-curricular experiences beckoned and were much more appealing. Eventually I was rumbled by my father, who found employment for me in an insurance agency office. I left school with no qualifications, but didn't feel that I needed any at this time.

I married young and had two wonderful daughters. But I soon started to get restless and needed some sort of stimulation for my brain. I searched for employment, not only for the finance we needed, but also for an interest and challenge. I would take temporary part-time work – cleaning offices or packing in factories. I enjoyed most of the jobs as they all provided new experiences and helped create different views of the world.

The first further education course I enrolled on was a literature appreciation course at the WEA – the Workers' Educational Association – in Leeds. It was not wholly successful. Although the seminars were interesting and I enjoyed the preparatory reading, I used to be so tired after completing jobs, organising two young children and travelling on the bus, that I found it hard not to fall asleep during the discussions. And although Kirsty at one-year-old was happy in the crêche, Jackie at two-and-a-half years hated it. However, the seeds were taking root and as I continued to search for future occupation, I quickly realised that I would need qualifications. I have vague memories of wandering into a local community centre in the old infant school building and talking about careers to someone. Perhaps I should be a librarian, as that was where my interests seemed to be. On making enquiries I found that the qualifications to be a librarian seemed to be difficult to gain, and it was the same for social work. What about teaching? Anyway, whatever career route I selected, I needed to study and take examinations. Onward to Park Lane College, which became a place I visited for the next three years, studying O level English Language, English Literature, History, R.E., Human Biology and A level English Literature. Thank you, Pat – wherever you are now – for that half-hour, two evenings a week looking after J & K – probably made the difference to where I am now. Steeped in our family folklore are the stories of how I used to catch seven buses a day, taking Jackie to school, Kirsty to nursery school, travelling to part-time office work in the city, back home again and then out to evening classes.

I then applied to Whitwood College to study for a teaching certificate and they turned me down! I remember it being an awful interview. I was twenty-five years old and I was a mature student with family commitments. Not necessarily a desirable commodity as a student teacher. James Graham College in Leeds awarded me a place on their Certificate in Education course. My year of entry – 1976 – they amalgamated with Leeds Polytechnic and I found myself sitting in a large hall with a couple of hundred students – all of whom seemed younger than me – at the Becketts Park site, wondering what on earth I was doing there.

I loved college. Education was now important, purposeful and stimulating.

I would have stayed at college for even longer than the four years it took me to get the B.Ed. Honours degree. However, I accepted it was time to leave and managed to get a job straight away in an infant school in Dewsbury. I continued to teach in Kirklees for the next ten years. At first I had temporary appointments and taught in two infant and two middle schools. This enabled me to gain a variety of valuable teaching experiences, before I gained a permanent position in an inner-city multicultural primary school.

I stayed at the school for six years and, now settled, I began to enrol on inservice courses and it became a natural process to undertake professional development to enable me to be better informed and more capable in teaching my class. I enrolled on a variety of curriculum courses over the years, including an interesting course entitled 'The Four Year Old in School'. Then my colleague, and friend, Jo and I decided to participate in an evening course entitled 'Communication Skills' – which involved analysing children's language use through watching a set of videos produced by Joan Tough. We continued to attend the course for a year, as much for meeting teachers from other schools and discussing different practice, as for the actual content. On completion of this course I decided that if I was going to invest so much attendance in a professional course, then I ought to study on one that would give me qualifications.

The RSA Diploma in Teaching English as a second language in multicultural classrooms was advertised in the LEA bulletin as being offered by Bradford and Ilkley Community College as a year's course with a term's secondment included. I sent off an application, was accepted and must have managed to get one of the final secondments on offer. The term's study was wonderful – it definitely makes a difference to be totally involved in study and change. About eight of us enrolled initially and we were from a variety of school backgrounds and from different educational authorities. Again I enjoyed the academic rigour that married practice and theory, with the expectation of reflection and study in assignments and in practice. The work was continued back in school, creating and implementing resources, assessing practice, evaluating teaching, application and effect. I was pleased to gain distinction for some of my work, to pass the course and was very excited to see my final dissertation in print (by this I mean typed up by the school secretary!).

Undertaking this course did make a real difference to my professional development. As new Section 11 posts were created to support second-language learning I attained promotion and became the Special Measures Coordinator in the school. Prior to the RSA Diploma I had always insisted on staying as a class teacher, which I had loved, but now I organised resources and teaching language for our bilingual children throughout the school. Another significant effect of the RSA was that the lecturers asked me to give presentations of my work to groups of teachers and students. A couple of years later I was seconded to the college half time and I combined teaching in school with lecturing in college on undergraduate courses. Soon I realised that I wanted, no needed, to move forward and decided to continue up the management ladder. I started applying for Deputy Headships and after several interviews achieved this in a local infant school. However, this was not a successful move. It was successful in that I learnt a great deal about professional ideology, reflection on practice and different management styles and professional relationships. But the job was unsuccessful in terms of personal satisfaction and enjoyment of the job. I had to continually self-evaluate and reflect on my practice, as my opinions and perceptions of an appropriate developmental curriculum for young children, alongside my role as a professional, were continually challenged.

Time to move again and this time into higher education full time, back at Bradford College. Professional development is an inherent part of teaching, whether in primary, secondary, further or higher education, and it has continued naturally and progressively for me. Now the attendance at conferences became an ongoing part of my furthering education and the enrolment on the M.Ed. programme at Bretton Hall was the next major step. It is not as though I was or am ambitious, or that I particularly wanted a further qualification, but that progression in education just seems to be an inherent part of what I should do. The Ed.D was the next progressive route, but unfortunately, although my research proposal was accepted, Bradford College ceased to fund higher degrees. Research was not amongst its priorities and I decided I could not fund myself at this time. But, that which is started must be continued, and I worked on my research of collaborative problem solving by bilingual pupils, with the exciting result of *Into the Enchanted Forest* being published four years later.

And now, as situations change and time moves on, I have begun a new and very challenging course of professional development in beginning this PhD.

The reason I have catalogued my CPD autobiography is because of the recent developments in my role at college, and because the field work and thinking have already begun. On acquiring, through my own request, the role of the Early Years Coordinator in the Department of Education at Bradford College, I have been widening my professional knowledge into hitherto uncharted areas (uncharted by me that is). The professional development achieved through being a RegNi – Registered Nursery Inspector – and inspecting a variety of settings, including playgroups, private daycare and independent schools, has widened my previously early year experiences, which had been in the context of LEA provision in nurseries and schools. Since beginning the inspections and since visiting a range of EY practice internationally in the USA, Poland, Portugal, The Netherlands and The Caribbean, I have been determined to also widen and further develop the experiences and knowledge of the students I teach, whether on undergraduate courses or on inservice programmes. In the last two years I have written and coordinated a new MA in Early Years and a new Advanced Study of Early Years route for BA Educational and BA QTS students. I have a strong interest in the development and professionalism of these students, not only because it is my job, but also because they will be teaching young children who deserve the most stimulating and developmentally appropriate education that can be offered. Some of the students have begun their CPD in adulthood, since perhaps helping in a playgroup or in school classrooms. Also, as I talked to the early years workers and teachers on my inservice modules in tutorials last week, I began to realise how they are now on an important rung of the ladder in their teaching careers. The majority of the students on this module have now decided to submit assignments and begin a programme to attain a Certificate or MA in Early Years. I can relate to the processes they are now engaged in and listen to their reflections, problems and ideological perspectives. I want to track their development and progress up the ladder of continuing professional development.

2

Reflective diary on the Personal and Professional Reflective Practice module

Mobalanle Cole

29 September 2011

Although I had attended classes for other modules, today was my first lecture on this course. I guess the fact that I struggled with remembering the 'name' of the module (which is a mouthful by the way) had created a fear of what to expect on the course. The tutor was able to help break the bubble by asking us to share a little bit about ourselves with someone next to us. Feedback to the general class was fun. One thing I loved about the tutor instantly was the constant way she smiled while talking. She ended the class by reading a part of her CPD Autobiography to us and challenged us to get writing as this was what the course was all about. I drove home that day trying to think of what and how to go about writing an autobiography.

6 October 2011

Came back to the next class with so much enthusiasm and although I was scared she might ask us to read our autobiography (which by the way I had not done) I was still excited being in class. As always, Avril didn't disappoint – it was indeed a fun time. She gave us a class exercise telling us to summarise 'who we are' through pictures cut out of a magazine and pasted onto a board. We were all running around, getting scissors, glues, sellotape and trying to put together something nice. I got home and showed my husband what I had done and he couldn't stop laughing – he asked what a Master's student was doing with a primary school exercise. Well that's what he thinks and that's what I thought initially but honestly it's harder to put things together that explain who you are.

13 October 2011

We had our lecture in the library today with Caroline and help from Erin (a library staff) and someone from the Skills for Learning department. The lady from Skills for Learning (can't remember her name) talked about the various help students could get as they provide skills for academic learning. She also introduced a book – *Quote and Unquote* – that could help us with referencing when we begin to do our writing. Erin took us through how we could access journals through the university library online and also told us that if we needed to access journals or books that are not available in the school, the library staff could help us source it from other libraries. I guess for the better part of the lectures my mind wasn't in class – I was due to go on holiday and my flight was for that night. Caroline also tried speaking to us about our dissertation topics. I can't seem to think of what to write my dissertation on.

20 October/27 October 2011

I regret booking a holiday during term time – I should have waited to see if I would be offered the admission before planning a holiday. My mind was in school all through the period of my holiday and on the most important things I would miss out on. I hope one of my friends in class would be able to explain to me what I had missed. The good thing though, is that I came up with my autobiography or so I thought.

3 November 2011

Thank God – back in class and like I thought I had missed quite a lot. Avril shared the teaching for the day with Caroline as she needed to leave early but not before she went to see if she could get us cakes from a retirement party that had just taken place. Well the cakes were all gone – so it was back to learning for us. Caroline asked us to do a little 'reflective' exercise – we talked in groups about what we had done in our professional life that has made a difference. I shared something in my group which they urged me to share with the entire class and I did. Caroline asked me how I would rate myself based on my experience and I humbly gave myself an 8. A lot of other people also shared their experiences and while they were talking and Caroline was feeding back I gradually started to have an idea of why I was in the class and what the module was all about – at long last! By the time the class finished that day I realised that what I thought I had written as my autobiography wasn't. It didn't contain the elements of what a professional autobiography should – self-evaluation, reflection and a thorough analysis of significant experiences. After class I was able to ask some of my course mates to explain what the digital paperchase and timeline was as I had missed the classes. Avril did ask some people to present their digital paperchase the next week – I hope I am able to understand and at least put something together afterwards.

10 November 2011

We had a guest speaker in from America who gave a lecture about The Changing Culture of American Childhood. She talked about how the images of childhood in America have evolved from the nineteenth century to date. The most touching part of her lecture was when she brought up a picture of a black girl, Ruby Bridges Hall, being escorted to school by US Marshals. I realised that if only one person could stand up and fight; it might be long and hard but freedom for all could be achieved through one person's action. The class ended with two students sharing their digital portfolio, which they did brilliantly, and through that I was able to go home and start putting paper and pictures together to work on my own paperchase. It was difficult as I had left most of the important things that contributed to my professional development back home in Nigeria when I relocated to the UK. I guess I would make do with the little I have. Spoke with one of the ladies that did the presentation after class and she really explained how to go about the paperchase and other type of writing involved in the course. Still worried about what to put in my portfolio and how to go about it. I need to put my shyness away and learn to ask questions more in class.

17 November 2011

No lectures today, but as we were advised, I spent the day putting together my timeline and paperchase . . . no way would I volunteer to present in class though. I was also able to borrow books from the reading list in the library and while reading, the module gradually made sense to me. I am happy I decided to take time to study during this time and not use it for something else.

24 November 2011

My best class ever! Before the class began I had the opportunity of looking through the former student's portfolio that was brought in by Avril. I now know how I would be putting my portfolio together. Four more students boldly presented their digital paperchase and it was amazing. It's back to the drawing board for me – I hope I could stand in front of the class like them and present what I have been doing to the class. Avril went through the lecture for the day – critical incidents – while she was talking, I was already writing what I intended to put in my portfolio under this type of writing in my head. I need to put my thoughts down as soon as I get home. We ended the class by looking at the Johari window. It was a tough exercise, because I found out that it was easy to say what I think of myself (which is mostly good) but listening to others giving feedback to you about what they think about you is a different ball game. It would be fun using the Johari window with someone you know and that knows you very well because it would give you the opportunity to reflect on what others have to say about you; if good you keep on in that path and if negative, you would be able to work on yourself in those areas to become a better person. Did a lot of writing into the night today! I'm so happy.

1 December 2011

Was unable to attend classes as I was indisposed, thanks to the weather that has refused to make up its mind – to move into winter or stay stuck in autumn.

8 December 2011

Well it's the final class and I must say I enjoyed every bit of it. Looking back to my first recording in this journal I can truly say I have gone through a learning process I never thought I would. I started the class with absolutely no idea what I was doing (or going to do) and ended the class with a smile on my face and great fulfilment. I was able to discuss my assignment with Avril for a few minutes and I felt a burden lifted off my shoulder when I confidently told her I had done quite a few writings. She did urge me to show the class my digital paperchase which as always (and not surprisingly) I refused. Thanks journal, it has been fun writing and reflecting and I have enjoyed this journey of experience and learning with you.

Avril Brock's timeline

A timeline of critical events during a lifelong process of continuing professional development

1952 1956 1957 1959 1963 1966 1967 1968 1969 1970 1971 1975 1976 1979 1980 1983 1986 1987 1989 1990 1991 1992 1993 1994 1997 1998 1999 2000 2001 2002 2003 2004 2005 2006 2007 2008

Mother died

Married

Jackie born   Kirsty born

Solo flight to Frankfurt

Bought first horse
Jackie graduated   Kirsty graduated
Moved to Coxley

Separated

Met Jonathan
Trekked in Nepal

Married Jonathan
Moved to Siavonga

Doris died   Riding accident

Father died
Jackie's wedding
Kirsty's wedding

First library visit
nursery/school
Junior school

Secondary school

Left

RSA typing Park Lane College

O levels + A level

Failed entry to Whitwood ITT

Enrolled Cert Ed

Leeds Polytechnic

Temporary Teacher Kirklees

RSA Diploma

Cert Ed

B.Ed[Hons] Degree

Permanent Carlton School

Lecturer Bradford College

Joan Tough's Communication Skills course

Deputy Headteacher St John's

Bradford College

Special Measures Coordinator

Permanent Lecturer Bradford

P/T school/college

Senior Lecturer Yr 2 tutor

Early Years Coordinator

Wrote Advanced Study & MA in Early Years

Tempus Project Poland

M.ED awarded
Into the Enchanted Forest published

California visits

Organised International EY conference

Began PhD

Moved to Leeds Met University

MA leader

Promoted to Principal Lecturer

Wrote 3 books & a journal article

PhD awarded

Mobalanle's timeline

A timeline of critical events that have shaped my professional life

Professional Life

Years: 1977 | 1986 | 1990 | 1994 | 1995 | 1997 | 1999 | 2000 | 2001 | 2002 | 2003 | 2004 | 2005 | 2006 | 2007 | 2009 | 2010 | 2011

Professional life events:

- Left Sec. Sch.
- Teaching practice experience
- Made a Prefect in Sec. Sch.
- Diploma in Secretarial Studies – Won 2 prizes
- BSc. (Ed.) Degree
- High School
- Ogun State Polytechnic to study Secretarial Studies
- 1st job – PA
- Devised a new way of teaching shorthand
- Started M.Ed (part time)
- 1st published journal article
- Course adviser
- Assistant Lecturer – Fed. College of Education
- Co-authored a book
- Lecturer III – Yaba College of Tech.
- New Job: Project Worker – Family & Children
- Began MACHS @ Leeds Met

Personal life events:

- Born into the world
- My Dad became a Prof. at age of 39
- Flight to Germany with my sisters
- Visited Orphanage
- Dad became Vice Chancellor – won the best VC award in Nigeria twice before end of tenure
- Met BJ
- Married
- Jola born
- Moved to UK
- Bolu born
- Baby P's death
- Became a British Citizen
- Bought 1st house

5

Avril Brock's digital paperchase

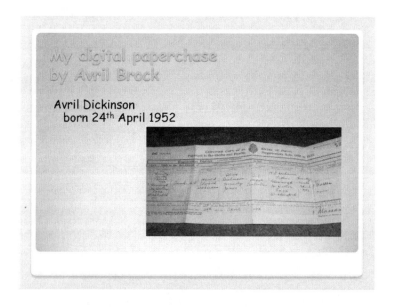

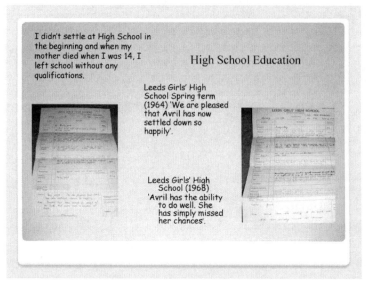

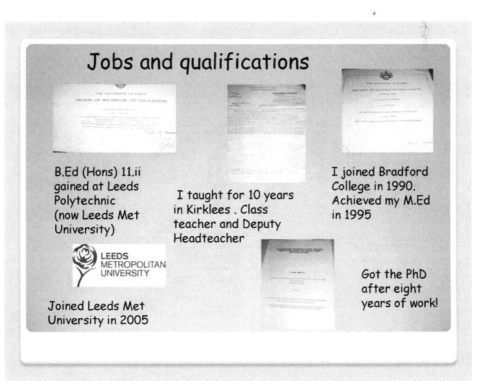

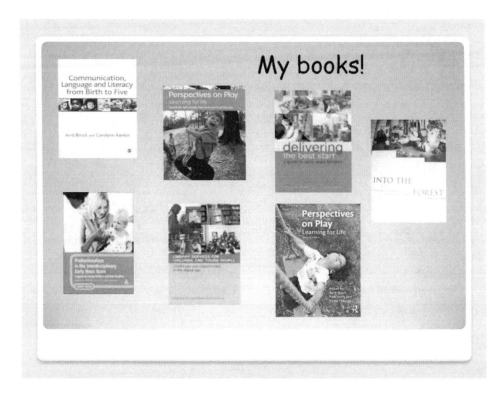

Pavla's paperchase

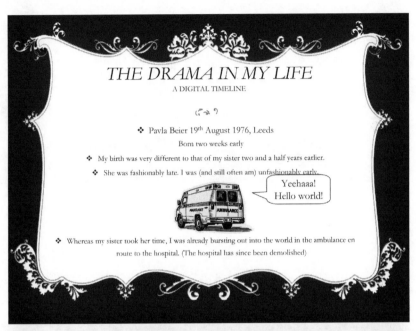

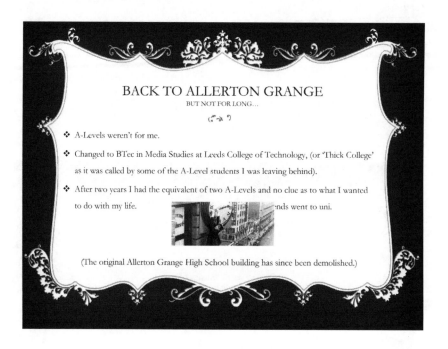

BACK TO ALLERTON GRANGE
BUT NOT FOR LONG...

- ❖ A-Levels weren't for me.
- ❖ Changed to BTec in Media Studies at Leeds College of Technology, (or 'Thick College' as it was called by some of the A-Level students I was leaving behind).
- ❖ After two years I had the equivalent of two A-Levels and no clue as to what I wanted to do with my life. ...nds went to uni.

(The original Allerton Grange High School building has since been demolished.)

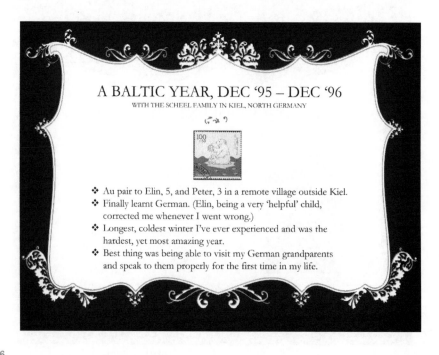

A BALTIC YEAR, DEC '95 – DEC '96
WITH THE SCHEEL FAMILY IN KIEL, NORTH GERMANY

- ❖ Au pair to Elin, 5, and Peter, 3 in a remote village outside Kiel.
- ❖ Finally learnt German. (Elin, being a very 'helpful' child, corrected me whenever I went wrong.)
- ❖ Longest, coldest winter I've ever experienced and was the hardest, yet most amazing year.
- ❖ Best thing was being able to visit my German grandparents and speak to them properly for the first time in my life.

HERE WE GO AGAIN...
MY FIRST BRUSH WITH LEEDS MET UNIVERSITY 1997-1998

❖ Did first year of BA(Hons) PR with Business German at LMU. Wasn't for me.

❖ Decided to do a drama related degree despite having always said I didn't want to be marked or tested on something I enjoyed.

❖ Changed to BA(Hons) Communication Arts: Specialism Drama at the College of Ripon and York St. John in Ripon.

❖ Spent four months at Stockholm University as part of my degree and made two of the best friends I have to this day.

(Most of the Ripon campus has since been demolished or turned in to luxury flats.)

WORLD OF WORK
AFTER GRADUATING IN 2001

❖ Worked as a 'jobbing' actor doing street theatre and theatre in education programmes in schools, as well as spending two months working with drama teachers in a school in India in 2004.

❖ Passion for working with children in schools grew and in 2006 I became a full-time member of The Theatre Company Blah Blah Blah, where I am now Assistant Artistic Director.

❖ Greatest challenge so far, performing in German at a festival in Frankfurt last year.

(The building in which we are based is currently under threat of being demolished.)

Index

Abdulmaali, K. 257
accountability 51, 130
Action for Children 81–2
action research 316, 336, 343, 350–5
active learning 182, 184
activity evaluations 40, 45–6
adjectives for the Johari window 331
adult-directed approach xvi
adult-initiated activities 188
adult-led activities 188
adults: bullying by 308–9; relationships
   between children and 213–14
advocacy 51, 130
aggressive play 275–80
Akerman, R. 256
alignment 145
Allen, G. 85, 104, 108, 332
Alterio, M. 323, 348
Anning, A. 61, 102, 146, 171, 216–17
Apprenticeships, Skills, Children and
   Learning Act 2009 103, 110
areas of learning and development 183,
   266
Armistead, J.L. 212–14
articulation 51, 130
assessment 217; of children's
   capabilities 286–9
assessment matrix 336, 337, 343
Association of Teachers and Lecturers
   (ATL) 169, 171
asylum-seeking children 303–5
Atkinson, R.J.C. 267
attachments, secure 205
attitude 66; beliefs and attitudes 342
August-born children 168
'auntie' (as expression of intimacy) 245
autism spectrum disorders (ASDs) 308
autobiographical writing 321–2, 359–67
autonomy 70, 72; relevance of personal
   autonomy for teachers with QTS 58–60
Avgitidou, S. 148
Avolio, B.J. 122

BA (Hons) students 315–16, 335–46
Bain, J. 43
Ball, M. 102
Bandura, A. 117
Barker, S. 266, 267
Barnardo's 311, 312
Basford, J. 188
Bass, B.M. 122
Baylis, S. 124
Bearne, E. 194–5
behaving professionally 66, 67
behavioural disorders 298
beliefs 342
belonging 145, 153; refugee and asylum
   children 305
Ben 10 Superhero 278, 279–80
Bennett, N. 60
Bercow Report 87
bereavement 254–9
bilingual learners 244–8
Bingham, S. 167, 170, 172
biological knowledge 257–8
Birth to Three Matters (*Bt3M*) 119, 120
black children: dealing with racist
   incidents 293–6; experiences in reception
   classes 234–9; supporting 236–7
Blake, S. 135–7
blogging 272
Blunkett, D. 102
Boddy, J. 24–5, 58
Bolton, G. 8, 39, 318, 327, 354
Bottle, G. 335
boys' underachievement in reading 242
Bradbury, H. 9–10, 40
Bradford 105, 109–10, 111; Integrated Care
   Pathway 108
Braun, V. 338
Brennan, C. 148
bridging cultures 145–6, 152–3
Broadhead, P. 147, 148
Brock, A. 23, 30, 171, 231–2, 242, 255,
   343; autobiography extract 359–63;

digital paperchase 372–4; ecological perspective 83, 84; professionalism 68–71, 72–3; tenets of ethical practice 57–8; timeline 368–9
Bronfenbrenner, U. 83, 149
Brooker, E. 183
Brooker, L. 145, 272
Brookfield, S. 342
Brown, S. 168–9
Brownlee, J.M. 344
Brucker, P. 282
Bruner, J. 148
bullying 306–10
Burt, A. 147
Business and Management (B&M) students 315–16, 335–46
Butler, F. 74
Buysse, V. 232–3
Byrne, D. 250–1

Cable, C. 68
Cameron, C. 24–5, 58
Cameron, D. 101, 104
capabilities: capable thinkers and learners 179, 184–6; observing and assessing 286–9
care xv–xvi; ethic of 56–8; pedagogy of 118–19
career development 353–4
Carlsson-Paige, N. 277
Carr, M. 146, 149–50, 217, 288
Cartwright, L. 34
Centre for Excellence and Outcomes in Children and Young People's Services (C4EO) 96
Centre for Research in Early Childhood (CREC) 86
challenging activities 157–8, 184–6
characteristics of effective learning 182, 184, 195, 270, 271
Chard, D. 283
Chernomas, W.M. 14–15
Chew, J. 192, 193
child-centred practice xv–xvi
child development 116–17; cognitive 88, 117, 170; impact of domestic violence 250–1; limitations of developmental perspectives 144; personal, social and emotional (PSED) 183, 297, 300; physical 138–9, 278, 279–80; social 170, 230–1
child-initiated activities 188, 264
child-led quality indicators 211–18, 219
child poverty 89–91, 103, 109–10, 112
Child Poverty Act 2010 109
child protection 251–3
childhood 211

Childline 306–7
children: capable learners and thinkers 179, 184–6; impact of policy on 82–4, 84–5; individuality 263–5; involvement in assessments 288–9; listening to 150–1; participation in developing an understanding of quality 211–18, 219; perspectives and play 150–8; quality perceived as children's happiness and enjoyment of their experiences 204, 211
Children and Family Court Advisory and Support Service (CAFCASS) 251
children's interests, following 179, 186–9
children's centre managers 60, 77, 101–14; see also Sure Start children's centres
children's rights 82, 117–18, 211, 303
Children's Society 230, 250
Children's Workforce Development Council (CWDC) 25, 56, 105, 348–9
choice 215
Clark, A. 211–12, 287
Clark, C. 242
Clarke, V. 338
classroom layout 179, 180–2
classroom organisation 179, 180–2
Claxton, G. 150
Cleave, S. 168–9
Clegg, N. 82, 104
Climbié, V. 103
Coalition Government 60, 82, 89, 355; Sure Start children's centres 103–7, 107–8, 109–10, 112
Cockburn, A. 266, 267–8
co-construction 188–9; evaluation of quality 215, 216–17; play 148–9, 155–6
cognitive development 88, 117, 170
Cohen, L. 149
cohesion, social 93
Cole, Mike 343, 344
Cole, Mobolanle: reflective diary 364–7; timeline 370–1
Coleyshaw, L. 215–16
collaborative reflection 341
collective action 93–4
Coltman, P. 186
Common Assessment Framework (CAF) 96
communication 87, 94, 136–7; using new technologies 270–4
communication and language 183
communities of learners 144–5, 147, 155, 161
competencies, babies' and toddlers' 117–18
complex reflection 342
Comprehensive Spending Review 101–2
confidence 353
conflict 147–8
connecting 246

consent 151
constructive practice 30–1
consultation 215
consumer price index (CPI) measure of
    inflation 109
contextual knowing 23
continuing professional development
    (CPD) 131
co-operation 93–4
copying 245–6
Corsaro, W. 147, 155
Cotton, T. 268
Craft, A. 332
Craven, P. 252
creating and thinking critically 182, 184
creativity 341–2
Cremin, T. 154
critical incidents 32–5
Critical Race Theory (CRT) 234, 237–8, 295
critical reflection 14–18, 19; promoting 18
critical relationships 35
critical thinking 13–14, 182, 184
cultural brokers 146, 153
cultural capital 67
culture: bridging home and school
    cultures 145–6, 152–3; refugee and asylum
    children 304
curriculum: development by co-
    construction 216–17; EYFS see
    early years foundation stage;
    National Curriculum 58, 271–2; and
    pedagogy 172–3, 174; play and 142–3

Dahlberg, G. 119
Daniels, J. 348
Dearnley, B. 135–7
death concepts 257–8; see also bereavement
deepening of reflection 315, 317–34
deficit model 167
defining reflective practice 339
Department for Children, Schools and
    Families (DCSF) 104
Department for Education 104
development: child see child development;
    professional see professional development
developmental theories 144
Dewey, J. 10, 45
dialogue 148–9
Dibb, L. 312
differentiation 179, 193–5
digital paperchases 323–5, 372–7
disclosures 251, 252
domestic violence 249–53
double consciousness 295
Drudy, S. 57
Drummond, M.J. 217
Duncan Smith, I. 89

Dunn, J. 231
Dye, D. 18
Dye, V. 329
Dyson, A. 94

early childhood care and education
    (ECCE) 1; policy 85–9; political
    perspective 81–2
early childhood care and education (ECCE)
    practitioners 1; diversity of qualifications
    and titles 51–6; see also under individual
    titles
Early Education 250
Early Education Pilot for Two Year Old
    Children 130
early intervention 95–6
Early Intervention Grant (EIG) 104–5, 106–7,
    299
early learning goals (ELGs) 168
Early Support Programme 96
early years educator (EYE) 52–4, 55
early years foundation stage (EYFS) 59, 145,
    309; adult-led activities xvi; assessment
    of two-year-olds 116; assessments 286–7;
    concept of time 266, 268; Curriculum
    Guidance for 58; graduate leadership 120;
    long-term planning 197–8; partnership
    with parents 207–8; personal, social and
    emotional development 300; physical
    development 138; play 143; quality as
    the effective implementation of 204–7,
    310; reception classroom 179, 182–4;
    safeguarding children 250, 252; school
    readiness 169; social development 231;
    technology 270
early years foundation stage profile
    (EYFSP) 168
Early Years Learning Consultancy team 131,
    140
early years professional (EYP) 25, 115–16,
    124, 347–8, 355; graduate leader role 78,
    115–29; reflections on practice for two-
    year-old children 78, 130–41
early years teacher (EYT) 53, 55, 59, 115–16,
    124; graduate leader role 78, 115–29
ECERS (Early Childhood Environment
    Rating Scale) audit 133–4
ecological perspective 83, 84
Edmond, N. 349
educare xv–xvi, 118–19
education 70, 71
educational achievement 89
Edwards, A. 171
Effective Pedagogy in the Early Years
    (EPPE) Project 59, 89, 183
Elbaz-Luwisch, F. 319–20
Emde, R.N. 298

Emery, C. 231
emotional disorders 297, 298
emotional intelligence 342
emotional well-being 94–5, 170, 172
emotions 348, 352–3, 354
empowerment 94
'Enabled to be Two' 131–2
enabling environments 132, 133–5
engagement: in the learning
    community 145, 155; levels of and
    reflective writing 39–40
English as an additional language 244–8
entrepreneurialism 341–2
environments, enabling 132, 133–5
Ephgrave, A. 182, 188
eportfolios 40, 43–5
Eraut, M. 12–13
ethic of care 56–8
ethics 71, 72; tenets of ethical practice 57–8
Evans, L. 345
Every Child Matters Framework 103, 107,
    300
everyday practice, reflecting on 24–8
evidence-based programmes 108
exploration 143, 182, 184
expressive arts and design 183

factory schools xv
Families in the Foundation Years 85
family: bridging home and school
    cultures 145–6, 152–3; domestic
    violence 249–53; life chances and
    educational achievement 88–9; see also
    parents
Family Nurse Partnership programme 94–5
family policy 77, 81–100
Federation of Prisoners' Families Support
    Group project 312
feedback 43
Feinstein, L. 90
Fekkes, M. 308
female non-traditional students 316, 347–56;
    barriers 354
Field, F. 85, 89, 104, 106
first language 304
Fisher, R. 283
Fishergate Primary School 159–61
Flewitt, R. 151, 186
food banks 90, 109
Fook, J. 14, 15, 318, 327
foundation degree programmes 348
foundation degree students: personal and
    professional development and the use of
    reflective practice 316, 347–56; reflective
    practice 315–16, 335–46
Foundations for Quality (Nutbrown
    Review) 53–4, 83

four-year-olds 168–9
free-flow play 180, 181–2
friendships 147, 229–33
frustration 352–3, 354
funding: early childhood education and
    care 87, 88; for SSCCs 102, 104–6;
    supporting children with mental health
    problems 299
funds of knowledge 146
further education (FE) provision 315–16,
    335–46

Gardner, F. 14, 15, 327
Garrick, R. 182, 190, 196
Garvey, D. 131
gender, and gun play 278
Ghaye, T. 320
Gibbs reflective cycle 16, 17
gifted and talented pupils 194
Giving All Children a Healthy Start in Life 95
Glass, N. 101–2, 103
go-kart building 152–3
Goleman, D. 299
Goodfellow, J. 319
Gouthro, P. 348
Gove, M. 59, 108
graduate leaders: reflections on practice for
    two-year-old children 78, 130–41; role 78,
    115–29; see also early years professional
    (EYP), early years teacher (EYT)
graphemes 282
Green, H. 297–8
Gregory, E. 246, 321
Griffiths, M. 258
groups 92–3; outdoor group challenge 185
Guasp, A. 307
guided participation 117–18
guilt 352–3, 354
Guite, H. 133–5
gun play 275–80

hair 234–5, 236
Hall, R. Bridges 366
Handy, C. 330–1
Hannikainen, M. 148
Hartnell-Young, E. 323
Hayes, D. 45
Haylock, D. 266, 267–8
health: mental 94–5, 297–302; physical 94–5
health visitors 94–5
Healthy Child Programme 94–5
Hedges, H. 146
Hickson, H. 8, 29
Hodgson, S. 25, 58, 349
Hodson, E. 188
home culture–school culture bridges 145–6,
    152–3

home visits 136
homophobic bullying 307–8
Hubbs and Brand matrix 336, 337, 343
Huitt, W. 231
Hunting, R. 267, 268
Hurst, V. 266

ideas, playing with 154–5
identity 152–3, 234–5, 304
images, metaphorical 327–8
imagination 145
imitation 245–6
impact of policy on children 82–4, 84–5
inclusion: managing children's needs 179,
    193–5; social 93
Index of Multiple Deprivation (IMD) 102
Individual Education Plan (IEP) 194, 195
individuality, children's 263–5
information: provision by SSCCs 94;
    sharing 111
information and communication
    technology 270–4
Ingham, H. 330–1
Ingram, H. 329
interdisciplinary teams 61, 66
internet 8
Isaacs, S. xv–xvi
ITERS (Infant and Toddler Environment
    Rating Scale) 133–4

Johari window 330–1, 366–7
Johnson, M. 327
joint involvement episodes 148, 150–1
Jones, M. 30
Joseph, J. 266
journaling 40–3; reflective logs 41, 340, 344

Katz, L. 68
Kay, J. 174
Keaton, A.F. 277
Keen, B. 283–4
Kennington, L. 272
key persons 121, 208–9
Kincheloe, J.L. 336
Kirklees Local Authority 130–41
knowing-in-action (tacit knowledge) 11–12,
    36
knowledge: children's perspective on
    quality in learning and knowing 213,
    214–15; context-specific 23; funds
    of 146; personal 12–13; practical 12–13;
    professional see professional knowledge
Kolb, D.A. 16, 17

labeling 305
Labour Government see New Labour
    Government

Lakoff, G. 327
Lamb Enquiry on Special Educational Needs
    and Parental Confidence 96
Lambert, S. 264
Langsted, O. 211
language development 87; stories
    and 241–2
layout: enabling environment 132, 133–5;
    reception classroom 179, 180–2
leadership 121–2; graduate leaders
    see graduate leaders; qualities 123;
    transformational 122
leadership for learning 122–3
leadership within 123
'Leading 2gether' professional
    symposium 131–2
learning: active 182, 184; children as
    capable learners 179, 184–6; children's
    perspectives on quality 213, 214–15;
    Rogoff's model 149, 153
learning communities 144–5, 147, 155,
    161
learning cycle 16, 17
learning journeys/stories 217, 219, 287–8
learning partner 28
'Learning to be Two' 131–2
Lee, C. 306
Leitch Review of Skills 348
Letters and Sounds 192
levels of engagement 39–40
Levin, D.E. 277
Lewis, J. 103
life chances 88–9
listening to children 150–1
literacy 183; see also reading
'living in the middle' 145–6
Livingstone, T. 230
logs, reflective 41, 340, 344
London Safeguarding Board 251, 252
long-term planning 197–8
Luft, J. 330, 331

MacNaughton, G. 52
managing children's needs 179, 193–5
Manning-Morton, J. 121, 131–2
Mantle, M. 342
marginalisation of black children 295
Marmot Review 84, 95, 106, 112
Marsh, J. 278
mathematics 183, 266
Mathers, S. 116
Maynard, T. 191
McDowall Clark, R. 123, 124
McGee, C. 251
McGillivray, G. 121
McGregor, D. 34, 45
McMillan, M. xv

media 270; terminology and racist incidents 294
medium-term planning 195
Medwell, J. 194, 196
Melhuish, E. 90, 95
Meltzer, H. 95
mental health 94–5, 297–302
mentors 9, 40
metaphors 327–8
microaggressions, racial 237–8
Miller, L. 68
Mills, J. 245
'mini-mes' 272
Montague-Smith, A. 266
Moon, J. 8, 13, 341, 348
More Affordable Childcare 82, 109
More Great Childcare (Truss Report) 53, 54, 82
Morpurgo, M. 242–3
Morris, P.A. 149
Morriss, M. 323
mosaic approach 212, 287
Moss, P. 119, 211–12, 287
mother tongue 244–5
movement play 137–9
Moyles, J. 15, 123, 124, 169, 173, 264
Munro Review of Child Protection 84, 95, 104
Murray, J. 123

NAEYC 271
Nagy, M. 257
National Children's Bureau (NCB) 91
National Curriculum 58, 271–2; EYFS *see* early years foundation stage
National Professional Qualification in Integrated Centre Leadership (NPQICL) 60
needs, managing children's 179, 193–5
networks 92–3
New Labour Government 89, 106, 349, 355; Sure Start children's centres 101–3
new technologies 270–4
New Zealand 117, 120, 145
Nocon, H. 146
non-traditional female students 316, 347–56; barriers 354
Nosy Crow 273
NSPCC 303
Nutbrown Review 53–4, 83

Oberhuemer, P. 61, 68
observation 158, 245–6; of children's capabilities 286–9; and listening to children playing 150–8
occupations 67
OECD 171, 172

of the moment reflection 15
Ofsted 9; Inspection Framework 107, 110–11; inspection process 48; self-evaluation form 9, 40, 47–8, 204–5, 206–7, 218; view of quality 204–7, 218, 219
Olusoga, Y. 231–2
open-ended resources 154–5, 159–61, 189–90, 237
organisation, classroom 179, 180–2
Osgood, J. 349
others, considering 340–1
outcomes-driven agenda 143
outdoor play provision 159–61; reception class 179, 189–91
outdoor team challenge 185

Paige-Smith, A. 332
paperchases, digital 323–5, 372–7
parents 89, 92, 134, 135; involvement in assessments 288–9; partnership with 135–7, 207–10; in prison 311–14; quality as parents' satisfaction 204, 207–10, 218; relationships with and child's mental health 300; strengthening ties with 135–7
'Parents in Early Years and Learning' (PEAL) training 136–7, 139
Parker, C. 191
Parker, I. 82
Parsons, S. 255, 256
participatory research 336
partnership with parents 135–7, 207–10
Pavla's paperchase 324, 375–7
Payler, J. 188–9
Payment By Results 108
Pebblepad Plus 44
pedagogy 118; of care 118–19; and curriculum 172–3, 174; reception class teacher's 79, 178–202
personal autonomy 58–60
Personal Independence Payments 109
personal knowledge 12–13
personal and professional development 30, 316, 347–56
Personal and Professional Reflective Practice (PPRP) module 317–34; reflective diary on 364–7
personal/professional timelines 325–7, 368–71
personal, social and emotional development (PSED) 183, 297, 300
Peters, S. 232
phonemes 282
phonics: systematic synthetic 281–5; teaching in the reception class 179, 191–3
phonics screening check 60, 168, 242
physical development 138–9, 183; focus plan based on *Ben 10* Superhero 278, 279–80

physical health 94–5
physical play 137–9
Piaget, J. 144
place for study 351–2
planning 179, 195–6, 197–8
play xv–xvi, 78, 142–65, 179; bridging
cultures 145–6, 152–3; and
curriculum 142–3; disclosure of domestic
violence 252; gun play 275–80; movement
play 137–9; and reciprocity 148–9,
155–6; refugee and asylum children 304;
resilience 149–50, 151, 157–8; story-
play 242, 243; understanding time 266
Play Plan 195
playing and exploring 182, 184
Plowden Report xvi
policy 1, 77, 81–100, 206; impact on
children 82–4, 84–5; and interdisciplinary
teams 61; prescriptive frameworks
58–60; reflection within a climate of policy
change 36; regarding Sure Start children's
centres 77, 91–4, 101–14
political action 94
portfolios 319–21; eportfolios 40, 43–5
'Positively Two' 131–2
possibility 151, 153–5
Potter, C. 25, 58, 349
Potts, S. 255
poverty 89–91, 103, 109–10, 112
Power, M. 242
power 147–8
practical knowledge 12–13
practice: leadership of 122–5; reflecting in
everyday practice 24–8
prescriptive frameworks 58–60
prime areas of learning and
development 183
prison, parents in 311–14
private daycare owner 47–8
professional artistry 11
professional development 9, 131; personal
and professional development 30, 316,
347–56
professional knowledge 12–13, 70, 71;
developing 22–3; development about
the teaching of phonics 283–5; model
of 23–4
professional roles 6, 28–9, 51–64; diversity of
qualifications and titles 51–6; meaning of
reflective practice 56–61
professionalisation 66, 67
professionalism 6, 28, 65–76, 121, 343–4,
348–9; defining 66–7; discourse of 67–8;
typology of 70–2
proficiency 66
programme of study (POS) 194
progressive universalism 106

prospective reflection 15
public spending cuts 103, 104–5, 106
Puppet Pals 272

qualifications 41, 52–4
qualified teacher status (QTS) 52, 53, 55,
124, 343–4; professional attributes 344;
relevance of personal autonomy 58–60
quality 79, 88, 203–21; children's
participation in developing an
understanding of 211–18, 219;
perspectives on 204–11
quality experiences 212–15

Race Relations Amendment Act 2000 293
racism: dealing with racist incidents 293–6;
experiences of black children in the
classroom 234–9
Rankin, C. 74, 242
Ranns, H. 355
reading 180; boys' underachievement 242;
importance of stories 240–3; teaching
phonics 179, 191–3; teaching using
systematic synthetic phonics 281–5
reception classes 79, 178–202; capable
thinkers and learners 179, 184–6;
classroom layout and organisation 179,
180–2; following children's interests 179,
186–9; four-year-olds in 168–9; managing
children's needs 179, 193–5; outdoor
provision 179, 189–91; phonics 179,
191–3; planning 179, 195–6, 197–8
reciprocal determinism 117
reciprocity 148–9, 151, 155–6
re-construction 148–9
Reed, M. 28–9
reflection 5, 7–21; critical 14–18, 19;
defining 7–8; how to reflect 9–10;
importance for ECCE practitioners 2, 5,
22–38; purposes of 8–9
reflection-in-action 11–12
reflection-on-action 11–12
reflection-on-practice 24–8
reflection-on-reflection 15, 18, 19, 31
reflective cycle models 16
reflective logs 41, 340, 344
reflective practice, definitions of 339
reflective practitioner 28–9
reflective skills, value of 338
reflective writing 5, 39–50, 349;
autobiographical 321–2, 359–67;
deepening reflection 315, 317–34; digital
paperchases 323–5, 372–7; for external
agencies 40–8; levels of engagement
39–40; personal/professional
timelines 325–7, 368–71; undergraduate
students 339–41, 344

refugee children 303–5
Reggio Emilia 117, 287–8
relationships: between children and
  adults 213–14; critical 35
'Researching Effective Pedagogy in the Early
  Years' (REPEY) study 173–4, 183
resentment 352–3, 354
resilience 251, 299; play 149–50, 151, 157–8
retail price index (RPI) measure of
  inflation 109
retrospective reflection 15
reward 71, 72
Richardson, A. 92–4
rights, children's 82, 117–18, 211, 303
ring-fencing 102, 104
risk 149–50, 157–8
Roberts-Holmes, G.P. 183
Rogers, S. 170, 181, 182
Rogoff, B. 117–18, 149, 153, 246
Rose, J. 170, 181, 182
Rose Review 192–3, 281
Rosen, M. 192
Ross, K. 278
Roulstone, S. 87
Ryan, M. 8

safeguarding procedures 251–3
Sawyer, R.K. 149
scaffolding 186
Scanlon, J.M. 14–15
Schön, D.A. 11–12
school culture–home culture bridges 145–6,
  152–3
school readiness 78, 82, 143, 166–77
school starting age 166, 168–9, 171
Schools Admission Policy 166
secure attachments 205
self-evaluation 28; Ofsted's self-evaluation
  form (SEF) 9, 40, 47–8, 204–5, 206–7, 218
semi-structured interviews 350
sequencing events 267
settings 87; leadership of 122–4
Shaw, Y. 137–9
Sheffield City Council 105
Shelton, M. 30
Shields, P. 208–9, 210
Shier, H. 215
short-term planning 196
silent pedagogy 35
silent period 244–8
simple reflection 342
Single Equality Act 2010 294
Siraj-Blatchford, I. 90, 174, 181
skills: professional 70, 72; undergraduate
  students' personal and professional skills
  development 353; value of reflective
  skills 338

Slaughter, V. 257–8
'sleeps', counting in 267
slow listening 151
Smart Notebook 44–5
Smith, A. 118
Smith, R. 208, 210
Smyth, J. 32
social agency, children's 211
social capital 91–4
social cohesion 93
social development 170, 230–1
Social and Emotional Aspects of Learning
  (SEAL) resources 299, 309
social inclusion 93
social networking media 43, 136, 208,
  273
solidarity 93
spaceship play 154–5
Spear-Swerling, L. 282
Special Educational Needs (SEN) 194, 195,
  298; bullying of children with 308
specific areas of learning and
  development 183
SPEEL study 173, 264
stages of implementation 215–16
stages of time 267
starting school 166–8; importance of first
  days 170–2; see also reception classes,
  school readiness
Statham, J. 256
'stay and play' sessions 134, 135, 136
stories 240–3
stress 36; bullying by adults under
  stress 308–9
structured uncertainty 29
study, time and place for 351–2
Study of Pedagogical Effectiveness in Early
  Learning (SPEEL) 173, 264
subjectivity of tutors 340
Sue, D.W. 237–8
Suggate, J. 268
Sule Tepetas, G. 306
Sullenberger, Captain 67
Sullivan, K. 306
superhero gun play 275–80
Supporting Families in the Foundation
  Years 84–5
Sure Start children's centres (SSCCs) 77,
  101–14; core purpose 107–8; development
  of social capital 91–4; funding 102,
  104–6; history 101–3; Ofsted Inspection
  Framework 110–11
Sure Start local programmes (SSLPs) 102,
  103, 104
Sure Start programme 83, 95
Sylva, K. 174
systematic synthetic phonics 281–5

tacit knowledge 11–12, 36
TACTYC (Association for the Professional
 Development of Early Years
 Educators) 167, 168, 171
Taggart, G. 56–7
Targeted Mental Health in Schools (TaMHS)
 project 299
Taylor, B. 250–1
Te Whāriki curriculum 117, 120, 145
teaching reflective practice 342
team challenge, outdoor 185
technology 270–4
telescope play 160–1
telling the time 268
ten-minute writing task 329–30
thinking: children as capable thinkers 179,
 184–6; critical 13–14, 182, 184
Thorp, M. 131–2
Thorpe, K. 43
Tickell, C. 84, 104
time: concept of 266–9; for study 351–2
timelines 325–7, 368–71
titles for ECCE practitioners 52–4
Tobin, J. 151
togetherness 148
Training and Development Agency
 (TDA) 344
transformational leadership 122
traumatic events 34–5
tree stumps 157–8
Troubled Families initiative 107–8
Truss, E. xvi, 107
Truss Report (*More Great Childcare*) 53, 54,
 82
Trussell Trust 90
trust 93
tutors 40; subjectivity of 340
two-year-olds 86–7, 87–8; assessment
 of 116; graduate leaders' reflections on
 practice for 78, 130–41; offer of 15 hours
 of free childcare for 105, 106–7, 130
typology of professionalism 70–2

undergraduate students *see* BA (Hons)
 students, foundation degree students
understanding of reflective practice 351
understanding the world 183
unemployment 109–10
UNICEF 249, 250

'Uniquely Two' 131–2
uniqueness 263–5
United Nations 249
United Nations Convention on the Rights of
 the Child (UNCRC) 82, 117, 211
Universal Credit 109
unqualified teachers 59
Utting, D. 89

values 31, 70, 72
Van Oers, B. 148
video-cued multivocal ethnography 151
violence: domestic 249–53; gun play
 275–80
Vlachou, M. 306
Vygotsky, L.S. 148, 246, 268

Waite, S. 191
Waldfogel, J. 90
Walker, D. 146
Washbrook, E. 90
water, explorations with 155–6
welfare reforms 109–10
well-being 297; emotional 94–5, 170, 172
Wenger, E. 145, 155
Wertsch, J.V. 145–6
West, L. 318
Whitebread, D. 167, 170, 172, 186
whiteness 236, 237, 238, 294, 295
Wild, M. 54, 82–3
Willis, D. 250
Wilson, A. 296
Winch, A. 329
Wolfe, S. 186
Wong, K. 15
Wood, E. 59–60, 188
work-based practice 349
worldview 34
Worthington, M. 169
writing, reflective *see* reflective writing
Wyse, D. 192

Young Children's Learning and
 Development (YCLD) students 315–16,
 335–46

Zablotsky, B. 308
Zone of Proximal Development (ZPD) 148,
 156